Saint Jean de Brébeuf Hymnal

Choral Supplement

For the first time in history, each verse is written out.

2019

WHILE de Brébeuf continued to pray in a commanding voice, to exhort the Hurons being tortured at nearby posts, to console Père Gabriel and the shackled prisoners, his tormentors stabbed him with javelin heads and sliced him with knives. Unmoved by their tormentings, he thundered at the top of his voice, "*Jésus taiteur!* Jesus, have mercy on us!" His plea rang out like a battle cry, and was answered by the Huron Believers, "*Jésus taiteur!*" Angered to insanity by his defiance, the Iroquois thrust torches against his face and into his mouth. He spat out the burning splinters, shook off the embers, and preached at his tormentors, especially at the renegade Hurons who were now revenging themselves on him. He exhorted them to believe in the God whom they had rejected. To show their hate, they burned and slashed him the more.

—From *The Life of Saint Jean de Brébeuf*

SAINT JEAN DE BRÉBEUF HYMNAL

CHORAL SUPPLEMENT

CATHOLIC CHURCH

Published with ecclesiastical approval.

The St. Jean de Brébeuf Hymnal
John Paul II Institute for Liturgical Renewal

Textual Copyrights

THE TEXTS in the Saint Jean de Brébeuf Hymnal—all of them—have undergone editorial revision, ranging from minimal to substantial, and as such are under copyright.[1] However, the pew edition carefully provides the source of each text, including even the page number (something no other hymnal does), making it easy for those who wish to consult the original texts. Modification of hymn texts for publication is standard practice. For example, John Mason Neale wrote "Draw nigh, draw nigh Emmanuel" in 1851; but when published, it became *O come, O come, Emmanuel*—and even the refrain was altered.[2] Nowhere can textual modification be seen more clearly than in the historic Roman Catholic primers:

Roman Catholic Primer (1706AD)

2. Born from above, and **Born for Man,**
From Virgin's Womb **his Life began:**
He liv'd on Earth, **and Preach'd, to sow**
The Seeds of Heav'nly Truth below:
Then seal'd his Mission from above
With strange Effects of Pow'r and Love.

4. **The Word made Flesh** for Love of Man,
With words, of Bread, made Flesh again:
Turn'd Wine to Blood unseen by sense
By Virtue of Omnipotence;
And here the Faithful rest secure
Whilst God can Vouch, and Faith ensure.

5. **To this mysterious Table now**
Our Knees, our Hearts and Sense we **bow;**
Let Ancient Rites resign their Place
To nobler Elements of Grace;
And Faith for all Defects supply,
Whilst Sense is lost in Mystery.

Roman Catholic Primer (1738AD)

2. For Man he came, was **born for Man;**
From a chaste Maid **his Life began;**
On Earth he liv'd **and preach'd, to sow—**
The Seeds of heav'nly Truth below;
And then with lasting Love to close
His Life, this wond'rous Way he chose.

4. **The Word made Flesh,** by Words he said,
Turns into Flesh substantial Bread;
Wine too he makes his Blood divine,
Tho' sense cry out, 'Tis Bread and Wine:
But Hearts sincere are here secur'd,
By Faith in Words of Truth assur'd.

5. **To this mysterious Table now**
Let Knees, and Heart, and Senses **bow:**
Let ancient Rites resign their Place
To nobler Elements of Grace:
What our weak senses can't descry,
Let stronger Faith the Want supply.

Nothing would have been easier than simply reproducing all texts unaltered, including archaic expressions unacceptable today.[3] Such a tempting course of action—deemed valid by several recent publications—would have significantly reduced our hymnal's production time; but we renounced such an approach because hymn texts must be received well by the faithful. Our textual changes always match the *style* of the poet, even when doing so necessitated adoption of highly idiosyncratic[4] capitalization conventions, and under no circumstances were theological truths diluted or obscured. Moreover, the notion of "change for the sake of change" was fiercely rejected, especially vis-à-vis hymns which are known and loved.

---

1 Even historic Roman Catholic primers have been carefully edited by our team. While the exact words, punctuation, and capitalization have been preserved, we have updated spelling where appropriate; for example, "sinne abyde" becomes *sin abide*, and so forth.

2 Consider, too, Dr. Neale's famous translation of *Quem Terra, Pontus, Sydera* ("The God whom earth, and sea, and sky"), published in 1851. When printed in *Hymns Ancient and Modern* (1861), every verse was altered considerably. For the 1972 edition of *Hymns Ancient and Modern*, it was again severely modified, and the second verse was inexplicably deleted.

3 For example, an extremely popular translation of *O Salutaris Hostia* (early 19th century) translated the phrase *bella premunt hostilia* as "intestine wars invade our breast."

4 Fr. Caswall unfailingly capitalizes "Thee" and "He" when referring to Christ, yet does not capitalize "thy" and "his."

NEXT TO the offering of the Eucharistical Sacrifice—which is the most sublime and the more essential act of divine worship—the singing of the praises of God and of the Lamb is unquestionably the noblest employment of a Christian. He who sings to God with a proper sense of devotion associates himself to the Choirs of Angels, and shares upon earth in the sweetest occupation of the blessed inhabitants of Heaven.

It cannot be doubted but that the most proper time for this holy exercise is when the faithful meet together in Church; and especially when the Lamb that was slain on the cross for the redemption of the world, comes down on our altars, and there continues to offer himself for us to his heavenly Father. […]

Besides a variety of Spiritual Canticles, the Catholic reader will have the satisfaction of finding a translation in verse, as literal as this kind of composition could permit, of those ancient hymns, which have been sung in the Catholic Church on the various festivals of our Lord, of the Blessed Virgin and of the Saints, through the year, for upwards of fourteen centuries…

—From the Preface to *Hymns for the use of the Catholic Church in the United States of America* (Baltimore, 1807)

Choral Supplement • Introduction

THE DICTIONARY definition for "supplement" is as follows: *Something that completes or enhances something else when added to it*. It is absolutely crucial to understand that you hold in your hands a Choral Supplement; you do not hold a "choral edition." Many companies publish "choral editions" which are identical to their pew books, except the hymns are printed SATB. Since we believe such an approach is flawed, we chose a different path. To understand our radically different approach, one must recall that the Brébeuf Hymnal is the antithesis of a theoretical exercise. It was created by and for priests and choirmasters working in real parishes across the globe. Our goal was to help Catholic parishes—even when that required a departure from convention. On the other hand, conventions which make sense and help choirs were retained.[1]

The SATB arrangements in this book are meant to enhance. We believe the default choice should be "German style" (unison + organ). In other words, the normal way to foster congregational singing is for a strong choir—not a cantor with microphone—to sing in unison with organ accompaniment. When "German style" is used, multifarious techniques can be employed: (a) alternating between men and women; (b) having the organist play interludes between verses; (c) transposing to a different key for the final verse; (d) using different harmonies for each verse, including a verse of just octaves, or a verse using beautiful dissonances; (e) using a soprano descant for the final verse.[2]

Each individual choirmaster must decide when SATB is appropriate. Such a decision will depend upon numerous factors, which will not be discussed here.[3] However, when SATB is chosen, it should be done well—and should constitute an improvement. If the harmonies have a deleterious effect on the music, the choirmaster should switch back to "German style" until the singers are ready. Many choirmasters have erroneously convinced themselves that SATB is *ipso facto* "better"—even when the result is cacophonous!

The competent choirmaster recognizes that "not all hymn tunes were created equal" when it comes to adding SATB harmonies. For example, it would be relatively easy to add SATB harmonies to #759 ("To Jesus Christ, Our Sovereign King"), and doing so does not run the

---

1 We do not condemn hymn editors who make different choices than we did. We strove, for example, to choose the perfect key for each hymn, yet we admit there can never be a "perfect" key that will satisfy every choir. To emphasize this reality, we sometimes included (optional) accompaniments transposed to a different key—when this could be done conveniently—to remind choirmasters to experiment. Depending upon the acoustics and time of day, transposing a semitone upwards or downwards can make quite a difference.

2 If harmonies had been included in the Brébeuf pew book, many of these beautiful options could not be used, which is a powerful reminder that harmonizations do not belong in a pew book. Something utterly repulsive—which must be eliminated wherever it exists—happens when members of the congregation sing a "harmonization" which does not match what is being played or sung. Such people fail to understand that every hymn tune has multiple harmonizations, which clash horribly when mixed.

3 If the SATB harmonies will confuse the congregation, "German style" is often a better choice.

risk of confusing one's congregation. Yet, certain other tunes are quite difficult to sing well in SATB—the operative phrase being "sing well."

Because singing SATB well with a volunteer choir is not easy, we have done everything possible to assist your choir. We have printed the hymns in such a way that throughout this entire book—consisting of 1,192 pages—only a minuscule number of hymns require a page turn. Even more significant is our placement of the hymn lyrics. Consider #363 from the choir edition of the ADOREMUS HYMNAL (Ignatius Press, 2011), which prints lyrics according to the "standard" procedure:

1. The glo - ry of these for - ty days We
2. A - lone and fast - ing Mo - ses saw The
3. So Dan - iel trained his mys - tic sight, De -
4. Then grant us, Lord, like them to be Full
5. O Fa - ther, Son, and Spir - it blest, To
cel - e - brate with songs of praise; For Christ, by whom all
lov - ing God who gave the law; And to E - li - jah,
liv - er'd from the li - on's might; And John, the Bride - groom's
oft in fast and prayer with thee; Our spir - its strength - en
thee be ev - ery prayer ad - drest; Who art in three - fold
things were made, Him - self has fast - ed and has prayed.
fast - ing came The steeds and char - i - ots of flame.
friend, be - came The her - ald of Mes - si - ah's name.
with thy grace, And give us joy to see thy face.
Name a - dored, From age to age, the on - ly Lord. A - men.

From the standpoint of convention, ADOREMUS did nothing wrong. But volunteer choirs find such arrangements difficult to read because of how the verses are stacked. Even more challenging is the way hymnals are printed in Great Britain, with harmonies printed on a different page from the lyrics.[4]

Every verse in this Choral Supplement has been painstakingly written out. Each verse was then formatted with an eye toward the singer's comprehension, meaning cramped and thoughtless spacing such as this:

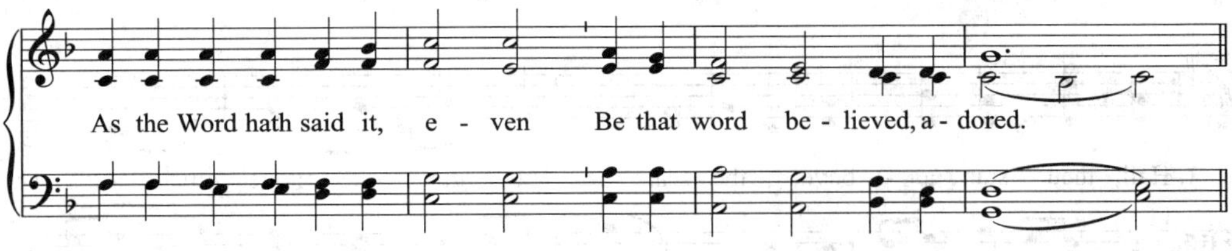
As the Word hath said it, e - ven Be that word be - lieved, a - dored.

…has been carefully changed to spacing such as this:

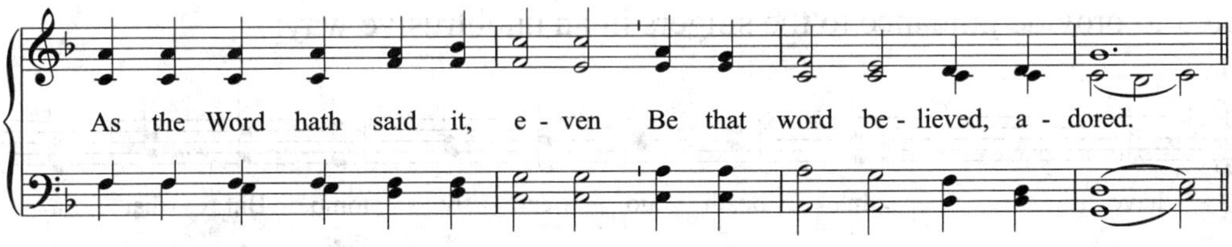
As the Word hath said it, e - ven Be that word be - lieved, a - dored.

Moreover, we rejected treating each hymn in a rigid, inflexible way. Occasionally, this meant placing the words higher or lower (vertically)—and this was a real bone of contention:

6. All__ glo - ry be to thee, O Lord, A Vir - gin's Son, by all a - dored;

The question was settled by testing the scores with real singers. Amazingly, not one singer noticed the unconventional placement, and it caused no issues whatsoever. Since our overriding goal was helping singers, there was nothing more to be said.

---

4 Some choirmasters will object, saying: "We sing the same hymns over and over, year after year, until the singers have the parts memorized; therefore, we have no problem with such an approach." But this objection does not address choirmasters who have no interest in singing the same hymns year after year. Indeed, Catholics should reject the idea of mindlessly and excessively repeating the same hymns—thereby refusing to grow musically and spiritually—because of laziness on the part of the hymnal editor. Rather, we should be open to learning new hymns from time to time.

Our scores have a particular approach to melismata slurs. We believe it will be self-evident to the singers, whereas explaining it makes it sound complicated. In essence, where it was possible to eliminate slurs—using eighth note beams instead—we did so.

Due to the particular way the SATB scores are printed in our Choral Supplement, it is sometimes necessary to "pull back" a word. For example, the word "the" (*Hail, thou star above the sea*) should be pulled back by Altos to the C-Sharp:

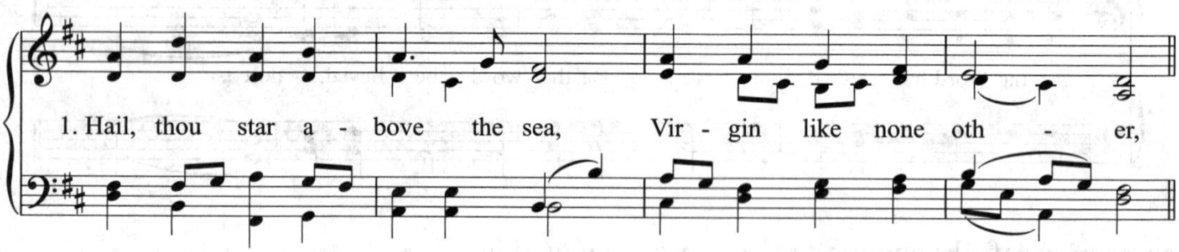
1. Hail, thou star a - bove the sea, Vir - gin like none oth - er,

In a handful of cases, "pulling back" lyrics was more complicated. In such instances, we attempted to provide guidance to the singers in an unobtrusive way:

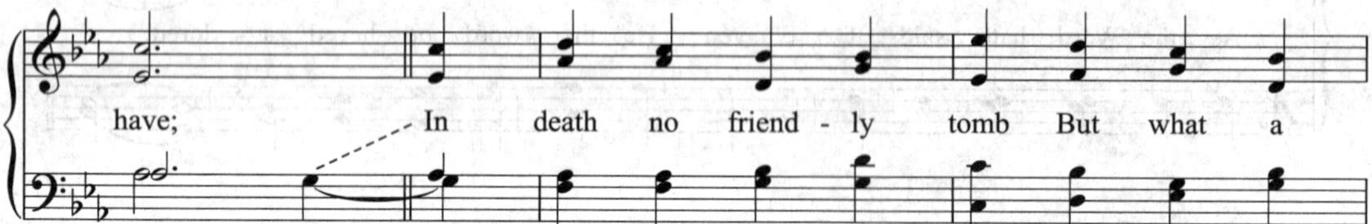
have; In death no friend - ly tomb But what a

In a very few instances, a "pulled back" word is indicated by an eighth note beam. In the following, for example, our recommendation is to have Altos sing "it" (*In royal majesty it stood*) beginning on the A-Natural:

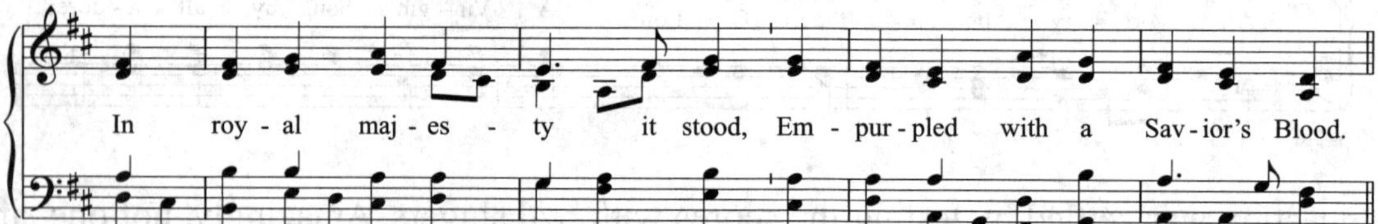
In roy - al maj - es - ty it stood, Em - pur - pled with a Sav - ior's Blood.

We would like to emphasize, however, that this is of minor importance. If a choirmaster prefers having Altos sing "it" on the D-Natural, no great harm will result.

Excluded from the Choral Supplement

CHOIR MEMBERS should normally sing from the Brébeuf pew edition, since (we emphasize again) "German style" will be the usual way hymns are sung. For SATB singing, needless to say, the choir must sing from the Choral Supplement.[1]

All preparation must be done from the pew edition, since that book contains:

- hymn recommendations according to liturgical season
- literal translations of hymn texts, which are very important
- theological and textual annotations
- complete information regarding the provenance of each hymn (text & melody)
- biographical information about translators and composers
- explanations for text sharing, melody sharing, and "common tunes"
- biographical information about Father Brébeuf, and why he was chosen as patron
- color pages reproducing important examples of the Catholic hymn tradition
- comprehensive indices not included in the Choral Supplement

Note: Many "unison" hymns cannot be found in this Choral Supplement.

Examples of "unison" hymns would be #242 (GONFALON ROYAL), #110 (JESU DULCIS MEMORIA), #292 (STARRY), #314 (BRETON), #323 (DAVOST), #348 (PANGE LINGUA PLAINSONG), and #703 (O FILII ET FILIAE).[2]

Moreover, many "text only" hymns in the pew edition were excluded from this Choral Supplement. For example, #437 (*Rex Sempiterne*, translated by Bishop Bagshawe) could be sung with a variety of melodies, and the Brébeuf pew book suggests eight additional possibilities.[3] That is yet another reason choir members should normally sing directly from the pew book, which—being an extremely thin and lightweight book—is slightly more pleasant to hold at Mass.

---

1 Because of this reality, some choirmasters prefer to give the Choral Supplement to every section except Soprano. This can lead to problems, however, if certain dynamics are required for each verse; yet, it cannot be denied that reducing clutter in a choir loft is a worthy goal. Incidentally, the Choral Supplement matches the harmonies in the organ edition—something utterly crucial.

2 We do not recommend SATB for these pieces, for multifarious reasons.

3 Exceptions are rare, but do exist. "Text only" hymns included in the Choral Supplement include: #683 *The Glory Of These Forty Days* (SPIRES / ERHALT UNS HERR); #838 *Soul Of My Savior* (ANIMA CHRISTI); #653 *O Come, O Come Emmanuel* (VENI EMMANUEL).

1. Now, from the ris - ing of the sun Un - to the ut - most bounds of earth,
We sing the praise of Christ our King, The Child of Mar - y's vir - gin - birth.
2. The bless - èd Found - er of the World, In form of guilt - y slave ar - rayed;
For flesh in flesh re - demp - tion wrought, Lest they should per - ish whom He made.
3. The splen - dor of ce - les - tial grace That bow - er fresh and fair il - lumes;
A Vir - gin's womb be - comes the shrine, Where God His hid - den throne as - sumes.
4. The chaste en - clo - sure of that frame Be - comes a tem - ple all di - vine;
In stain - less pu - ri - ty she bore The Son of God with - in that shrine.

5. The time ful - filled, she gave Him birth Whom Ga - bri - el had once fore - told;
And whom, when yet with - in the womb, Saint John ex - ult - ed to be - hold.
6. A man - ger was His low - ly bed, Dis - dain - ing not on hay to lie;
And mea - ger milk sup - port - ed Him Who feeds the ra - vens when they cry.
7. The choirs of heav'n ex - ult with joy, And an - gels sing be - fore His throne;
The Shep - herd of our souls su - preme To shep - herds makes His Glo - ry known.
8. O Je - sus Vir - gin - born, to Thee E - ter - nal glo - ry be con - fessed,
With Fa - ther and with Spir - it, Lord For ev - er in one God - head blest.

007 BRESSANI — *A Solis Ortus Cardine* — English Translation by Father Wallace

1. Now, from the ris - ing of the sun Un - to the ut - most bounds of__ earth,
We__ sing the praise of Christ our King, The Child of Mar - y's vir - gin - birth.
2. The__ bless - èd Found - er of the World, In form of guilt - y slave ar - rayed;
For__ flesh in flesh re - demp - tion wrought, Lest they should per - ish whom He made.
3. The__ splen - dor of ce - les - tial grace That bow - er fresh and fair il - lumes;
A__ Vir - gin's womb be - comes the shrine, Where God His hid - den throne as - sumes.
4. The__ chaste en - clo - sure of that frame Be - comes a tem - ple all di - vine;
In__ stain - less pu - ri - ty she bore The Son of God with - in that shrine.

#97 has (optional) organ accompaniment at a lower key.

5. The_ time ful-filled, she gave Him birth Whom Ga-bri-el had once fore-told;
And_ whom, when yet with-in the womb, Saint John ex-ult-ed to be-hold.
6. A___ man-ger was His low-ly bed, Dis-dain-ing not on hay to___ lie;
And_ mea-ger milk sup-port-ed Him Who feeds the ra-vens when they cry.
7. The_ choirs of heav'n ex-ult with joy, And an-gels sing be-fore His__throne;
The_ Shep-herd of our souls su-preme To shep-herds makes His Glo-ry known.
8. O___ Je-sus Vir-gin-born, to Thee E-ter-nal glo-ry be con-fessed,
With_ Fa-ther and with Spir-it, Lord For ev-er in one God-head blest.

 O INVIDENDA MARTYRUM — *A Solis Ortus Cardine* — English Translation by Father Wallace

5. The time ful-filled, she gave Him birth Whom Ga - bri - el had once fore-told;
And whom, when yet with - in the womb, Saint John ex - ult - ed to be - hold.
6. A man - ger was His low - ly bed, Dis-dain - ing not on hay to lie;
And mea - ger milk sup - port - ed Him Who feeds the ra - vens when they cry.
7. The choirs of heav'n ex - ult with joy, And an - gels sing be - fore His throne;
The Shep - herd of our souls su - preme To shep-herds makes His Glo - ry known.
8. O Je - sus Vir - gin - born, to Thee E - ter - nal glo - ry be con fessed,
With Fa - ther and with Spir - it, Lord For ev - er in one God - head blest.

009 OLD HUNDREDTH — *A Solis Ortus Cardine* — English Translation by Father Wallace

5. The time ful - filled, she gave Him birth Whom Ga - bri - el had once fore - told;
And whom, when yet with - in the womb, Saint John ex - ult - ed to be - hold.
6. A man - ger was His low - ly bed, Dis - dain - ing not on hay to lie;
And mea - ger milk sup - port - ed Him Who feeds the ra-vens when they cry.
7. The choirs of heav'n ex - ult with joy, And an - gels sing be - fore His throne;
The Shep-herd of our souls su - preme To shep-herds makes His Glo - ry known.
8. O Je - sus Vir - gin - born, to Thee E - ter - nal glo - ry be con - fessed,
With Fa - ther and with Spir - it, Lord For ev - er in one God - head blest.

 WHITEHEAD — *A Solis Ortus Cardine* — English Translation by Father Wallace

5. The time ful - filled, she gave Him birth Whom Ga - bri - el had once fore - told;
And whom, when yet with - in the womb, Saint John ex - ult - ed to be - hold.
6. A man - ger__ was His low - ly bed, Dis - dain - ing not on hay to lie;
And mea - ger milk sup - port - ed Him Who feeds the ra - vens when they cry.
7. The choirs of__heav'n ex - ult with joy, And an - gels sing be - fore His throne;
The Shep - herd of our souls su - preme To shep - herds makes His Glo - ry known.
8. O Je - sus__ Vir - gin - born, to Thee E - ter - nal glo - ry be con - fessed,
With Fa - ther and with Spir - it, Lord For ev - er in one God - head blest.

011 CANON VIII — *A Solis Ortus Cardine* — English Translation by Father Wallace

* *The beginning of the Canon is placed in brackets in SOPRANO and TENOR.*

5. The time ful - filled, she gave Him birth Whom Ga - bri - el had once fore - told;
And whom, when yet with - in the womb, Saint John ex - ult - ed to be - hold.
6. A man - ger was His low - ly bed, Dis - dain - ing not on hay to lie;
And mea - ger milk sup - port - ed Him Who feeds the ra - vens when they cry.
7. The choirs of heav'n ex - ult with joy, And an - gels sing be - fore His throne;
The Shep - herd of our souls su - preme To shep - herds makes His Glo - ry known.
8. O Je - sus Vir - gin - born, to Thee E - ter - nal glo - ry be con - fessed,
With Fa - ther and with Spir - it, Lord For ev - er in one God - head blest.

012 ALTONA — *A Solis Ortus Cardine* — English Translation by Father Wallace

5. The time ful-filled, she gave Him birth Whom Ga - bri - el had_ once fore - told;
And whom, when yet_ with - in_ the womb, Saint John ex - ult - ed to_ be - hold.
6. A man-ger was His low - ly bed, Dis - dain - ing not on_ hay to lie;
And mea - ger milk sup - port - ed Him Who feeds the ra - vens when they cry.
7. The choirs of heav'n ex - ult with joy, And an - gels sing be - fore His throne;
The Shep - herd of_ our souls su - preme To shep - herds makes His Glo - ry known.
8. O Je - sus Vir - gin - born, to Thee E - ter - nal glo - ry_ be con - fessed,
With Fa - ther and_ with Spir - it, Lord For ev - er in one God-head blest.

 ALTONA — *Hostis Herodes Impie* — English Translation by Archbishop Bagshawe

1. That God Him-self as King should come, Why, cru - el Her - od,— fear - est thou?
He takes no earth - ly realms a - way, Who doth with Heav'n - ly ones_ en - dow.
2. The Ma - gi saw the star re - vealed, And fol - lowed as it___ went be - fore;
The true Light by_ its light_ they seek, And as true God by gifts a - dore.

* *A transposed organ accompaniment has been provided for optional use.*

3. The pure and Heav'n - ly Lamb of God, In - to the lim - pid__ wa - ters went,
And washed and cleansed us from__ our sins, All pure Him - self, and in - no - cent.
4. The wa - ter - jars blush ros - y red, New prod - i - gy of__ Pow'r Di - vine!
The wa - ter its__ own na - ture changed, When bid - den to pour forth as wine.
5. Who to the Gen - tiles wast re - vealed, O Christ, may glo - ry__ be to Thee,
With Fa - ther and__ with Ho - ly Ghost, Now, and for all E - ter - ni - ty.

1. Why, cru - el Her - od, dost thou fear, Lest Christ, our God and King ap - pear?
He who can heav'n - ly crowns be - stow Comes not to seize thy throne be - low.
2. The Wise Men, guid - ed by the star, Pur - sued their way from realms a - far;
Lit by that light, the Light they seek; Their gifts the pre - sent God be - speak.

* *A transposed organ accompaniment has been provided for optional use.*

3. Un - to the pure and cleans-ing stream Then came the Lamb, the Lord Su-preme;
That He, to whom no sin was known, Might cleanse His peo - ple from their own.
4. Be - hold a new dis - play of might, As Ca - na's wa - ters red - den bright;
He spoke the word, and forth there flowed A stream that na - ture ne'er be-stowed.
5. To Christ, who did the Gen-tiles call, Be end - less glo - ry paid by all;
To God the Fa - ther we re - peat The same, and to the Par - a - clete.

027 EISENACH — *Ad Cenam Agni Providi* — English Translation by Father Fitzpatrick

1. As_ at the Lamb's high feast we sit, And, clad in white, par - take of it,
Since we have passed the dark Red Sea, Our hymns for Christ,_ our Lead - er, be.
2. To_ us, with char - i - ty di - vine, He doth His Sa - cred Blood as - sign:
His hal-lowed Bod - y, as a priest, His love ap - points our host and feast.
3. Awed,_ by the door posts marked with blood, The dev - as - ta - ting An - gel stood;
The sea is part - ed, then it flows To - geth - er, drown - ing Is - raël's foes.
4. The_ Christ is now our Pasch in - deed: Our Vic - tim He, for us to plead;
And He, since pure with pure is fed, Sin - cer - i - ty's_ un - leav-ened Bread.

5. O__ Thou true Vic - tim in the skies, Be - fore Thee, hell sub - ject - ed lies,
By Thee are loos - ened death's cold chains, Thru Thee the soul_ life's guer - don gains.
6. Thou,_ Christ vic - to - rious o'er the grave Un - furl'st Thy ban - ner, there to wave,
And, op'n - ing Heav'n, dost in Thy might The Prince of dark - ness put to flight.
7. O__ Je - sus, that Thou may - est thus Be end - less Pas - chal joy to us,
Keep us, who now new life be - gin, Free from the woe - ful death of sin.
8. To__ God the Fa - ther glo - ry be, The Son, from death a - ris - en free,
The Par - a - clete, from day to day, While age - less ag - es pass a - way.

LASST UNS ERFREUEN — *Ad Cenam Agni Providi* — English Translation by Father Fitzpatrick

1. As at the Lamb's high feast we sit, And, clad in white, par-take of it,
O___ praise Him! Al-le-lu - ia! Since we have passed the dark Red Sea,
Our hymns for Christ, our Lead-er, be. R. Let us praise Him, let us
praise Him: Al-le-lu - ia, al-le-lu - ia, al-le-lu - - ia!
2. To us, with char-i-ty di-vine, He doth His Sa-cred Blood as-sign:
O___ praise Him! Al-le-lu - ia! His hal-lowed Bod-y, as a priest,
His love ap-points our host and feast. R. Let us praise Him, let us
praise Him: Al-le-lu - ia, al-le-lu - ia, al-le-lu - - ia!

3. Awed, by the door posts marked with blood, The dev-as-ta-ting An-gel stood;
O___ praise Him! Al-le-lu-ia! The sea is part-ed, then it flows
To-geth-er, drown-ing Is-raël's foes. R. Let us praise Him, let us
praise Him: Al-le-lu-ia, al-le-lu-ia, al-le-lu-ia!
4. The Christ is now our Pasch in-deed: Our Vic-tim He, for us to plead;
O___ praise Him! Al-le-lu-ia! And He, since pure with pure is fed,
Sin-cer-i-ty's un-leav-ened Bread. R. Let us praise Him, let us
praise Him: Al-le-lu-ia, al-le-lu-ia, al-le-lu-ia!

5. O Thou true Vic-tim in the skies, Be - fore Thee, hell sub-ject-ed lies,
O__ praise Him! Al-le-lu - ia! By Thee are loos-ened death's cold chains,
Through Thee the soul life's guer-don gains. R. Let us praise Him, let us
praise Him: Al-le-lu - ia, al-le-lu - ia, al-le-lu - - ia!
6. Thou, Christ vic - to-rious o'er the grave Un - furl'st Thy ban-ner, there to wave,
O___ praise Him! Al-le-lu - ia! And, op'n-ing Heav'n, dost in Thy might
The Prince of dark-ness put to flight. R. Let us praise Him, let us
praise Him: Al-le-lu - ia, al-le-lu - ia, al-le-lu - - ia!

7. O Je - sus, that Thou may - est thus Be end - less Pas - chal joy to us,
O praise Him! Al - le - lu - ia! Keep us, who now new life be - gin,
Free from the woe - ful death of sin. R. Let us praise Him, let us
praise Him: Al - le - lu - ia, al - le - lu - ia, al - le - lu - ia!
8. To God the Fa - ther glo - ry be, The Son, from death a - ris - en free,
O praise Him! Al - le - lu - ia! The Par - a - clete, from day to day,
While age - less ag - es pass a - way. R. Let us praise Him, let us
praise Him: Al - le - lu - ia, al - le - lu - ia, al - le - lu - ia!

030 ALTONA — *Ad Cenam Agni Providi* — English Translation by Father Fitzpatrick

#18 has (optional) organ accompaniment at a higher key.

5. O Thou true Vic - tim in the skies, Be - fore Thee, hell sub - ject - ed lies,
By Thee are loos - ened death's cold chains, Thru Thee the soul life's guer - don gains.
6. Thou, Christ vic - to - rious o'er the grave Un - furl'st Thy ban - ner,_ there to wave,
And, op'n - ing Heav'n, dost in_ Thy might The Prince of dark - ness put_ to flight.
7. O Je - sus, that Thou may - est thus Be end - less Pas - chal_ joy to us,
Keep us, who now_ new life_ be - gin, Free from the woe - ful death of sin.
8. To God the Fa - ther glo - ry be, The Son, from death a - ris - en free,
The Par - a - clete, from day_ to day, While age - less ag - es pass_ a - way.

032 WHITEHALL — *Ad Cenam Agni Providi* — English Translation by Father Husenbeth

1. Come to the re - gal feast dis - played In robes of pur - est white ar - rayed,
The Red sea's threat - 'ning per - ils past, And sing to Christ se - cure at last.
2. The Lamb's pure blood, the pledge of love, Is free - ly giv'n us from a - bove;
His bod - y now in glo - rious state, As priest, his love will im - mo - late.
3. The doors which show the san - guine dye The a - veng - ing an - gel pass - es by:
The wa - ters of the deep di - vide: The foe is whelmed be - neath the tide.
4. Christ is the Pasch we sac - ri - fice, Pure vic - tim to the Fa - ther's eyes,
Ap - proach - ing with un - sul - lied mind, May all his grace and mer - cy find.

#102 has (optional) organ accompaniment at a higher key.

033 DUGUET — *Ad Cenam Agni Providi* — English Translation by Father Husenbeth

5. Ce - les - tial vic - tim, spot - less, true, Who hell's dark vic - tim o - ver - threw,
From chains of death our souls re - lieved, And life's per - en - nial crown re - ceived.
6. Vic - tor of hell, Christ ris'n dis - plays His tro - phies bright with glo - ry's rays,
And o - p'ning heav'n, he binds his__ chain A - round the king of hell's do - main.
7. O Je - sus! that our faith - ful mind In thee pure pas - chal joy may find,
From dead - ly sin re - deem us__ free, And grant us life re - newed in thee.
8. To God the Fa - ther, to the Son, Who rose from death, his vic - t'ry won,
And Ho - ly Spir - it, hymns of__ praise And glo - ry sem - pi - ter - nal raise.

034 MELCOMBE — *Ad Cenam Agni Providi* — English Translation by Father Husenbeth

5. Ce - les - tial vic - tim, spot - less, true, Who hell's dark vic - tim o - ver - threw,
From chains of death our souls re - lieved, And life's per - en - nial crown re - ceived.
6. Vic - tor of hell, Christ ris'n dis - plays His tro - phies bright with glo - ry's rays,
And o - p'ning heav'n, he binds his chain A - round the king of hell's do - main.
7. O Je - sus! that our faith - ful mind In thee pure pas - chal joy may find,
From dead - ly sin re - deem us free, And grant us life re - newed in thee.
8. To God the Fa - ther, to the Son, Who rose from death, his vic - t'ry won,
And Ho - ly Spir - it, hymns of praise And glo - ry sem - pi - ter - nal raise.

036 SALZBURG — *Ad Cenam Agni Providi* — English Translation by Campbell of Skerrington

1. At the Lamb's high feast we sing Praise to our vic - to - rious King,
Who hath washed us in the tide Flow - ing from his pierc - ѐd side.
Praise we him_whose love di - vine Gives the guests his blood for wine,
Gives his bod - y for the feast, Love the Vic - tim, Love the Priest.
2. Where the Pas-chal blood is poured, Death's dark an - gel sheathes his sword;
Is-rael's hosts tri - um - phant go Through the wave that drowns the foe.
Christ, the Lamb, whose blood was shed, Pas - chal vic - tim, Pas-chal bread;
With sin - cer - i - ty and love Eat we man - na from a - bove.

3. Might - y Vic - tim from on high, Pow'rs of hell be - neath thee lie;
Death is con-quered in the fight; Thou hast brought us life and light.
Now thy ban - ner thou dost wave; Van - quished Sa - tan and the grave;
An - gels join his praise to tell, See o'er - thrown the prince of hell.
4. Pas - chal tri - umph, Pas - chal joy, On - ly sin can this de - stroy;
From the death of sin set free, Souls re - born, dear Lord, in thee.
Hymns of glo - ry, songs of praise, Fa - ther, un - to thee we raise;
Ris - en Lord, all praise to thee, Ev - er with the Spir - it be.

 PASCHAL LAMB — *Ad Cenam Agni Providi* — English Translation by Campbell of Skerrington

3. Might - y Vic - tim from on high, Pow'rs of hell be - neath thee lie;
Death is con-quered in the fight; Thou hast brought us__ life and light.
Now thy ban - ner thou dost wave; Van-quished Sa - tan and the grave;
An - gels join his praise to tell, See o'er-thrown the__ prince of hell.
4. Pas - chal tri - umph, Pas - chal joy, On - ly sin can this de - stroy;
From the death of sin set free, Souls re - born, dear_ Lord, in thee.
Hymns of glo - ry, songs of praise, Fa - ther, un - to thee we raise;
Ris - en Lord, all praise to thee, Ev - er with the__ Spir - it be.

038 ST GEORGE — *Ad Cenam Agni Providi* — English Translation by Campbell of Skerrington

3. Might - y Vic - tim from on high, Pow'rs of hell be - neath thee lie;
Death is con - quered in the fight; Thou hast brought us life and light.
Now thy ban - ner thou dost wave; Van - quished Sa - tan and the grave;
An - gels join his praise to tell, See o'er-thrown the prince of hell.
4. Pas - chal tri - umph, Pas - chal joy, On - ly sin can this de - stroy;
From the death of sin set free, Souls re - born, dear Lord, in thee.
Hymns of glo - ry, songs of praise, Fa - ther, un - to thee we raise;
Ris - en Lord, all praise to thee, Ev - er with the Spir - it be.

039 ORIENTIS PARTIBUS — *Ad Cenam Agni Providi* — English Translation by Campbell of Skerrington

1. At the Lamb's high feast we sing Praise to our vic - to - rious King, Who hath washed us in the tide Flow - ing from his pierc - èd side. Chri - ste Red - em - ptor
2. Praise we him whose love di - vine Gives the guests his blood for wine, Gives his bod - y for the feast, Love the Vic - tim, Love the Priest. Chri - ste Red - em - ptor
3. Where the Pas - chal blood is poured, Death's dark an - gel sheathes his sword; Is - rael's hosts tri - um - phant go Through the wave that drowns the foe. Chri - ste Red - em - ptor
4. Christ, the Lamb, whose blood was shed, Pas - chal vic - tim, Pas - chal bread; With sin - cer - i - ty and love Eat we man - na from a - bove. Chri - ste Red - em - ptor

5. Might - y Vic - tim from on high, Pow'rs of hell be - neath thee lie; Death is con-quered
in the fight; Thou hast brought us life and light. Chri - ste Red - em - ptor
6. Now thy ban - ner thou dost wave; Van-quished Sa - tan and the grave; An - gels join his
praise to tell, See o'er-thrown the prince of hell. Chri - ste Red - em - ptor
7. Pas - chal tri - umph, Pas - chal joy, On - ly sin can this de - stroy; From the death of
sin set free, Souls re - born, dear Lord, in thee. Chri - ste Red - em - ptor
8. Hymns of glo - ry, songs of praise, Fa - ther, un - to thee we raise; Ris - en Lord, all
praise to thee, Ev - er with the Spir - it be. Chri - ste Red - em - ptor

1. At the Lamb's high feast we_ sing Al - le - lu - ia.
Praise to our vic - to - rious_ King, Al - - le - lu - - ia.
Who hath washed us in_ the_ tide Al - le - lu - ia.
Flow - ing from his pierc - èd_ side. Al - - le - lu - ia.
2. Praise we him whose love di - vine Al - le - lu - ia. Gives the guests his
blood for_ wine, Al - le - lu - ia. Gives his bod - y for_ the_ feast,
Al - le - lu - ia. Love the Vic - tim, Love the_Priest. Al - le - lu - ia.

3. Where the Pas-chal blood is poured, Al - le - lu - ia.
Death's dark an-gel sheathes his sword; Al - le - lu - ia.
Is-rael's hosts tri - um - phant go Al - le - lu - ia.
Through the wave that drowns the foe. Al - le - lu - ia.
4. Christ, the Lamb, whose blood was shed, Al - le - lu - ia. Pas-chal vic-tim,
Pas-chal bread; Al - le - lu - ia. With sin-cer-i-ty and love
Al - le - lu - ia. Eat we man-na from a-bove. Al - le - lu - ia.

5. Might - y Vic - tim from on__ high, Al - - le - lu - ia.
Pow'rs of hell be - neath thee__ lie; Al - - le - lu - ia.
Death is con-quered in__ the__ fight; Al - le - lu - ia.
Thou hast brought us life and__ light. Al - - le - lu - ia.
6. Now thy ban - ner thou dost__ wave; Al - le - lu - ia. Van-quished Sa - tan
and the__ grave; Al - le - lu - ia. An - gels join his praise to__ tell,
Al - le - lu - ia. See o'er - thrown the prince of__ hell. Al - le - lu - ia.

7. Pas - chal tri - umph, Pas - chal_ joy, Al - - le - lu - ia.
On - ly sin can this de - stroy; Al - - le - lu - ia.
From the death of sin_ set_ free, Al - le - lu - ia.
Souls re - born, dear Lord, in_ thee. Al - - le - lu - ia.
8. Hymns of glo - ry, songs of_praise, Al - le - lu - ia. Fa - ther, un - to
thee we_ raise; Al - le - lu - ia. Ris - en Lord, all praise to_ thee,
Al - le - lu - ia. Ev - er with the Spir - it_ be. Al - le - lu - ia.

041 SAVANNAH — *Ad Cenam Agni Providi* — English Translation by Campbell of Skerrington

1. At the__ Lamb's high feast_ we sing Praise to__ our vic - to - rious King,
Who hath washed us__ in the tide Flow - ing from his__ pierc - èd side.
2. Praise we__ him whose love_ di - vine Gives the__ guests his blood_ for wine,
Gives his bod - y__ for the feast, Love the Vic - tim,_ Love the Priest.
3. Where the__ Pas - chal blood is poured, Death's dark_ an - gel sheathes his sword;
Is - rael's hosts tri - um - phant go Through the wave that_ drowns the foe.
4. Christ, the__ Lamb, whose blood was shed, Pas - chal_ vic - tim, Pas - chal bread;
With sin - cer - i - ty and love Eat we man - na__ from a - bove.

5. Might - y Vic - tim from on high, Pow'rs of hell be - neath thee lie;
Death is con - quered in the fight; Thou hast brought us life and light.
6. Now thy ban - ner thou dost wave; Van - quished Sa - tan and the grave;
An - gels join his praise to tell, See o'er-thrown the prince of hell.
7. Pas - chal tri - umph, Pas - chal joy, On - ly sin can this de - stroy;
From the death of sin set free, Souls re - born, dear Lord, in thee.
8. Hymns of glo - ry, songs of praise, Fa - ther, un - to thee we raise;
Ris - en Lord, all praise to thee, Ev - er with the Spir - it be.

 GROSSER GOTT 7B — *Ad Cenam Agni Providi* — English Translation by Campbell of Skerrington

This pairing (Text+Tune) appeared in *Arundel Hymns* (1898), a hymnal endorsed by Pope Leo XIII.

3. Might - y Vic - tim from_ on high, Pow'rs of hell_ be - neath thee lie;_
Death is con - quered in_ the fight; Thou hast brought us life_ and light._
Now thy ban - ner thou dost wave; Van - quished Sa - tan and_ the grave;
An - gels join_ his praise to tell, See o'er - thrown the prince of hell.
4. Pas - chal tri - umph, Pas - chal joy, On - ly sin_ can this_ de - stroy;
From the death of sin_ set free, Souls re - born,_ dear Lord, in thee._
Hymns of glo - ry, songs of praise, Fa - ther, un - to thee_ we raise;
Ris - en Lord, all praise to thee, Ev - er with_ the Spir - it be.

043 ST VENANTIUS — *Ad Cenam Agni Providi* — English Translation by E. R. Charles

1. The Sup - per of__ the Lamb to share, We come in ves - ture white and fair,
The Red_ Sea crossed, our hymn we sing To Christ, our Cap - tain and our King.
2. His ho - ly bod - y on the cross, Parched, on__ that al - tar hung for us;
Par - tak - ing of__ His sa - cred blood, We live_ up - on__ the liv - ing God.
3. Pro - tect - ed in__ the Pas - chal night From the__ de - stroy - ing an - gel's might,
And by__ a pow'r - ful hand set free From Phar - aoh's bit - ter slav - er - y.

4. For Christ our Pass - o - ver is slain. The Lamb is of - fered not__ in vain;
Sin - cer - i - ty's__ un - leav - ened bread, His flesh He gave, His blood He shed.
5. O Vic - tim ev - er wor - thy, who Didst all__ the bonds of hell__ un - do,
Didst ran - som cap - tives from the foe And life,__ thy gift,__ a - fresh be - stow!
6. When Christ from out__ the tomb a - rose, Vic - tor__ o'er hell__ and all__ His foes,
The ty - rant down in chains He threw, And plant - ed Par - a - dise a - new.

044 DEVONSHIRE — *Ad Cenam Agni Providi* — English Translation by E. R. Charles

4. For Christ our Pass - o - ver is slain. The Lamb is of - fered not in vain;
Sin - cer - i - ty's un - leav - ened bread, His flesh He gave, His blood He shed.
5. O Vic - tim ev - er wor - thy, who Didst all the bonds of__ hell un - do,
Didst ran - som cap - tives from the foe And life, thy gift, a - fresh be - stow!
6. When Christ from out the tomb a - rose, Vic - tor o'er hell and__ all His foes,
The ty - rant down in chains He threw, And plant - ed Par - a - dise_ a - new.

 HILDERSTONE — *Ad Cenam Agni Providi* — English Translation by E. R. Charles

1. The Sup-per of the Lamb to share, We come in ves-ture white and fair,
The Red Sea crossed, our hymn we sing To Christ, our_ Cap-tain and our King.
2. His ho-ly bod-y on the cross, Parched, on that al-tar hung for us;
Par-tak-ing of His sa-cred blood, We live up-on the liv-ing God.
3. Pro-tect-ed in the Pas-chal night From the de-stroy-ing an-gel's might,

* *A transposed organ accompaniment has been provided for optional use.*

And by a pow'r-ful hand set free From Phar - aoh's_ bit - ter slav - er - y.
4. For Christ our Pass - o - ver is slain. The Lamb is of - fered not in vain;
Sin - cer - i - ty's un - leav-ened bread, His flesh He_ gave, His blood He shed.
5. O Vic-tim ev - er wor - thy, who Didst all the bonds of hell un - do,
Didst ran-som cap-tives from the foe And life, thy_ gift, a - fresh be-stow!
6. When Christ from out the tomb a-rose, Vic - tor o'er hell and all His foes,
The ty-rant down in chains He threw, And plant - ed_ Par - a - dise a - new.

046 KEMPEN — *Ad Cenam Agni Providi* — English Translation by E. R. Charles

Melody © World Library Publications. Used with permission.

4. For Christ our Pass - o - ver is slain. The Lamb is of - fered not_ in vain;
Sin - cer - i - ty's un - leav-ened bread, His flesh He gave, His blood He shed.
5. O Vic - tim ev - er wor - thy, who Didst all_ the bonds of hell_ un - do,
Didst ran - som cap - tives from the foe And life, thy gift,_ a - fresh_ be - stow!
6. When Christ from out the tomb a - rose, Vic - tor_ o'er hell and all_ His foes,
The ty - rant down in chains He threw, And plant - ed Par - a - dise_ a - new.

 HERZLIEBSTER JESU — *Ad Preces Nostras Deitatis* — English Translation by McDougall

1. God, of thy pit - y, un - to us thy chil - dren Bend down thine ear in thine own lov - ing -
kind - ness, And all thy peo - ple's prayers and vows as - cend - ing Hear, we be - seech thee.
2. Look down in mer - cy from thy seat of glo - ry, Pour on our
souls the ra - diance of thy pres - ence, Drive from our wea - ry
hearts the shades of dark - ness, Light - en our foot - steps.
3. Free us from sin by might of thy great lov - ing, Cleanse thou the
sor - did, loose the fet-tered spir - it, Spare eve - ry sin - ner,
raise with thine own right hand All who are fall - en.

4. Reft of thy guid - ing we are lost in dark - ness, Drowned in the great wide sea of sin we
per - ish, But we are led by thy strong hand to climb the As-cents of heav - en.
5. Christ, ver - y light and good-ness, life of all things, Joy of the
whole world, in - fi - nite in kind - ness, Who by the crim - son
flow - ing of thy life - blood From death hast saved us,
6. Plant, sweet-est Je - sus, at our sup - pli - ca - tion Deep in our
hearts thy char - i - ty: up - on us Faith's ev - er - last - ing
light be poured, and in - crease Grant us of lov - ing.

7. Grant to our souls a ho - ly fount of weep - ing, Grant to us strength to aid us in our
fast - ing, And all the thou - sand hosts of e - vil ban - ish Far from thy peo - ple.
8. Bruised by thine heel may Sa - tan and his le - gions Far from our
minds be driv - en, that are guid - ed By the in - dwell - ing
of the Ho - ly Spir - it Sent from thy heav - en.
9. Glo - ry to God the Fa - ther ev - er - last - ing, Glo - ry for
ev - er to the Sole - be - got - ten, With whom the Ho - ly
Spir - it through the ag - es Reign - eth co - e - qual.

ISTE CONFESSOR — *Ad Preces Nostras Deitatis* — English Translation by McDougall

4. Reft of thy guid - ing we are lost in dark - ness, Drowned in the great wide sea of sin we
per - ish, But we are led by thy strong hand to climb the As - cents of heav - en.
5. Christ, ver - y light and good - ness, life of all things,
Joy of the whole world, in - fi - nite in kind - ness, Who by the
crim - son flow - ing of thy life - blood From death hast saved us,
6. Plant, sweet-est Je - sus, at our sup - pli - ca - tion
Deep in our hearts thy char - i - ty: up - on us Faith's ev - er -
last - ing light be poured, and in - crease Grant us of lov - ing.

7. Grant to our souls a ho - ly fount of weep - ing, Grant to us strength to aid us in our
fast - ing, And all the thou - sand hosts of e - vil ban - ish Far from thy peo - ple.
8. Bruised by thine heel may Sa - tan and his le - gions
Far from our minds be driv - en, that are guid - ed By the in -
dwell - ing of the Ho - ly Spir - it Sent from thy heav - en.
9. Glo - ry to God the Fa - ther ev - er - last - ing,
Glo - ry for ev - er to the Sole - be - got - ten, With whom the
Ho - ly Spir - it through the ag - es Reign - eth co - e - qual.

 ST RITA — *Adoro Te Devote, Latens Deitas* — English Translation by Monsignor Henry

1. Tru - ly I a - dore Thee, hid - den De - i - ty,
That be - neath these fig - ures hid - est ver - i - ly:
Sub - ject is my spir - it whol - ly to Thy sway,
For in con - tem - plat - ing Thee it faints a - way.
2. Taste and touch and vi - sion are de - ceived in Thee, And the hear - ing
on - ly can safe wit - ness be. I be - lieve what - ev - er from the
Lord is heard: Noth - ing can be tru - er than Truth's ver - y word.

3. On the cross was hid - den but the De - i - ty;
Nor is here the Man - hood e - ven ours to see:
Yet these both con - fess - ing with the same be - lief,
I will make pe - ti - tion like the dy - ing thief.
4. Though Thy wounds as Thom - as saw, I see not now,
Thee my lips shall ev - er Lord and God a - vow.
Grant that I may ev - er more and more be - lieve,
Hope in Thee and love Thee bar - ring all re - prieve.

5. O Me - mo - rial bless - èd of the Sav - ior's death,
O true Bread that giv - eth man his vi - tal breath,
Let mine un - der - stand - ing live on Thee a - lone,
And let it for - ev - er but Thy sweet - ness own.
6. Pel - i - can most ten - der, Je - sus, Lord and God, Wash my guilt - y
spir - it in Thy Pre - cious Blood: One sole drop a - vail - eth all the
world to win From its ban of bond-age and its stain of sin.

7. Je - sus, Whom but veil - èd see I here be - low,
Cede the draft, I pray Thee, that I thirst for so—
That, the veil once riv - en, in Thy fond em - brace
I may see Thy glo - ry ev - er face to face.

059 UNE VAINE CRAINTE — *Adoro Te Devote, Latens Deitas* — English Translation by Monsignor Henry

1. Tru - ly I a - dore Thee, hid - den De - i - ty, That be - neath these
fig - ures hid - est ver - i - ly: Sub - ject is my spir - it
whol - ly to Thy sway, For in con - tem - plat - ing Thee it faints a - way.
2. Taste and touch and vi - sion are de-ceived in Thee, And the hear - ing
on - ly can safe wit - ness be. I be - lieve what - ev - er
from the Lord is heard: Noth - ing can be tru - er than Truth's ver - y word.
3. On the cross was hid - den but the De - i - ty; Nor is here the

Man - hood e - ven ours to see: Yet these both con - fess - ing
with the same be - lief, I will make pe - ti - tion like the dy - ing thief.
4. Though Thy wounds as Thom - as saw, I see not now, Thee my lips shall
ev - er Lord and God a - vow. Grant that I may ev - er
more and more be - lieve, Hope in Thee and love Thee bar - ring all re - prieve.
5. O Me - mo - rial bless - èd of the Sav - ior's death, O true Bread that
giv - eth man his vi - tal breath, Let mine un - der - stand - ing

live on Thee a - lone, And let it for - ev - er but Thy sweet - ness own.
6. Pel - i - can most ten - der, Je - sus, Lord and God, Wash my guilt - y
spir - it in Thy Pre - cious Blood: One sole drop a - vail - eth
all the world to win From its ban of bond - age and its stain of sin.
7. Je - sus, Whom but veil - èd see I here be - low, Cede the draft, I
pray Thee, that I thirst for so— That, the veil once riv - en,
in Thy fond em - brace I may see Thy glo - ry ev - er face to face.

CUDDESDON — *Adoro Te Devote, Latens Deitas* — English Translation by Monsignor Henry **060**

1. Tru - ly I a - dore Thee, hid-den De - i - ty, That be-neath these
fig - ures hid - est ver - i - ly: Sub - ject is my spir - it
whol - ly to Thy sway, For in con - tem - plat - ing Thee it faints a - way.
2. Taste and touch and vi - sion are de-ceived in Thee, And the hear - ing
on - ly can safe wit - ness be. I be - lieve what - ev - er
from the Lord is heard: Noth - ing can be tru - er than Truth's ver - y word.
3. On the cross was hid - den but the De - i - ty; Nor is here the

Man - hood e - ven ours to see: Yet these both con - fess - ing
with the same be - lief, I will make pe - ti - tion like the dy - ing thief.
4. Though Thy wounds as Thom - as saw, I see not now, Thee my lips shall
evi - er Lord and God a - vow. Grant that I may ev - er
more and more be - lieve, Hope in Thee and love Thee bar - ring all re - prieve.
5. O Me - mo - rial bless - èd of the Sav - ior's death, O true Bread that
giv - eth man his vi - tal breath, Let mine un - der - stand - ing

live on Thee a - lone, And let it for - ev - er but Thy sweet - ness own.
6. Pel - i - can most ten - der, Je - sus, Lord and God, Wash my guilt - y
spir - it in Thy Pre-cious Blood: One sole drop a - vail - eth
all the world to win From its ban of bond-age and its stain of sin.
7. Je - sus, Whom but veil - èd see I here be - low, Cede the draft, I
pray Thee, that I thirst for so— That, the veil once riv - en,
in Thy fond em - brace I may see Thy glo - ry ev - er face to face.

 TOULON — *Adoro Te Devote, Latens Deitas* — English Translation by Archbishop Bagshawe

1. I wor - ship Thee de - vout - ly, who dost hide With - in these fig - ures,
Hid - den De - i - ty, And ut - ter - ly sub - ject my heart to Thee,
To com - pre - hend Thee, fail - ing ut - ter - ly.
2. Though sight, and
taste, and touch, do fail in Thee, Yet may we trust to what from Thee we
hear; I do be - lieve in what God's Son hath said, Nought tru - er than that
word of Truth most clear.
3. Up - on the Cross the De - i - ty was
hid, But here His Hu - man Na - ture lies con - cealed, Yet, both be -

liev - ing, that I sup - pli - cate, For which the Thief from off his
cross ap - pealed.
4. Thy wounds, like Thom - as, I do not be - hold,
Yet Thee, as God, I wor-ship and a - dore, O make me with more
faith in Thee be - lieve, And hope in Thee, and love Thee, more and
more.
5. I now be - hold Thee, hid - den un - der veils,
O grant my prayer, that I Thy Face may see, Re - vealed in glo - ry,
sight for which I thirst, To make me bless - èd for E - ter - ni - ty.

063 FARLEY CASTLE — *Adoro Te Devote* — English Translation by Archbishop Bagshawe

1. I worship Thee devoutly, who dost hide
Within these figures, Hidden Deity,
And utterly subject my heart to Thee,
To comprehend Thee, failing utterly.
2. Though sight, and taste, and touch, do fail in Thee,
Yet may we trust to what from Thee we hear;
I do believe in what God's Son hath said,
Nought truer than that word of Truth most clear.
3. Upon the Cross the Deity was hid,
But here His Human Nature lies concealed,
Yet, both be -

liev - ing, that I sup - pli - cate, For which the Thief from off his
cross ap - pealed.
4. Thy wounds, like Thom - as, I do not be - hold,
Yet Thee, as God, I wor - ship and a - dore, O make me
with more faith in Thee be - lieve, And hope in Thee, and love Thee,
more and more.
5. I now be - hold Thee, hid - den un - der veils,
O grant my prayer, that I Thy Face may see, Re - vealed in
glo - ry, sight for which I thirst, To make me bless - èd for E - ter - ni - ty.

 ALL SOULS — *Adoro Te Devote* — English Translation by Archbishop Bagshawe

liev - ing, that I sup - pli - cate, For which the Thief from off his
cross ap - pealed.
4. Thy wounds, like Thom - as, I do not be - hold,
Yet Thee, as God, I wor - ship and a - dore, O make me
with more faith in Thee be - lieve, And hope in Thee, and love Thee,
more and more.
5. I now be - hold Thee, hid-den un - der veils,
O grant my prayer, that I Thy Face may see, Re - vealed in glo - ry,
sight for which I thirst, To make me bless-èd for E - ter - ni - ty.

SONG 24 — *Adoro Te Devote* — English Translation by Archbishop Bagshawe

liev - ing, that I sup - pli - cate, For which the Thief from off his
cross ap - pealed.
4. Thy wounds, like Thom - as, I do not be - hold,
Yet Thee, as God, I wor - ship and a - dore, O make me
with more faith in Thee be - lieve, And hope in Thee, and love Thee,
more and more.
5. I now be - hold Thee, hid - den un - der veils,
O grant my prayer, that I Thy Face may see, Re - vealed in
glo - ry, sight for which I thirst, To make me bless - èd for E - ter - ni - ty.

066 EVENTIDE — *Adoro Te Devote* — English Translation by Archbishop Bagshawe

liev - ing, that I sup - pli - cate, For which the Thief from off his
cross ap - pealed.
4. Thy wounds, like Thom - as, I do not be - hold,
Yet Thee, as God, I wor - ship and a - dore, O make me with
more faith in Thee be - lieve, And hope in Thee, and love Thee,
more and more.
5. I now be - hold Thee, hid - den un - der veils,
O grant my prayer, that I Thy Face may see, Re - vealed in glo - ry,
sight for which I thirst, To make me bless - èd for E - ter - ni - ty.

1. God - head here in hid - ing, whom I do a - dore, Masked by these bare
shad - ows, shape and noth - ing more, See, Lord, at thy ser - vice
low lies here a heart Lost, all lost in won - der at the God thou art.
2. See - ing, touch - ing, tast - ing are in thee de - ceived: How says trust - y
hear - ing? That shall be be - lieved. What God's Son has told me,
take for truth I do— Truth him - self speaks tru - ly, or there's noth - ing true.
3. On the Cross thy God - head made no sign to men; Here thy ver - y

man - hood steals from hu - man ken; Both are my con - fes - sion,
both are my be - lief, And I pray the same prayer as the dy - ing thief.
4. I am not like Thom - as, wounds I can - not see, But can plain - ly
call thee Lord and God as he; This faith each day deep - er
be my hold - ing of, Dai - ly make me hard - er hope and dear - er love.
5. O thou our re - mind - er of Christ cru - ci - fied, Liv - ing Bread, the
life of us for whom he died, Lend this life to me then:

feed and feast my mind, There be thou the sweet - ness man was meant to find.
6. Bring the ten - der tale true of the Pel - i - can, Bathe me, Je - sus
Lord, in what thy bos - om ran— Blood that but one drop of
has the worth to win All the world for - give - ness of its world of sin.
7. Je - sus, whom I look at shroud-ed here be - low, I be-seech thee
send me what I long for so, Some day to gaze on thee
face to face in light And be blest for ev - er with thy glo - ry's sight.

FIORILLO — *Adoro Te Devote* — English Translation by C. K. Paul **070**

1. Hum - bly I a - dore Thee, Hid - den De - i - ty, Who be - neath these
fig - ures hid - est ver - i - ly: Whol - ly in sub - mis - sion
Thee my spir - it hails, For in con - tem - plat - ing Thee it whol - ly fails.
2. See - ing, tast - ing, touch - ing are in Thee de - ceived, And a - lone the
hear - ing safe - ly is be - lieved: All the Son of God said
I ac - cept and hold, Tru - est truth that must be which the Truth has told.
3. Once 'twas God-head on - ly hid - den on the Tree, Now the Man-hood

al - so is not here to see; Both I now be - lieve, and
vow-ing my be - lief, Seek I what of old sought the re-pent-ant thief.
4. On Thy wounds, like Thom - as, though I do not gaze, Yet, my Lord, I
know Thee, and con-fess al - ways; Give me in Thee ev - er
faith all faiths a - bove, Give me hope in - creas - ing, give me great-er love.
5. O Thou high me - mo - rial of my Lord who died, Liv - ing Bread, for
mor - tals Thou dost life pro - vide; Grant through Thee my soul's life

nev - er more may waste, Give in it Thy sa - vor sweet-ly to my taste.
6. Pel - i - can of mer - cy, Je - sus, Lord and God, Cleanse me, wretch-ed
sin - ner, in Thy Pre-cious Blood; One drop, and one on - ly,
might a - vail to win Par-don, full, a - bound - ing, for the whole world's sin.
7. Je - sus, whom thus dim - ly un - der veils I see, Grant the boon I
thirst for, grant my prayer to me, That, veils rent a - sun - der,
I may see by Grace, Fi - nal - ly the glo - ry of Thy ver - y Face.

074 FULDA — *Agnoscat Omne Saeculum* — English Translation by the editors

1. He who is life's re - ward draws near, Let all the world con - fess him here:
The ruth - less foe - man's yoke is past, Re - demp - tion hath ap - peared at last.
2. Ful - fill-ment of I - sa - iah's strain A Vir - gin mer - its to at - tain:
The same an An - gel came to greet The Ho - ly Ghost hath left re - plete.
3. The bless-èd Mar - y hath con-ceived By that true word which she be - lieved:
And he whom worlds can - not com - prise With - in a maid - en's bod - y lies.
4. There springs a branch from Jes - se's root, And lo, his rod puts forth its fruit:
The Moth - er, though she tru - ly bore, A - bides a Vir - gin, as be - fore.

* *Some choirmasters will transpose this hymn to a higher key.*

5. He at whose wish the light_ was made, Yet will-ing-ly in man - ger laid,
Who with his Fa - ther spread the skies, Now swad - dled by_ his Moth - er lies.
6. Com - mand-ments ten, the Law_ he gave, A heed-less world to teach_ and save,
Who, man be - come, a bonds - man is_ Of that same Law_whose gift_ was his.
7. The lat-ter Ad - am wash - es clear Where once the for - mer chose_ to smear:
That which the proud man for - feit - ed_ The low - li - est_ up - holds in - stead.
8. Now light is born and strength re - newed, The night dis-pelled and death_ sub - dued:
Come and be - lieve,_ ye na - tions, then,_ That Mar - y brings their God_ to men.

078 MELCOMBE — *Auctor Beate Saeculi* — English Translation by Father Popplewell

1. O bless - èd Fram - er of the world, O Christ, all things who dost re - deem,
art ver - y God of ver - y God, the gleam-ing of the Fa - ther's gleam:
2. Thy love it was did thee con-strain on thee to take our mor - tal clay,
the lat - ter Ad - am, to re-store that which the for - mer took a - way.
3. Thy love it was did earth, and sea, and stars with boun - teous craft - ing make,
took pit - y when our fa - thers strayed, and did our own con - fine-ments break.

4. Let not that force of no - ble love from out its prop - er seat de - part:
and let the na - tions draw the grace of par - don at that spring, thy Heart:
5. The which for this once suf - fered wounds, and e'en for this the bit - ter spear:
our - selves, who were in filth - y state, while wa - ter ran with blood, to clear.
6. Let praise the Fa - ther, and the Son, and Ho - ly Ghost this day at - tend,
as glo - ry, might and rule be-seem the same, nor ev - er - more shall end.

079 KEMPEN — *Auctor Beate Saeculi* — English Translation by Father Popplewell

4. Let not that force of no - ble love from out__ its prop - er seat__ de - part:
and let the na - tions draw the grace of par - don at__ that spring, thy Heart:
5. The which for this once suf - fered wounds, and e'en__ for this the bit - ter spear:
our-selves, who were in filth - y state, while wa - ter ran__ with blood, to clear.
6. Let praise the Fa - ther, and the Son, and Ho - ly Ghost this day__ at - tend,
as glo - ry, might and rule be - seem the same, nor ev - er - more shall end.

080 BESSEMER — *Auctor Beate Saeculi* — English Translation by Father Popplewell

4. Let not that force of no - ble love from out its prop - er seat de - part:
and let the na - tions draw the grace of par - don at that spring, thy Heart:
5. The which for this once suf - fered wounds, and e'en for this the bit - ter spear:
our - selves, who were in filth - y state, while wa - ter ran with blood, to clear.
6. Let praise the Fa - ther, and the Son, and Ho - ly Ghost this day at - tend,
as glo - ry, might and rule be - seem the same, nor ev - er - more shall end.

081 WAREHAM — *Auctor Beate Saeculi* — English Translation by Father Popplewell

4. Let not_ that force of no - ble love from out_ its prop - er seat_ de - part:
and let_ the_ na - tions draw the grace of_ par - don at_ that spring, thy Heart:
5. The which for this once suf - fered wounds, and e'en_ for this_ the bit - ter spear:
our - selves, who_ were in filth - y state, while wa - ter ran_ with blood, to clear.
6. Let praise the Fa - ther, and_ the Son, and Ho - ly Ghost this day_ at - tend,
as glo - ry,_ might and rule be - seem the_ same, nor ev - er - more shall end.

082 WINCHESTER NEW — *Auctor Beate Saeculi* — English Translation by Father Popplewell

4. Let not that force of no - ble love from out its prop - er seat de - part:
and let the na - tions draw the grace of par - don at that spring, thy Heart:
5. The which for this once suf - fered wounds, and e'en for this the bit - ter spear:
our - selves, who were in filth - y state, while wa - ter ran with blood, to clear.
6. Let praise the Fa - ther, and the Son, and Ho - ly Ghost this day at - tend,
as glo - ry, might and rule be - seem the same, nor ev - er - more shall end.

084 SEÁN — *Auctor Beate Saeculi* — English Translation by Monsignor Henry

1. Blest Au - thor of the world, Re - deem - er of our race,
Thou ver - y God of God, Light of the Fa - ther's face:
2. 'Twas love that bade Thee take Our__ frame of mor - tal clay,
New Ad - am for the Old, His thiev - ing to re - pay.
3. Thy love that build - ed fair The__ earth, the sea, the stars;
That pit - ied old - en faults, And broke our pris - on - bars:

4. O may Thy Heart re - tain For__ e'er such won-drous love!
Let all ap-proach the Fount, And Thy sweet mer - cy prove.
5. For this a - lone the lance Set__ free Its sav - ing flood,
To wash our sins a - way In wa - ter and in blood.
6. To Fa - ther and to Son And_ Ho - ly Spir - it be
The king-dom and the pow'r Through all e - ter - ni - ty.

1. O Christ, who didst the world cre - ate, And man hast by re - demp - tion freed,
Light of the Fa - ther's Light art Thou, True God from God Thou dost pro - ceed.
2. A mor - tal bod - y to as - sume, Thy won - drous love didst Thee con - strain,
To give what the old Ad - am took, As the new Ad - am, back a - gain.
3. That Love the mak - er was of earth And sea and stars in old - en time,
Our fa - ther's er - rors it for - gave, It breaks for us the bonds of crime.

4. Let not that might - y no - ble Love, To e'er de - part from out Thy Heart;
Let na - tions drink that pard-'ning grace, Which this sweet Foun - tain doth im - part.
5. For this the lance did pierce It through, For this Its wounds It did en - dure,
To cleanse us from our filth - y stains, It poured forth Blood and Wa - ter pure.
6. Glo - ry to Fa - ther and to Son, And to the Ho - ly Spir - it, be,
Let pow'r and hon - or be to Them, And may They reign e - ter - nal - ly.

091 EISENACH — *Audi Benigne Conditor* — English Translation by Father Fitzpatrick

1. O deign to hear, Cre - a - tor Kind,
Our prayers with heart - felt tears com - bined, While on, in ho - ly
fast - ing, glide The for - ty days of Lent - en - tide.
2. Each heart is man - i - fest to Thee:
Thou know - est our in - fir - mi - ty: Re - pent - ant now we
seek Thy face, Vouch - safe to us Thy par - d'ning grace.
3. Our sins are mul - ti - plied and great,

But spare us in our help - less state; And for thy name's re -
nown and praise Our souls to health and vir - tue raise.
4. Grant that our bod - y's ev - 'ry sense
May con - quered be through ab - sti - nence, That so our hearts, which
fast from sin, May find no food for fault there - in.
5. This, Ho - ly Trin - i - ty, who art A per - fect U - ni - ty, im - part;
That they who are Thine own may see How fruit - ful shall their fast - ing be.

 MELCOMBE — *Audi Benigne Conditor* — English Translation by Father Fitzpatrick

1. O deign to hear, Cre - a - tor Kind, Our prayers with heart - felt tears com - bined,
While on, in ho - ly fast - ing, glide The for - ty days of Lent - en - tide.
2. Each heart is man - i - fest to Thee: Thou know - est our in - fir - mi - ty:
Re - pent - ant now we seek Thy face, Vouch - safe to us Thy par - d'ning grace.

* *A transposed organ accompaniment has been provided for optional use.*

3. Our sins are mul - ti - plied and great, But spare us in our help - less state;
And for thy name's re - nown and praise Our souls to health and vir - tue raise.
4. Grant that our bod - y's ev - 'ry sense May con - quered be through ab - sti - nence,
That so our hearts, which fast from sin, May find no food for fault there - in.
5. This, Ho - ly Trin - i - ty, who art A per - fect U - ni - ty, im - part;
That they who are Thine own may see How fruit - ful shall their fast - ing be.

 SAXONY — *Audi Benigne Conditor* — English Translation by Father Fitzpatrick

3. Our sins are mul - ti - plied and great, But spare us in our help - less state;
And for thy name's re - nown and praise Our souls to health and vir - tue raise.
4. Grant that our bod - y's ev - 'ry sense May con - quered be through ab - sti - nence,
That so our hearts, which fast from sin, May find no food for fault there - in.
5. This, Ho - ly Trin - i - ty, who art A per - fect U - ni - ty, im - part;
That they who are Thine own may see How fruit - ful shall their fast - ing be.

 WAREHAM — *Audi Benigne Conditor* — English Translation by Father Fitzpatrick

* *A transposed organ accompaniment has been provided for optional use.*

095 NOTRE DAME — *Audi Benigne Conditor* — English Translation by Father Fitzpatrick

* *A transposed organ accompaniment has been provided for optional use.*

 ALFRETON — *Audi Benigne Conditor* — English Translation by Father Fitzpatrick

** A lower accompaniment (D-Major) is provided in the Brébeuf Organ Edition—for optional use.*
—This is in addition to the (G-Major) transposed version included here—for optional use.

3. Our sins are mul - ti - plied and great, But spare us in our help - less_ state;
And for thy name's re - nown and praise Our souls to health and vir - tue raise.
4. Grant that our bod - y's ev - 'ry sense May con-quered be through ab - sti - nence,
That so our hearts, which fast from sin, May find no food for fault there - in.
5. This, Ho - ly Trin - i - ty, who art A per - fect U - ni - ty, im - part;
That they who are Thine own may see How fruit - ful shall their fast - ing be.

097 BRESSANI — *Audi Benigne Conditor* — English Translation by Father Fitzpatrick

* *A transposed organ accompaniment has been provided for optional use.*

098 KEMPEN — *Audi Benigne Conditor* — English Translation by Father Fitzpatrick

1. O deign to hear, Cre - a - tor Kind, Our prayers with heart - felt tears_ com bined,
While on, in ho - ly fast-ing, glide The for - ty days_ of Lent - en - tide.
2. Each heart is man - i - fest to Thee: Thou know-est our in - fir - mi - ty:
Re-pent - ant now we seek Thy face, Vouch-safe to us__ Thy par - d'ning grace.
3. Our sins are mul - ti - plied and great, But spare us in our help - less state;

And for thy name's re - nown and praise Our souls to health and vir - tue raise.
4. Grant that our bod - y's ev - 'ry sense May con - quered be through ab - sti - nence,
That so our hearts, which fast from sin, May find no food_ for fault_ there - in.
5. This, Ho - ly Trin - i - ty, who art A per - fect U - ni - ty,__ im - part;
That they who are Thine own may see How fruit - ful shall_ their fast - ing be.

099 HILDERSTONE — *Audi Benigne Conditor* — English Translation by Father Fitzpatrick

* *A transposed organ accompaniment has been provided for optional use.*

1. O deign to hear, Cre - a - tor Kind, Our prayers with heart - felt
tears com bined, While on, in ho - ly fast - ing, glide The for - ty
days of Lent - en - tide.
2. Each heart is man - i - fest to
Thee: Thou know - est our in - fir - mi - ty: Re - pent - ant
now we seek Thy face, Vouch - safe to us Thy par - d'ning grace.
3. Our sins are mul - ti - plied and great, But spare us in our help - less state;

And for thy name's re - nown and praise Our souls to health and vir - tue raise.
4. Grant that our bod - y's ev - 'ry sense May con - quered be__ through
ab - sti - nence, That so our hearts,_ which fast__ from sin,__ May find no
food_ for fault__ there - in.
5. This, Ho - ly Trin - i - ty,__ who
art A per - fect U - ni - ty, im - part; That they who
are__ Thine own__ may see__ How fruit - ful shall_ their fast - ing be.

101 BESSEMER — *Audi Benigne Conditor* — English Translation by Father Fitzpatrick

help - less state; And for thy name's re - nown and praise
Our souls to health and vir - tue raise.
4. Grant that our bod - y's
ev - 'ry sense May con-quered be through ab - sti - nence, That
so our hearts, which fast from sin, May find no food for
fault there - in.
5. This, Ho - ly Trin - i - ty, who
art A per - fect U - ni - ty, im - part; That they who
are Thine own may see How fruit - ful shall their fast - ing be.

1. O deign to hear, Cre - a - tor Kind, Our prayers with heart - felt tears com - bined,
While on, in ho - ly fast - ing, glide The for - ty days of Lent - en - tide.
2. Each heart is man - i - fest to Thee: Thou know - est our in - fir - mi - ty:
Re - pent - ant now we seek Thy face, Vouch - safe to us Thy par - d'ning grace.

* *A transposed organ accompaniment has been provided for optional use.*

 AGINCOURT — *Audi Benigne Conditor* — English Translation by Father Potter

* *A transposed organ accompaniment has been provided for optional use.*

3. Much have we sinned, and to ex - cess, But spare us, Lord, who thus con - fess;
And for the glo - ry of thy name, Thy sav - ing mer - cy now pro - claim.
4. As sav - ing fasts our flesh sub - due, May thy_ sweet grace our_ hearts re - new,
That vice may thus_ un - fed re - main, And we from sin and guilt ab - stain.
5. Grant us, O sa - cred Trin - i - ty, Grant us,_ O per - fect U - ni - ty,
That these our fasts_ may fruit-ful prove Of end - less bliss, in realms a - bove.

105 TRINITY COLLEGE — *Audi Benigne Conditor* — English Translation by Father Potter

1. Be - nign Cre - a - tor of the spheres, Hear thou the prayers, be - hold the tears,
That in this ho - ly sea - son we With Lent - en fas - tings, pour to thee.
2. Thy pierc - ing eye our hearts doth scan, And mea - sure all the woes of man;
Whilst now, we sor - r'wing turn to thee, From sin's foul bur - den set us free.

* *A transposed organ accompaniment has been provided for optional use.*

1. Be - nign Cre - a - tor of the spheres, Hear thou the prayers, be - hold the tears,
That in this ho - ly sea-son we With Lent - en fas-tings, pour to thee.
2. Thy pierc - ing eye our hearts doth scan, And mea - sure all the woes of man;
Whilst now, we sor - r'wing turn to thee, From sin's foul bur-den set us free.

* *A transposed organ accompaniment has been provided for optional use.*

107 CANON VIII — *Audi Benigne Conditor* — English Translation by Father Potter

* *The beginning of the Canon is placed in brackets in SOPRANO and TENOR.*

3. Much have we sinned, and to ex - cess, But spare us, Lord, who thus con - fess;
And for the glo - ry of thy name, Thy sav - ing mer - cy now pro - claim.
4. As sav - ing fasts our flesh sub - due, May thy sweet grace our hearts re - new,
That vice may thus un - fed re - main, And we from sin and guilt ab - stain.
5. Grant us, O sa - cred Trin - i - ty, Grant us, O per - fect U - ni - ty,
That these our fasts may fruit - ful prove Of end - less bliss, in realms a - bove.

1. Be - nign_ Cre - a - tor of the spheres, Hear thou_ the prayers, be - hold_ the tears,
That in___ this ho - ly sea - son we With Lent - en fas - tings, pour to thee.
2. Thy pierc - ing eye_ our hearts doth scan, And mea - sure all__ the woes of man;
Whilst now,_ we sor - r'wing turn_ to thee, From sin's_ foul bur - den set us free.

* *A transposed organ accompaniment has been provided for optional use.*

109 BRESLAU — Audi Benigne Conditor — English Translation by Father Potter

3. Much have we sinned, and to ex - cess, But spare us, Lord, who_ thus con - fess;
And for the glo - ry of thy name, Thy sav - ing mer - cy now pro - claim.
4. As sav - ing fasts our flesh sub - due, May thy sweet grace our_ hearts re - new,
That vice may thus un - fed re - main, And we from sin and guilt ab - stain.
5. Grant us, O sa - cred Trin - i - ty, Grant us, O per - fect_ U - ni - ty,
That these our fasts may fruit - ful prove Of end - less bliss, in realms a - bove.

1. Hail, Star of o - cean, hail; God's Moth - er full of love,
And ev - er Vir - gin pure, Blest Gate of Heav'n a - bove.
2. Since from Saint Ga - briel's lips, To thee that "A - ve" came,
Es - tab - lish us in peace, Trans - pos - ing E - va's name.
3. Un - loose the sin - ner's chains, Light to the blind re - store,
Drive far a - way our ills, And all good things im - plore.
4. A Moth - er show thy - self, Through thee, our prayers may He

Ac - cept, who born for us, Deigned to be born of thee.
5. O all - ex - cel - ling Maid, With_ spe - cial meek-ness graced,
O free us from our sins, And keep us al - ways chaste.
6. Pure lives for us ob - tain, And_ a safe way pre - pare,
That we may Je - sus see, And His joy ev - er share.
7. To God the Fa - ther praise, And_ glo - ry to the Son,
And to the Ho - ly Ghost, To Three be hon - or One.

117 ST MARTIN — *Ave Maris Stella* — English Translation by Monsignor Knox

1. Star of o - cean, lead us; God for moth - er claims thee,
Ev - er - Vir - gin names thee; Gate of heav - en, speed us.
2. "A - ve" to thee cry - ing Ga - briel went be - fore us;
Peace do thou re - store us, E - va's knot un - ty - ing.
3. Loose the bonds that chain us, Dark - ened eyes en - light - en,
Cloud - ed pros - pects bright - en, Heav - en's mer - cies gain us.
4. For thy sons thou car - est; Of - fer Christ our pray - ing—

Still thy word o - bey - ing— Whom on earth thou bar - est.
5. Pur - er, kind - er maid - en God did nev - er fash - ion;
Pure - ness and com - pas - sion Grant to hearts sin - lad - en.
6. From that sin re - lease us, Shield us, heav'n - ward far - ing—
Heav'n, that is but shar - ing In thy joy with Je - sus.
7. Hon - or, praise and mer - it To our God ad - dress we;
Three in One con - fess we, Fa - ther, Son, and Spir - it.

1. Hail, thou star a - bove the sea, Vir - gin like none oth - er,
Door to high fe - lic - i - ty, God's own gra - cious Moth - er.
With that "A - ve," which to thee Ga - bri - el has spo - ken,
E - va's name re - verse, that we Peace en - joy un - bro - ken.

* *A transposed organ accompaniment has been provided for optional use.*

2. Blind are we: let us see day; Guilt - y we: un - bind us;
Drive all e - vil things a - way; Gain the good as - signed us.
Prove thy - self a moth - er thus; Pray, at our pe - ti - tion,
Till He hears who, born for us, Showed thee all sub - mis - sion.
3. First of vir - gins, who of all Art most meek and low - ly, Make us, free of
e - vil's pall, Chaste and gen - tle whol - ly. Let our lives grow pure a - pace,
Guide and guard our go - ing, Till, be - hold - ing Je - sus' face, Ours be bliss o'er flow - ing.

 TEMPUS ADEST FLORIDUM — *Ave Maris Stella* — English Translation by Father Fitzpatrick

1. Hail, thou star a - bove the sea, Vir - gin like none oth - - er,
Door to high fe - lic - i - ty, God's own gra - cious Moth - er.
With that "A - ve," which to thee Ga - bri - el has spo - ken,
E - va's name re - verse, that we Peace en - joy un - bro - - ken.

A transposed organ accompaniment has been provided for optional use.

1. Hail, thou star a - bove the sea, Vir - gin like none oth - er,
Door to high fe - lic - i - ty, God's own gra - cious Moth - er.
With that "A - ve," which to thee Ga - bri - el has spo - ken,
E - va's name re - verse, that we Peace en - joy un - bro - ken.
2. Blind are we: let us see day; Guilt - y we: un - bind us;
Drive all e - vil things a - way; Gain the good as - signed us.

Prove thy - self a moth - er thus; Pray, at our pe - ti - tion,
Till He hears who, born for us, Showed thee all sub - mis - sion.
3. First of vir - gins, who of all Art most meek and low - ly,
Make us, free of e - vil's pall, Chaste and gen - tle whol - ly.
Let our lives grow pure a - pace, Guide and guard our go - ing,
Till, be - hold - ing Je - sus' face, Ours be bliss o'er flow - ing.

 JESU LEIDEN PEIN UND TOD — *Ave Maris Stella* — English Translation by Father Fitzpatrick

1. Hail, thou star a - bove the sea, Vir - gin like none oth - er,
Door to high fe - lic - i - ty, God's own gra - cious Moth - er.
With that "A - ve," which to thee Ga - bri - el___ has spo - ken,
E - va's name re - verse, that we Peace en - joy un - bro - ken.
2. Blind are we: let us see day; Guilt - y we: un - bind us;
Drive all e - vil things a - way; Gain the good as - signed us.

Prove thy - self a moth - er thus; Pray, at our pe - ti - tion,
Till He hears who, born for us, Showed thee all sub - mis - sion.
3. First of vir - gins, who of all Art most meek and low - ly,
Make us, free of e - vil's pall, Chaste and gen - tle whol - ly.
Let our lives grow pure a - pace, Guide and guard our go - ing,
Till, be - hold - ing Je - sus' face, Ours be bliss o'er flow - ing.

1. Hail, thou star a - bove the sea, Vir - gin like none oth - er,
Door to high fe - lic - i - ty, God's own gra - cious Moth - er.
With that "A - ve," which to thee Ga - bri - el has spo - ken,
E - va's name re - verse, that we Peace en - joy un - bro - ken.

* *A transposed organ accompaniment has been provided for optional use.*

1. Hail, thou star a - bove the sea, Vir - gin like none oth - er, Door to high fe -
lic - i - ty, God's own gra - cious Moth - er. Vir - go Ma - rí - a!
2. With that "A - ve," which to thee Ga - bri - el has spo - ken, E - va's
name re - verse, that we Peace en - joy un - bro - ken. Vir - go Ma - rí - a!
3. Blind are we: let us see day; Guilt - y we: un - bind us; Drive all e - vil
things a - way; Gain the good as - signed us. Vir - go Ma - rí - a!
4. Prove thy - self a moth - er thus; Pray, at our pe - ti - tion, Till He hears who,

born for us, Showed thee all sub - mis - sion. Vir - go Ma - rí - a!
5. First of vir - gins, who of all Art most meek and low - ly, Make us,
free of e - vil's pall, Chaste and gen - tle whol - ly. Vir - go Ma - rí - a!
6. Let our lives grow pure a - pace, Guide and guard our go - ing, Till, be -
hold - ing Je - sus' face, Ours be bliss o'er flow - ing. Vir - go Ma - rí - a!
7. Glo - ry to the Fa - ther be, And the Christ su - per - nal, And the Spir - it:
to the Three E - qual praise e - ter - nal. Vir - go Ma - rí - a!

WÜRTEMBURG E6 — *Ave Maris Stella* — English Translation by Father Fitzpatrick

1. Hail, thou star a - bove the sea, Vir - gin like none oth - er, Door to
high fe - lic - i - ty, God's own gra - cious Moth - er. Al - le - lu - ia.
2. With that "A - ve," which to thee Ga - bri - el has spo - ken, E - va's
name re - verse, that we Peace en - joy un - bro - ken. Al - le - lu - ia.
3. Blind are we: let us see day; Guilt - y we: un - bind us; Drive all
e - vil things a - way; Gain the good as - signed us. Al - le - lu - ia.
4. Prove thy - self a moth - er thus; Pray, at our pe - ti - tion, Till He

hears who, born for us, Showed thee all_ sub - mis - sion. Al - le - lu - ia.
5. First of vir - gins, who of all Art most meek and low - ly, Make us,
free of e - vil's pall, Chaste and gen - tle whol - ly. Al - le - lu - ia.
6. Let our lives grow pure a - pace, Guide and guard our go - ing, Till, be -
hold-ing Je - sus' face, Ours be bliss o'er flow - ing. Al - le - lu - ia.
7. Glo - ry to the Fa - ther be, And the Christ su - per - nal, And the
Spir - it: to the Three E - qual praise e - ter - nal. Al - le - lu - ia.

 MONKLAND E6 — *Ave Maris Stella* — English Translation by Father Fitzpatrick

1. Hail, thou star a - bove the_ sea, Vir - gin like none oth - er,
Door to_ high fe - lic - i - ty, God's own_ gra - cious Moth - er.
2. With that "A - ve," which to_ thee Ga - bri - el has spo - ken,
E - va's_ name re - verse, that we Peace en - joy un - bro - ken.
3. Blind are we: let us_ see_ day; Guilt - y we: un - bind_ us;
Drive all_ e - vil things a - way; Gain the_ good as - signed_ us.
4. Prove thy - self a moth - er_ thus; Pray, at our pe - ti - tion,

Till He__ hears who, born for us, Showed thee__ all sub - mis - sion.
5. First of vir - gins, who_ of__ all Art most meek and low - ly,
Make us,__ free of e - vil's pall, Chaste and__ gen - tle whol - ly.
6. Let our lives grow pure_ a - pace, Guide and guard our go - ing,
Till, be - hold - ing Je - sus' face, Ours be__ bliss o'er flow - ing.
7. Glo - ry to the Fa - ther_ be, And the Christ su - per - nal,
And the__ Spir - it: to the Three E - qual_ praise e - ter - nal.

1. Hail, thou star a - bove the sea, Vir - gin like none oth - er,
Door to high fe - lic - i - ty, God's own gra - cious Moth - er.
2. With that "A - ve," which to thee Ga - bri - el has spo - ken,
E - va's name re - verse, that we Peace en - joy un - bro - ken.
3. Blind are we: let us see day; Guilt - y we: un - bind us;
Drive all e - vil things a - way; Gain the good as - signed us.
4. Prove thy - self a moth - er thus; Pray, at our pe - ti - tion,

Till He hears who, born for us, Showed thee all sub - mis - sion.
5. First of vir - gins, who of all Art most meek and low - ly,
Make us, free of e - vil's pall, Chaste and gen - tle whol - ly.
6. Let our lives grow pure a - pace, Guide and guard our go - ing,
Till, be - hold - ing Je - sus' face, Ours be bliss o'er flow - ing.
7. Glo - ry to the Fa - ther be, And the Christ su - per - nal,
And the Spir - it: to the Three E - qual praise e - ter - nal.

1. Hail, thou star a - bove the sea, Vir - gin like none oth - er,
Door to high fe - lic - i - ty, God's own gra - cious Moth - er.
2. With that "A - ve," which to thee Ga - bri - el has spo - ken,
E - va's name re - verse, that we Peace en - joy un - bro - ken.
3. Blind are we: let us see day; Guilt - y we: un - bind us;
Drive all e - vil things a - way; Gain the good as - signed us.
4. Prove thy - self a moth - er thus; Pray, at our pe - ti - tion,

Till He hears who, born for us, Showed thee all sub - mis - sion.
5. First of vir - gins, who of all Art most meek and low - ly,
Make us, free of e - vil's pall, Chaste and gen - tle whol - ly.
6. Let our lives grow pure a - pace, Guide and guard our go - ing,
Till, be - hold - ing Je - sus' face, Ours be bliss o'er flow - ing.
7. Glo - ry to the Fa - ther be, And the Christ su - per - nal,
And the Spir - it: to the Three E - qual praise e - ter - nal.

ST MARTIN — *Ave Maris Stella* — English Translation by Riley

1. Hail, O Star that point - est T'ward the port of heav - en,
Thou to whom as Maid - en God for Son was giv - en.
2. When the sal - u - ta - tion Ga - bri - el had spo - ken,
Peace was shed up - on us, E - va's bonds were bro - ken.
3. Bound by Sa - tan's fet - ters, Health and vi - sion need - ing,
God will aid and light us At thy gen - tle plead - ing.
4. Je - sus' ten - der Moth - er, Make thy sup - pli - ca - tion

Un - to him who chose thee At his In - car - na - tion;
5. That, O match-less Vir - gin, Pass - ing meek and low - ly,
Thy dear Son may make us Blame - less, chaste and ho - ly.
6. So, as now we jour - ney, Aid our weak en - deav - or,
Till we gaze on Je - sus, And re - joice for ev - er.
7. Fa - ther, Son and Spir - it, Three in One con - fess - ing,
Give we e - qual glo - ry, E - qual praise and bless - ing.

129 RAVENSHAW — *Ave Maris Stella* — English Translation by Riley

Un - to him who chose thee At his In - car - na - tion;
5. That, O match - less Vir - gin, Pass - ing meek and low - ly,
Thy dear Son may make us Blame - less, chaste and ho - ly.
6. So, as now we jour - ney, Aid our weak en - deav - or,
Till we gaze on Je - sus, And re - joice for ev - er.
7. Fa - ther, Son and Spir - it, Three in One con - fess - ing,
Give we e - qual glo - ry, E - qual praise and bless - ing.

AVE RADIX — *Ave Maris Stella* — English Translation by Riley

Un - to him who chose thee At his In - car - na - tion;
5. That, O match - less Vir - gin, Pass - ing meek and low - ly,
Thy dear Son may make us Blame - less, chaste and ho - ly.
6. So, as now we jour - ney, Aid our weak en - deav - or,
Till we gaze on Je - sus, And re - joice for ev - er.
7. Fa - ther, Son and Spir - it, Three in One con - fess - ing,
Give we e - qual glo - ry, E - qual praise and bless - ing.

131 WALTHAM FOREST — *Ave Maris Stella* — English Translation by Riley

Un - to him who chose thee At his In - car - na - tion;
5. That, O match - less Vir - gin, Pass - ing meek and low - ly,
Thy dear Son may make us Blame - less, chaste and ho - ly.
6. So, as now we jour - ney, Aid our weak en - deav - or,
Till we gaze on Je - sus, And re - joice for ev - er.
7. Fa - ther, Son and Spir - it, Three in One con - fess - ing,
Give we e - qual glo - ry, E - qual praise and bless - ing.

1. Bright Moth - er of our Mak - er, hail, Thou Vir - gin ev - er blest;
The o - cean's star, by which we sail, And gain the port of rest:
2. Whilst we this "A - ve" thus to thee, From Ga - briel's mouth re - hearse;
Pre - vail that peace our lot may be, And E - va's name re - verse.
3. Re - lease our long en - tan - gled mind, From all the snares of ill;
With heav'n - ly light in - struct the blind, And all our vows ful - fill.
4. Ex - ert for us a moth - er's care, And us thy chil - dren own;

Pre - vail with Him to hear our pray'r, Who chose to be thy son.
5. O spot - less maid, whose vir - tues shine, With bright - est pu - ri - ty;
Each ac - tion of our lives re - fine, And make us pure like thee.
6. Pre - serve our lives un - stain'd with ill; And guard us in our way;
That Christ one day our souls may fill With joys that ne'er de - cay.
7. To God the Fa - ther, end - less praise; To God the Son, the same;
And, Ho - ly Ghost, whose e - qual rays One e - qual glo - ry claim.

133 RICHMOND — *Ave Maris Stella* — Historic Catholic Translation (1807)

1. Bright Moth-er of our Mak - er, hail, Thou Vir - gin ev - er blest;
The o - cean's star, by which we sail, And gain the port of rest:
2. Whilst we this "A - ve" thus to thee, From Ga - briel's mouth re - hearse;
Pre - vail that peace our lot may be, And E - va's name re - verse.
3. Re - lease our long en - tan - gled mind, From all the snares of ill;
With heav'n - ly light in - struct the blind, And all our vows ful - fill.
4. Ex - ert for us a moth - er's care, And us thy chil - dren own;

Pre - vail with Him to hear our pray'r, Who chose to be thy son.
5. O spot-less maid, whose vir - tues shine, With bright - est pu - ri - ty;
Each ac - tion of our lives re - fine, And make us pure like thee.
6. Pre - serve our lives un - stain'd with ill; And guard us in our way;
That Christ one day our souls may fill With joys that ne'er de - cay.
7. To God the Fa - ther, end - less praise; To God the Son, the same;
And, Holy Ghost, whose e - qual rays One e - qual glo - ry claim.

1. Bright Moth - er of our Mak - er, hail, Thou Vir - gin ev - er blest;
The o - cean's star, by which we sail, And gain the port of rest:
2. Whilst we this "A - ve" thus to thee, From Ga - briel's mouth re - hearse;
Pre - vail that peace our lot may be, And E - va's name re - verse.
3. Re - lease our long en - tan - gled mind, From all the snares of ill;
With heav'n - ly light in - struct the blind, And all our vows ful - fill.
4. Ex - ert for us a moth - er's care, And us thy chil - dren own;

Pre - vail with Him to hear our pray'r, Who chose to be thy son.
5. O spot - less maid, whose vir - tues shine, With bright - est pu - ri - ty;
Each ac - tion of our lives re - fine, And make us pure like thee.
6. Pre - serve our lives un - stain'd with ill; And guard us in our way;
That Christ one day our souls may fill With joys that ne'er de - cay.
7. To God the Fa - ther, end - less praise; To God the Son, the same;
And, Ho - ly Ghost, whose e - qual rays One e - qual glo - ry claim.

AVE VIRGO VIRGINUM — *Ave Vivens Hostia* — English Translation by Monsignor Knox

1. Hail, true Vic - tim, life and light Un - to sin - ners lend - ing—
Ev - 'ry old - er form and rite Hath in thee its end - ing—
Spot - less in the Fa - ther's sight Ev - er - more as - cend - ing,
Ho - ly church in bit - ter fight Ev - er - more be - friend - ing.
2. Hail, true Man - na from the sky— Is - rael nev - er knew thee;
Pil - grims, for the day's sup - ply, Dai - ly hom - age do thee;
When our souls in sick - ness lie, Yields that sick - ness to thee;
Chris - tians, when they come to die, Live im - mor - tal through thee.

3. Hail, Christ's Bod - y— gift he made, His own death fore - show - ing,
(God - head un - der earth - ly shade Like a jew - el glow - ing),
Sa - cred mem - 'ries, ne'er to fade, On his Church be - stow - ing,
When to earth fare - well he bade, To his Pas - sion go - ing.
4. Je - sus tru - ly in this place God and Man re - sid - eth;
Him no shad - ow doth re - place, Him no rent di - vid - eth,
Ver - y flesh, al - though his face, Glo - ri - fied, he hid - eth;
Gar - nered in this lit - tle space All of Christ a - bid - eth.

5. Seen in heav'n by bless-èd eyes This his bod-y reign-eth;
Form of bread, in oth-er wise, Here its scope con-tain-eth;—
Mys-t'ry he a-lone de-scries Who the same or-dain-eth;
Well may he such thing de-vise Whom no pow'r re-strain-eth.
6. Plead, true Vic-tim, in our stead To the Fa-ther cry-ing,
Thou, thy chil-dren's dai-ly bread, Dai-ly health sup-ply-ing;
Ban-quet for the ex-ile spread, Grant us life un-dy-ing;
May our love from thine be fed, Self and sense de-ny-ing!

1. Hail, true Vic-tim, life and light Un - to sin - ners lend - ing—
Ev - 'ry old - er form and rite Hath in thee its end - ing—
Spot-less in the Fa-ther's sight Ev - er - more as - cend - ing,
Ho - ly church in bit - ter fight Ev - er - more be - friend - ing.
2. Hail, true Man-na from the sky— Is - rael nev - er knew thee;
Pil-grims, for the day's sup-ply, Dai - ly hom - age do thee;

When our souls in sick-ness lie, Yields that sick - ness to thee;
Chris- tians, when they come to die, Live im - mor - tal through thee.
3. Hail, Christ's Bod - y— gift he made, His own death forc - show - ing,
(God-head un - der earth - ly shade Like a jew - el glow - ing),
Sa-cred mem - 'ries, ne'er to fade, On his Church be - stow - ing,
When to earth fare - well he bade, To his Pas - sion go - ing.

4. Je - sus tru - ly in this place God and Man re - sid - eth;
Him no shad - ow doth re - place, Him no rent di - vid - eth,
Ver - y flesh, al - though his face, Glo - ri - fied, he hid - eth;
Gar - nered in this lit - tle space All of Christ a - bid - eth.
5. Seen in heav'n by bless - èd eyes This his bod - y reign - eth;
Form of bread, in oth - er wise, Here its scope con - tain - eth;—

Mys - t'ry he__ a - lone de - scries Who the same or - dain - eth;
Well may he such thing de - vise Whom no pow'r re - strain - eth.
6. Plead, true Vic-tim, in our stead To the Fa - ther cry - ing,
Thou, thy chil-dren's dai - ly bread, Dai - ly health sup - ply - ing;
Ban - quet for__ the ex - ile spread, Grant us life un - dy - ing;
May our love from thine be fed, Self and sense de - ny - ing!

1. Hail, true Vic - tim, life and light Un - to sin - ners lend - ing—
Ev - 'ry old - er form and rite Hath in thee its end - ing—
Spot - less in the Fa - ther's sight Ev - er - more as - cend - ing,
Ho - ly church in bit - ter fight Ev - er - more be-friend - ing.
2. Hail, true Man - na from the sky— Is - rael nev - er knew thee;
Pil - grims, for the day's sup - ply, Dai - ly hom - age do thee;
When our souls in sick - ness lie, Yields that sick - ness to thee;
Chris - tians, when they come to die, Live im - mor - tal through thee.

3. Hail, Christ's Bod- y—gift he made, His own death fore - show - ing,
(God - head un - der earth - ly shade Like a jew - el glow - ing),
Sa - cred mem- 'ries, ne'er to fade, On his Church be - stow - ing,
When to earth fare - well he bade, To his Pas - sion go - ing.
4. Je - sus tru - ly in this place God and Man re - sid - eth;
Him no shad - ow doth re - place, Him no rent di - vid - eth,
Ver - y flesh, al - though his face, Glo - ri - fied, he hid - eth;
Gar - nered in this lit - tle space All of Christ a - bid - eth.

5. Seen in heav'n by bless - èd eyes This his bod - y reign - eth;
Form of bread, in oth - er wise, Here its scope con - tain - eth;—
Mys - t'ry he a - lone de - scries Who the same or - dain - eth;
Well may he such thing de - vise Whom no pow'r re - strain - eth.
6. Plead, true Vic - tim, in our stead To the Fa - ther cry - ing,
Thou, thy chil - dren's dai - ly bread, Dai - ly health sup - ply - ing;
Ban - quet for the ex - ile spread, Grant us life un - dy - ing;
May our love from thine be fed, Self and sense de - ny - ing!

145 NUN KOMM E4 — *Ave Vivens Hostia* — English Translation by Monsignor Knox

3. Hail, Christ's Bod - y— gift_ he made, His own death fore - show - ing, (God - head un - der
earth - ly__ shade Like a jew - el glow - ing), Sa - cred mem- 'ries, ne'er to fade,
On his Church be - stow - ing, When to earth fare - well he__ bade, To his Pas - sion go - ing.
4. Je - sus tru - ly in__ this place God and Man re - sid - eth;
Him no shad - ow doth re - place, Him no rent di - vid - eth,
Ver - y flesh, al - though his face, Glo - ri - fied, he hid - eth;
Gar - nered in this lit - tle__ space All of Christ a - bid - eth.

5. Seen in heav'n by bless - èd eyes This his bod - y reign - eth; Form of bread, in
oth - er wise, Here its scope con - tain - eth; Mys - t'ry he a - lone de - scries
Who the same or - dain - eth; Well may he such thing de - vise Whom no pow'r re - strain - eth.
6. Plead, true Vic - tim, in our stead To the Fa - ther cry - ing,
Thou, thy chil - dren's dai - ly bread, Dai - ly health sup - ply - ing;
Ban - quet for the ex - ile spread, Grant us life un - dy - ing;
May our love from thine be fed, Self and sense de - ny - ing!

CHRISTUS CHRISTUS CHRISTUS IST — *Ave Vivens Hostia* — English Transl. by Monsignor Knox **146**

1. Hail, true Vic - tim, life and light Un - to sin - ners lend - ing— Ev - 'ry old - er
form and rite Hath in thee its end - ing— Spot - less in the Fa - ther's sight
Ev - er - more as - cend - ing, Ho - ly church in bit - ter fight Ev - er - more be - friend - ing.
2. Hail, true Man - na from the sky— Is - rael nev - er knew thee;
Pil - grims, for the day's sup - ply, Dai - ly hom - age do thee;
When our souls in sick - ness lie, Yields that sick - ness to thee;
Chris - tians, when they come to die, Live im - mor - tal through thee.

3. Hail, Christ's Bod - y— gift he made, His own death fore - show - ing, (God - head un - der
earth - ly shade Like a jew - el glow - ing), Sa - cred mem- 'ries, ne'er to fade, On his
Church be - stow - ing, When to earth fare - well he bade, To his Pas - sion go - ing.
4. Je - sus tru - ly in this place God and Man re - sid - eth;
Him no shad - ow doth re - place, Him no rent di - vid - eth,
Ver - y flesh, al - though his face, Glo - ri - fied, he hid - eth;
Gar - nered in this lit - tle space All of Christ a - bid - eth.

5. Seen in heav'n by bless - èd eyes This his bod - y reign - eth; Form of bread, in
oth - er wise, Here its scope con - tain - eth;— Mys - t'ry he a - lone de - scries Who the
same or - dain - eth; Well may he such thing de - vise Whom no pow'r re - strain - eth.
6. Plead, true Vic - tim, in our stead To the Fa - ther cry - ing,
Thou, thy chil - dren's dai - ly bread, Dai - ly health sup - ply - ing;
Ban - quet for the ex - ile spread, Grant us life un - dy - ing;
May our love from thine be fed, Self and sense de - ny - ing!

147 JESU LEIDEN PEIN UND TOD — *Ave Vivens Hostia* — English Translation by Monsignor Knox

3. Hail, Christ's Bod - y— gift he made, His own death fore-show - ing, (God-head un-der
earth-ly shade Like a jew-el glow - ing), Sa-cred mem-'ries, ne'er to fade, On his
Church be - stow - ing, When to earth fare-well he bade, To his Pas-sion go - ing.
4. Je - sus tru - ly in this place God and Man re - sid - eth;
Him no shad - ow doth re - place, Him no rent di - vid - eth,
Ver - y flesh, al - though his face, Glo - ri - fied, he hid - eth;
Gar - nered in this lit - tle space All of Christ a - bid - eth.

5. Seen in heav'n by bless - èd eyes This his bod - y reign - eth; Form of bread, in
oth - er wise, Here its scope con - tain - eth;— Mys-t'ry he a - lone de-scries Who the
same_ or - dain - eth; Well may he such thing de - vise Whom no pow'r re - strain - eth.
6. Plead, true Vic - tim, in our stead To the Fa - ther cry - ing,
Thou, thy chil-dren's dai - ly bread, Dai - ly health sup - ply - ing;
Ban-quet for the ex - ile spread, Grant us life_ un - dy - ing;
May our love from thine be fed, Self and sense de - ny - ing!

ACH WIE KURZ — *Ave Vivens Hostia* — English Translation by Monsignor Knox

3. Hail, Christ's Bod - y— gift he made, His own death fore - show - ing, (God - head un - der
earth - ly shade Like a jew - el glow - ing), Sa - cred mem - 'ries, ne'er to fade, On his
Church be - stow - ing, When to earth fare - well he bade, To his Pas - sion go - ing.
4. Je - sus__ tru - ly in this place God and Man re - sid - eth;
Him no__ shad - ow doth re - place, Him no rent di - vid - eth,
Ver - y flesh, al - though his face, Glo - ri - fied, he hid - eth;
Gar - nered in this lit - tle space All of Christ a - bid - eth.

5. Seen in__ heav'n by bless - èd eyes This his bod - y reign - eth; Form of__ bread, in
oth - er wise, Here its scope con - tain - eth;— Mys - t'ry he a - lone de - scries Who the
same or - dain - eth; Well may he such thing de - vise Whom no pow'r re - strain - eth.
6. Plead, true__ Vic - tim, in our stead To the Fa - ther cry - ing,
Thou, thy__ chil - dren's dai - ly bread, Dai - ly health sup - ply - ing;
Ban - quet for the ex - ile spread, Grant us life un - dy - ing;
May our love from thine be fed, Self and sense de - ny - ing!

GOTT SEI DANK E6 — *Ave Vivens Hostia* — English Translation by Monsignor Henry

1. Hail, Thou liv - ing Vic - tim blest, Truth and Life su - per - nal, Old - en
types in Thee con-fessed Find their end e - ter - nal. Al - le - lu - ia.
2. In - fi - nite through Thee the praise To the Fa - ther giv - en, While Thy
love the Church ar - rays As an earth - ly heav - en. Al - le - lu - ia.
3. Hail, Thou an - cient Mer - cy - seat, Source of grace and fa - vor; Pre - cious
Oint-ment - box re - plete With ce - les - tial sa - vor: Al - le - lu - ia.

4. Thou the God-man tru - ly art In di - vine com - plete - ness: Fed on
Thee, the lov - ing heart Knows Thy rap - tured sweet - ness. Al - le - lu - ia.
5. Hail, Thou Man - na from the skies, Yet more tru - ly giv - en To the
pil - grim soul that sighs For her prom - ised Heav - en: Al - le - lu - ia.
6. Mys - tic med - i - cine Thou art For the wound - ed spir - it; Healed by
Thee, may eve - ry heart End - less life in - her - it. Al - le - lu - ia.

1. Hail, Thou liv - ing Vic - tim blest, Truth and Life su - per - nal,
Old - en types in Thee con - fessed Find their end e - ter - nal.
2. In - fi - nite through Thee the praise To the Fa - ther giv - en,
While Thy love the Church ar - rays As an earth - ly heav - en.
3. Hail, Thou an - cient Mer - cy - seat, Source of grace and fa - vor;
Pre - cious Oint - ment - box re - plete With ce - les - tial sa - vor:

4. Thou the God - man tru - ly art In di - vine com - plete - ness:
Fed on Thee, the lov - ing heart Knows Thy rap - tured sweet - ness.
5. Hail, Thou Man - na from the skies, Yet more tru - ly giv - en
To the pil - grim soul that sighs For her prom - ised Heav - en:
6. Mys - tic med - i - cine Thou art For the wound - ed spir - it;
Healed by Thee, may eve - ry heart End - less life in - her - it.

1. Hail, Thou liv - ing Vic - tim blest, Truth and Life su - per - nal, Old - en
types in Thee con-fessed Find their end e - ter - nal. Je - su Sal - vá - tor.
2. In - fi - nite through Thee the praise To the Fa - ther giv - en, While Thy
love the Church ar - rays As an earth - ly heav - en. Je - su Sal - vá - tor.
3. Hail, Thou an - cient Mer - cy - seat, Source of grace and fa - vor; Pre - cious
Oint - ment - box re - plete With ce - les - tial sa - vor: Je - su Sal - vá - tor.

4. Thou the God - man tru - ly art In di - vine com - plete - ness: Fed on
Thee, the lov - ing heart Knows Thy rap - tured sweet - ness. Je - su Sal - vá - tor.
5. Hail, Thou Man - na from the skies, Yet more tru - ly giv - en To the
pil - grim soul that sighs For her prom - ised Heav - en: Je - su Sal - vá - tor.
6. Mys - tic med - i - cine Thou art For the wound - ed spir - it; Healed by
Thee, may eve - ry heart End - less life in - her - it. Je - su Sal - vá - tor.

1. O Christ, Thy ser - vants deign to spare, For whom their Vir - gin - Pa - tron
speaks Be - fore Thy bar of grace, and there The Fa - ther's kind in -
dul - gence seeks. Al - le - lu - ia.
2. Ye bless - èd hosts who
are ar - rayed In cir - cles nine of le - gions bright, Who gave and
give us time - ly aid: Our fu - ture let no e - vil blight.
Al - le - lu - ia.
3. Ye Proph - ets and A - pos - tles, plead
For us be - fore our Judge se - vere To show us mer - cy,
as in - deed We mourn our guilt with grief sin - cere. Al - le - lu - ia.

4. Ye Mar - tyrs pur - ple - clad, and all Re - ward - ed in the white - robed
band Who faith con - fessed, from ex - ile call Us on - ward to our
na - tive land. Al - le - lu - ia.
5. O joy - ous choir of
Vir - gins chaste, With all whom earth has sent on high, Once dwell - ers
of the de - sert waste, Su - per - nal thrones to us sup - ply.
Al - le - lu - ia.
6. Drive out the false and faith - less race
From where the bounds of faith are set, That there may be in
eve - ry place One Shep - herd and one sheep - fold yet. Al - le - lu - ia.

157 OLD HUNDREDTH — *Christe Redemptor Omnium* — English Translation by Father Fitzpatrick

1. O Christ, Thy ser - vants deign to spare, For whom their Vir - gin - Pa - tron speaks
Be - fore Thy bar of grace, and there The Fa - ther's kind in - dul - gence seeks.
2. Ye bless - èd hosts who are ar - rayed In cir - cles nine of le - gions bright,
Who gave and give us time - ly aid: Our fu - ture let no e - vil blight.
3. Ye Proph - ets and A - pos - tles, plead For us be - fore our Judge se - vere
To show us mer - cy, as in - deed We mourn our guilt with grief sin - cere.

4. Ye Mar - tyrs pur - ple - clad, and all Re - ward - ed in the white - robed band
Who faith con - fessed, from ex - ile call Us on - ward to our na - tive land.
5. O joy - ous choir of Vir - gins chaste, With all whom earth has sent on high,
Once dwell - ers of the de - sert waste, Su - per - nal thrones to us sup - ply.
6. Drive out the false and faith - less race From where the bounds of faith are set,
That there may be in eve - ry place One Shep - herd and one sheep - fold yet.

1. O Christ, Thy ser - vants deign to spare, For whom their Vir - gin - Pa - tron speaks
Be - fore Thy bar of grace, and there The Fa - ther's kind in - dul - gence seeks.
2. Ye bless - èd hosts who are ar - rayed In cir - cles nine of le - gions bright,
Who gave and give us time - ly aid: Our fu - ture_ let no e - vil blight.
3. Ye Proph - ets and A - pos - tles, plead For us be - fore our Judge se - vere

* *A transposed organ accompaniment has been provided for optional use.*

To show us mer - cy, as in - deed We mourn our__ guilt with grief sin - cere.
4. Ye Mar - tyrs pur - ple - clad, and all Re - ward - ed in the white - robed band
Who faith con - fessed, from ex - ile call Us on - ward to our na - tive land.
5. O joy - ous choir of Vir - gins chaste, With all whom earth has sent on high,
Once dwell - ers of the de - sert waste, Su - per - nal__ thrones to us sup - ply.
6. Drive out the false and faith - less race From where the bounds of faith are set,
That there may be in eve - ry place One Shep - herd__ and one sheep - fold yet.

 CROMER — *Christe Redemptor Omnium* — English Translation by Father Fitzpatrick

4. Ye Mar-tyrs pur - ple - clad, and all Re - ward - ed in the__ white-robed band
Who faith con-fessed, from ex - ile call Us on - ward to our__ na - tive land.
5. O joy - ous choir of__ Vir - gins chaste, With all whom earth has__ sent on high,
Once dwell - ers of the de - sert waste, Su - per - nal thrones to__ us sup - ply.
6. Drive out the false and__ faith-less race From where the bounds of__ faith are set,
That there may be in eve - ry place One Shep-herd and one__ sheep-fold yet.

161 ROCKINGHAM — *Christe Redemptor Omnium* — English Translation by Father Fitzpatrick

4. Ye Mar - tyrs pur - ple - clad, and all Re - ward - ed in the
white - robed band Who faith con - fessed, from ex - ile call Us
on - ward to our na - tive land.
5. O joy - ous
choir of Vir - gins chaste, With all whom earth has sent on
high, Once dwell - ers of the de - sert waste, Su - per - nal
thrones to us sup - ply.
6. Drive out the false and faith - less
race From where the bounds of faith are set, That there may
be in eve - ry place One Shep - herd and one sheep - fold yet.

1. O Christ, Thy ser - vants deign to spare, For whom their Vir - gin - Pa - tron speaks
Be - fore Thy bar of grace, and there The Fa - ther's kind in - dul - gence seeks.
2. Ye bless - èd hosts who are ar - rayed In cir - cles nine of___ le - gions bright,
Who gave and give us time - ly aid: Our fu - ture let no e - vil blight.
3. Ye Proph - ets and A - pos - tles, plead For us be - fore our___ Judge se - vere

* A transposed organ accompaniment has been provided for optional use.

1. O Christ, Re - deem-er of man - kind, thy ser-vants here pro - tect and spare,
who hear-est with a lov - ing mind the bless-èd ev - er - Vir - gin's prayer.
2. Ye bless - èd hosts who see his face, the Spir - its of the heav'n-ly home,
a - way from us all e - vils chase, the past and pre - sent, and to come.
3. O Proph-ets of the Judge e - terne, A - pos-tles of the Lord most high,
de - liv - er - ance, for which we yearn, we beg your pa - tron - age sup - ply.
4. God's Mar-tyrs who have won re - nown, Con - fes-sors all in bright ar - ray,

be - seech for us to win the crown and us to realms a - bove con - vey.
5. Ye choirs of ho - ly Vir - gins fine, of Monks who lived by sa - cred vow,
with all the Saints in prayer com - bine, a part - ner - ship with Christ en - dow.
6. Do ye all un - be - lief ex - pel from eve - ry land of Chris - tian claim,
that we to Christ our praise may tell in bound - en trib - ute to his name.
7. The un - beg - ot - ten Fa - ther praise, and laud the sole - be - got - ten Son;
to God the Ho - ly Spir - it raise the same, as end - less ag - es run.

165 DUGUET — *Christe Redemptor Omnium* — English Translation by Littledale

1. O Christ, Re - deem - er of man - kind, thy ser - vants here pro - tect and spare,
who hear - est with a lov - ing_ mind the bless - èd ev - er - Vir - gin's prayer.
2. Ye bless - èd hosts who see his face, the Spir - its of the heav'n - ly home,
a - way from us all e - vils_ chase, the past and pre - sent, and to come.
3. O Proph - ets of the Judge e - terne, A - pos - tles of the Lord most high,
de - liv - er - ance, for which we_ yearn, we beg your pa - tron - age sup - ply.
4. God's Mar - tyrs who have won re - nown, Con - fes - sors all in bright ar - ray,

be - seech for us to win the_ crown and us to realms a - bove con - vey.
5. Ye choirs of ho - ly Vir - gins fine, of Monks who lived by sa - cred vow,
with all the Saints in prayer com - bine, a part - ner - ship with Christ en - dow.
6. Do ye all un - be - lief ex - pel from eve - ry land of Chris - tian claim,
that we to Christ our praise may_ tell in bound - en trib - ute to his name.
7. The un - beg - ot - ten Fa - ther praise, and laud the sole - be - got - ten Son;
to God the Ho - ly Spir - it_ raise the same, as end - less ag - es run.

WHITEHALL — *Christe Redemptor Omnium* — English Translation by Littledale

#102 has (optional) organ accompaniment at a higher key.

be - seech for us to win the crown and us to realms a - bove con - vey.
5. Ye choirs of ho - ly Vir - gins fine, of Monks who lived by sa - cred vow,
with all the Saints in prayer com - bine, a part - ner - ship with Christ en - dow.
6. Do ye all un - be - lief ex - pel from eve - ry land of Chris - tian claim,
that we to Christ our praise may tell in bound - en trib - ute to his name.
7. The un - beg - ot - ten Fa - ther praise, and laud the sole - be - got - ten Son;
to God the Ho - ly Spir - it raise the same, as end - less ag - es run.

 KEMPEN — *Christe Redemptor Omnium* — Historic Catholic Translation (1684ad)

1. Of all Re-deem - er, Christ, be pleased thy ser - vants to pre - serve and aid,
by her most ho - ly prayers ap - peased who ev - er was_ a spot - less Maid.
2. And you, O bless - èd com - pa - nies of spir - its, which in heav - en dwell,
at hand and past ca - lam - i - ties, and all that are_ to come, re - pel.
3. Th'e - ter - nal Judge - 's Proph - ets blest, and you_ A - pos - tles of_ his choice,
O by your prayers do we re - quest to be pre - served, with hum - ble voice.
4. You Mar - tyrs, whose re - nown is great, of God, our Lord's Con - fes - sors bright,

your in - ter - ces - sion we en - treat to raise us up__ to heav'n-ly light.
5. You ho - ly Vir - gins' spot - less choirs and Monks that lived in will - ing pain,
and all you Saints, with joint de - sires im - plore that we__ with Christ re - main.
6. The wick - ed in - fi - dels a - way do drive from grounds where faith_ doth grow,
that we with joy to Christ may pay those prais - es which to him__ we owe.
7. To Fa - ther e - ven as to Son, un - sired_ and sole - be - got - ten, be
with Ho - ly Ghost, all glo - ry done for ag - es ev - er - last - ing - ly.

169 AGINCOURT — *Christe Redemptor Omnium* — Historic Catholic Translation (1684ad)

your in - ter - ces - sion we en - treat to raise us up to heav'n-ly light.
5. You ho - ly Vir - gins' spot-less choirs and Monks that lived in willing pain,
and all you Saints, with joint de - sires im-plore that we with Christ re - main.
6. The wick - ed in - fi - dels a - way do drive from grounds where faith doth grow,
that we with joy to Christ may pay those prais - es which to him we owe.
7. To Fa - ther e - ven as to Son, un - sired and sole - be - got-ten, be
with Ho - ly Ghost, all glo-ry done for ag - es ev - er - last-ing - ly.

1. Of all Re-deem - er, Christ, be pleased thy ser - vants to pre - serve and aid,
by her most ho - ly prayers ap - peased who ev - er was a spot - less Maid.
2. And you, O bless - èd com - pa - nies of spir - its, which in__ heav - en dwell,
at hand and past__ ca - lam - i - ties, and all that are to come, re - pel.
3. Th'e - ter - nal Judge - 's Proph-ets blest, and you A - pos - tles__ of his choice,
O by your prayers do we__ re - quest to be pre-served, with hum - ble voice.
4. You Mar-tyrs, whose re - nown is great, of God, our Lord's Con - fes - sors bright,

#18 has (optional) organ accompaniment at a higher key.

your in - ter - ces - sion we__ en - treat to raise us up to heav'n - ly light.
5. You ho - ly Vir - gins' spot - less choirs and Monks that lived in__ will - ing pain,
and all you Saints, with joint de - sires im - plore that we with Christ re - main.
6. The wick - ed in - fi - dels a - way do drive from grounds where faith doth grow,
that we with joy__ to Christ may pay those prais - es which to him_ we owe.
7. To Fa - ther e - ven as to Son, un - sired and sole - be - got - ten, be
with Ho - ly Ghost, all glo - ry done for ag - es ev - er - last - ing - ly.

1. O__ Christ, thy gracious mer - cy be to us, thy low - ly ser - vants, shown,
for whom a Vir - gin Pa - tron - ess is plead - ing at__ thy Fa - ther's throne.
2. Ye__ bless - èd hosts in cir - cles nine of ser - ried row and bright ar - ray,
our pre - sent harms, as those to come or past, con - front and chase a - way.
3. A - pos - tles, too, and Proph - ets, bid the Judge whom guile would nev - er move
that see - ing sin - ners' con - trite tears, he may to them his pit - y prove.
4. Ye__ Mar - tyrs, pur - pled with your blood, Con - fes - sors, all en - robed in white,

do us, in ex - ile here be - low, to seek our home on high in - vite.
5. O__ choir of Vir-gins fair and pure, and ye who from the de-sert sand
at - tained the stars, for us ob - tain with you a place in heav-en's land.
6. Our_ foe de - ceit-ful deign to drive from faith-ful dwell-ings far a-way,
that we may all, in one true fold, one law-ful Pas - tor's rule o - bey.
7. To__ God the Fa-ther glo - ry be, And to the Fa-ther's on - ly Son,
And to the Ho - ly Par - a - clete, While ev - er - last - ing ag - es run.

173 MELCOMBE — *Christe Redemptor Omnium* — English Translation by Archbishop Bagshawe

1. O Christ, thy gra cious mer - cy be to us, thy low - ly ser-vants, shown,
for whom a Vir - gin Pa - tron-ess is plead - ing at thy Fa-ther's throne.
2. Ye bless-èd hosts in cir - cles nine of ser - ried row and bright ar - ray,
our pre - sent harms, as those to come or past, con - front and chase a - way.
3. A - pos - tles, too, and Proph-ets, bid the Judge whom guile would nev - er move
that see - ing sin - ners' con - trite tears, he may to them his pit - y prove.
4. Ye Mar-tyrs, pur-pled with your blood, Con - fes - sors, all en - robed in white,

do us, in ex - ile here be-low, to seek our home on high in - vite.
5. O choir of Vir-gins fair and pure, and ye who from the de - sert sand
at - tained the stars, for us ob-tain with you a place in heav-en's land.
6. Our foe de - ceit - ful deign to drive from faith - ful dwell - ings far a - way,
that we may all, in one true fold, one law - ful Pas-tor's rule o - bey.
7. To God the Fa - ther glo - ry be, And to the Fa - ther's on - ly Son,
And to the Ho - ly Par - a-clete, While ev - er - last - ing ag - es run.

 MEIN SEEL O GOTT — *Christe Redemptor Omnium* — English Translation by Archbishop Bagshawe

1. Je - sus, thy gra - cious mer - cy be to us, thy low - ly ser - vants, shown,
for whom a Vir - gin Pa - tron - ess is plead - ing at thy Fa - ther's throne.
2. Ye bless-èd hosts in cir-cles nine of ser-ried row and bright ar - ray,
our pre - sent harms, as those to come or past, con - front and chase a - way.
3. A - pos - tles, too, and Proph-ets, bid the Judge whom guile would nev - er move
that see - ing sin - ners' con - trite tears, he may to them his pit - y prove.
4. Ye Mar-tyrs, pur - pled with your blood, Con - fes - sors, all en - robed in white,

do us, in ex - ile here be - low, to seek our home on high in - vite.
5. O choir of Vir - gins fair and pure, and ye who from the de - sert sand
at-tained the stars, for us ob - tain with you a place in heav - en's land.
6. Our foe de - ceit - ful deign to drive from faith-ful dwell - ings far a - way,
that we may all, in one true fold, one law-ful Pas - tor's rule o - bey.
7. To God the Fa - ther glo - ry be, And to the Fa - ther's on - ly Son,
And to the Ho - ly Par - a - clete, While ev - er - last - ing ag - es run.

175 NÜRNBERG — *Christe Redemptor Omnium* — English Translation by Archbishop Bagshawe

1. Je - sus, thy gra - cious mer - cy be to us,__ thy low - ly ser - vants, shown,
for whom a Vir - gin_ Pa - tron - ess is plead - ing_ at__ thy Fa - ther's throne.
2. Ye bless-ed hosts in cir - cles nine of ser - ried row_ and bright_ ar - ray,
our pre - sent harms,__ as__ those to come or past,__ con - front and chase a - way.
3. A - pos - tles, too, and Proph - ets, bid the Judge_ whom guile_ would nev - er move
that see-ing sin - ners' con - trite tears, he may__ to__ them his pit - y prove.
4. Ye Mar-tyrs, pur - pled with__ your blood, Con - fes - sors, all__ en - robed in white,

do us, in ex - ile_ here be - low, to seek___ our_ home on high_ in - vite.
5. O choir of Vir - gins fair___ and pure, and ye__ who from_ the de - sert sand
at-tained the stars,___ for_ us ob - tain with you___ a__ place in heav - en's land.
6. Our foe de - ceit - ful deign__ to drive from faith - ful dwell - ings far__ a - way,
that we may all,___ in_ one true fold, one law - ful_ Pas - tor's rule_ o - bey.
7. To God the Fa - ther glo - ry be, And to___ the Fa - ther's on - ly Son,
And to the Ho - ly_ Par - a - clete, While ev - er - last - ing ag - es run.

WAREHAM — *Christe Redemptor Omnium* — English Translation by Archbishop Bagshawe

do us,__ in__ ex - ile here be - low, to__ seek_ our home on high_ in - vite.
5. O choir of Vir - gins fair__ and pure, and ye__ who from the de - sert sand
at - tained the_ stars, for us ob - tain with you_ a place in heav - en's land.
6. Our foe__ de - ceit - ful deign to drive from faith - ful dwell-ings far__ a - way,
that we__ may all, in one true fold, one_ law - ful Pas - tor's rule_ o - bey.
7. To God_ the Fa - ther glo - ry be, And to__ the Fa - ther's on - ly Son,
And to__ the_ Ho - ly Par - a - clete, While ev - er - last - ing ag - es run.

1. Cre - a - tor of the star - ry height, The faith - ful's ev - er - last - ing light,
O Christ, Re - deem - er of man - kind, Our hum - ble prayers vouch - safe to mind.
2. Thy love that pit - ied from on high A guilt - y race fore - doomed to die,
Was pleased that sen - tence to re - peal, Those fail - ing en - er - gies to heal.
3. So, at the e - ven - tide of earth, From that bride - cham - ber of Thy birth

* Stemless accompaniment matches the stemmed version.

Our mor - tal flesh Thou didst as - sume, Born of a spot - less Vir - gin's womb.
4. Such is Thy glo - ry in its might That, when Thy name in heav - en's height
Is heard, or down in hell, to Thee All bend a - like on trem - bling knee.
5. O Christ, who at the lat - ter day Shalt be our Judge, we hum - bly pray,
Such arms of heav'n - ly grace to send, As from our foes may us de - fend.
6. To God the Fa - ther, God the Son, And God the Spir - it, Three in One,
Laud, hon - or, might, and glo - ry be From age to age e - ter - nal - ly.

183 WHITEHALL — *Conditor Alme Siderum* — English Translation by Monsignor Knox

1. Cre - a - tor of the star - ry height, The faith - ful's ev - er - last - ing light,
O Christ, Re - deem - er of man - kind, Our hum - ble prayers vouch - safe to mind.
2. Thy love that pit - ied from on high A guilt - y race fore - doomed to die,
Was pleased that sen - tence to re - peal, Those fail - ing en - er - gies to heal.
3. So, at the e - ven - tide of earth, From that bride - cham - ber of Thy birth
Our mor - tal flesh Thou didst as - sume, Born of a spot - less Vir - gin's womb.

4. Such is Thy glo - ry in its might That, when Thy name in heav - en's height
Is heard, or down in hell, to Thee All bend a - like on trem-bling knee.
5. O Christ, who at the lat - ter day Shalt be our Judge, we hum - bly pray,
Such arms of heav'n - ly grace to send, As from our foes may us de - fend.
6. To God the Fa - ther, God the Son, And God the Spir - it, Three in One,
Laud, hon - or, might, and glo - ry be From age to age e - ter - nal - ly.

1. Cre - a - tor of the star - ry height, The faith - ful's ev - er - last - ing light,
O Christ, Re - deem - er of_ man - kind,_ Our hum - ble prayers vouch - safe_ to mind.
2. Thy love that pit - ied from on high A guilt - y race_ fore - doomed to die,
Was pleased that sen - tence to_ re - peal,_ Those fail - ing en - er - gies_ to heal.
3. So, at the e - ven - tide_ of earth, From that bride - cham - ber of Thy birth
Our mor - tal flesh_ Thou didst_ as - sume, Born of a spot - less Vir - gin's womb.

4. Such is Thy glo - ry in__ its might That, when Thy name in heav - en's height
Is heard, or down in hell,_ to Thee All bend a - like_ on trem - bling knee.
5. O Christ, who at the lat - ter day Shalt be our Judge, we hum - bly pray,
Such arms of heav'n-ly grace to send, As from our foes_ may us__ de - fend.
6. To God the Fa - ther, God_ the Son, And God the Spir - it, Three in One,
Laud, hon - or, might, and glo - ry be__ From age to age_ e - ter - nal - ly.

KEMPEN — *Conditor Alme Siderum* — English Translation by Monsignor Knox

4. Such is Thy glo - ry in its might That, when Thy name in heav - en's height
Is heard, or down in hell, to Thee All bend a - like_ on trem - bling knee.
5. O Christ, who at the lat - ter day Shalt be_ our Judge, we hum - bly pray,
Such arms of heav'n - ly grace to send, As from our foes_ may us_ de - fend.
6. To God the Fa - ther, God the Son, And God_ the Spir - it, Three in One,
Laud, hon - or, might, and glo - ry be From age to age_ e - ter - nal - ly.

187 LA ROCHELLE — *Conditor Alme Siderum* — English Translation by Monsignor Knox

1. Cre - a - tor of the star - ry height, The faith - ful's ev - er - last - ing light,
O Christ, Re - deem - er of man - kind, Our hum - ble prayers vouch - safe_ to mind.
2. Thy love that pit - ied from on high A guilt - y race fore - doomed to die,
Was pleased that sen - tence to re - peal, Those fail - ing en - er - gies_ to heal.
3. So, at the e - ven - tide of earth, From that bride - cham - ber of Thy birth

* *A transposed organ accompaniment has been provided for optional use.*

Our mor-tal flesh Thou didst as-sume, Born of a spot-less Vir-gin's womb.
4. Such is Thy glo-ry in its might That, when Thy name in heav-en's height
Is heard, or down in hell, to Thee All bend a-like on trem-bling knee.
5. O Christ, who at the lat-ter day Shalt be our Judge, we hum-bly pray,
Such arms of heav'n-ly grace to send, As from our foes may us__ de-fend.
6. To God the Fa-ther, God the Son, And God the Spir-it, Three in One,
Laud, hon-or, might, and glo-ry be From age to age e-ter-nal-ly.

1. Cre - a - tor of the star - ry height, The faith-ful's ev - er - last-ing light,
O Christ, Re - deem - er of man-kind, Our hum-ble prayers vouch - safe to mind.
2. Thy love that pit - ied from on high A guilt-y race fore - doomed to die,
Was pleased that sen - tence to re - peal, Those fail-ing en - er - gies to heal.
3. So, at the e - ven-tide of earth, From that bride - cham - ber of Thy birth
Our mor-tal flesh Thou didst as - sume, Born of a spot - less Vir-gin's womb.

4. Such is Thy glo - ry in its might That, when Thy name in heav-en's height
Is heard, or down in hell, to Thee All bend a - like on trem-bling knee.
5. O Christ, who at the lat-ter day Shalt be our Judge, we hum-bly pray,
Such arms of heav'n - ly grace to send, As from our foes may us de - fend.
6. To God the Fa - ther, God the Son, And God the Spir - it, Three in One,
Laud, hon-or, might, and glo - ry be From age to age e - ter-nal - ly.

190 NUN KOMM DER HEIDEN HEILAND — *Conditor Alme Siderum* — English Transl. by Campbell

1. Mak - er of the star - ry sphere, To the faith - ful, Light most dear,
Je - sus, Sav - ior, Lord of___ all, Heark - en to thy peo - ple's call.
2. When our na - ture faint - ing lay, Crushed by Sa - tan's cru - el sway,
Blest phy - si - cian, 'twas thy___ love Brought us heal - ing from_ a - bove.
3. In the bless - èd Mar - y's womb, Pur - est flesh thou didst as - sume,
That to God a - bove might rise The all - ho - ly sac - ri - fice.

4. Un - to heav'n ex - alt - ed now, At thy sa - cred name shall bow
All that on the earth do__ dwell, All in heav - en, all__ in hell.
5. Thou, who on the judg - ment - day Our most se - cret thoughts shall weigh,
Shield us now with pit - y ing_ care, Guard us from temp - ta - tion's snare.
6. Hon - or, glo - ry, love_ and praise, Be through nev - er - end - ing days,
To the Fa - ther and the__ Son And the Spir - it, Three in One.

191 MONKLAND — *Conditor Alme Siderum* — English Translation by Campbell of Skerrington

1. Mak - er of the star - ry__ sphere, To the faith - ful, Light most dear,
Je - sus,__ Sav - ior, Lord of all, Heark - en__ to thy peo - ple's call.
2. When our na - ture faint - ing__ lay, Crushed by Sa - tan's cru - el sway,
Blest phy - si - cian, 'twas thy love Brought us__ heal - ing from a - bove.
3. In the bless - èd Mar - y's__womb, Pur - est flesh thou didst as - sume,
That to__ God a - bove might rise The all - ho - ly sac - ri - fice.

4. Un - to heav'n ex - alt - ed__ now, At thy sa - cred name shall bow
All that__ on the earth do dwell, All in__ heav - en, all in hell.
5. Thou, who on the judg - ment - day Our most se - cret thoughts shall weigh,
Shield us__ now with pit - y ing care, Guard us__ from temp - ta - tion's snare.
6. Hon - or, glo - ry, love_ and_praise, Be through nev - er - end - ing days,
To the__ Fa - ther and the Son And the__ Spir - it, Three in One.

1. Mak - er of the star - ry sphere, To the faith - ful, Light most dear,
Je - sus, Sav - ior, Lord of all, Heark - en to thy peo - ple's call.
2. When our na - ture faint - ing lay, Crushed by Sa - tan's cru - el sway,
Blest phy - si - cian, 'twas thy love Brought us heal - ing from a - bove.
3. In the bless - èd Mar - y's womb, Pur - est flesh thou didst as - sume,
That to God a - bove might rise The all - ho - ly sac - ri - fice.

4. Un - to heav'n ex - alt - ed now, At thy sa - cred name shall bow
All that on the earth do dwell, All in heav - en, all in hell.
5. Thou, who on the judg - ment - day Our most se - cret thoughts shall weigh,
Shield us now with pit - y ing care, Guard us from temp - ta - tion's snare.
6. Hon - or, glo - ry, love and praise, Be through nev - er - end - ing days,
To the Fa - ther and the Son And the Spir - it, Three in One.

193 ALS CHRISTUS MIT SEINER LEHR — *Conditor Alme Siderum* — English Translation by Campbell

1. Mak - er of the star - ry sphere, To the faith - ful, Light most dear,
Je - sus, Sav - ior, Lord of all, Heark - en to thy peo - ple's call.
2. When our na - ture faint - ing lay, Crushed by Sa - tan's cru - el sway,
Blest phy - si - cian, 'twas thy love Brought us heal - ing from a - bove.
3. In the bless - èd Mar - y's womb, Pur - est flesh thou didst as - sume,
That to God a - bove might rise The all - ho - ly sac - ri - fice.

4. Un - to heav'n ex - alt - ed now, At thy sa - cred name shall bow
All that on the earth do dwell, All in heav - en, all in hell.
5. Thou, who on the judg - ment - day Our most se - cret thoughts shall weigh,
Shield us now with pit - y ing care, Guard us from temp - ta - tion's snare.
6. Hon - or, glo - ry, love and praise, Be through nev - er - end - ing days,
To the Fa - ther and the Son And the Spir - it, Three in One.

1. Mak - er of the star - ry sphere, To the faith - ful, Light most dear,
Je - sus, Sav - ior, Lord of all, Heark - en to thy peo - ple's call.
2. When our na - ture faint - ing lay, Crushed by Sa - tan's cru - el sway,
Blest phy - si - cian, 'twas thy love Brought us heal - ing from a - bove.
3. In the bless - èd Mar - y's womb, Pur - est flesh thou didst as - sume,
That to God a - bove might rise The all - ho - ly sac - ri - fice.

4. Un - to heav'n ex - alt - ed now, At thy sa - cred name shall bow
All that on the earth do dwell, All in heav - en, all in hell.
5. Thou, who on the judg - ment - day Our most se - cret thoughts shall weigh,
Shield us now with pit - y ing care, Guard us from temp - ta - tion's snare.
6. Hon - or, glo - ry, love and praise, Be through nev - er - end - ing days,
To the Fa - ther and the Son And the Spir - it, Three in One.

 GOTT SEI DANK — *Die Parente Temporum* — English Translation by Baker

1. On this day, the first of days, God the Fa-ther's name we praise; Who, cre-
a-tion's Lord and spring Did the world from dark-ness bring. Al - le - lu - ia.
2. On this day th'E - ter - nal Son O - ver death His tri-umph won; On this
day the Spir - it came With His gifts of liv - ing flame. Al - le - lu - ia.
3. O that fer - vent love to - day May in eve - ry heart have sway, Teach-ing
us to praise a - right God, the source of life and light. Al - le - lu - ia.
4. Fa - ther, who didst fash - ion me Im - age of Thy - self to be, Fill me
with Thy love di - vine, Let my ev - 'ry thought be Thine. Al - le - lu - ia.

5. Ho - ly Je - sus, may I be Dead and bur - ied here with Thee; And, by
love in - flamed, a - rise Un - to Thee a sac - ri - fice. Al - le - lu - ia.
6. Thou, who dost all gifts im - part, Shine, sweet Spir - it, in my heart; Best of
gifts Thy - self be - stow; Make me burn Thy love to know. Al - le - lu - ia.
7. God, the bless - èd Three in One, Dwell with - in my heart a - lone; Thou dost
give Thy - self to me; May I give my - self to Thee. Al - le - lu - ia.
8. E - qual praise to Fa - ther, Son And to Spir - it now be done: Who us
made, and Who us bought, Who by love is our sup - port. Al - le - lu - ia.

201 ALS CHRISTUS MIT SEINER LEHR — *Die Parente Temporum* — English Translation by Baker

1. On this day, the first of days, God the Fa - ther's name we praise;
Who, cre - a - tion's Lord and spring Did the world from dark - ness bring.
2. On this day th'E - ter - nal Son O - ver death His tri - umph won;
On this day the Spir - it came With His gifts of liv - ing flame.
3. O that fer - vent love to - day May in eve - ry heart have sway,
Teach - ing us to praise a - right God, the source of life and light.
4. Fa - ther, who didst fash - ion me Im - age of Thy - self to be,
Fill me with Thy love di - vine, Let my ev - 'ry thought be Thine.

5. Ho - ly Je - sus, may I be Dead and bur - ied here with Thee;
And, by love in - flamed, a - rise Un - to Thee a sac - ri - fice.
6. Thou, who dost all gifts im - part, Shine, sweet Spir - it, in my heart;
Best of gifts Thy - self be - stow; Make me burn Thy love to know.
7. God, the bless - èd Three in One, Dwell with - in my heart a - lone;
Thou dost give Thy - self to me; May I give my - self to Thee.
8. E - qual praise to Fa - ther, Son And to Spir - it now be done:
Who us made, and Who us bought, Who by love is our sup - port.

1. On this day, the first of days, God the Fa-ther's name we praise;
Who, cre - a - tion's Lord and spring Did the world from dark - ness bring.
2. On this day th'E - ter - nal Son O - ver death His tri - umph won;
On this day the Spir - it came With His gifts of liv - ing flame.
3. O that fer - vent love to - day May in eve - ry heart have sway,
Teach - ing us to praise a - right God, the source of life and light.
4. Fa - ther, who didst fash - ion me Im - age of Thy - self to be,
Fill me with Thy love di - vine, Let my ev - 'ry thought be Thine.

* *A higher accompaniment is provided in the Brébeuf Organ Edition—for optional use.*

5. Ho - ly Je - sus, may I be Dead and bur - ied here___ with Thee;
And, by love in - flamed, a - rise Un - to Thee a sac - ri - fice.
6. Thou, who dost all gifts im - part, Shine, sweet Spir - it, in___ my heart;
Best of gifts Thy - self be - stow; Make me burn Thy love to___ know.
7. God, the bless - èd Three in One, Dwell with - in my heart___ a - lone;
Thou dost give Thy - self to me; May I give my - self to___ Thee.
8. E - qual praise to Fa - ther, Son And to Spir - it now___ be done:
Who us made, and Who us bought, Who by love is our sup - port.

1. On this day, the first of days, God the Fa - ther's name we praise;
Who, cre - a - tion's Lord and spring Did the world from dark - ness bring.
2. On this day th'E - ter - nal Son O - ver death His tri - umph won;
On this day the Spir - it came With His gifts of liv - ing flame.
3. O that fer - vent love to - day May in eve - ry heart have sway,
Teach - ing us to praise a - right God, the source of life and light.
4. Fa - ther, who didst fash - ion me Im - age of Thy - self to be,
Fill me with Thy love di - vine, Let my ev - 'ry thought be Thine.

5. Ho - ly Je - sus, may I be Dead and bur - ied here with Thee;
And, by love in - flamed, a - rise Un - to Thee a sac - ri - fice.
6. Thou, who dost all gifts im - part, Shine, sweet Spir - it, in my heart;
Best of gifts Thy - self be - stow; Make me burn Thy love to know.
7. God, the bless - èd Three in One, Dwell with - in my heart a - lone;
Thou dost give Thy - self to me; May I give my - self to Thee.
8. E - qual praise to Fa - ther, Son And to Spir - it now be done:
Who us made, and Who us bought, Who by love is our sup - port.

1. On this day, the first of__ days, Al - - le - lu - ia. God the Fa-ther's
name we__praise; Al - le - lu - ia. Who, cre - a - tion's Lord and__spring
Al - le - lu - ia. Did the world from dark-ness bring. Al - le - lu - ia.
2. On this day th'E - ter - nal__ Son Al - le - lu - ia. O - ver death His
tri - umph won; Al - le - lu - ia. On this day the Spir - it__came
Al - le - lu - ia. With His gifts of liv - ing__flame. Al - le - lu - ia.

3. O that fer-vent love to - day Al - le - lu - ia. May in eve - ry
heart have_ sway, Al - le - lu - ia. Teach - ing us to praise a - right
Al - le - lu - ia. God, the source of life and_ light. Al - le - lu - ia.
4. Fa - ther, who didst fash - ion_ me Al - le - lu - ia. Im - age of Thy-
self to_ be, Al - le - lu - ia. Fill me with Thy love_ di - vine,
Al - le - lu - ia. Let my ev - 'ry thought be_ Thine. Al - le - lu - ia.

5. Ho - ly Je - sus, may I ___ be Al - le - lu - ia. Dead and bur - ied
here with Thee; Al - le - lu - ia. And, by love in - flamed, a - rise
Al - le - lu - ia. Un - to Thee a sac - ri - fice. Al - le - lu - ia.
6. Thou, who dost all gifts im - part, Al - le - lu - ia. Shine, sweet Spir - it,
in my ___ heart; Al - le - lu - ia. Best of gifts Thy - self ___ be - stow;
Al - le - lu - ia. Make me burn Thy love to ___ know. Al - le - lu - ia.

7. God, the bless - èd Three in__ One, Al - le - lu - ia. Dwell with - in my
heart a - lone; Al - le - lu - ia. Thou dost give Thy - self_ to__ me;
Al - le - lu - ia. May I give my - self to__ Thee. Al - le - lu - ia.
8. E - qual praise to Fa - ther,_ Son Al - le - lu - ia. And to Spir - it
now be__ done: Al - le - lu - ia. Who us made, and Who us__ bought,
Al - le - lu - ia. Who by love is our sup - port. Al - le - lu - ia.

205 WÜRTEMBURG — *Die Parente Temporum* — English Translation by Baker

1. On this day, the first of days, God the Fa - ther's name we praise;
Who, cre - a - tion's Lord and spring Did the world from dark - ness bring.
Al - le - lu - ia.
2. On this day th'E - ter - nal Son O - ver death His tri - umph won; On this day the Spir - it came With His gifts of liv - ing flame. Al - le - lu - ia.
3. O that fer - vent love to - day May in eve - ry heart have sway, Teach - ing us to praise a - right God, the source of life and light. Al - le - lu - ia.

4. Fa - ther, who didst fash - ion me Im - age of Thy - self to be,
Fill me with Thy love di - vine, Let my ev - 'ry thought be Thine.
Al - le - lu - ia.
5. Ho - ly Je - sus, may I be
Dead and bur - ied here with Thee; And, by love in - flamed, a - rise
Un - to Thee a sac - ri - fice. Al - le - lu - ia.
6. Thou, who dost all gifts im - part, Shine, sweet Spir - it, in my heart;

Best of gifts Thy - self be - stow; Make me burn_ Thy love to know.
Al - le - lu - ia.
7. God, the bless - èd Three in One,
Dwell with - in my heart a - lone; Thou dost give Thy - self to me;
May I give_ my - self to Thee. Al - - le - lu - ia.
8. E - qual praise to Fa - ther, Son And to Spir - it now be done: Who us
made, and Who us bought, Who by love is our sup - port. Al - le - lu - ia.

1. On this day, the__ first of days, God the Fa - ther's name we__ praise;
Who, cre - a - tion's Lord and spring Did the world from dark - ness_ bring,
Did the world from dark - ness bring.
2. On this day th'E - ter - nal Son
O - ver death His tri - umph won;
On this day the__ Spir - it came
With His gifts of liv - ing__ flame,
With His gifts of__ liv - ing flame.
3. O that fer - vent_ love to - day May in eve - ry heart have_ sway,

Teach-ing us to praise a - right God, the source of life and light,
God, the source of life and light.
4. Fa - ther, who didst fash - ion me
Im - age of Thy - self to be,
Fill me with Thy love di - vine,
Let my ev - 'ry thought be Thine,
Let my ev - 'ry thought be Thine.
5. Ho - ly Je - sus, may I be
Dead and bur - ied here with Thee;
And, by love in - flamed, a - rise
Un - to Thee a sac - ri - fice,
Un - to Thee a sac - ri - fice.
6. Thou, who dost all gifts im - part,

Shine, sweet Spir - it, in my__ heart; Best of gifts Thy - self be - stow;
Make me burn Thy love to__ know, Make me burn Thy__ love to know.
7. God, the bless - èd__ Three in One, Dwell with-in my heart a - lone;
Thou dost give Thy - self to me; May I give my - self to__ Thee,
May I give my - self to Thee.
8. E - qual praise to__ Fa - ther, Son
And to Spir - it now be__ done: Who us made, and__ Who us bought,
Who by love is our sup - port, Who by love is__ our sup - port.

208 ST ANNE — *Die Parente Temporum* — English Translation by Cooke

1. This day the Fa - ther, Source of all, Put forth cre - a - tive might;
He spoke, and called the world He made From dark - ness in - to light.
2. This day the Son tri - um - phant left The grave, and death o'er - came;
The Spir - it came in hu - man hearts To sow His fruit - ful flame.
3. Let love in - flame with fer - vent glow Our hearts, this first of days;
That we to Him Who gives us life May pay our debt of praise.
4. O Fa - ther, in God's im - age Thou In love didst fash - ion me;

Thee may I love with all my heart, And med - i - tate on Thee.
5. O Son, vouch - safe that I may die With Thee, and with Thee rise;
For Thee, con - sumed by love, may be A ho - ly sac - ri - fice.
6. O Ho - ly Ghost, Thy - self the best Of gifts Thou dost be - stow;
Burn, Fire of love, in me, that I May burn Thy love to know.
7. God of my heart, Thrice Ho - ly God, Whose grace my prayers im - plore,
To Thee I vow my - self; and Thee Will love for ev - er - more.

1. This day the Fa - ther, Source of all, Put forth cre - a - tive might;
He spoke, and called the world He made From dark - ness in - to light.
2. This day the Son tri - um - phant left The grave, and death o'er - came;
The Spir - it came in hu - man hearts To sow His fruit - ful flame.
3. Let love in - flame with fer - vent glow Our hearts, this first of days;
That we to Him Who gives us life May pay our debt of praise.
4. O Fa - ther, in God's im - age Thou In love didst fash - ion me;

Thee may I love with all my heart, And med - i - tate on Thee.
5. O Son, vouch - safe that I may die With Thee, and with Thee rise;
For Thee, con - sumed by love, may be A ho - ly sac - ri - fice.
6. O Ho - ly Ghost, Thy - self the best Of gifts Thou dost be - stow;
Burn, Fire of love, in me, that I May burn Thy love to know.
7. God of my heart, Thrice Ho - ly God, Whose grace my prayers im - plore,
To Thee I vow my - self; and Thee Will love for ev - er - more.

210 ST JAMES — *Die Parente Temporum* — English Translation by Cooke

Thee may I love with all my heart, And med - i - tate on Thee.
5. O Son, vouch-safe that I may die With Thee, and with Thee rise;
For Thee, con-sumed by love, may be A ho - ly sac - ri - fice.
6. O Ho - ly Ghost, Thy - self the best Of gifts Thou dost be - stow;
Burn, Fire of love, in me, that I May burn_ Thy love to know.
7. God of my heart, Thrice Ho - ly God, Whose grace my prayers im - plore,
To Thee I vow my - self; and Thee Will love_ for ev - er - more.

214 ALTONA — *Ex More Docti Mystico* — English Translation by Father Fitzpatrick

1. By ho - ly cus - tom taught, we raise Our minds and hearts the__ Lord to serve,
And through the space of for - ty days The fasts and laws of Lent ob - serve.
2. The law first set these days a - side; The Proph - ets act - ed__ in ac - cord;
Then Christ the sea - son sanc - ti - fied, Time's Mak - er, and time's on - ly Lord.
3. There - fore, let us more spar - ing - ly Both food, and drink, and__ talk en - joy,
And sleep and joc - u - lar - i - ty More strict - ly than we do,__ em - ploy.

#18 has (optional) organ accompaniment at a higher key.

4. And let us shun each e - vil thought That un - der - mines the_ rest - less soul,
And bring the tempt - er's pow'r to nought By spir - its bound in close_ con - trol.
5. We kneel be - fore Thee, Lord, and weep; Thine ire is just; our_ judge Thou art;
We cry with sup - pliant voice, and keep Our hope in Thee, with hum - bled heart.
6. We of - ten by our e - vil deeds, O God, Thy clem - en - cy of - fend;
For - giv - er, then, up - on_ our needs Pour down Thy mer - cies with - out end.

7. Re - mem - ber that, though prone to fall, From Thine own hands at first we came:
We beg Thee, let none take of all The hon - or due to Thine own Name.
8. For - give the e - vil we have done; The bless - ing that we need, in - crease;
In - flame our hearts all sin to shun, And keep our souls in end - less peace.
9. Hear us, O Trin - i - ty sub - lime, And un - di - vid - ed U - ni - ty;
So let this con - se - crat - ed time Bring forth Thy fruits a - bun - dant - ly.

1. By ho - ly cus - tom taught, we raise Our minds and hearts the Lord to serve,
And through the space of for - ty days The fasts and laws of Lent ob - serve.
2. The law first set these days a - side; The Proph - ets act - ed in ac - cord;
Then Christ the sea - son sanc - ti - fied, Time's Mak - er, and time's on - ly Lord.
3. There - fore, let us more spar - ing - ly Both food, and drink, and talk en - joy,
And sleep and joc - u - lar - i - ty More strict - ly than we do, em - ploy.

4. And let us shun each e - vil thought That un - der - mines the rest - less soul,
And bring the tempt-er's pow'r to nought By spir - its bound in close con - trol.
5. We kneel be - fore Thee, Lord, and weep; Thine ire is just; our judge Thou art;
We cry with sup-pliant voice, and keep Our hope in Thee, with hum-bled heart.
6. We of - ten by our e - vil deeds, O God, Thy clem - en - cy of - fend;
For - giv - er, then, up - on our needs Pour down Thy mer - cies with - out end.

7. Re - mem - ber that, though prone to fall, From Thine own hands at first we came:
We beg Thee, let none take of all The hon - or due to Thine own Name.
8. For - give the e - vil we have done; The bless - ing that we need, in - crease;
In - flame our hearts all sin to shun, And keep our souls in end - less peace.
9. Hear us, O Trin - i - ty sub - lime, And un - di - vid - ed U - ni - ty;
So let this con - se - crat - ed time Bring forth Thy fruits a - bun - dant - ly.

EISENACH — *Ex More Docti Mystico* — English Translation by Father Fitzpatrick

4. And_ let us shun each e - vil thought That un - der-mines the rest - less soul,
And bring the tempt - er's pow'r to nought By spir - its bound in close con - trol.
5. We_ kneel be - fore Thee, Lord, and weep; Thine ire is just; our judge Thou art;
We cry with sup - pliant voice, and keep Our hope in Thee, with hum-bled heart.
6. We_ of - ten by our e - vil deeds, O God, Thy clem - en - cy of - fend;
For - giv - er, then, up - on our needs Pour down Thy mer - cies with - out end.

7. Re - mem - ber that, though prone to fall, From Thine own hands at first we came:
We beg Thee, let none take of all The hon - or due_ to Thine own Name.
8. For - give the e - vil we have done; The bless-ing that we need, in-crease;
In - flame our hearts all sin to shun, And keep our souls in end-less peace.
9. Hear us, O Trin - i - ty sub - lime, And un - di - vid - ed U - ni - ty;
So let this con - se - crat - ed time Bring forth Thy fruits a - bun - dant - ly.

1. By ho - ly cus - tom taught, we raise Our minds and hearts the Lord to serve,
And through the space of for-ty days The fasts_ and laws of Lent ob - serve.
2. The law first set these days a - side; The Proph - ets act - ed in ac - cord;
Then Christ the sea - son sanc-ti - fied, Time's Mak - er, and time's on-ly Lord.
3. There - fore, let us more spar- ing - ly Both food, and drink, and talk en - joy,
And sleep and joc - u - lar - i - ty More strict - ly than we do, em - ploy.

4. And let us shun each e-vil thought That un-der-mines the rest-less soul,
And bring the tempt-er's pow'r to nought By spir-its bound in close con-trol.
5. We kneel be-fore Thee, Lord, and weep; Thine ire is just; our judge Thou art;
We cry with sup-pliant voice, and keep Our hope in Thee, with hum-bled heart.
6. We of-ten by our e-vil deeds, O God, Thy clem-en-cy of-fend;
For-giv-er, then, up-on our needs Pour down Thy mer-cies with-out end.

7. Re - mem - ber that, though prone to fall, From Thine own hands at first we came:
We beg Thee, let none take of all The hon - or due to Thine own Name.
8. For - give the e - vil we have done; The bless - ing that_ we need, in - crease;
In - flame our hearts all sin to shun, And keep_ our souls in end - less peace.
9. Hear us, O Trin - i - ty sub - lime, And un - di - vid - ed U - ni - ty;
So let this con - se - crat-ed time Bring forth_ Thy fruits a - bun-dant - ly.

ST CROSS — *Ex More Docti Mystico* — English Translation by Father Fitzpatrick

1. By ho - ly cus - tom taught, we raise Our minds and hearts the Lord to serve, And through the space of for - ty days The fasts and laws of Lent ob - serve.
2. The law first set these days a - side; The Proph-ets act - ed in ac - cord; Then Christ the sea - son sanc - ti - fied, Time's Mak-er, and time's on - ly Lord.
3. There - fore, let us more spar - ing - ly Both food, and drink, and talk en - joy, And sleep and joc - u - lar - i - ty More strict - ly

than we do, em - ploy.
4. And let us shun each e - vil thought That un-der-mines the rest - less soul, And bring the tempt - er's pow'r to nought By spir-its bound in close con - trol.
5. We kneel be - fore Thee, Lord, and weep; Thine ire is just; our judge Thou art; We cry with sup - pliant voice, and keep Our hope in Thee, with hum - bled heart.
6. We of - ten by our e - vil deeds, O God, Thy clem - en - cy of - fend; For - giv - er,

then, up - on our needs Pour down Thy mer - cies with - out end.
7. Re - mem-ber that, though prone to fall, From Thine own hands at first we came:
We beg Thee, let none take of all The hon-or due to Thine own Name.
8. For - give the e - vil we have done; The bless-ing that we need, in - crease;
In - flame our hearts all sin to shun, And keep our souls in end - less peace.
9. Hear us, O Trin - i - ty sub - lime, And un - di - vid - ed U - ni - ty;
So let this con - se - crat - ed time Bring forth Thy fruits a - bun - dant - ly.

1. By ho - ly cus - tom taught, we raise Our minds and hearts the
Lord to serve, And through the space of for - ty days The fasts and
laws of Lent ob - serve.
2. The law first set these
days a - side; The Proph - ets act - ed in ac - cord; Then Christ the
sea - son sanc - ti - fied, Time's Mak - er, and time's on - ly Lord.
3. There - fore, let us more spar - ing - ly Both food, and drink, and
talk en - joy, And sleep and joc - u - lar - i - ty More strict - ly

than we do, em - ploy.
4. And let us shun each
e - vil thought That un - der - mines the rest - less soul, And bring the
tempt - er's pow'r to nought By spir - its bound in close con - trol.
5. We kneel be - fore Thee, Lord, and weep; Thine ire is just; our
judge Thou art; We cry with sup - pliant voice, and keep Our hope in
Thee, with hum - bled heart.
6. We of - ten by our
e - vil deeds, O God, Thy clem - en - cy of - fend; For - giv - er,

then, up - on__ our needs Pour down Thy mer - cies with - out end.
7. Re - mem - ber that, though prone to fall, From Thine own hands at first_ we came:
We beg Thee, let none take_ of all The hon - or due to Thine_ own Name.
8. For - give_ the e - vil we have done; The bless - ing that we need, in - crease;
In - flame our hearts all sin__ to shun, And keep our souls in end - less peace.
9. Hear us,__ O Trin - i - ty sub - lime, And un - di - vid - ed U - ni - ty;__
So let this con - se - crat - ed time Bring forth Thy fruits a - bun - dant - ly.

1. By ho - ly cus - tom taught, we raise Our minds and hearts the Lord to
serve, And through the space of for - ty days The fasts and laws of
Lent ob - serve.
2. The law first set these days a - side;
The Proph-ets act - ed in ac - cord; Then Christ the sea - son sanc - ti -
fied, Time's Mak - er, and time's on - ly Lord.
3. There - fore, let
us more spar - ing - ly Both food, and drink, and talk en - joy,
And sleep and joc - u - lar - i - ty More strict - ly than we do, em - ploy.

4. And let us shun each e - vil thought That un - der - mines the rest - less
soul, And bring the tempt - er's pow'r to nought By spir - its bound in
close con - trol.
5. We kneel be - fore Thee, Lord, and weep;
Thine ire is just; our judge Thou art; We cry with sup - pliant voice, and
keep Our hope in Thee, with hum - bled heart.
6. We of - ten
by our e - vil deeds, O God, Thy clem - en - cy of - fend; For - giv - er,
then, up - on our needs Pour down Thy mer - cies with - out end.

7. Re - mem-ber that, though prone to fall, From Thine own hands at first we
came: We beg Thee, let none take of all The hon - or due to
Thine own Name.
8. For-give the e - vil we have done; The bless - ing
that we need, in - crease; In - flame our hearts all sin to
shun, And keep our souls in end-less peace.
9. Hear us, O
Trin - i - ty sub - lime, And un - di - vid - ed U - ni - ty; So let this
con - se - crat - ed time Bring forth Thy fruits a - bun - dant - ly.

1. By__ ho - ly cus - tom taught, we raise Our minds and hearts the Lord to__ serve,
And__ through the space of for - ty days The fasts and laws of Lent ob - serve.
2. The__ law first set these days a - side; The Proph - ets act - ed in ac - cord;
Then_ Christ the sea - son sanc - ti - fied, Time's Mak - er, and time's on - ly Lord.
3. There - fore, let us more spar - ing - ly Both food, and drink, and talk en - joy,
And__ sleep and joc - u - lar - i - ty More strict - ly than we do, em - ploy.

4. And_ let us shun each e - vil thought That un - der-mines the rest - less_ soul,
And_ bring the tempt-er's pow'r to nought By spir - its bound in close con - trol.
5. We_ kneel be - fore Thee, Lord, and weep; Thine ire is just; our judge Thou_ art;
We_ cry with sup-pliant voice, and keep Our hope in Thee, with hum - bled heart.
6. We_ of - ten by our e - vil deeds, O God, Thy clem - en - cy of - fend;
For - giv - er, then, up - on our needs Pour down Thy mer - cies with - out end.

7. Re - mem - ber that, though prone to fall, From Thine own hands at first we__ came:
We__ beg Thee, let none take of all The hon - or due to Thine own Name.
8. For - give the e - vil we have done; The bless - ing that we need, in - crease;
In - flame our hearts all sin to shun, And keep our souls in end - less peace.
9. Hear_ us, O Trin - i - ty sub - lime, And un - di - vid - ed U - ni - ty;
So__ let this con - se - crat - ed time Bring forth Thy fruits a - bun - dant - ly.

223 MELCOMBE — *Ex More Docti Mystico* — English Translation by Father Fitzpatrick

4. And let us shun each e - vil thought That un - der - mines the rest - less soul,
And bring the tempt - er's pow'r to nought By spir - its bound in close con - trol.
5. We kneel be - fore Thee, Lord, and weep; Thine ire is just; our judge Thou art;
We cry with sup-pliant voice, and keep Our hope in Thee, with hum-bled heart.
6. We of - ten by our e - vil deeds, O God, Thy clem - en - cy of - fend;
For - giv - er, then, up - on our needs Pour down Thy mer-cies with-out end.

7. Re - mem - ber that, though prone to fall, From Thine own hands at first we came:
We beg Thee, let none take of all The hon - or due to Thine own Name.
8. For - give the e - vil we have done; The bless - ing that we need, in - crease;
In - flame our hearts all sin to shun, And keep our souls in end - less peace.
9. Hear us, O Trin - i - ty sub - lime, And un - di - vid - ed U - ni - ty;
So let this con - se - crat - ed time Bring forth Thy fruits a - bun - dant - ly.

TRINITY COLLEGE — *Ex More Docti Mystico* — English Translation by Father Fitzpatrick **224**

1. By ho - ly cus - tom taught, we raise Our minds and hearts the Lord to serve,
And through the space of for - ty days The fasts and laws of Lent ob - serve.
2. The law first set these days a - side; The Proph - ets act - ed in ac - cord;
Then Christ the sea - son sanc - ti - fied, Time's Mak - er, and time's on - ly Lord.
3. There - fore, let us more spar - ing - ly Both food, and drink, and talk en - joy,
And sleep and joc - u - lar - i - ty More strict - ly than we do, em - ploy.

4. And let us shun each e - vil thought That un - der - mines the rest - less soul,
And bring the tempt - er's pow'r to nought By spir - its bound in close con - trol.
5. We kneel be - fore Thee, Lord, and weep; Thine ire is just; our judge Thou art;
We cry with sup - pliant voice, and keep Our hope in Thee, with hum - bled heart.
6. We of - ten by our e - vil deeds, O God, Thy clem - en - cy of - fend;
For - giv - er, then, up - on our needs Pour down Thy mer - cies with - out end.

7. Re - mem - ber that, though prone to fall, From Thine own hands at first we came:
We beg Thee, let none take of all The hon - or due to Thine own Name.
8. For - give the e - vil we have done; The bless - ing that we need, in - crease;
In - flame our hearts all sin to shun, And keep our souls in end - less peace.
9. Hear us, O Trin - i - ty sub - lime, And un - di - vid - ed U - ni - ty;
So let this con - se - crat - ed time Bring forth Thy fruits a - bun - dant - ly.

1. When the Pa - triarch was re-turn - ing Crown'd with_ tri - umph from the fray,
Him the peace - ful king of Sa - lem Came to_ meet up - on his way;
Meek - ly bear - ing_ Bread and_ Wine, Ho - ly Priest - hood's aw - ful sign.

* *A transposed organ accompaniment has been provided for optional use.*

2. On the truth thus dim - ly shad-ow'd Lat - er__ days a lus - ter shed;
When the great High - Priest e - ter - nal, Un - der__ forms of Wine and Bread,
For the world's im - mor - tal__ food Gave His Flesh and gave His Blood.
3. Wond-'rous gift! The Word who fash-ion'd All things by His might di - vine,
Bread in - to His Bod - y chang-es, In - to__ His own Blood the wine;
What though sense no__ change per-ceives, Faith ad - mires, a - dores, be - lieves.

4. He who once to die a Vic - tim On the_ Cross, did not re - fuse,
Day by day, up - on our al - tars, That same Sac - ri - fice re - news;
Through His ho - ly_ Priest - hood's hands, Faith - ful to_ His last com - mands.
5. While the peo - ple all u - nit - ing In the_ Sac - ri - fice sub - lime,
Of - fer Christ to His high Fa - ther, Of - fer_ up them - selves with Him;
Then to - geth - er_ with the_ Priest On the liv - ing Vic - tim feast.

1. When the Pa - triarch was re - turn - ing Crown'd with tri - umph from the fray,
Him the peace - ful king of Sa - lem Came to meet up - on his way;
Meek - ly bear - ing Bread and Wine, Ho - ly Priest-hood's aw - ful sign.

2. On the truth thus dim - ly shad - ow'd Lat - er days a lus - ter shed;
When the great High - Priest e - ter - nal, Un - der forms of Wine and Bread,
For the world's im - mor - tal food Gave His Flesh and gave His Blood.
3. Wond - 'rous gift! The Word who fash - ion'd All things by His might di - vine,
Bread in - to His Bod - y chang - es, In - to His own Blood the wine;
What though sense no change per - ceives, Faith ad - mires, a - dores, be - lieves.

* *A transposed organ accompaniment has been provided for optional use.*

4. He who once to die a Vic - tim On the Cross, did not re - fuse,
Day by day, up - on our al - tars, That same Sac - ri - fice re - news;
Through His ho - ly Priest - hood's hands, Faith - ful to His last com - mands.
5. While the peo - ple all u - nit - ing In the Sac - ri - fice sub - lime,
Of - fer Christ to His high Fa - ther, Of - fer up them - selves with Him;
Then to - geth - er with the Priest On the liv - ing Vic - tim feast.

1. When the Pa - triarch was re - turn - ing Crown'd with tri - umph from the fray,
Him the peace - ful king of Sa - lem Came to meet_ up - on his way;
Meek - ly bear - ing Bread and Wine, Ho - ly Priest-hood's aw - ful sign.
2. On the truth thus dim - ly shad - ow'd Lat - er days_ a lus - ter shed;
When the great High - Priest e - ter - nal, Un - der forms of Wine and Bread,
For the world's im - mor - tal food Gave His Flesh and gave His Blood.
3. Wond - 'rous gift! The Word who fash - ion'd All things by_ His might di - vine,

Bread in - to His Bod - y chang - es, In - to His__ own Blood the wine;
What though sense no change per- ceives, Faith ad - mires, a - dores, be - lieves.
4. He who once to die a Vic - tim On the Cross, did not re - fuse,
Day by day, up - on our al - tars, That same Sac - ri - fice re - news;
Through His ho - ly Priest - hood's hands, Faith - ful to His last com - mands.
5. While the peo - ple all u - nit - ing In the Sac - ri - fice sub - lime,
Of - fer Christ to His high Fa - ther, Of - fer up__ them - selves with Him;
Then to - geth - er with the Priest On the liv - ing Vic - tim feast.

 ICH BEGEHR NICHT MEHR — *Hoste Dum Victo Triumphans* — English Transl. by Father Caswall

1. When the__ Pa - triarch was re - turn - ing Crown'd with tri - umph from the fray,
Him the__ peace - ful king of__ Sa - lem Came to meet up - on his way;
Meek - ly__ bear - ing Bread and Wine, Ho - ly Priest-hood's aw - ful sign.

2. On the__ truth thus dim - ly__ shad - ow'd Lat - er days a lus - ter shed;
When the__ great High - Priest e - ter - nal, Un - der forms of Wine and Bread,
For the__ world's im - mor - tal food Gave His Flesh and gave His Blood.
3. Wond - 'rous__ gift! The Word who__ fash - ion'd All things by His might di - vine,
Bread in - to His Bod - y__ chang - es, In - to His own Blood the wine;
What though sense no change per - ceives, Faith ad - mires, a - dores, be - lieves.

4. He who_ once to die a_ Vic - tim On the Cross, did not re - fuse,
Day by_ day, up - on our_ al - tars, That same Sac - ri - fice re - news;
Through His_ ho - ly Priest - hood's hands, Faith - ful to His last com - mands.
5. While the_ peo - ple all u - nit - ing In the Sac - ri - fice sub - lime,
Of - fer_ Christ to His high_ Fa - ther, Of - fer up them - selves with Him;
Then to - geth - er with the Priest On the liv - ing Vic - tim feast.

1. When, the foe laid low, re - tir - ing, A - bra - ham vic - to - rious went,
then Mel - chis - e - dech be - fore him, Sa - lem's liege mag - nif - i - cent,
came, and act - ing on his priest - hood, wine and bread did there pre - sent.
2. Truth that an - cient shad - ow hint - ed clear - ly shines be - fore our gaze:
see, our new High Priest the pat - tern of Mel - chis - e - dech dis - plays,
un - der bread and wine his bod - y with his blood for us out - lays.

3. Won - drous change the Word pro - duc - es, all cre - a - tion's foun - tain - head,
in - to blood is wine con - vert - ed, e - ven as to flesh is bread:
feel - ing fails, but to our think - ing strength by loft - y faith is wed.
4. As in gor - y wise he of - fered to the Fa - ther once of yore,
so him - self he du - ly ren - ders dai - ly, vic - tim as be - fore,
by the hands of those who serve him, on our al - tars, with - out gore.

5. Draw - ing nigh the hal - lowed pre - cincts, there the ho - ly peo - ple stand,
Christ un - to the sov-'reign Fa - ther and them - selves with Christ re - mand,
by his flesh and blood thus yield - ed feed then from a shep-herd's hand.
6. High - est praise to God the Fa - ther, who has made all things of naught,
high - est praise be to his Off - spring, who us with his blood has bought,
to the Spir - it, by whose boun - teous breath we thrive, the same be wrought.

BRESLAU — *Jam Christe Sol Justitiae* — English Translation by Donahoe

1. O Sun of our sal - va - tion, rise, Il - lume our souls with_ light di - vine;
Drive night and dark - ness from the skies, And let thy day of mer - cy shine.
2. Grant that we may with stream - ing tears Wash from the heart all_ stain of sin,
And freed from world - ly joys and fears, Kin - dle the fire of love there - in.

* *A transposed organ accompaniment has been provided for optional use.*

3. Seal up the fount of sin, and bring The sigh of sor - row_ and the smart;
So shall the rod of pen - ance wring With soft'n-ing grief the har-dened heart.
4. Thy day of glo - ry comes; the glow Shall eve - ry hol - low_ fill and height;
And we re - joic - ing, Lord, shall go In safe - ty, guid - ed by thy light.
5. Be - nig - nant Trin - i - ty, to thee The world shall bow; the_ weak and strong
Shall call up - on thy name; and we, Re - newed in grace, lift up the song.

ROCKINGHAM — *Jam Christe Sol Justitiae* — English Translation by Donahoe

1. O Sun of our sal - va - tion, rise, Il - lume our souls with
light di - vine; Drive night and dark - ness from the skies,
And let thy day of mer - cy shine.
2. Grant that we
may with stream - ing tears Wash from the heart all stain of sin,
And freed from world - ly joys and fears, Kin - dle the
fire of love there - in.
3. Seal up the fount of
sin, and bring The sigh of sor - row and the smart;

So shall the rod of pen - ance wring With soft'n - ing
grief the har - dened heart.
4. Thy day of glo - ry
comes; the glow Shall eve - ry hol - low fill and height;
And we re - joic - ing, Lord, shall go In safe - ty, guid - ed
by thy light.
5. Be - nig - nant Trin - i - ty, to thee
The world shall bow; the weak and strong Shall call up - on thy
name; and we, Re - newed in grace, lift up the song.

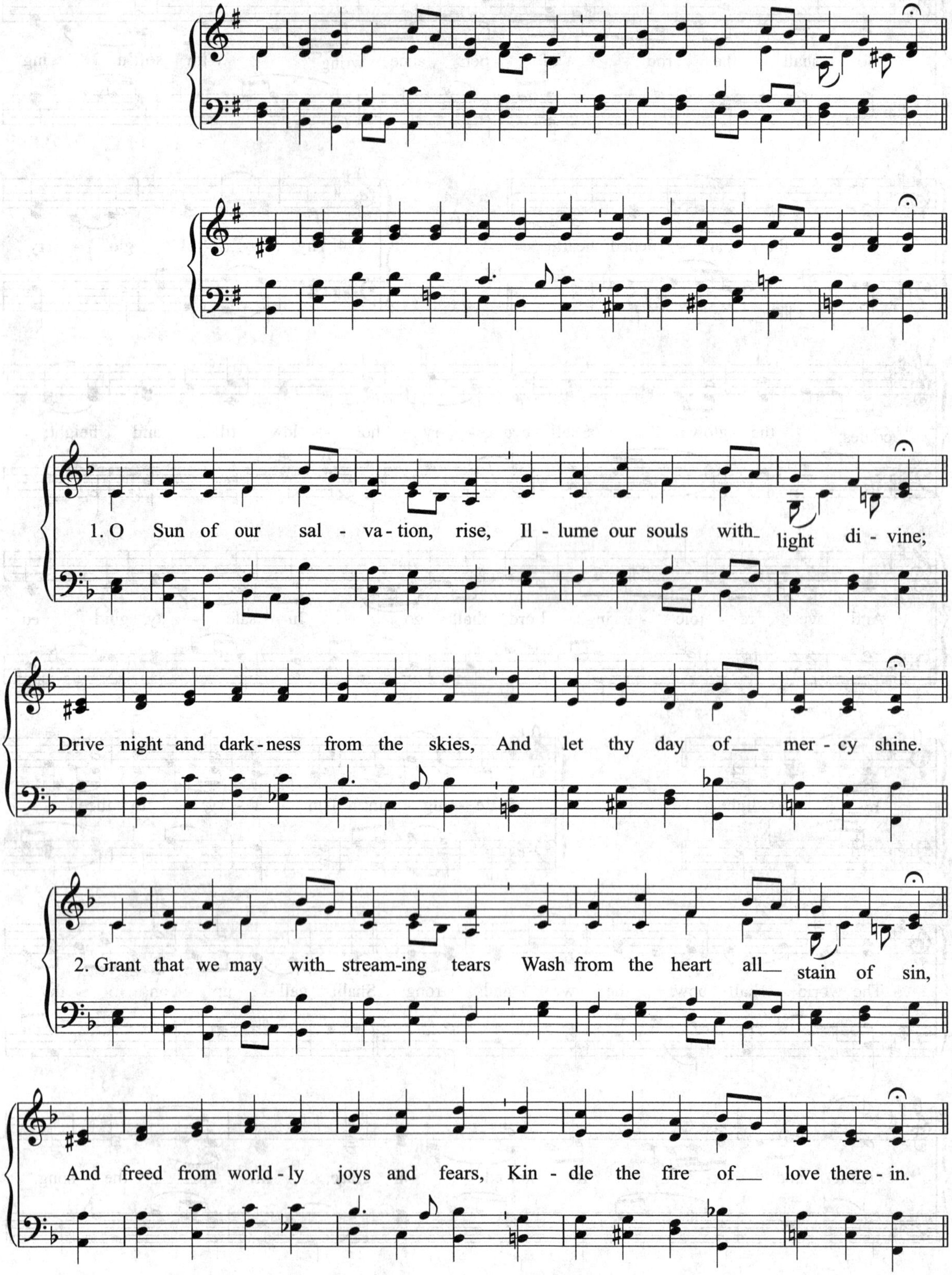
1. O Sun of our sal - va - tion, rise, Il - lume our souls with light di - vine;
Drive night and dark - ness from the skies, And let thy day of mer - cy shine.
2. Grant that we may with stream-ing tears Wash from the heart all stain of sin,
And freed from world - ly joys and fears, Kin - dle the fire of love there - in.

* A transposed organ accompaniment has been provided for optional use.

239 HILDERSTONE — *Jam Christe Sol Justitiae* — English Translation by Donahoe

* A transposed organ accompaniment has been provided for optional use.

1. O Sun of our sal - va - tion, rise, Il - lume our souls with
light di - vine; Drive night and dark - ness from the skies,
And let thy day of mer - cy shine.
2. Grant that we may with
stream-ing tears Wash from the heart all stain of sin, And freed from
world - ly joys and fears, Kin - dle the fire of love there - in.

* *A transposed organ accompaniment has been provided for optional use.*

1. Thy rays, O Sun of Jus-tice, send And all our sin-ful shad-ows rend;
With vir - tue light our souls once more, And un - to earth Thy day re - store.
2. The time ac-cept - a - ble is here; Make our re-pent-ant hearts sin-cere;
Con-vert us with Thy kind-ly care, Whom Thy long-suf-f'ring mer - cies spare.
3. Grant that for all our deep of-fense We of - fer Thee meet pen-i-tence;
That Thy be-nign and sov-'reign grace May these our griev-ous sins ef - face.

4. Thy Day draws near, that Day of bliss, When teem - ing Na - ture
blooms a - fresh; May we re - joice there - in, O Lord,
To Thy sweet fa - vor then re - stored.
5. Kind Trin - i - ty, for ev - er - more Let all Thy crea - tures
Thee a - dore, As, new by par - don, Thee we raise
A new - made can - ti - cle of praise.

EISENACH — *Jam Christe Sol Justitiae* — English Translation by Chambers

* *A transposed organ accompaniment has been provided for optional use.*

3. Grant_ that for all our deep of - fense We of - fer Thee meet pen - i - tence;
That Thy be - nign and sov - 'reign grace May these our griev - ous sins ef - face.
4. Thy___ Day draws near, that Day of bliss, When teem - ing Na - ture blooms a - fresh;
May we re - joice there - in, O Lord, To Thy sweet fa - vor then re - stored.
5. Kind_ Trin - i - ty, for ev - er - more Let all Thy crea - tures Thee a - dore,
As, new by par - don, Thee we raise A new-made can - ti - cle of praise.

KEMPEN — Jam Christe Sol Justitiae — English Translation by Chambers

1. Thy rays, O Sun of Jus - tice, send And all__ our sin - ful shad - ows rend;
With vir - tue light our souls once more, And un - to earth Thy day__ re - store.
2. The time ac - cept - a - ble is here; Make our__ re - pent - ant hearts sin - cere;
Con - vert us with Thy kind-ly care, Whom Thy long - suf - f'ring mer - cies spare.
3. Grant that for all our deep of - fense We of - fer Thee meet pen - i - tence;
That Thy be - nign and sov'reign grace May these our griev - ous sins__ ef - face.

4. Thy Day draws near, that Day of bliss, When teem - ing
Na - ture blooms a - fresh; May we re - joice there - in, O Lord,
To Thy sweet fa - vor then re - stored.
5. Kind Trin - i - ty, for ev - er - more Let all Thy
crea - tures Thee a - dore, As, new by par - don, Thee we raise
A new - made can - ti - cle of praise.

AGINCOURT — *Jam Christe Sol Justitiae* — English Translation by Chambers

1. Thy rays, O Sun of Jus - tice, send And all__ our sin - ful__
shad-ows rend; With vir - tue light_ our souls once more, And un - to
earth Thy day re - store.
2. The time ac - cept - a - ble is
here; Make our__ re - pent - ant_ hearts sin - cere; Con - vert us
with_ Thy kind - ly care, Whom Thy long - suf - f'ring mer-cies spare.
3. Grant that for all our deep of - fense We of - fer Thee_ meet_

pen - i - tence; That Thy be - nign_ and sov-'reign grace May these our
griev - ous sins ef - face.
4. Thy Day draws near, that Day of
bliss, When teem - ing Na - ture_ blooms a - fresh; May we re -
joice_ there - in, O Lord, To Thy sweet fa - vor then re - stored.
5. Kind Trin - i - ty, for ev - er - more
Let all___ Thy crea - tures_ Thee a - dore, As, new by
par - don, Thee we raise A new - made can - ti - cle of praise.

247 ALFRETON — *Jam Christe Sol Justitiae* — English Translation by Chambers

1. Thy rays, O Sun of Jus - tice, send And all our sin - ful shad - ows_ rend;
With vir - tue light our souls once more, And un - to earth Thy day re - store.
2. The time ac - cept - a - ble is here; Make our re - pent - ant hearts sin - cere;
Con - vert us with Thy kind - ly care, Whom Thy long - suf - f'ring mer - cies spare.

* *A transposed organ accompaniment has been provided for optional use.*

1. Thy rays, O Sun of Jus - tice, send And all our sin - ful
shad - ows rend; With vir - tue light our souls once more,
And un - to earth Thy day re - store.
2. The time ac - cept - a -
ble is here; Make our re - pent - ant hearts sin - cere; Con - vert us
with Thy kind - ly care, Whom Thy long - suf - f'ring mer - cies spare.
3. Grant that for all our deep of - fense We of - fer Thee meet

pen - i - tence; That Thy be - nign_ and sov - 'reign grace May these our
griev - ous sins_ ef - face.
4. Thy Day draws near, that Day_ of
bliss, When teem - ing Na - ture blooms a - fresh; May we re -
joice_ there - in,_ O Lord,_ To Thy sweet fa - vor then_ re - stored.
5. Kind Trin - i - ty, for ev - er - more Let all Thy crea - tures Thee a - dore,
As, new by par - don, Thee we raise_ A new - made can - ti - cle_ of praise.

250 ALTONA — *Jam Christe Sol Justitiae* — English Translation by Archbishop Bagshawe

1. O Je - sus, our sal - va - tion's Sun, Shine Thou our in - most hearts with - in,
Dis - pel the night; let bright - er day Now for the dark - ened world be - gin.
2. Grant in this time ac - cept - a - ble That we with tears may cleanse for Thee
The vic - tim of our heart, and then Burn it with glad - some char - i - ty.

* *A transposed organ accompaniment has been provided for optional use.*

3. The ver - y source that poured forth guilt, Shall with in - ces - sant_ weep-ing flow,
If har - dened heart be made to melt By rod of pen - i - ten - tial woe.
4. The day will come, Thy day, when all Thou wilt in fresh - est_ bloom re - new;
Then our glad souls let Thy_ right hand Lead back, and with true life_ en - due.
5. May all the world be - fore Thee fall And wor - ship, Trin - i - ty Di - vine,
May we new songs of wor - ship sing, And with new grac - es ev - er shine.

1. Ye peo - ple, cease from tears, Your prayers are heard a - bove;
And from his throne in heav'n ap - pears The God of peace and love.
2. O'er Ju - dah's si - lent plains, An - gel - ic voic - es sing,
An - nounc - ing in tri - um - phant strains The birth - day of our king.
3. The faith - ful shep - herds hear, And haste the Babe to greet;
Let us like them with joy draw near, And wor - ship at his feet.
4. But, full of strange sur - prise, What spec - ta - cle is seen?
An In - fant in the man - ger lies, His par - ents poor and mean.

5. Do not we here be - hold The Son of God most high,
Who doth with - in his hand en - fold The earth and sea and sky?
6. Faith pen - e - trates the veil, And through the cloud drawn o'er,
Sees him whom an - gels trem - bling hail, The God whom they a - dore.
7. O Babe, thy birth de - spised And low - ly man - ger tell,
To flee from all be - low that's prized, And with the meek to dwell.
8. From sin - ful shame and pride Guard us, thou Child di - vine;
Then wilt thou in our hearts a - bide, Thy cra - dle and thy shrine.

 LA ROCHELLE — *Jesu Nostra Redemptio* — English Translation by Father Fitzpatrick

1. Re - deem - er of our fall - en state, Thou, Je - sus, joy of eve - ry heart,
Who didst Thy ran-somed world cre - ate, Pure light to faith - ful souls_ Thou art.
2. What clem - en - cy Thy heart o'er - came, That Thou wouldst bear our load of sin?
And, sin - less, die a death of shame, From death and hell our souls_ to win?

* *A transposed organ accompaniment has been provided for optional use.*

3. Thou dost the gates of hell with-stand, Its cap-tives from their fet-ters free,
As vic-tor sit at God's right hand, And reign with Him tri-um-phant-ly.
4. Com-pelled by pit-y, let Thy grace Our loss-es and our ills re-pair;
And may the vi-sion of Thy face With us its bless-èd ra-diance share.
5. Our guide to Heav-en and the road, Be Thou the goal to which we tend;
Our joy in this our sad a-bode, Our life's re-ward which ne'er shall end.

 ROGERS PARK — *Jesu Nostra Redemptio* — English Translation by Father Fitzpatrick

* *A transposed organ accompaniment has been provided for optional use.*

1. Re - deem - er of our fall - en state, Thou, Je - sus, joy of eve - ry___ heart,
Who_ didst Thy ran-somed world cre - ate, Pure light to faith - ful souls Thou art.
2. What__ clem - en - cy Thy heart o'er-came, That Thou wouldst bear our load of__ sin?
And,_ sin - less, die a death of shame, From death and hell our souls to win?

* *A transposed organ accompaniment has been provided for optional use.*

1. Sav - ior of all, for ev - er One With God the Fa - ther; on - ly Son,
Whom he a - lone, when time was not, Past our im - ag - in - ing, be - got,
2. Splen - dor and light of his own fire, E - ter - nal hope of man's de - sire,
Look down and hear the prayers that we In world-wide hom - age make to thee.
3. Au - thor of life, re - mem-ber still In for-mer times thy lov - ing will,
Our mor - tal na - ture to as - sume, Born of a spot - less Vir-gin's womb.
4. Each wan-ing year doth tes - ti - fy That from thy Fa - ther's throne on high

Thou, and no oth - er, on this morn Didst come to save a world for - lorn.
5. Earth, sea, and sky, thy three - fold plan, And all that heav - en's vault doth span,
Ech - o thy praise in mute ac - cord To greet the ad - vent of their Lord.
6. And we in turn, whose life to save That hal - lowed blood re - demp - tion gave,
On this, the birth day of our King New songs of sal - u - ta - tion bring.
7. Je - sus, of Vir - gin Moth - er born, Praise be to thee this ho - ly morn;
Praise to the Fa - ther end - less - ly And his life - giv - ing Spir - it be.

267 FULDA — *Jesu Redemptor Omnium* — English Translation by Monsignor Knox

1. Sav - ior of all, for ev - er One With God the Fa - ther; on - ly Son,
Whom he a - lone, when time was not, Past our im - ag - in - ing, be - got,
2. Splen - dor and light of his own fire, E - ter - nal hope of man's de - sire,
Look down and hear the prayers that we In world - wide hom - age make to thee.
3. Au - thor of life, re - mem - ber still In for - mer times thy lov - ing will,
Our mor - tal na - ture to as - sume, Born of a spot - less Vir - gin's womb.
4. Each wan - ing year doth tes - ti - fy That from thy Fa - ther's throne on high

Thou, and no oth - er, on this morn Didst come to save_ a world for - lorn.
5. Earth, sea, and sky, thy three - fold plan, And all that heav - en's vault_ doth span,
Ech - o thy praise in mute ac - cord_ To greet the ad - vent of_ their Lord.
6. And we in turn, whose life_ to save That hal - lowed blood re - demp - tion gave,
On this, the birth_ day of our King_ New songs of sal - u - ta - tion bring.
7. Je - sus, of Vir - gin Moth - er born, Praise be to thee this ho - ly morn;
Praise to the Fa - ther end - less - ly_ And his life - giv - ing Spir - it be.

268 MEIN SEEL O GOTT — *Jesu Redemptor Omnium* — English Translation by Monsignor Knox

Thou, and no oth - er, on this morn Didst come to save a world for - lorn.
5. Earth, sea, and sky, thy three-fold plan, And all that heav - en's vault doth span,
Ech - o thy praise in mute ac - cord To greet the ad - vent of their Lord.
6. And we in turn, whose life to save That hal-lowed blood re - demp - tion gave,
On this, the birth day of our King New songs of sal - u - ta - tion bring.
7. Je - sus, of Vir - gin Moth-er born, Praise be to thee this ho - ly morn;
Praise to the Fa - ther end - less - ly And his life - giv - ing Spir - it be.

269 CUPERTINO — *Jesu Redemptor Omnium* — English Translation by Monsignor Knox

Thou, and no oth-er, on this morn Didst come to save a world for-lorn.
5. Earth, sea, and sky, thy three-fold plan, And all that heav-en's vault doth span,
Ech-o thy praise in mute ac-cord To greet the ad-vent of their Lord.
6. And we in turn, whose life to save That hal-lowed blood re-demp-tion gave,
On this, the birth day of our King New songs of sal-u-ta-tion bring.
7. Je-sus, of Vir-gin Moth-er born, Praise be to thee this ho-ly morn;
Praise to the Fa-ther end-less-ly And his life-giv-ing Spir-it be.

1. Sav - ior of all, for ev - er__ One With God the Fa - ther; on - ly__ Son,
Whom he a - lone, when time was_ not, Past our im - ag - in - ing, be - got,
2. Splen - dor and light of his own fire, E - ter - nal hope of man's de - sire,
Look down and hear the prayers that_ we In world - wide hom - age make to thee.
3. Au - thor of life, re - mem - ber__ still In for-mer times thy lov - ing__ will,
Our mor-tal na - ture to as - sume, Born of a spot - less Vir - gin's womb.
4. Each wan-ing year doth tes - ti - fy That from thy Fa - ther's throne on__ high

Thou, and no oth - er, on this_ morn Didst come to save a world for - lorn.
5. Earth, sea, and sky, thy three - fold_ plan, And all that heav - en's vault doth_ span,
Ech - o thy praise in mute ac - cord To greet the ad - vent of their Lord.
6. And we in turn, whose life to_ save That hal-lowed blood re - demp - tion_ gave,
On this, the birth day of our_ King New songs of sal - u - ta - tion bring.
7. Je - sus, of Vir - gin Moth - er_ born, Praise be to thee this ho - ly_ morn;
Praise to the Fa - ther end - less - ly And his life - giv - ing Spir - it be.

1. O Christ, Re-deem - er of the world, Be - fore the ear - liest_ dawn of light
From ev - er - last - ing ag - es born, Im - mense in glo - ry as_ in might.
2. Im - mor - tal Hope of all man-kind, In whom the Fa - ther's face we see;
Hear Thou the prayers thy peo - ple pour This day through-out the world to Thee.
3. Re - mem - ber, O Cre - a - tor Lord, That in the Vir - gin's_ sa - cred womb
Thou wast con - ceiv'd, and of_ her flesh Didst our mor - tal - i - ty_ as - sume.
4. This day to that di - vine e - vent Doth year by year its_ wit - ness bear:

Thou mad - est, by__ Thy Fa - ther sent, The world's re - demp - tion Thine own care.
5. O Day! to which the seas and sky, And earth and Heav - en__ wel - come sing;
O Day! which heal'd our mis - er - y, And brought on earth sal - va - tion's King.
6. We too, whose souls Thy Pre - cious Blood, Hath cleans - èd from their_ sin - ful stain,
A trib - ute to__ Thy birth_ day pay, Rais - ing our hymn with joy - ous strain.
7. Je - sus, the Vir - gin's on - ly Son, Be praise and glo - ry__ giv'n to Thee,
With Fa - ther and_ with Spir - it one, In time and in e - ter - ni - ty.

ST GEORGE — *Jesu Redemptor Omnium* — English Translation by Campbell of Skerrington

Now thy Church, each cir - cling year, Cel - e-brates that love so dear;
Love that brought thee here a - lone, For the guilt - y to a - tone.
3. Let not earth a - lone re - joice, Seas and skies u - nite their voice
In a new song, to the morn When the Lord of life was born.
Ran - somed by the ho - ly tide Shed from thy most pre - cious side,
Joy - ful let us hail the morn When the Lord of life was born.

275 PASCHAL LAMB — *Jesu Redemptor Omnium* — English Translation by Campbell of Skerrington

1. Lamb, whose blood for all men streamed, Light, that shone ere morn - ing beamed,
God and God's e - ter - nal Son, Ev - er with the__ Fa - ther one;
Splen - dor of the Fa - ther's light, Star of hope for ev - er bright,
Heark - en to the prayers that flow From thy ser - vants here be - low.
2. Lord, re - mem - ber that for love Thou didst leave thy throne a - bove,
Man's frail na - ture to as - sume In the ho - ly__ Vir - gin's womb.

Now thy Church, each cir - cling year, Cel - e - brates that love so dear;
Love that brought thee here a - lone, For the guilt - y___ to a - tone.
3. Let not earth a - lone re - joice, Seas and skies u - nite their voice
In a new song, to the morn When the Lord of___ life was born.
Ran - somed by the ho - ly tide Shed from thy most pre - cious side,
Joy - ful let us hail the morn When the Lord of___ life was born.

1. Lamb, whose blood for all men streamed, Light, that shone ere morn - ing beamed,
God and God's e - ter - nal Son, Ev - er with the Fa - ther one;
Splen-dor of the Fa-ther's light, Star of hope for ev - er bright,
Heark-en to the prayers that flow From thy ser - vants here be - low.
2. Lord, re - mem - ber that for love Thou didst leave thy throne a - bove,
Man's frail na - ture to as - sume In the ho - ly Vir - gin's womb.

Now thy Church, each cir - cling year, Cel - e - brates that love so dear;
Love that brought thee here a - lone, For the guilt - y to a - tone.
3. Let not earth a - lone re - joice, Seas and skies u - nite their voice
In a new song, to the morn When the Lord of life was born.
Ran-somed by the ho - ly tide Shed from thy most pre - cious side,
Joy - ful let us hail the morn When the Lord of life was born.

1. Sing, O earth, for thy re-demp-tion! Lo, his__ race of sor-row run,
Christ the Sanc - tu - ar - y en-ters, Priest and__ vic-tim both in one,
There to make our__ peace with God, By ob - la - tion of his blood.

* *A transposed organ accompaniment has been provided for optional use.*

2. Priest be-neath the Law, and guilt - y, For the guilt - y cease to plead!
Goats and ox - en, shad - ows emp - ty, Of the which is no more need:
None so frail as these could win Peace with God, could par - don sin.
3. Hail to thee, High Priest e - ter - nal, Ho - ly, in - fi - nite, di - vine:
Mys - tic fig - ures once en - shroud - ed Thee, all sin - less who dost shine!
Thou art he whose blood a - lone Can for guilt - y man a - tone.

4. With the Ho - ly Ghost a-noint - ed, Thou the__ name of Christ dost bear,
God that flesh dost free - ly fur - nish Which thou__ didst thy - self pre - pare,
On the al - tar__ of the__ rood, God and Vir - gin - Moth-er's brood.
5. Those who thee in fu - ry tor - ment Yield thee__ ser - vice un - a - wares;
As thy blood they shed, it cleans - es All the__ world, its crime re - pairs.
Love con - sumes that__ thou dost__ bring, While it prompts the of - fer - ing.

6. High - est praise to God the Fa - ther, Who hath_ made all things of naught;
High - est praise his Son at - trib - ute, Who us__ with his blood hath bought;
E - qual praise, thou_ Breath di - vine Whence we live_ and move, be thine!

1. God need - eth not the cleans - ing wave, But giv - eth it the pow'r to save;
His sin - less flesh, bap - tized there - in, Hath hal - lowed it to cleanse from sin.
2. The sa - cred foun - tain long fore - told For all un - clean - ness here be - hold;
For thus the Lord his death ap - plies, And with his blood the spir - it dyes.

* *A transposed organ accompaniment has been provided for optional use.*

3. For bathed in that bap - tis - mal flood, The soul is dyed with Je - sus' blood;
And clothed in robes which bright - ly glow, Sur - pas - sing far the pur - est snow.
4. Filled with the Ho - ly Ghost, on Earth The Vir - gin to our God gave birth!
Filled with the Ho - ly Ghost are we New - born in wa - ter, Christ, to Thee!
5. O Christ, to thee all praise we pay, For thou hast washed our sins a - way;
The Fa - ther e - qual - ly a - dore, And Ho - ly Spir - it ev - er - more.

 ALTONA — *O Sola Magnarum Urbium* — English Translation by Father Fitzpatrick

1. O Beth - le - hem, thou dost sur - pass All oth - er cit - ies__ in re - nown;
Thy priv - i - lege_ a - lone it was To call from Heav'n our Sav - ior down.
2. A star, out - shin - ing in its light And beau - ty the re - volv - ing sun,
Pro - claims to earth the God of might, Who now His mor - tal course will run.
3. The Ma - gi, who His face be - hold, for Him their East - ern__ gifts have spread;
In in - cense, myrrh and roy - al gold, They, pros - trate, all their vows have said.

4. His God - head and His Sov - 'reign - ty, The in - cense and the
gold re - veal, The dust of myrrh fore - tells the tomb,
Which shall His mor - tal form con - ceal.
5. Be glo - ry, Je - sus, un - to Thee Re - vealed for Gen - tile
eyes to greet, Be like - wise praised e - ter - nal - ly
The Fa - ther and the Par - a - clete.

1. O Beth - le - hem, thou dost sur - pass All oth - er cit - ies in re - nown;
Thy priv - i - lege a - lone it was To call from Heav'n our Sav - ior down.
2. A star, out - shin - ing in its light And beau - ty the re - volv - ing sun,
Pro - claims to earth the God of might, Who now His mor - tal course will run.

* *A transposed organ accompaniment has been provided for optional use.*

293 ST MARK — *O Sola Magnarum Urbium* — English Translation by Father Fitzpatrick

1. O Beth - le - hem, thou dost_ sur - pass All oth - er cit - ies in_ re - nown;
Thy priv - i - lege a - lone_ it was To call_ from Heav'n our Sav - ior down.
2. A star, out - shin - ing in_ its light And beau - ty the re - volv - ing sun,
Pro - claims to earth the God_ of might, Who now_ His mor - tal course_ will run.

* *A transposed organ accompaniment has been provided for optional use.*

3. The Ma - gi, who His face_ be - hold, for Him_ their East - ern
gifts_ have spread; In in - cense, myrrh and roy - al gold, They,
pros - trate, all_ their vows have said.
4. His God - head and His
Sov - 'reign - ty, The in - cense and the gold_ re - veal, The dust_ of
myrrh fore - tells_ the tomb, Which shall_ His mor - tal form_ con - ceal.
5. Be glo - ry, Je - sus, un - to Thee Re - vealed for Gen - tile eyes_ to greet,
Be like - wise praised e - ter - nal - ly The Fa - ther and_ the Par - a - clete.

1. O Beth - le - hem, thou dost sur - pass All oth - er cit - ies in re - nown;
Thy priv - i - lege a - lone it was To call from Heav'n our Sav - ior down.
2. A star, out - shin - ing in its light And beau - ty the re - volv - ing sun,
Pro - claims to earth the God of might, Who now His mor - tal course will run.

* *A transposed organ accompaniment has been provided for optional use.*

296 STUTTGART — *O Sola Magnarum Urbium* — English Translation by Father Caswall

1. Beth - le - hem! of nobl - est cit - ies None can once with thee com - pare;
Thou a - lone the Lord from Heav - en Didst for us In - car - nate bear.
2. Fair - er than the sun at morn - ing Was the star that told his birth;
To the lands their God an - nounc - ing, Hid be - neath a form of earth.

* *A transposed organ accompaniment has been provided for optional use.*

3. By its lam - bent beau - ty guid - ed, See, the East - ern kings ap - pear;
See them bend, their gifts to of - fer, Gifts of in - cense, gold, and myrrh.
4. Of - fer - ings of hid - den mean - ing: In - cense doth the God dis - close;
Gold a roy - al child pro - claim - eth; Myrrh a fu - ture tomb fore - shows.
5. Ho - ly Je - sus, in thy bright - ness To the Gen - tile world dis - play'd,
With the Fa - ther, and the Spir - it, End - less praise to Thee be paid.

297 BRONZEVILLE — *O Sola Magnarum Urbium* — English Translation by Father Caswall

1. Beth - le - hem! of nobl - est cit - ies None can once with thee com - pare;
Thou a - lone the Lord from Heav - en Didst for us In - car - nate bear.
2. Fair - er than the sun at morn - ing Was the star that told his birth;
To the lands their God an - nounc - ing, Hid be - neath a form of earth.
3. By its lam - bent beau - ty guid - ed, See, the East - ern kings ap - pear;
See them bend, their gifts to of - fer, Gifts of in - cense, gold, and myrrh.

4. Of - fer - ings of hid - den mean - ing: In - cense doth the God dis - close;
Gold a roy - al child pro - claim - eth; Myrrh a fu - ture tomb fore - shows.

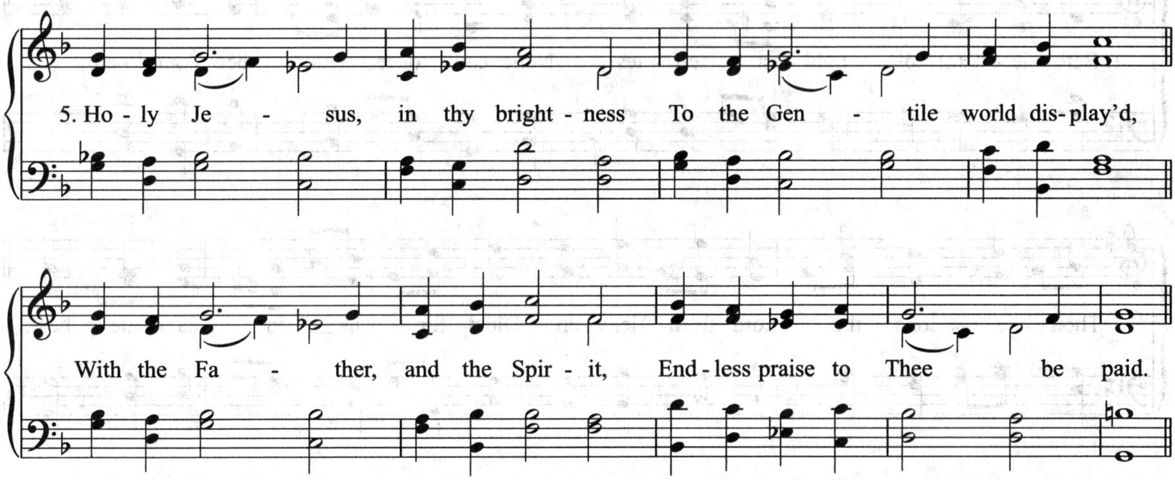
5. Ho - ly Je - sus, in thy bright - ness To the Gen - tile world dis - play'd,
With the Fa - ther, and the Spir - it, End - less praise to Thee be paid.

 CROSS OF JESUS — *O Sola Magnarum Urbium* — English Translation by Father Caswall

3. By its lam - bent beau - ty guid - ed, See, the East - ern kings ap - pear;
See them bend, their gifts to of - fer, Gifts of in - cense, gold, and myrrh.
4. Of - fer - ings of hid - den mean - ing: In - cense doth the God dis - close;
Gold a roy - al child pro - claim - eth; Myrrh a fu - ture tomb fore - shows.
5. Ho - ly Je - sus, in thy bright - ness To the Gen - tile world dis - play'd,
With the Fa - ther, and the Spir - it, End - less praise to Thee be paid.

299 WALTHAM — *O Sola Magnarum Urbium* — English Translation by Father Caswall

* *A transposed organ accompaniment has been provided for optional use.*

1. Beth - le - hem! of nobl - est cit - ies None can once with thee com - pare;
Thou a - lone the Lord from Heav - en Didst for us In - car - nate bear.
2. Fair - er than the sun at morn - ing Was the star that told his birth;
To the lands their God an - nounc - ing, Hid be - neath a form of earth.

3. By its lam - bent beau - ty guid - ed, See, the East - ern kings ap - pear;
See them bend, their gifts to of - fer, Gifts of in - cense, gold, and myrrh.
4. Of - fer - ings of hid - den mean - ing: In - cense doth the God dis - close;
Gold a roy - al child pro - claim - eth; Myrrh a fu - ture tomb fore - shows.
5. Ho - ly Je - sus, in thy bright - ness To the Gen - tile world dis - play'd,
With the Fa - ther, and the Spir - it, End - less praise to Thee be paid.

 ST BERNARD — *O Sola Magnarum Urbium* — English Translation by Donahoe

1. A sa - cred town is___ Beth - le - hem, Its walls are won - drous fair;
For Je - sus, our sal - va - tion, came And made his birth - place there.
2. The star that leads the___ sag - es three Is bright as ear - ly day,
And in its light their God they see En - robed in mor - tal clay.

* *A transposed organ accompaniment has been provided for optional use.*

3. They bow to earth as___ they be - hold, And o - rient of - f'rings bring,
The myrrh, the frank - in - cense, the gold, As God, as man, as king.
4. Un - to the King the___ gold - en hoard, As trib - ute they pre - fer;
The in - cense to the death - less Lord, To mor - tal man the myrrh.
5. To thee, O Christ, be___ glo - ry meet; Thy name all lands a - dore;
Un - to the Sire and Par - a - clete Like glo - ry ev - er - more.

BRISTOL — *O Sola Magnarum Urbium* — English Translation by Donahoe

1. A sa - cred town is Beth - le - hem, Its walls are won - drous fair;
For Je - sus, our sal - va - tion, came And made his birth - place there.
2. The star that leads the sag - es three Is bright as ear - ly day,
And in its light their God they see En - robed in mor - tal clay.
3. They bow to earth as they be - hold, And o - rient of - f'rings bring,
The myrrh, the frank - in - cense, the gold, As God, as man, as king.

4. Un - to the King the gold - en hoard, As trib - ute they pre - fer;
The in - cense to the death - less Lord, To mor - tal man the myrrh.
5. To thee, O Christ, be glo - ry meet; Thy name all lands a - dore;
Un - to the Sire and Par - a - clete Like glo - ry ev - er - more.

ERSCHIENEN IST — *O Sola Magnarum Urbium* — English Translation by H. Trend

1. The nobl - est cit - ies on the earth Must yield, O Beth - le - hem, to
thee; 'Twas thine to give mys - te - rious Birth To Christ, th'In - car - nate
De - i - ty. Al - le - lu - ia.
2. More glo - rious than the Sun at morn,
Thy Her - ald star its rays un - furled, Pro - claim - ing that the Babe was
born, Whose Pow'r should save a dy - ing world. Al - le - lu - ia.
3. Drawn by its guid - ing light from far, The Sag - es
at His Cra - dle meet, With Gold, and Frank - in - cense, and Myrrh,

To wor - ship at His sa - cred Feet. Al - le - lu - ia.
4. Nor vain their mys - tic Of - fer - ing: The In - cense
owned the Child as God; The Gold did hom - age to the King;
The Myrrh His Death and Bur - ial showed. Al - le - lu - ia.
5. Who to the Gen - tiles wast re - vealed, All glo - ry,
Je - sus, be to Thee, With Fa - ther and with Ho - ly Ghost,
Now, and for all E - ter - ni - ty. Al - le - lu - ia.

312 RUNNELLS — *Pange Lingua* (6th century) — English Translation by Father Caswall

1. Sing, my tongue, the Sav-ior's glo - ry; Tell his tri-umph far and wide;
Tell a-loud the fa-mous sto - ry Of his Bod-y Cru - ci-fied:
How, up-on the Cross a Vic - tim, Van-quish-ing in death, He died.
2. Eat-ing of the Tree for-bid - den, Man had sunk in Sa - tan's snare,
When his pit - y - ing Cre-a - tor Did this sec-ond Tree pre-pare;
Des-tin'd, man-y ag-es lat - er, That first e-vil to re - pair.

3. Such the or - der God ap - point - ed When for sin He would a - tone;
To the ser - pent thus op - pos - ing Ploys yet deep - er than his own,
Thence the rem - e - dy pro - cur - ing, Whence the fa - tal wound had come.
4. So, when now at length the full - ness Of the sa - cred time drew nigh,
Then the Son, the world's Cre - a - tor, Left his Fa - ther's throne on high;
From a Vir - gin's womb ap - pear - ing, Cloth'd in our mor - tal - i - ty.

5. All with-in a low-ly man - ger, Lo, a ten-der babe he lies;
See his gen - tle Vir-gin moth - er Lull to sleep his in - fant cries;
While the limbs of God In - car - nate Round with swath-ing bands she ties.
6. Thus did Christ to per-fect man - hood In our mor-tal flesh at-tain:
Then of his free choice He go - eth To a death of bit - ter pain;
As a Lamb, up-on the al - tar Of the Cross, for us is slain.

7. Lo, with gall his thirst He quench - es: See the thorns up - on his brow;
Nails his ten - der flesh are rend - ing, See, his side is o - pen'd now;
Whence, to cleanse the whole cre - a - tion, Streams of blood and wa - ter flow!
8. Faith - ful Cross, a - bove all oth - er One and on - ly no - ble Tree:
None in fo - liage, none in blos - som, None in fruit com - pares with thee:
Sweet - est wood, and sweet - est i - ron, Sweet - est weight sus - tain - ing free.

9. Loft - y tree, bend down thy branch - es, To em-brace thy sa - cred load;
Oh, re - lax the na-tive ten - sion Of that all too rig - id wood;
Gen - tly, gen - tly bear the mem - bers Of thy dy - ing King and God.
10. Tree, which sole - ly wast found wor - thy Earth's great Vic-tim to sus-tain;
Har-bor from the rag-ing tem - pest, Ark, that saved the world a - gain,
Tree, with sa - cred Blood a - noint - ed Of the Lamb for sin - ners slain.

1. Sing, my tongue, that glo - rious com - bat, When, vic - to - rious in the fray,
Christ our Lord a tro - phy made Him Of the Cross where - on He lay;
Tell how then the world's Re - deem - er, Im - mo - lat - ed, won the day.
2. Our Cre - a - tor, grieved that Ad - am Sin up - on us all had brought,
When he ate the fruit for - bid - den Which for man with death was fraught,
Marked a tree, for the re - triev - al Of the harm a tree had wrought.

3. For, the work of our sal - va - tion Or - dered well, de - mand - ed this:
To de - feat the craft - y trai - tor, Ar - ti - fice by ar - ti - fice,
Thence the rem - e - dy pro - cur - ing Where the foe had worked a - miss.
4. There - fore, in its des - tined full - ness When the bless - èd time be - fell,
Came the world's own Mak - er, sent us From His Fa - ther's cit - a - del:
Born in flesh He came, pro - ceed - ing From an ev - er - vir - gin cell.

5. Ly - ing in a nar - row man - ger, Hark! His in - fant cries en - treat;
Limb by limb the Vir - gin - Moth - er Clothes her new - born Ba - by sweet,
With her swad - dling bands en - clos - ing Of our God the hands and feet.
6. Thir - ty years of life e - laps - ing, Time had made that frame ma - ture;
Now, His long - ap - point - ed Pas - sion Christ wills free - ly to en - dure:
On the Cross the Lamb is lift - ed, Lo! the Vic - tim they se - cure.
7. Of the gall He drinks, out - wea - ried; Thorns, and nails, and spear have vied,

Till the blood and wa - ter is - sue From His gen - tle riv - en side:
Earth and sea and stars, all crea - tures Cleans - ing find with - in the tide.
8. Faith - ful Cross! of all the for - est Thou art far the nobl - est tree;
None of all its growth pro - duc - es Leaf or flow'r, or fruit, like thee:
Sweet thy wood is, sweet thy nails are, And thy Bur - den, sweet is He.
9. Bend thy branch - es, tree so loft - y; Let thy stub - born heart re - lent:
Hence-forth soft - er be and pli - ant, Con - quer - ing thy na - ture's bent;

That the King may stretch His mem - bers On thy ten - der trunk's ex - tent.
10. Thou, to bear the world's one Vic - tim, Wert the on - ly wor - thy bed;
When we, ship-wrecked, had no ha - ven, Like the Ark wert thou in - stead,
With the Sa - cred Blood a - noint - ed By the Lamb's pure Bod - y shed.
11. Sem - pi - ter - nal praise be giv - en Un - to God, the One in Three;
To the Fa - ther, Son, and Spir - it, E - qual glo - ry ren - dered be;
Yea, the Tri - une Name be hal - lowed Eve - ry - where, e - ter - nal - ly.

318 ST LEONARD — *Pange Lingua* (6th century) — English Translation by Father Fitzpatrick

1. Sing, my__ tongue, that glo - rious_ com - bat, When, vic - to - rious in the fray,
Christ our__ Lord a tro - phy__ made Him Of the Cross where - on He lay;
Tell how_ then the world's Re - deem - er, Im - mo - lat - ed, won the day.
2. Our Cre - a - tor, grieved that__ Ad - am Sin up - on us all had brought,
When he__ ate the fruit for - bid - den Which for man with death was fraught,
Marked a__ tree, for the re - triev - al Of the__ harm_ a tree had wrought.

3. For, the work of our sal - va - tion Or - dered well, de - mand - ed this:
To de - feat the craft - y trai - tor, Ar - ti - fice by ar - ti - fice,
Thence the rem - e - dy pro - cur - ing Where the foe had worked a - miss.
4. There - fore, in its des - tined full - ness When the bless - èd time be - fell,
Came the world's own Mak - er, sent us From His Fa - ther's cit - a - del:
Born in flesh He came, pro - ceed - ing From an ev - er - vir - gin cell.

5. Ly - ing__ in a nar - row__ man - ger, Hark! His in - fant cries en - treat;
Limb by__ limb the Vir - gin - Moth - er Clothes her new - born Ba - by sweet,
With her__ swad-dling bands en - clos - ing Of our__ God__ the hands and feet.
6. Thir - ty__ years of life e - laps - ing, Time had made that frame ma - ture;
Now, His__ long - ap - point - ed__ Pas - sion Christ wills free - ly to en - dure:
On the__ Cross the Lamb is lift - ed, Lo! the__ Vic - tim they se - cure.
7. Of the__ gall He drinks, out - wea - ried; Thorns, and nails, and spear have vied,

Till the blood and wa - ter is - sue From His gen - tle riv - en side:
Earth and sea and stars, all crea - tures Cleans - ing find with - in the tide.
8. Faith - ful Cross! of all the for - est Thou art far the nobl - est tree;
None of all its growth pro - duc - es Leaf or flow'r, or fruit, like thee:
Sweet thy wood is, sweet thy nails are, And thy Bur - den, sweet is He.
9. Bend thy branch - es, tree so loft - y; Let thy stub - born heart re - lent:
Hence - forth soft - er be and pli - ant, Con - quer - ing thy na - ture's bent;

That the__ King may stretch His mem - bers On thy__ ten - der trunk's ex - tent.
10. Thou, to__ bear the world's one__ Vic - tim, Wert the on - ly wor - thy bed;
When we,__ ship - wrecked, had no__ ha - ven, Like the Ark wert thou in - stead,
With the__ Sa - cred Blood a - noint - ed By the__ Lamb's pure Bod - y shed.
11. Sem - pi - ter - nal praise be__ giv - en Un - to God, the One in Three;
To the__ Fa - ther, Son, and__ Spir - it, E - qual glo - ry ren - dered be;
Yea, the__ Tri - une Name be hal - lowed Ev - ry - where, e - ter - nal - ly.

1. Sing, my tongue, that glo - rious com - bat, When, vic - to - rious in the fray,
Christ our Lord a tro - phy made Him Of the Cross where - on He lay;
Tell how then the world's Re - deem - er, Im - mo - lat - ed, won the day.
2. Our Cre - a - tor, grieved that Ad - am Sin up - on us all had brought,
When he ate the fruit for - bid - den Which for man with death was fraught,
Marked a tree, for the re - triev - al Of the harm a tree had wrought.

3. For, the work of our sal - va - tion Or - dered well, de - mand - ed this:
To de - feat the craft - y trai - tor, Ar - ti - fice by ar - ti - fice,
Thence the rem - e - dy pro - cur - ing Where the foe had worked a - miss.
4. There - fore, in its des - tined full - ness When the bless - èd time be - fell,
Came the world's own Mak - er, sent us From His Fa - ther's cit - a - del:
Born in flesh He came, pro - ceed - ing From an ev - er - vir - gin cell.

5. Ly - ing in a nar - row man - ger, Hark! His in - fant cries en - treat;
Limb by limb the Vir - gin - Moth - er Clothes her new - born Ba - by sweet,
With her swad - dling bands en - clos - ing Of our God the hands and feet.
6. Thir - ty years of life e - laps - ing, Time had made that frame ma - ture;
Now, His long - ap - point - ed Pas - sion Christ wills free - ly to en - dure:
On the Cross the Lamb is lift - ed, Lo! the Vic - tim they se - cure.
7. Of the gall He drinks, out - wea - ried; Thorns, and nails, and spear have vied,

Till the blood and wa - ter is - sue From His gen - tle riv - en side:
Earth and sea and stars, all crea - tures Cleans - ing find with - in the tide.
8. Faith - ful Cross! of all the for - est Thou art far the nobl - est tree;
None of all its growth pro - duc - es Leaf or flow'r, or fruit, like thee:
Sweet thy wood is, sweet thy nails are, And thy Bur - den, sweet is He.
9. Bend thy branch - es, tree so loft - y; Let thy stub - born heart re - lent:
Hence - forth soft - er be and pli - ant, Con - quer - ing thy na - ture's bent;

That the King may stretch His mem - bers On thy ten - der trunk's ex - tent.
10. Thou, to bear the world's one Vic - tim, Wert the on - ly wor - thy bed;
When we, ship - wrecked, had no ha - ven, Like the Ark wert thou in - stead,
With the Sa - cred Blood a - noint - ed By the Lamb's pure Bod - y shed.
11. Sem - pi - ter - nal praise be giv - en Un - to God, the One in Three;
To the Fa - ther, Son, and Spir - it, E - qual glo - ry ren - dered be;
Yea, the Tri - une Name be hal - lowed Eve - ry - where, e - ter - nal - ly.

322 REGENT SQUARE — *Pange Lingua* (6th century) — English Translation by Father Schrader

1. Let our tongues sing out the sto - ry: Fear - some bat - tle, des - p'rate war!
Laud the Cross, the pre - cious tro - phy Of the Sav - ior— of the world,
Tell of sac - ri - fice and glo - ry, Praise the tri - umph of the Lord.

2. God, our Mak - er, griev - ing with us At our fa - ther's treach - er - y:
Ad - am, made in his own im - age, Ate of that for - bid - den tree;
Duped by Sa - tan, man would per - ish, Dead - ly fruit its fruit would see.

3. Yet our Fa - ther deigned to save us, Mark - ing out that fate - ful wood,
In a plan of res - cue won - drous Foiled the cun - ning of our foe,
From our bane a cure he gave us, From great e - vil, great - est good!
4. When the ag - es reached their full - ness, From his throne a - bove the sky
He came down a - mid our weak - ness, Born to suf - fer and to die;
Mar - y first with joy em - braced him, In the flesh the Son most high.

5. Liv - ing with us, God al-might - y, Comes of age and man-hood's strength.
Hands and arms, once swad - dled tight - ly, Now em-brace the Cross-'s weight.
He, the Lamb, a cost - ly Vic - tim, Climbs the mount of sac - ri - fice.
6. See the gall, the nails, the spit - ting, Ter - ri - ble and bless - èd rood!
Mar - y, too, in sor - row watch-ing As her Son is cru - ci - fied;
Gen - tle bod - y, pierced and bleed - ing, Springs of life where Life has died.

7. All the u - ni - verse is mourn- ing: Dark - ness falls, the plan - ets shake,
Till that ra - diant East - er morn - ing Sees the liv - ing Lord a - wake:
Glo - ry be to Christ the Vic - tor, Glo - ry to our ris - en King!

1. Let our tongues sing out the sto - ry: Fear - some bat - tle, des - p'rate war!
Laud the Cross, the pre - cious tro - phy Of the Sav - ior of the world,
Tell of sac - ri - fice and glo - ry, Praise the tri - umph of the Lord.
2. God, our Mak - er, griev - ing with us At our fa - ther's treach - er - y:
Ad - am, made in his own im - age, Ate of that__ for - bid - den tree;
Duped by Sa - tan, man would per - ish, Dead - ly fruit its fruit would see.
3. Yet our Fa - ther deigned to save us, Mark - ing out__ that fate - ful wood,

In a plan of res - cue won-drous Foiled the cun - ning of our foe,
From our bane a cure he gave us, From great e - vil, great - est good!
4. When the ag - es reached their full-ness, From his throne a - bove the sky
He came down a - mid our weak-ness, Born to suf - fer and to die;
Mar - y first with joy em-braced him, In the flesh the Son most high.
5. Liv - ing with us, God al-might - y, Comes of age and man-hood's strength.
Hands and arms, once swad - dled tight - ly, Now em - brace the Cross - 's weight.

He, the Lamb, a cost - ly Vic - tim, Climbs the mount of sac - ri - fice.
6. See the gall, the nails, the spit - ting, Ter - ri - ble__ and bless - èd rood!
Mar - y, too, in sor - row watch - ing As her Son__ is cru - ci - fied;
Gen - tle bod - y, pierced and bleed - ing, Springs of life where Life has died.
7. All the u - ni - verse is mourn - ing: Dark - ness falls,_ the plan - ets shake,
Till that ra - diant East - er morn - ing Sees the liv - ing Lord a - wake:
Glo - ry be to Christ the Vic - tor, Glo - ry to our ris - en King!

1. Let our tongues sing out the sto - ry: Fear-some bat - tle, des-p'rate war!
Laud the Cross, the pre - cious tro - phy Of the Sav - ior of the world,
Tell of sac - ri - fice and glo - ry, Praise the tri - umph of the Lord.
2. God, our Mak - er, griev - ing with us At our fa - ther's treach - er - y:
Ad - am, made in his own im - age, Ate of that for - bid - den tree;
Duped by Sa - tan, man would per - ish, Dead - ly fruit its fruit would see.
3. Yet our Fa - ther deigned to save us, Mark-ing out that fate - ful wood,

In a plan of res - cue won - drous Foiled the cun - ning of our foe,
From our bane a cure he gave us, From great e - vil, great - est good!
4. When the ag - es reached their full - ness, From his throne a - bove the sky
He came down a - mid our weak - ness, Born to suf - fer and to die;
Mar - y first with joy em - braced him, In the flesh the Son most high.
5. Liv - ing with us, God al - might - y, Comes of age and man - hood's strength.
Hands and arms, once swad - dled tight - ly, Now em - brace the Cross - 's weight.

He, the Lamb, a cost - ly Vic - tim, Climbs the mount of sac - ri - fice.
6. See the gall, the nails, the spit - ting, Ter - ri - ble and bless-èd rood!
Mar - y, too, in sor - row watch-ing As her Son is cru - ci - fied;
Gen - tle bod - y, pierced and bleed - ing, Springs of life where Life has died.
7. All the u - ni - verse is mourn - ing: Dark-ness falls, the plan - ets shake,
Till that ra - diant East - er morn - ing Sees the liv - ing Lord a - wake:
Glo - ry be to Christ the Vic - tor, Glo - ry to our ris - en King!

1. Sing, my tongue, of war - fare end - ed, Of the Vic - tor's lau - reled crown;
Let the Cross, his tro - phy splen - did, Be the theme of high re - nown;
How a bro - ken world was mend - ed, Life re - stored by life laid down.
2. God, for man's re - bel - lion griev - ing, When the world his hands had made
Per - ished by a fruit's de - ceiv - ing, In that hour his coun - sel laid,
By a tree the race re - priev - ing Whom a tree long since be - trayed.

3. Man's e - ter - nal health con - triv - ing Wrought he with un - fail - ing art,
Wis - dom 'gainst the wis - dom striv - ing Of the tempt - er's guile - ful heart;
From that source the balm de - riv - ing Where the foe had steeped his dart.
4. There - fore, when that hal - lowed hour Time to its ful - fill - ment brought,
From his Fa - ther's heav'n - ly tow - er Came he, who the worlds had wrought,
From his Moth - er's se - cret bow - er, Clothed in flesh, and wel - come sought.

5. See a help - less in - fant cry - ing, Whom a man - ger doth en - fold;
See his Vir - gin Moth - er ty - ing Rags a - bout him in the cold;
Bound both hand and feet, and ly - ing 'Mid the beasts, your God be - hold!
6. Now, his years of life per - fect - ed, Our a - tone-ment's price to be,
By the doom long since e - lect - ed, Bound and nailed to set us free,
Christ, our Vic - tim, hangs re - ject - ed On the Cross of Cal - va - ry.
7. Gall he drinks; his strength sub - du - ing, Reed and thorn and nail and spear

Plot his gen - tle frame's un - do - ing; Blood and wa - ter thence ap - pear,
With their cleans - ing tide re - new - ing Earth and sea and star - ry sphere.
8. Hail, true Cross, of beau - ty rar - est, King of all the for - est trees;
Leaf and flow'r and fruit thou bear - est, Medi - cine for a world's dis - ease;
Fair - est wood, and i - ron fair - est, Yet more fair, who hung on these.
9. Bend thy branch - es down to meet him, Bend that stub - born heart of thine;
Let thy na - tive force, to greet him, All its rug - ged - ness re - sign;

Gen - tly let thy wood en - treat him, Roy - al suff - 'rer, and di - vine.
10. Vic - tim of our race, he deign - èd On thy arms to lay his head;
Thou the ark, whose ref - uge gain - èd, Sin - ful man no more may dread;
Ark, whose planks are deep - ly stain - èd With the blood the Lamb hath shed.
11. Hon - or, glo - ry, might and mer - it To the e - ter - nal Trin - i - ty,
Fa - ther, Son, and Ho - ly Spir - it, Throned in heav - en e - qual - ly;
All that doth the world in - her - it, Praise one God in Per - sons three.

1. Sing, my tongue, of war - fare_ end - ed, Of the Vic-tor's lau - reled crown;
Let the Cross, his tro - phy_ splen - did, Be the theme of high re - nown;
How a bro-ken world was mend - ed, Life re-stored by life laid_ down.
2. God, for man's re - bel - lion_ griev - ing, When the world his hands had_ made
Per-ished by a fruit's de - ceiv - ing, In that hour his coun - sel_ laid,
By a tree the race re - priev - ing Whom a tree long since be - trayed.

3. Man's e - ter-nal health con - triv - ing Wrought he with un - fail - ing art,
Wis-dom 'gainst the wis - dom striv - ing Of the tempt-er's guile - ful heart;
From that source the balm de - riv - ing Where the foe had steeped his dart.
4. There-fore, when that hal - lowed hour Time to its ful - fill - ment brought,
From his Fa-ther's heav'n - ly tow - er Came he, who the worlds had wrought,
From his Moth-er's se - cret bow - er, Clothed in flesh, and wel - come sought.

5. See a help-less in - fant_ cry - ing, Whom a man-ger doth en - fold;
See his Vir-gin Moth - er___ ty - ing Rags a-bout him in the__ cold;
Bound both hand and feet, and ly - ing 'Mid the beasts, your God be - hold!
6. Now, his years of life per - fect - ed, Our a-tone-ment's price to__ be,
By the doom long since e - lect - ed, Bound and nailed to set us__ free,
Christ, our Vic-tim, hangs re - ject - ed On the Cross of Cal - va - ry.
7. Gall he drinks; his strength sub - du - ing, Reed and thorn and nail and_ spear

Plot his gen - tle frame's un - do - ing; Blood and wa - ter thence ap - pear,
With their cleans - ing tide re - new - ing Earth and sea and star - ry__ sphere.
8. Hail, true Cross, of beau - ty__ rar - est, King of all the for - est__ trees;
Leaf and flow'r and fruit thou_ bear - est, Med*i* - cine for a world's dis - ease;
Fair - est wood, and i - ron fair - est, Yet more fair, who hung on__ these.
9. Bend thy branch - es down to__ meet him, Bend that stub - born heart of__ thine;
Let thy na - tive force, to__ greet him, All its rug - ged - ness re - sign;

Gen-tly let thy wood en - treat him, Roy-al suff-'rer, and di - vine.
10. Vic - tim of our race, he deign - èd On thy arms to lay his head;
Thou the ark, whose ref - uge gain - èd, Sin-ful man no more may dread;
Ark, whose planks are deep - ly stain - èd With the blood the Lamb hath shed.
11. Hon - or, glo-ry, might and mer - it To the e-ter - nal Trin - i - ty,
Fa-ther, Son, and Ho - ly Spir - it, Throned in heav-en e - qual - ly;
All that doth the world in - her - it, Praise one God in Per - sons three.

DULCE CARMEN — *Pange Lingua* (6th century) — English Translation by Macgill

1. Sing the Cross! the con - flict tell - ing, Crown'd with glo - ry more than woe;
Sing the bat - tle and the tri - umph, Tell its fame_ to___ all be - low,
How by death the world's Re - deem - er O - ver - threw and bound His foe.
2. Touch'd with pit - y for the ru - in Of our first - made fa - ther's fall,
When the fa - tal fruit he tast - ed, By one bite_ de - stroy - ing all;
God mark'd out the tree of Cal - v'ry, E - den's_ tree to match with - al.

3. Law could on - ly yield our res - cue As the fruit of pains and toils;
Art by art, the great Re - stor - er Foiled, and took_ the__ Trai - tor's spoils;
Thus His heal - ing balm He gath - ered Where_ the__ foe had spread his wiles.
4. At the time a - fore ap - point - ed, Com - ing in His Fa - ther's name,
In the womb of Vir - gin Moth - er Clothed in flesh,_ with_ fee - ble frame;
Born a man, the world's Cre - a - tor From_ the__ throne of glo - ry came.

5. Hark, and see, the wail - ing In - fant In a man - ger mean is found:
Child all low - ly, God all ho - ly, Whom no robes of light sur - round,
But who by a bless - ed Vir - gin Close in swad-dling has been bound.
6. Thir - ty win - ters has He num - bered Here on earth in quest of me;
Yea, my soul! thy great Re - deem - er Ag - o - niz - ing on the tree,
As the Lamb of God, up - lift - ed, Bleeds, and bows that head for thee.
7. Faint - ing, lo! the gall He tast - eth; See the thorns, the nails, the spear,

From His ebb - ing life are draw - ing Crim - son blood and__ wa - ter clear!
Fit for cleans - ing souls, and cleans - ing Earth, and__ sea, and star - ry sphere.
8. Faith - ful Cross of Christ, we hail thee; Of all trees on earth most fair;
None in all the for - est yield - eth Leaf, or flow'r, or__ fruit so rare.
Sweet - est wood, and sweet - est i - ron, Sweet - est__ bur - den fit to bear.
9. Tree of aw - ful beau - ty, bend thee. Bend; thy stub - born branch - es bring
Soft - ly round the form thou bear - est; O'er His head_ thy__ shad - ow fling;

Gen - tly in thine arms up - hold Him, For of glo - ry He is King.
10. Wor - thy Thou to bear the ran - som Of a ship - wreck'd world art found,
And to be our Ark of safe - ty, For ce - les - tial har - bor bound;
Sa - cred, hence, that blood has made thee, As it flowed and wrapt thee round.
11. Glo - ry, glo - ry, ev - er - last - ing, To the bless - èd Trin - i - ty,
Praise to Thee, E - ter - nal Fa - ther, Praise, E - ter - nal Son, to Thee,
Praise to Thee, E - ter - nal Spir - it, Three in One, and One in Three!

1. Come then, my soul, and glad - ly sing The happy com - bat of our King,
Which on the Cross He fought: Where He, the all - vic - to - rious Lamb,
Sin, death and hell it - self o'er - came, And our full safe - ty wrought.
2. He saw with pit - y our sad fate, When our first par - ents rash - ly ate
Of that un - hap - py tree: He saw and marked the dead - ly wound,
And soon this sov - 'reign bal - sam found To save our souls by thee.

3. This way our cure_ re - quired, as fit That_ heav'n's high wis - dom should out - wit
The dire black art of hell: And from the source of all our bane
A_ pow'r - ful an - ti - dote be ta'en The poi - son to ex - pel.
4. When the blest time_ was ful - ly come, The_ Fa - ther from His glo - rious home
Sent His e - ter - nal Son: He that cre - at - ed heav'n and earth,
Of_ a poor Vir - gin took His birth, And our_ frail flesh put on.

5. The ten - der In - fant, as He lies In__ the cold man - ger, shrinks and cries
As lit - tle chil - dren use: While His chaste Moth - er binds His hands,
His__ feet, His legs in swath - ing bands; Nor does_ He worse re - fuse.
6. He does not on - ly not re - fuse, But_ out of pure love free - ly choose
Death on this bit - ter Cross; Where He, the sin - less Lamb, was slain,
E - ter - nal life for us to gain, And so__ re - pair our loss.
7. Be - hold the gall_ and vin - e - gar, The_ mock-ing reed and cru - el spear,

Their hate, His love dis - play: Be - hold the Bod - y cold and wan, Whence
streams of blood and wa - ter ran To wash our stains a - way.
8. Hail, ho - ly Cross, to thee we bow, To whose blest Fruit our lives we owe;
Our earth bears no such tree: Dear are the nails, and dear the wood
On which our dear Lord shed his blood 'Twas heav'n that plant - ed thee.
9. Bend, gen - tle tree, O quick - ly bend Thy sof - tened branch - es, and sus - pend
Thy na - tive stub - born heart: O give at least this small re - lief

To__ God of heav'n, but Man of grief, At least_ a - bate His smart.
10. 'Twas thou a - lone_ wert wor - thy thought To__ bear Him, Who our ran - som
brought And on thee paid it down: 'Twas He a - lone_ and His dear Blood
That_ saved us from the com - mon flood, Which else_ the world would drown.
11. All glo - ry to__ the sa - cred Three, One_ un - di - vid - ed De - i - ty,
All hon - or, bliss and praise! O may we still_ a - dore Thy name,
Thy_ pow'r and good - ness still pro - claim Be - yond the end of days.

1. In Pas - chal feast, the end of an - cient rite An en - trance was to
nev - er - end - ing grace: Types yield to truth, dim glimps - es to the light,
Per - form - ing deed pres - ag - ing signs did chase; Christ's fi - nal meal was
foun - tain of our good, For mor - tal fare He gave im - mor - tal food.
2. They saw, they heard, they felt Him sit - ting near, Un - seen, un - felt, un -
heard, they Him re - ceiv'd: No dif - f'rent thing, though dif - f'rent it ap - pear,
Though sens - es fail, yet faith is not de - ceiv'd; And if the won - der
of the work be new, Be - lieve the work - er, for his word is true.

3. Though blind men see no light, the sun doth shine,
Sweet is the sweet, though fe-ver'd taste de-ny,
Pearls pre-cious are, though trod-den on by swine:
All truths are true, though not all men them try;
The best un-to the bad doth work the worst,
In-stead of bless-ing, make the more ac-curs'd.
4. The an-gels' eyes, whom veils can-not de-ceive,
Might best dis-close what best they did dis-cern:
Men must, with meek and si-lent faith, re-ceive
More than they can by sense or rea-son learn;
God's pow'r our proofs, His works our wit ex-ceed,
Proud rea-son oft to fa-tal lapse doth lead.

5. The God of hosts in slen - der host doth dwell, Yea, God and man, with
all to ei - ther due: The God who rules the heav'ns and ri - fled hell,
The man whose death did us to life re - new; The God and man who
is the an - gels' bliss In form of bread and wine our nur - ture is.
6. One soul in man is all in eve - ry part, One face at once in
man - y mir - rors shines, One fear - ful noise doth make a thou - sand start,
One eye at once of count - less things de - fines: If na - ture proofs of
one in man - y frame, In strong - er sort may God per - form the same.

7. God is at hand at once in eve - ry place, Yet God in eve - ry
place is ev - er one: So may there be, by su - per - nat - 'ral grace,
One man in man - y spac - es, fill - ing none; Since an - gels may ef -
fects of bod - ies show, On bod - ies God may an - gels' gifts be - stow.
8. What God as au - thor made, He al - ter may, No change so hard as
mak - ing all of nought: If Ad - am fash - ion'd were of earth - ly clay,
To sa - cred flesh of Christ may bread be wrought; This may he do who
made, by strength di - vine, A snake of Mo - ses' wand, of wa - ter wine.

1. In Pas-chal feast, the end of an-cient rite An en-trance was to nev-er-end-ing
grace: Types yield to truth, dim glimps-es to the light, Per-form-ing deed pres-
ag-ing signs did chase; Christ's fi-nal meal was foun-tain of our good, For mor-tal
fare He gave im-mor-tal food.
2. They saw, they heard, they felt Him sit-ting near,
Un-seen, un-felt, un-heard, they Him re-ceiv'd: No dif-f'rent thing, though
dif-f'rent it ap-pear, Though sens-es fail, yet faith is not de-ceiv'd; And if the
won-der of the work be new, Be-lieve the work-er, for his word is true.

3. Though blind men see no light, the sun doth shine, Sweet is the sweet, though fe-ver'd taste de-
ny, Pearls pre-cious are, though trod-den on by swine: All truths are true, though
not all men them try; The best un - to the bad doth work the worst, In - stead of
bless-ing, make the more ac - curs'd.
4. The an-gels' eyes, whom veils can-not de-ceive,
Might best dis - close what best they did dis - cern: Men must, with meek and
si-lent faith, re - ceive More than they can by sense or rea-son learn; God's pow'r our
proofs, His works our wit ex - ceed, Proud rea-son oft to fa - tal lapse doth lead.

5. The God of hosts in slen-der host doth dwell, Yea, God and man, with all to ei-ther
due: The God who rules the heav'ns and ri-fled hell, The man whose death did
us to life re-new; The God and man who is the an-gels' bliss In form of
bread and wine our nur-ture is.
6. One soul in man is all in eve-ry part,
One face at once in man-y mir-rors shines, One fear-ful noise doth make a thou-sand
start, One eye at once of count-less things de-fines: If na-ture
proofs of one in man-y frame, In strong-er sort may God per-form the same.

7. God is at hand at once in eve-ry place, Yet God in eve - ry place is ev-er
one: So may there be, by su-per-nat-'ral grace, One man in man - y
spac-es, fill-ing none; Since an-gels may ef-fects of bod-ies show, On bod-ies
God may an-gels' gifts be - stow.
8. What God as au - thor made, He al-ter may,
No change so hard as mak-ing all of nought: If Ad-am fash-ion'd were of earth-ly
clay, To sa-cred flesh of Christ may bread be wrought; This may he
do who made, by strength di - vine, A snake of Mo-ses' wand, of wa - ter wine.

1. Sing, my tongue, the Sav - ior's glo - ry, Of his Flesh the mys - t'ry sing;
Of the Blood, all price ex - ceed - ing, Shed by our im - mor - tal King,
Des - tin'd, for the world's re - demp - tion, From a no - ble womb to spring.
2. Of a pure and spot - less Vir - gin Born for us on earth be - low,
He, as Man with man con - vers - ing, Stay'd, the seeds of truth to sow;
Then He clos'd in sol - emn or - der Won - drous - ly his life of woe.

3. On the night of that Last Sup - per, Seat - ed with his cho - sen band,
He the pas - chal vic - tim eat - ing, First ful - fils the Law's com - mand;
Then, as Food to all his breth - ren Gives Him - self with his own hand.
4. The In - car - nate Word now chang - es Bread to flesh at His com - mand,
And the wine be - comes His life - blood. Sens - es fail to un - der - stand;
But the heart that is in ear - nest Can by faith its doubt with - stand.

5. Down in ad - o - ra - tion fall - ing, This great Sac - ra - ment we hail;
O - ver an - cient forms of wor - ship New - er rites of grace pre - vail;
Faith re - minds us Christ is pre - sent When our fee - ble sens - es fail.
6. To the Ev - er - last - ing Fa - ther, And the Son who reigns on high,
With the Ho - ly Ghost pro - ceed - ing Forth from Each e - ter - nal - ly,
Be sal - va - tion, hon - or, bless - ing, Might, and end - less maj - es - ty.

1. Sing, my tongue, the Sav - ior's glo - ry, Of his Flesh the mys - t'ry sing;
Of the Blood, all price ex-ceed - ing, Shed by our im - mor - tal King,
Des - tin'd, for the world's re - demp - tion, From a no - ble womb to spring.
2. Of a pure and spot - less Vir - gin Born for us on earth be - low,
He, as Man with man con-vers - ing, Stay'd, the seeds of truth to sow;
Then He clos'd in sol - emn or - der Won-drous - ly his life of woe.

3. On the night of that Last Sup - per, Seat-ed with his cho - sen band,
He the pas - chal vic-tim eat - ing, First ful-fils the Law's com-mand;
Then, as Food to all his breth - ren Gives Him - self with his own hand.
4. The In-car - nate Word now chang - es Bread to flesh at His com-mand,
And the wine be - comes His life - blood. Sens-es fail to un - der-stand;
But the heart that is in ear - nest Can by faith its doubt with - stand.

5. Down in ad - o - ra - tion fall - ing, This great Sac - ra - ment___ we hail;
O - ver an - cient forms of wor - ship New - er rites of grace___ pre - vail;
Faith re - minds us Christ is pre - sent When our fee - ble sens - es fail.
6. To the Ev - er - last - ing Fa - ther, And the Son who reigns___ on high,
With the Ho - ly Ghost pro - ceed - ing Forth from Each e - ter - nal - ly,
Be sal - va - tion, hon - or, bless - ing, Might, and end - less maj - es - ty.

 PICARDY — *Pange Lingua* (Aquinas) — English Translation by Father Caswall

1. Sing, my tongue, the Sav - ior's_ glo - ry, Of his Flesh the mys - t'ry_ sing;
Of the Blood, all price ex - ceed - ing, Shed by our im - mor - tal_ King,
Des- tin'd, for the world's re - demp - tion, From a no - ble womb to_ spring.
2. Of a pure and spot - less_ Vir - gin Born for us on earth be - low,
He, as Man with man con - vers - ing, Stay'd, the seeds of truth to_ sow;
Then He clos'd in sol - emn or - der Won-drous-ly his life of_ woe.

3. On the night of that Last_ Sup - per, Seat-ed with his cho - sen_ band,
He the pas-chal vic - tim_ eat - ing, First ful-fils the Law's com - mand;
Then, as Food to all his breth - ren Gives Him-self with his own_ hand.
4. The In - car-nate Word now_ chang - es Bread to flesh at His com - mand,
And the wine be-comes His_ life - blood. Sens-es fail to un - der - stand;
But the heart that is in ear - nest Can by faith its doubt with - stand.

5. Down in ad - o - ra - tion__ fall - ing, This great Sac - ra - ment we__ hail;
O - ver an - cient forms of__ wor - ship New - er rites of grace pre - vail;
Faith re - minds us Christ is pre - sent When our fee - ble sens - es__ fail.
6. To the Ev - er - last - ing__ Fa - ther, And the Son who reigns on high,
With the Ho - ly Ghost pro - ceed - ing Forth from Each e - ter - nal - ly,
Be sal - va - tion, hon - or, bless - ing, Might, and end - less maj - es - ty.

1. Sing, my tongue, the Sav - ior's glo - ry, Of his Flesh the mys - t'ry sing;
Of the Blood, all price ex-ceed - ing, Shed by our im - mor - tal King,
Des - tin'd, for the world's re-demp - tion, From a no - ble womb to spring.
2. Of a pure and spot - less Vir - gin Born for us on earth be - low,
He, as Man with man con - vers - ing, Stay'd, the seeds of truth to sow;
Then He clos'd in sol - emn or - der Wondrous - ly his life of woe.

3. On the night of that Last Sup - per, Seat - ed with_ his cho - sen band,
He the pas - chal vic - tim eat - ing, First ful - fils_ the Law's com - mand;
Then, as Food to all his breth - ren Gives Him - self with his own hand.
4. The In - car - nate Word now chang - es Bread to flesh_ at His com - mand,
And the wine be - comes His life - blood. Sens - es fail_ to un - der - stand;
But the heart that is in ear - nest Can by faith its doubt with - stand.

5. Down in ad - o - ra - tion fall - ing, This great Sac - ra - ment we hail;
O - ver an - cient forms of wor - ship New - er rites_ of grace pre - vail;
Faith re - minds us Christ is pre - sent When our fee - ble sens - es fail.
6. To the Ev - er - last - ing Fa - ther, And the Son_ who reigns on high,
With the Ho - ly Ghost pro-ceed - ing Forth from Each_ e - ter - nal - ly,
Be sal - va - tion, hon - or, bless - ing, Might, and end - less maj - es - ty.

1. Hail, the bod - y bright and glo - rious, Mys-ter - y of love di - vine;
Hail, the blood that flows vic - to - rious From the true, the liv - ing vine;
Hail, our ran - som mer - i - to - rious, Flow'r and root of Da - vid's line.
2. Born for us and to us giv - en Of a Vir - gin pure as snow—
He, as man, with man con-vers - ing, Stay'd, the seeds of truth to sow;
Then at length in won-drous or - der, Closed His so - journ here be - low.

3. On the night be - fore His Pas - sion, Seat-ed with His cho - sen band,
Je - sus, with the Law com-ply - ing, Keeps the feast its rites de - mand;
Then, more pre - cious food sup - ply - ing, Gives Him - self with His own hand.
4. Earth - ly things to things of heav - en Changed by God's in - car - nate Word,
Flesh and blood in mys-t'ry giv - en, We be-lieve with faith as - sured;
As the Word hath said it, e - ven Be that word be - lieved, a - dored.

5. Then be - fore His al - tar bow - ing, Let our hearts the Lord re - vere;
Faith her aid to vi - sion lend - ing, Tells that He un - seen is near;
An - cient types and shad - ows end - ing, Christ our pas - chal Lamb is here.
6. To the Trin - i - ty be glo - ry Ev - er - last - ing, as is meet:
E - qual to the Fa - ther, e - qual To the Son and Par - a - clete:
Bless - èd U - ni - ty, whose prais - es All cre - at - ed things re - peat.

1. Pan - ge lin - gua glo - ri - ó - si Cór - po - ris my - sté - ri - um
San - gui - nís - que pre - ti - ó - si, Quem in mun - di pré - ti - um
Fru - ctus ven - tris ge - ne - ró - si, Rex ef - fú - dit gén - ti - um.
2. No - bis da - tus, no - bis na - tus Ex in - tá - cta Vír - gi - ne,
Et in mun - do con - ver - sá - tus, Spar - so ver - bi sé - mi - ne,
Su - i mo - ras in - co - lá - tus Mi - ro clau - sit ór - di - ne.

3. In su-pré - mae no-cte coe - nae Re-cúm-bens cum frá - tri-bus,
Ob-ser-vá - ta le-ge ple - ne Ci-bis in le-gá - li-bus,
Ci-bum tur-bae du - o - dé - nae Se dat su - is má - ni - bus.
4. Ver-bum ca - ro, pa-nem ve - rum Ver-bo car-nem éf - fi-cit,
Fit-que san - guis Chri-sti me - rum, Et si sen-sus dé - fi-cit,
Ad fir-mán-dum cor sin - cé - rum So-la fi-des súf - fi - cit.

5. Tan - tum er - go Sa - cra - mén - tum Ve - ne - ré - mur cér - nu - i:
Et an - tí - quum do - cu - mén - tum No - vo ce - dat rí - tu - i:
Prae - stet fi - des sup - ple - mén - tum Sén - su - um de - fé - ctu - i.
6. Ge - ni - tó - ri, Ge - ni - tó - que Laus et ju - bi - lá - ti - o,
Sa - lus, ho - nor, vir - tus quo - que Sit et be - ne - dí - cti - o:
Pro - ce - dén - ti ab u - tró - que Com - par sit lau - dá - ti - o.

 GAUFESTRE — *Pange Lingua* (Aquinas) — English Translation by Campbell of Skerrington

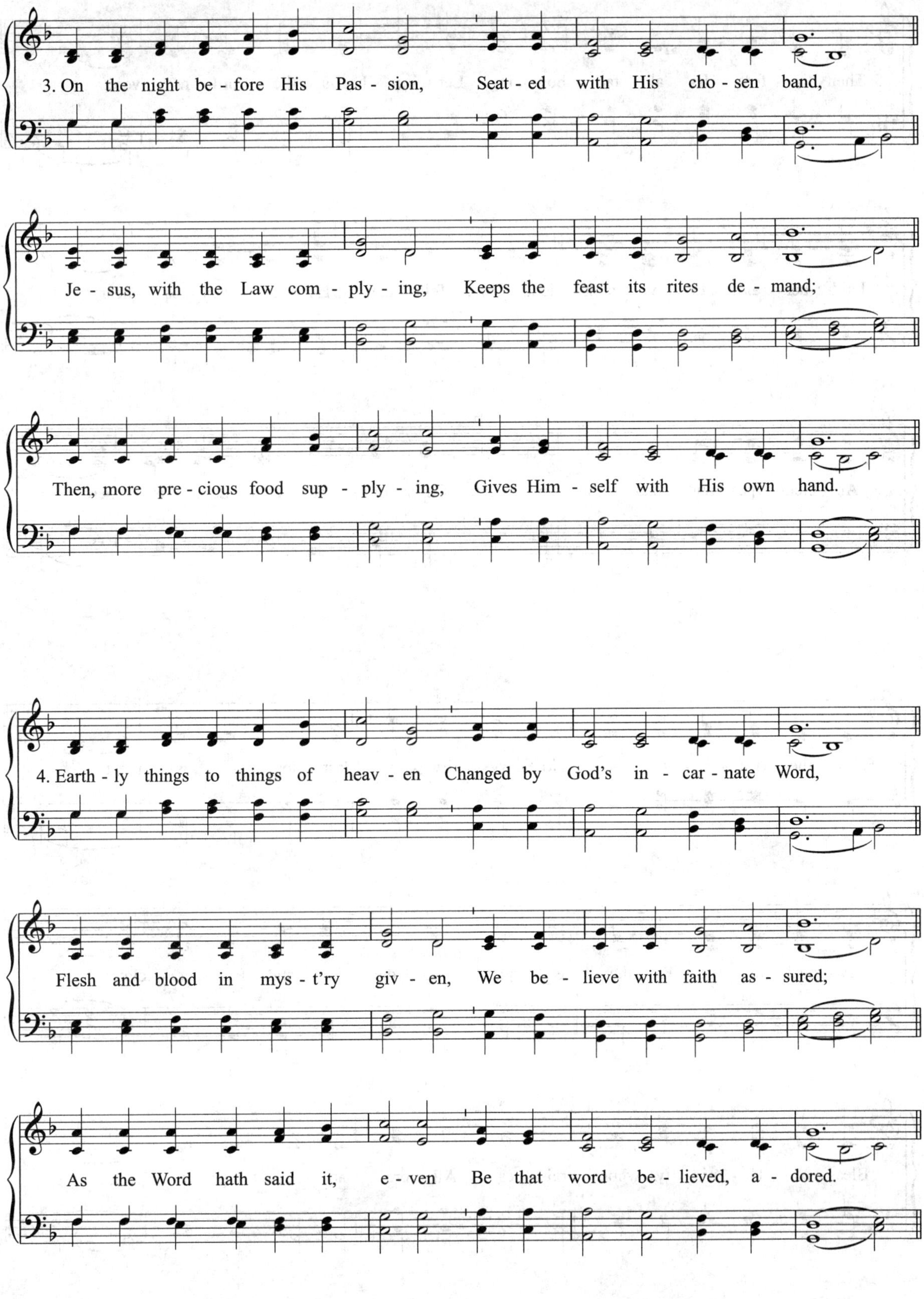
3. On the night be - fore His Pas - sion, Seat - ed with His cho - sen band,
Je - sus, with the Law com - ply - ing, Keeps the feast its rites de - mand;
Then, more pre - cious food sup - ply - ing, Gives Him - self with His own hand.
4. Earth - ly things to things of heav - en Changed by God's in - car - nate Word,
Flesh and blood in mys - t'ry giv - en, We be - lieve with faith as - sured;
As the Word hath said it, e - ven Be that word be - lieved, a - dored.

5. Then be - fore His al - tar bow - ing, Let our hearts the Lord re - vere;
Faith her aid to vi - sion lend - ing, Tells that He un - seen is near;
An - cient types and shad - ows end - ing, Christ our pas - chal Lamb is here.
6. To the Trin - i - ty be glo - ry Ev - er - last - ing, as is meet:
E - qual to the Fa - ther, e - qual To the Son and Par - a - clete:
Bless - èd U - ni - ty, whose prais - es All cre - at - ed things re - peat.

1. Pan - ge lin - gua glo - ri - ó - si Cór - po - ris my - sté - ri - um
San - gui - nís - que pre - ti - ó - si, Quem in mun - di pré - ti - um
Fru - ctus ven - tris ge - ne - ró - si, Rex ef - fú - dit gén - ti - um.
2. No - bis da - tus, no - bis na - tus Ex in - tá - cta Vír - gi - ne,
Et in mun - do con - ver - sá - tus, Spar - so ver - bi sé - mi - ne,
Su - i mo - ras in - co - lá - tus Mi - ro clau - sit ór - di - ne.

3. In su - pré - mae no - cte coe - nae Re - cúm - bens cum frá - tri - bus,
Ob - ser - vá - ta le - ge ple - ne Ci - bis in le - gá - li - bus,
Ci - bum tur - bae du - o - dé - nae Se dat su - is má - ni - bus.
4. Ver - bum ca - ro, pa - nem ve - rum Ver - bo car - nem éf - fi - cit,
Fit - que san - guis Chri - sti me - rum, Et si sen - sus dé - fi - cit,
Ad fir - mán - dum cor sin - cé - rum So - la fi - des súf - fi - cit.

5. Tan - tum er - go Sa - cra - mén - tum Ve - ne - ré - mur cér - nu - i:
Et an - tí - quum do - cu - mén - tum No - vo ce - dat rí - tu - i:
Prae - stet fi - des sup - ple - mén - tum Sén - su - um de - fé - ctu - i.
6. Ge - ni - tó - ri, Ge - ni - tó - que Laus et ju - bi - lá - ti - o,
Sa - lus, ho - nor, vir - tus quo - que Sit et be - ne - dí - cti - o:
Pro - ce - dén - ti ab u - tró - que Com - par sit lau - dá - ti - o.

1. Hail, the bod - y bright and glo - rious, Mys - ter - y of love di - vine;
Hail, the blood that flows vic - to - rious From the true, the liv - ing vine;
Hail, our ran - som mer - i - to - rious, Flow'r and root of Da - vid's line.
2. Born for us and to us giv - en Of a Vir - gin pure as snow—
He, as man, with man con - vers - ing, Stay'd, the seeds of truth to sow;
Then at length in won - drous or - der, Closed His so - journ here be - low.

3. On the night be - fore His Pas - sion, Seat - ed with His cho - sen band,
Je - sus, with the Law com - ply - ing, Keeps the feast its rites de - mand;
Then, more pre - cious food sup - ply - ing, Gives Him - self with His own hand.
4. Earth - ly things to things of heav - en Changed by God's in - car - nate Word,
Flesh and blood in mys - t'ry giv - en, We be - lieve with faith as - sured;
As the Word hath said it, e - ven Be that word be - lieved, a - dored.

5. Then be - fore His al - tar bow - ing, Let our hearts the Lord re - vere;
Faith her aid to vi - sion lend - ing, Tells that He un - seen is near;
An - cient types and shad - ows end - ing, Christ our pas - chal Lamb is here.
6. To the Trin - i - ty be glo - ry Ev - er - last - ing, as is meet:
E - qual to the Fa - ther, e - qual To the Son and Par - a - clete:
Bless - èd U - ni - ty, whose prais - es All cre - at - ed things re - peat.

1. Hail, the body bright and glorious, Mystery of love divine;
Hail, the blood that flows victorious From the true, the living vine;
Hail, our ransom merii-torious, Flow'r and root of David's line.
2. Born for us and to us given Of a Virgin pure as snow—
He, as man, with man conversing, Stay'd, the seeds of truth to sow;
Then at length in wondrous order, Closed His sojourn here below.

3. On the__ night be - fore His__ Pas - sion, Seat - ed with His cho - sen band,
Je - sus,__ with the Law com - ply - ing, Keeps the feast its rites de - mand;
Then, more__ pre - cious food sup - ply - ing, Gives Him - self__ with His own hand.
4. Earth - ly__ things to things of__ heav - en Changed by God's in - car - nate Word,
Flesh and__ blood in mys - t'ry__ giv - en, We be - lieve with faith as - sured;
As the__ Word hath said it, e - ven Be that__ word be - lieved, a - dored.

5. Then be - fore His al - tar__ bow - ing, Let our hearts the Lord re - vere;
Faith her__ aid to vi - sion__ lend - ing, Tells that He un - seen is near;
An - cient__ types and shad - ows end - ing, Christ our__ pas - chal Lamb is here.
6. To the__ Trin - i - ty be__ glo - ry Ev - er - last - ing, as is meet:
E - qual__ to the Fa - ther,__ e - qual To the Son and Par - a - clete:
Bless - èd__ U - ni - ty, whose prais - es All cre - at - ed things re - peat.

364 LAUDA ANIMA — *Pange Lingua* (Aquinas) — English Translation by Campbell of Skerrington

3. On the night be - fore His Pas - sion, Seat - ed with His cho - sen band,
Je - sus, with the Law com - ply - ing, Keeps the feast its rites de - mand;
Then, more pre - cious food sup - ply - ing, Gives Him - self with His own hand.
4. Earth - ly things to things of heav - en Changed by God's in - car - nate Word,
Flesh and blood in mys - t'ry giv - en, We be - lieve with faith as - sured;
As the Word hath said it, e - ven Be that word be - lieved, a - dored.

5. Then be - fore His al - tar bow - ing, Let our hearts the Lord re - vere;
Faith her aid to vi - sion lend - ing, Tells that He un - seen is near;
An - cient types and shad - ows end - ing, Christ our pas - chal Lamb is here.
6. To the Trin - i - ty be glo - ry Ev - er - last - ing, as is meet:
E - qual to the Fa - ther, e - qual To the Son and Par - a - clete:
Bless - èd U - ni - ty, whose prais - es All cre - at - ed things re - peat.

ORIEL — *Pange Lingua* (Aquinas) — English Translation by Campbell of Skerrington **365**

1. Hail, the bod - y bright and glo - rious, Mys - ter - y of love di - vine;
Hail, the blood that flows vic - to - rious From the true, the liv - ing vine;
Hail, our ran - som mer - i - to - rious, Flow'r and root of Da - vid's line.
2. Born for us and to us giv - en Of a Vir - gin pure as snow—
He, as man, with man con - vers - ing, Stay'd, the seeds of truth to sow;
Then at length in won - drous or - der, Closed His so - journ here be - low.

3. On the night be - fore His Pas - sion, Seat - ed with His cho - sen band,
Je - sus, with the Law com - ply - ing, Keeps the feast its rites de - mand;
Then, more pre - cious food sup - ply - ing, Gives Him - self with His own hand.
4. Earth - ly things to things of heav - en Changed by God's in - car - nate Word,
Flesh and blood in mys - t'ry giv - en, We be - lieve with faith as - sured;
As the Word hath said it, e - ven Be that word be - lieved, a - dored.

5. Then be - fore His al - tar bow - ing, Let our hearts the Lord re - vere;
Faith her aid to vi - sion lend - ing, Tells that He un - seen is near;
An - cient types and shad - ows end - ing, Christ our pas - chal Lamb is here.
6. To the Trin - i - ty be glo - ry Ev - er - last - ing, as is meet:
E - qual to the Fa - ther, e - qual To the Son and Par - a - clete:
Bless - èd U - ni - ty, whose prais - es All cre - at - ed things re - peat.

367 AUSTRIA B7 — *Pange Lingua* (Aquinas) — English Translation by Campbell of Skerrington

3. On the night be - fore His Pas - sion, Seat - ed with His cho - sen_ band,
Je - sus, with_ the Law com - ply - ing, Keeps the feast its rites de - mand;
Then, more pre - cious food sup - ply - ing, Gives Him - self_ with_ His own_ hand.
4. Earth - ly things to things of heav - en Changed by God's in - car - nate_ Word,
Flesh and blood in mys - t'ry giv - en, We be - lieve with faith as - sured;
As the Word hath said it, e - ven Be that_ word be - lieved, a - dored.

5. Then be - fore His al - tar bow - ing, Let our hearts the Lord re - vere;
Faith her aid_ to vi - sion lend - ing, Tells that He un - seen is near;
An - cient types and shad - ows end - ing, Christ our_ pas - chal_ Lamb is_ here.
6. To the Trin - i - ty be glo - ry Ev - er - last - ing, as is_ meet:
E - qual to_ the Fa - ther, e - qual To the Son and Par - a - clete:
Bless - èd U - ni - ty, whose prais - es All cre - at - ed_ things re - peat.

PICARDY — *Pange Lingua* (Aquinas) — English Translation by Campbell of Skerrington **368**

1. Hail, the bod - y bright and__ glo - rious, Mys-ter - y of love di - vine;
Hail, the blood that flows vic - to - rious From the true, the liv - ing__ vine;
Hail, our ran - som mer - i - to - rious, Flow'r and root of Da - vid's line.
2. Born for us and to us__ giv - en Of a Vir-gin pure as__ snow—
He, as man, with man con - vers - ing, Stay'd, the seeds of truth to__ sow;
Then at length in won - drous or - der, Closed His so - journ here be - low.

3. On the night be - fore His_ Pas - sion, Seat - ed with His cho - sen_ band,
Je - sus, with the Law com - ply - ing, Keeps the feast its rites de - mand;
Then, more pre - cious food sup - ply - ing, Gives Him - self with His own hand.
4. Earth - ly things to things of_ heav - en Changed by God's in - car - nate_ Word,
Flesh and blood in mys - t'ry_ giv - en, We be - lieve with faith as - sured;
As the Word hath said it, e - ven Be that word be lieved, a - dored.

5. Then be - fore His al - tar__ bow - ing, Let our hearts the Lord re - vere;
Faith her aid to vi - sion__ lend - ing, Tells that He un - seen is__ near;
An-cient types and shad - ows end - ing, Christ our pas-chal Lamb is__ here.
6. To the Trin - i - ty be__ glo - ry Ev - er - last - ing, as is__ meet:
E-qual to the Fa - ther,__ e - qual To the Son and Par - a - clete:
Bless-èd U - ni - ty, whose prais - es All cre - at - ed things re - peat.

369 DULCE CARMEN — *Pange Lingua* (Aquinas) — English Translation by Campbell of Skerrington

1. Hail, the bod - y bright and glo - rious, Mys - ter - y of love di - vine;
Hail, the blood that flows vic - to - rious From the true,_ the_ liv - ing vine;
Hail, our ran - som mer - i - to - rious, Flow'r_ and_ root of Da - vid's line.
2. Born for us and to us giv - en Of a Vir - gin pure as snow—
He, as man, with man con - vers - ing, Stay'd, the seeds of_ truth to sow;
Then at length in won - drous or - der, Closed_ His_ so - journ here be - low.

3. On the night be - fore His Pas - sion, Seat - ed with His cho - sen band,
Je - sus, with the Law com - ply - ing, Keeps the feast_ its_ rites de - mand;
Then, more pre - cious food sup - ply - ing, Gives_ Him - self with His own hand.
4. Earth - ly things to things of heav - en Changed by God's in - car - nate Word,
Flesh and blood in mys - t'ry giv - en, We be - lieve_ with_ faith as - sured;
As the Word hath said it, e - ven Be_ that_ word be - lieved, a - dored.

5. Then be - fore His al - tar bow - ing, Let our hearts the Lord re - vere;
Faith her aid to vi - sion lend - ing, Tells that He__ un - seen is near;
An - cient types and shad - ows end - ing, Christ__ our__ pas - chal Lamb is here.
6. To the Trin - i - ty be glo - ry Ev - er - last - ing, as is meet:
E - qual to the Fa - ther, e - qual To the Son__ and__ Par - a - clete:
Bless - èd U - ni - ty, whose prais - es All__ cre - at - ed things re - peat.

REGENT SQUARE — *Pange Lingua* (Aquinas) — English Translation by Campbell of Skerrington

3. On the night be - fore His Pas - sion, Seat - ed with His cho - sen band,
Je - sus, with the Law com-ply - ing, Keeps the feast its rites de - mand;
Then, more pre-cious food sup-ply - ing, Gives Him - self with His own hand.
4. Earth - ly things to things of heav - en Changed by God's in - car - nate Word,
Flesh and blood in mys - t'ry giv - en, We be - lieve with faith as - sured;
As the Word hath said it, e - ven Be that word be - lieved, a - dored.

5. Then be - fore His al - tar bow - ing, Let our hearts the Lord re - vere;
Faith her aid to vi - sion lend - ing, Tells that He un - seen is near;
An - cient types and shad - ows end - ing, Christ our pas - chal Lamb is here.
6. To the Trin - i - ty be glo - ry Ev - er - last - ing, as is meet:
E - qual to the Fa - ther, e - qual To the Son and Par - a - clete:
Bless - èd U - ni - ty, whose prais - es All cre - at - ed things re - peat.

 EISENACH — *Quem Terra, Pontus, Aethera* — English Translation by Prior Aylward

1. Whom_ earth and sea and sky pro - claim The Rul - er of their tri - ple frame,
He, un - to whom their prais - es rise, With - in the womb of Mar - y lies.
2. Her_ womb, the seat of ev - 'ry grace, Is now the Lord's a - bid - ing place;
That Lord to whom the sun by day, The moon by night,_ their hom - age pay.
3. O_ hap - py Moth - er that thou art, Close un - der-neath thy beat - ing heart
Lies the Cre - a - tor - God, who planned The world he holds_ with - in his hand.

4. Blest_ by the her-ald - an - gel's tongue, O'er thee God's shad-'wing Spir-it hung
And filled thy womb—whence is-sued forth The Long-de - sir'd_ of all the earth.
5. O__ Mar - y, Moth-er of all Grace And Mer-cy to our sin-ful race,
Drive back the foe; and to thy Son Lead thou our souls_ when life is done.
6. All__ glo - ry be to thee, O Lord, A Vir-gin's Son, by all a-dored;
And e-qual praise for ev - er greet The Fa-ther and_ the Par - a - clete.

 DUGUET — *Quem Terra, Pontus, Aethera* — English Translation by Prior Aylward

4. Blest by the her - ald - an - gel's tongue, O'er thee God's shad-'wing Spir - it hung
And filled thy womb—whence is - sued forth The Long - de - sir'd of all the earth.
5. O Mar - y, Moth - er of all Grace And Mer - cy to our sin - ful race,
Drive back the foe; and to thy Son Lead thou our souls when life is done.
6. All glo - ry be to thee, O Lord, A Vir - gin's Son, by all a - dored;
And e - qual praise for ev - er greet The Fa - ther and the Par - a - clete.

 WHITEHALL — *Quem Terra, Pontus, Aethera* — English Translation by Prior Aylward

4. Blest by the her - ald - an - gel's tongue, O'er thee God's shad-'wing Spir - it hung
And filled thy womb— whence is - sued forth The Long - de - sir'd of all the earth.
5. O Mar - y, Moth - er of all Grace And Mer - cy to our sin - ful race,
Drive back the foe; and to thy Son Lead thou our souls when life is done.
6. All glo - ry be to thee, O Lord, A Vir - gin's Son, by all a - dored;
And e - qual praise for ev - er greet The Fa - ther and the Par - a - clete.

379 MELCOMBE — *Quem Terra, Pontus, Aethera* — English Translation by Prior Aylward

4. Blest by the her - ald - an - gel's tongue, O'er thee God's shad - 'wing Spir - it hung
And filled thy womb—whence is - sued forth The Long - de - sir'd of all the earth.
5. O Mar - y, Moth - er of all Grace And Mer - cy to our sin - ful race,
Drive back the foe; and to thy Son Lead thou our souls when life is done.
6. All glo - ry be to thee, O Lord, A Vir - gin's Son, by all a - dored;
And e - qual praise for ev - er greet The Fa - ther and the Par - a - clete.

380 KEMPEN — *Quem Terra, Pontus, Aethera* — English Translation by Prior Aylward

4. Blest by the her - ald - an - gel's tongue, O'er thee_ God's shad - 'wing Spir - it hung
And filled thy womb— whence is - sued forth The Long - de - sir'd_ of all_ the earth.
5. O Mar - y, Moth - er of all Grace And Mer - cy to our sin - ful race,
Drive back the foe; and to thy Son Lead thou our souls_ when life_ is done.
6. All glo - ry be to thee, O Lord, A Vir - gin's Son, by all_ a - dored;
And e - qual praise for ev - er greet The Fa - ther and_ the Par - a - clete.

 TRINITY COLLEGE — *Quem Terra, Pontus, Aethera* — English Translation by Father Fitzpatrick

1. The Lord, whom earth, and sea, and sky Re - vere, a - dore and mag - ni - fy,
Who o'er this tri - une sys - tem reigns, To dwell in Mar - y's clois - ter deigns!
2. Whom sun, and moon, and all things serve, Nor ev - er from this du - ty swerve,
He makes that womb, which heav'n - ly grace Im - bues, his vir - gin lodg - ing - place.

* A transposed organ accompaniment has been provided for optional use.

3. A moth - er bless - èd, who can claim With - in the cof - fer of her frame
To keep her Mak - er, who has spann'd The whole world with His in - fant hand!
4. Bless - èd by God's own mes - sage made, And fruit - ful 'neath His spir - it's shade
She was, of whom con - ceived came He, Whom all the na - tions longed to see.
5. Je - sus the Vir - gin's on - ly Son, With Fa - ther and with spir - it One,
Be praise and glo - ry giv'n to Thee In time and in e - ter - ni - ty.

1. The Lord, whom earth, and sea, and sky Re - vere, a - dore and mag - ni - fy, Who o'er this tri - une sys - tem reigns, To dwell in Mar - y's clois - ter deigns!
2. Whom sun, and moon, and all things serve, Nor ev - er from this du - ty swerve, He makes that womb, which heav'n - ly grace Im - bues, his vir - gin lodg - ing - place.
3. A moth - er bless - èd, who can claim With - in the cof - fer of her frame

To keep her Mak - er, who_ has spann'd The whole world
with His in - fant hand!
4. Bless - èd_ by God's own
mes - sage made, And fruit - ful 'neath His spir - it's shade_
She was, of whom con - ceived_ came He, Whom all the na - tions
longed_ to see.
5. Je - sus_ the Vir - gin's on - ly Son,
With Fa - ther and with spir - it One,_ Be praise and glo - ry
giv'n_ to Thee In time and in e - ter - ni - ty.

385 SAXONY — *Quem Terra, Pontus, Aethera* — English Translation by Father Fitzpatrick

1. The Lord, whom earth, and sea, and sky Re - vere, a - dore and mag - ni - fy,
Who o'er this tri - une sys - tem reigns, To dwell in Mar - y's clois - ter deigns!
2. Whom sun, and moon, and all things serve, Nor ev - er from this du - ty swerve,
He makes that womb, which heav'n-ly grace Im - bues, his vir - gin lodg - ing - place.
3. A moth - er bless - èd, who can claim With - in the cof - fer of her frame
To keep her Mak - er, who has spann'd The whole world with His in - fant hand!

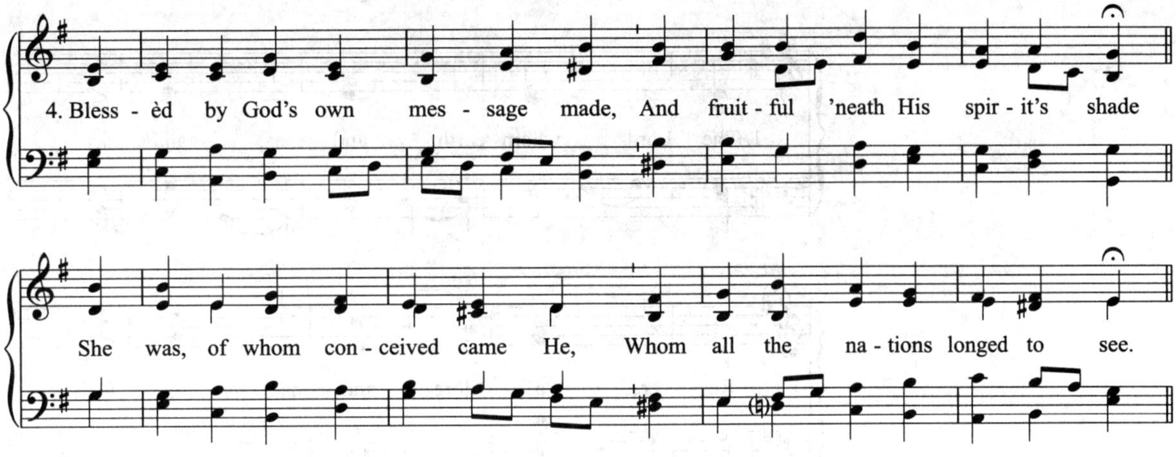
4. Bless - èd by God's own mes - sage made, And fruit - ful 'neath His spir - it's shade
She was, of whom con - ceived came He, Whom all the na - tions longed to see.

5. Je - sus the Vir - gin's on - ly Son, With Fa - ther and with spir - it One,
Be praise and glo - ry giv'n to Thee In time and in e - ter - ni - ty.

1. The Lord, whom earth, and sea, and sky

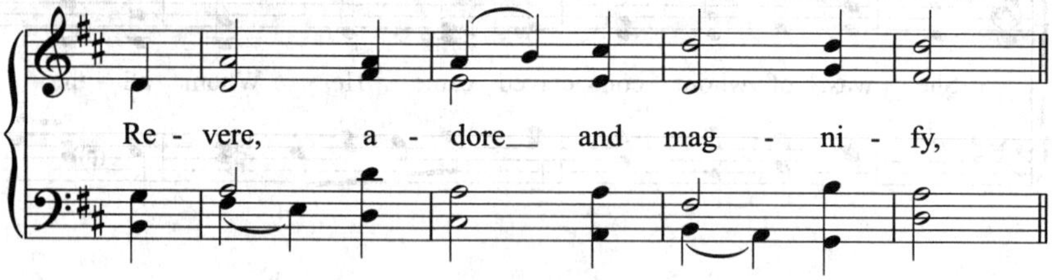
Re - vere, a - dore__ and mag - ni - fy,

Who o'er this tri - une sys - tem reigns,

To dwell in Mar - y's clois - ter deigns!

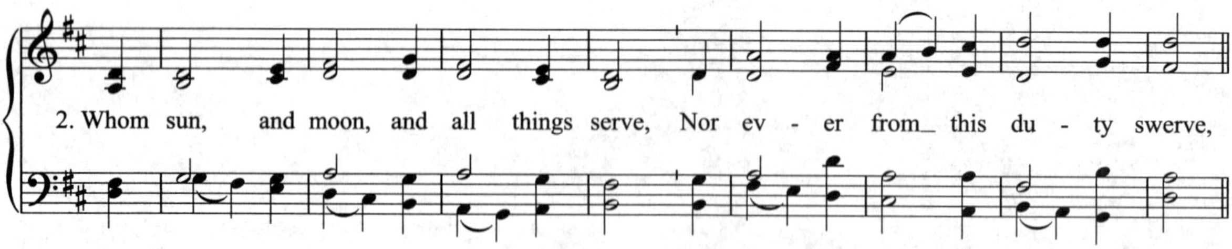
2. Whom sun, and moon, and all things serve, Nor ev - er from_ this du - ty swerve,

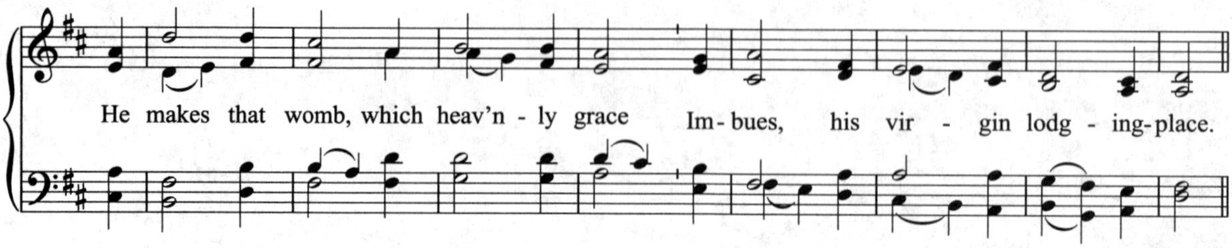
He makes that womb, which heav'n - ly grace Im- bues, his vir - gin lodg - ing-place.

3. A moth - er bless - èd, who can claim With - in the cof - fer of her frame
To keep her Mak - er, who has spann'd The whole world with His in - fant hand!
4. Bless - èd by God's own mes - sage made, And fruit - ful 'neath His spir - it's shade
She was, of whom con ceived came He, Whom all the na - tions longed to see.
5. Je - sus the Vir - gin's on - ly Son, With Fa - ther and_ with spir - it One,
Be praise and glo - ry giv'n to Thee In time and in e - ter - ni - ty.

388 ALL SAINTS — *Quem Terra, Pontus, Aethera* — This version is suitable for Christmas.

1. Sing we Him whose won - drous sto - ry Air, and — earth, and seas pro - claim,
Rul - er of the realms of glo - ry, To the — world be - low who came:
Je - sus ho - ly, — who was — born Ear - ly on — the Christ-mas morn.
2. What though sun and moon a - dore Him, While suc - ceed - ing e - ons move,
Yet a mor - tal Maid - en bore Him, Graced by — rare su - per - nal love:
Lo, the Mak - er — of the — skies In a nar - row man - ger lies!
3. Moth - er of the world's Cre - a - tor, Hap - py — Moth - er, Maid - en mild!

He who holds the frame of na - ture In His hands be - came her Child,
Set - tled by her lull - a - by, In her arms was pleased to lie.
4. Blest by An - gel's sal - u - ta - tion, Fruit - ful by the Spir - it's might,
Christ, the hope of eve - ry na - tion, God and man, she brought to light
At the prov - i - den - tial tide, Him for whom the ag - es sighed.
5. Hark, the heav'n - ly host re - joic - es With ex - ult - ant hymns of praise:
Let our grate - ful hearts and voic - es Add their bur - den to those lays,
With that mul - ti - tude to cry Peace to men from God on high!

389 IRBY — *Quem Terra, Pontus, Aethera* — This version is suitable for Christmas.

1. Sing we Him whose won - drous sto - ry Air, and earth, and seas_ pro - claim,
Rul - er of the realms of__ glo - ry, To the world be - low__ who_ came:
Je - sus ho - ly, who was born Ear - ly on the Christ - mas_ morn.
2. What though sun and moon_ a - dore Him, While suc - ceed - ing e - ons_ move,
Yet a mor - tal Maid - en__ bore Him, Graced by rare su - per - nal__ love:
Lo, the Mak - er of the skies In a nar - row man - ger_ lies!

3. Moth - er of the world's Cre - a - tor, Hap - py Moth - er, Maid - en__ mild!
He who holds the frame_ of__ na - ture In His hands be - came her__ Child,
Set - tled by her lull - a - by, In her arms was pleased to__ lie.
4. Blest by An - gel's sal - u - ta - tion, Fruit - ful by the Spir - it's__ might,
Christ, the hope of eve - ry__ na - tion, God and man, she brought to__ light
At the prov - i - den - tial tide, Him for whom the ag - es__ sighed.
5. Hark, the heav'n - ly host__ re - joic - es With ex - ult - ant hymns of__ praise:

Let our grate - ful hearts and_ voic - es Add their bur - den to_ those lays,
With that mul - ti - tude to cry Peace to men from God_ on_ high!

BROCKHAM — *Quem Terra, Pontus, Aethera* — Historic Catholic Translation (1807)

1. The Sov'reign God whose hands sus - tain The heav'n - ly orbs, the earth, the main;
Whose gen - er - a - tion none can tell, In thee, O Mar - y, chose to_ dwell.
2. He, whom the sun and moon o - bey, To whom all crea - tures hom - age pay,
The might - y Rul - er of the skies, In thee con - ceal'd, an in - fant_ lies.

3. Thrice hap - py Maid, whom Heav - en's choice Has made the source of
all our joys; Since he, by whom we move and live, From thee would
life and food re - ceive.
4. An an - gel brings the
hap - py news; The Ho - ly Ghost, thy heav'n - ly spouse, Thee co - vers
with his fruit - ful shade, And Christ's blest Moth - er thou art made.
5. O Mar - y, full of grace di - vine, Thy glo - ries now the stars out - shine;
Lo! thy Cre - a - tor and thy God Draws from thy bod - y life and food.

6. O gra-cious Moth - er of man-kind, What Eve had lost, in thee we find;
The way to heav'n is now by thee To mourn - ing sin - ners o - pen'd_ free.
7. Thou art the gate of heav'n-ly light, Through which the con - qu'ring
Prince of might Comes, cap - tive man - kind to re - deem; Ye, Na - tions,
sound the glo - rious_ theme.
8. May age to age for -
ev - er sing The Vir - gin's Son and an - gels' King; And praise with
the ce - les - tial host, The Fa - ther Son and Ho - ly___ Ghost.

LA ROCHELLE — *Quem Terra, Pontus, Aethera* — Historic Catholic Translation (1807)

1. The Sov-'reign God whose hands sus-tain The heav'n-ly orbs, the earth, the main;
Whose gen-er-a-tion none can tell, In thee, O Mar-y, chose to dwell.
2. He, whom the sun and moon o-bey, To whom all crea-tures hom-age pay,
The might-y Rul-er of the skies, In thee con-ceal'd, an in-fant lies.
3. Thrice hap-py Maid, whom Heav-en's choice Has made the source of all our joys;
Since he, by whom we move and live, From thee would life and food_ re-ceive.
4. An an-gel brings the hap-py news; The Ho-ly Ghost, thy heav'n-ly spouse,
Thee co-vers with his fruit-ful shade, And Christ's blest Moth-er thou_ art made.

5. O Mar - y, full of grace di - vine, Thy glo - ries now the stars out - shine;
Lo! thy Cre - a - tor and thy God Draws from thy bod - y life__ and food.
6. O gra - cious Moth - er of man - kind, What Eve had lost, in thee we find;
The way to heav'n is now by thee To mourn-ing sin - ners o - pen'd free.
7. Thou art the gate of heav'n - ly light, Through which the con-qu'ring Prince of might
Comes, cap - tive man - kind to re - deem; Ye, Na - tions, sound the glo - rious theme.
8. May age to age for - ev - er sing The Vir - gin's Son and an - gels' King;
And praise with the ce - les - tial host, The Fa - ther Son and Ho - ly Ghost.

ALTONA — *Quem Terra, Pontus, Aethera* — Historic Catholic Translation (1807)

394

** A transposed organ accompaniment has been provided for optional use.*

1. The Sov-'reign God whose hands sus-tain The heav'n-ly orbs, the_ earth, the main;
Whose gen-er-a-tion none_ can tell, In thee, O Mar-y, chose to dwell.
2. He, whom the sun and moon o-bey, To whom all crea-tures hom-age pay,
The might-y Rul-er of_ the skies, In thee con-ceal'd, an in-fant lies.

3. Thrice hap - py Maid, whom Heav - en's choice Has made the source of___
all our joys; Since he, by whom we move and live, From thee would
life and food_ re - ceive.
4. An an - gel brings the
hap - py news; The Ho - ly Ghost, thy__ heav'n - ly spouse, Thee co - vers
with_ his fruit - ful shade, And Christ's blest Moth - er thou_ art made.
5. O Mar - y, full of grace di - vine, Thy glo - ries now the_ stars out - shine;
Lo! thy Cre - a - tor and_ thy God Draws from thy bod - y life_ and food.

6. O gra-cious Moth - er of man-kind, What Eve had lost, in__ thee we find;
The way to heav'n is now_ by thee To mourn-ing sin - ners o - pen'd free.
7. Thou art the gate of heav'n - ly light, Through which the con- qu'ring
Prince of might Comes, cap - tive man - kind to__ re - deem; Ye, Na - tions,
sound the glo - rious theme.
8. May age to age for -
ev - er sing The Vir - gin's Son and__ an - gels' King;
And praise with the__ ce - les - tial host, The Fa - ther Son and Ho - ly Ghost.

396 HILDERSTONE — *Quem Terra, Pontus, Aethera* — English Translation by Father Caswall

** A transposed organ accompaniment has been provided for optional use.*

1. The Lord, whom earth, and sea, and sky, With one a - dor - ing voice pro- claim;
Who rules them all in maj - es - ty; En - clos'd Him - self in Mar - y's frame.
2. Lo! in a hum - ble Vir - gin's womb, O'er - sha - dowed by Al - might - y pow'r;
He whom the stars, and sun, and moon, Each serve in their ap - point - ed hour.

3. O Moth - er blest, to whom was giv'n With - in thy bod - y to con - tain
The Ar - chi - tect of earth and Heav'n, Whose hands the__ u - ni - verse sus - tain.
4. To thee was sent an An - gel down; In thee the Spir - it was en - shrin'd;
Of thee was born that Might - y One, The long - de - sir'd of all man - kind.
5. O Je - sus, born of Vir - gin bright, Im - mor - tal glo - ry be to Thee;
Praise to the Fa - ther in - fi - nite, And Par - a - clete e - ter - nal - ly.

399 EISENACH — *Quem Terra, Pontus, Aethera* — English Translation by Neale

1. The God whom earth and sea and sky
A - dore and laud and mag - ni - fy, Whose might they own, whose
praise they tell, In Ma - ry's bod - y deigned to dwell.
2. O Moth - er blest, the cho - sen shrine
Where - in the Ar - chi - tect di - vine, Whose hand con - tains the
earth and sky, Vouch - safed, as in his ark, to lie!

3. Blest_ in the mes - sage Ga - briel brought;
Blest by the work the Spir - it wrought: From whom the great De -
sire of earth Took hu - man flesh_ and hu - man birth.
4. All_ hon - or, laud, and glo - ry be,
O Je - sus, Vir - gin - born, to thee! All glo - ry, as is
ev - er meet, To Fa - ther and_ to Par - a - clete.

1. O___ Lord, in per - fect bliss a - bove Thou couldst not need cre - at - ed___ love;
And_ yet Thou didst Thy pow'r dis - play, And earth's foun - da - tions firm - ly lay.
2. Things_ that were not, at Thy com - mand, In per - fect bliss be - fore Thee_ stand;
And_ all to their Cre - a - tor raise A won - drous har - mo - ny of praise.
3. But_ e - ven while the world came forth In all the beau - ty of its___ birth,
In___ Thy deep thought Thou didst be - hold An - oth - er world of nobl - er mold.

#97 has (optional) organ accompaniment at a lower key.

4. For__ Thou didst will that Christ should frame A new cre - a - tion by His__ Name;
Its__ seed, the liv - ing word of grace He scat - ters wide in eve - ry place;
5. Its__ home, when time shall be no more, In heav'n with Thee for ev - er - more;
Ac - cept - ed in Thy bound - less love To share His throne and joy a - bove.
6. O__ Fa - ther, Son, and Spir - it blest, One God in heav'n and earth con - fessed,
Pre - serve, di - rect, and sanc - ti - fy Thy realm be - low, Thy realm on high.

 TRINITY COLLEGE — *Rebus Creatis Nil Egens* — English Translation by the editors

1. O Lord, in per - fect bliss a - bove Thou couldst not need cre - at - ed love;
And yet Thou didst Thy pow'r dis - play, And earth's foun - da - tions firm - ly lay.
2. Things that were not, at Thy com - mand, In per - fect bliss be - fore Thee stand;
And all to their Cre - a - tor raise A won - drous har - mo - ny of praise.
3. But e - ven while the world came forth In all the beau - ty of its birth,
In Thy deep thought Thou didst be - hold An - oth - er world of nobl - er mold.

#105 has (optional) organ accompaniment at a lower key.

405 BESSEMER — *Rebus Creatis Nil Egens* — English Translation by the editors

4. For Thou didst will that Christ should frame A new cre - a - tion by His Name;
Its seed, the liv - ing word of grace He scat - ters wide in eve - ry place;
5. Its home, when time shall be no more, In heav'n with Thee for ev - er - more;
Ac - cept - ed in Thy bound-less love To share His throne and joy a - bove.
6. O Fa - ther, Son, and Spir - it blest, One God in heav'n and earth con - fessed,
Pre - serve, di - rect, and sanc - ti - fy Thy realm be - low, Thy realm on high.

406 WHITEHALL — *Rebus Creatis Nil Egens* — English Translation by the editors

4. For Thou didst will that Christ should frame A new cre - a - tion by His Name;
Its seed, the liv - ing word of grace He scat - ters wide in eve - ry place;
5. Its home, when time shall be no more, In heav'n with Thee for ev - er - more;
Ac - cept - ed in Thy bound - less love To share His throne and joy a - bove.
6. O Fa - ther, Son, and Spir - it blest, One God in heav'n and earth con - fessed,
Pre - serve, di - rect, and sanc - ti - fy Thy realm be - low, Thy realm on high.

 IOANNES — *Rebus Creatis Nil Egens* — English Translation by the editors

4. For Thou didst will that Christ_ should frame A new cre - a - tion
by His Name; Its seed, the liv - ing word_ of grace_ He scat - ters
wide_ in eve - ry place;
5. Its home, when time shall be_ no
more, In heav'n with Thee_ for ev - er - more; Ac - cept - ed
in_ Thy bound - less love_ To share His throne and joy_ a - bove.
6. O Fa - ther, Son, and Spir - it blest, One God in heav'n and earth con fessed,
Pre - serve, di - rect,_ and sanc - ti - fy_ Thy realm be - low,_ Thy realm on high.

 ALTONA — *Rebus Creatis Nil Egens* — English Translation by the editors

#18 has (optional) organ accompaniment at a higher key.

4. For Thou didst will that Christ should frame A new cre - a - tion_ by His Name;
Its seed, the liv - ing word of grace He scat-ters wide in eve - ry place;
5. Its home, when time shall be no more, In heav'n with Thee for_ ev - er - more;
Ac - cept - ed in_ Thy bound - less love To share His throne and joy_ a - bove.
6. O Fa - ther, Son, and Spir - it blest, One God in heav'n and_ earth con - fessed,
Pre - serve, di - rect, and sanc - ti - fy Thy realm be - low, Thy realm_ on high.

 BRISTOL — *Rebus Creatis Nil Egens* — English Translation by Campbell of Skerrington

4. Its Mak - er Christ, our Lord and God, Its frame His truth and grace,
And, far as foot of man hath trod, It finds a rest - ing place.
5. And when the course of time has run His lov - ing call will ring,
And it will rise, e'er with the Son To dwell, the sov-'reign King.
6. Thy new cre - a - tion, Lord, di - rect, Till fixed a - bove se - cure;
O Fa - ther, from its foes pro - tect; O, cleanse it, Spir - it Pure.

411 ST FLAVIAN — *Rebus Creatis Nil Egens* — English Translation by Campbell of Skerrington

4. Its Mak - er Christ, our Lord and God, Its frame His truth and grace,
And, far as foot of man hath trod, It finds a rest - ing place.
5. And when the course of time has run His lov - ing call will ring,
And it will rise, e'er with the Son To dwell, the sov - 'reign King.
6. Thy new cre - a - tion, Lord, di - rect, Till fixed a - bove se - cure;
O Fa - ther, from its foes pro - tect; O, cleanse it, Spir - it Pure.

1. To crown that per - fect bliss of__ Thine, Cre - a - tion nought can give;
Yet__ issu - ing from Thy se - cret shrine, Thou bid'st a world to live.
2. The morn - ing stars to - geth - er__ sing, The sons of God re - joice,
For__ earth and skies to be - ing spring At Thy cre - at - ing Voice.
3. But while so fair to out - ward_ view A - rose the earth and skies,
A__ fair - er world Thy will fore - knew Here - af - ter to a - rise.

4. Its Mak - er Christ, our Lord and_ God, Its frame His truth and grace,
And,_ far as foot of man hath trod, It finds a rest - ing place.
5. And when the course of time has_ run His lov - ing call will ring,
And_ it will rise, e'er with the Son To dwell, the sov - 'reign King.
6. Thy new cre - a - tion, Lord, di - rect, Till fixed a - bove se - cure;
O___ Fa - ther, from its foes pro - tect; O, cleanse it, Spir - it Pure.

413 WINDSOR — *Rebus Creatis Nil Egens* — English Translation by Campbell of Skerrington

4. Its Mak - er Christ, our Lord and God, Its frame His truth and grace,
And, far as foot of man hath trod, It finds a rest - ing place.
5. And when the course of time has run His lov - ing call will ring,
And it will rise, e'er with the Son To dwell, the sov - 'reign King.
6. Thy new cre - a - tion, Lord, di - rect, Till fixed a - bove se - cure;
O Fa - ther, from its foes pro - tect; O, cleanse it, Spir - it Pure.

414 ST FULBERT — *Rebus Creatis Nil Egens* — English Translation by Campbell of Skerrington

4. Its Mak - er Christ, our Lord and God, Its frame His truth and grace,
And, far as foot of man hath trod, It finds a rest - ing place.
5. And when the course of time has run His lov - ing call will ring,
And it will rise, e'er with the Son To dwell, the sov - 'reign King.
6. Thy new cre - a - tion, Lord, di - rect, Till fixed a - bove se - cure;
O Fa - ther, from its foes pro - tect; O, cleanse it, Spir - it Pure.

415 WINCHESTER OLD — *Rebus Creatis Nil Egens* — English Translation by Campbell of Skerrington

1. To crown that per - fect bliss of Thine, Cre - a - tion nought can give;
Yet issu - ing from Thy se - cret shrine, Thou bid'st a world to live.
2. The morn - ing stars to - geth - er sing, The sons of God re - joice,
For earth and skies to be - ing spring At Thy cre - at - ing Voice.
3. But while so fair to out - ward view A - rose the earth and skies,
A fair - er world Thy will fore - knew Here - af - ter to a - rise.

4. Its Mak - er Christ, our Lord and God, Its frame His truth and grace,
And, far as foot of man hath trod, It finds a rest - ing place.
5. And when the course of time has run His lov - ing call will ring,
And it will rise, e'er with the Son To dwell, the sov - 'reign King.
6. Thy new cre - a - tion, Lord, di - rect, Till fixed a - bove se - cure;
O Fa - ther, from its foes pro - tect; O, cleanse it, Spir - it Pure.

 ST ANNE — *Rebus Creatis Nil Egens* — English Translation by Campbell of Skerrington

4. Its Mak - er Christ, our Lord and God, Its frame His truth and grace,
And, far as foot of man hath trod, It finds a rest - ing place.
5. And when the course of time has run His lov - ing call will ring,
And it will rise, e'er with the Son To dwell, the sov - 'reign King.
6. Thy new cre - a - tion, Lord, di - rect, Till fixed a - bove se - cure;
O Fa - ther, from its foes pro - tect; O, cleanse it, Spir - it Pure.

422 ALFRETON — *Rex Sempiterne Domine* — English Translation by Father Fitzpatrick

1. To Thee, O ev - er - last - ing King, And Mak - er of the worlds, we sing,
Who, with the Fa - ther ev - er one, Wert ev - er His co - e - qual Son.
2. Cre - a - tor who, when earth be - gan, To Thine own im - age mad - est man,
Thou didst, in Ad - am, wed to clay A spir - it no - ble ev - 'ry way.
3. And when, with en - vy man - y - wiled, The dev - il had our race de - filed,
Made Man, man's like - ness un - to Thee Thou didst re - store with mas - ter - y.
4. Now born a - gain from out the tomb, As once, from Mar - y's vir - gin womb,

Thou bidd - est us our - selves be - stir And quit with Thee the sep - ul - chre.
5. E - ter - nal Shep - herd, who dost purge The flock in Thy bap - tis - mal_ surge:
This is the bath from which a - rise Pure thoughts, and where sin bur - ied lies.
6. Re - deem - er, on the Cross up - raised, Long ow - ing to our - selves, be_praised
That there Thy Blood sal - va - tion's price Paid lav - ish - ly in sac - ri - fice.
7. May end - less worlds the glo - ries tell Of Christ, who van - quished death and_ hell;
And one e - ter - nal praise re - peat The Fa - ther and the Par - a - clete.

 ERSCHIENEN IST — *Rex Sempiterne Domine* — English Translation by Father Fitzpatrick

1. To Thee, O ev - er - last - ing King, And Mak - er of the worlds, we sing, Who, with the Fa - ther ev - er one, Wert ev - er His co - e - qual Son. Al - le - lu - ia.
2. Cre - a - tor who, when earth be - gan, To Thine own im - age madest man, Thou didst, in Ad - am, wed to clay A spir - it no - ble ev - 'ry way. Al - le - lu - ia.

3. And when, with en - vy man - y - wiled, The dev - il
had our race de - filed, Made Man, man's like - ness un - to Thee
Thou didst re - store with mas - ter - y. Al - le - lu - ia.
4. Now born a - gain from out the tomb, As once, from
Mar - y's vir - gin womb, Thou bidd - est us our - selves be - stir
And quit with Thee the sep - ul - chre. Al - le - lu - ia.

5. E - ter - nal Shep - herd, who dost purge The flock in
Thy bap - tis - mal surge: This is the bath from which a - rise
Pure thoughts, and where sin bur - ied lies. Al - le - lu - ia.
6. Re - deem - er, on the Cross up - raised, Long ow - ing
to our - selves, be praised That there Thy Blood sal - va - tion's price
Paid lav - ish - ly in sac - ri - fice. Al - le - lu - ia.

7. May end - less worlds the glo - ries tell Of Christ, who
van - quished death and hell; And one__ e - ter - nal praise re - peat
The Fa - ther and the Par - a - clete. Al - le - lu - ia.

GRÉLON — *Rex Sempiterne Domine* — English Translation by Father Fitzpatrick

Thou bidd - est us our - selves be - stir And quit with Thee the sep - ul - chre.
5. E - ter - nal Shep - herd, who dost purge The flock in Thy bap - tis - mal surge:
This is the bath from which a - rise Pure thoughts, and where sin bur - ied lies.
6. Re - deem - er, on the Cross up - raised, Long ow - ing to our - selves, be praised
That there Thy Blood sal - va - tion's price Paid lav - ish - ly in sac - ri - fice.
7. May end - less worlds the glo - ries tell Of Christ, who van - quished death and hell;
And one e - ter - nal praise re - peat The Fa - ther and the Par - a - clete.

425 DEUS TUORUM MILITUM — *Rex Sempiterne Domine* — English Translation by Father Fitzpatrick

Thou bidd - est us our - selves be - stir And quit_ with Thee_ the sep - ul - chre.
5. E - ter - nal Shep - herd, who_ dost purge The flock in Thy_ bap - tis - mal surge:
This is the bath from which a - rise Pure thoughts, and where sin bur - ied lies.
6. Re - deem - er, on the Cross up - raised, Long ow - ing to___ our - selves, be praised
That there Thy Blood sal - va - tion's price Paid lav - ish - ly___ in sac - ri - fice.
7. May end - less worlds the glo - ries tell Of Christ, who van - quished death and
hell; And one e - ter - nal praise re - peat The Fa - ther and_ the Par - a - clete.

1. To Thee, O ev - er - last - ing King, And Mak - er of the worlds,_ we sing,
Who, with the Fa - ther ev - er one, Wert ev - er His_ co - e - qual Son.
2. Cre - a - tor who, when earth be - gan, To Thine_ own im - age mad - est man,
Thou didst, in Ad - am, wed to clay A spir - it no - ble ev - 'ry way.
3. And when, with en - vy man - y - wiled, The dev - il had our race_ de - filed,
Made Man, man's like - ness un - to Thee Thou didst re - store_ with mas - ter - y.
4. Now born a - gain from out the tomb, As once,_ from Mar - y's vir - gin womb,

Thou bidd - est us our-selves be - stir And quit with Thee the sep - ul - chre.
5. E - ter - nal Shep - herd, who dost purge The flock in Thy bap - tis - mal surge:
This is the bath from which a - rise Pure thoughts, and where sin bur - ied lies.
6. Re - deem - er, on the Cross up - raised, Long ow - ing to our - selves, be praised
That there Thy Blood sal - va - tion's price Paid lav - ish - ly in sac - ri - fice.
7. May end - less worlds the glo - ries tell Of Christ, who van - quished death and hell;
And one e - ter - nal praise re - peat The Fa - ther and the Par - a - clete.

427 CANON VIII — *Rex Sempiterne Domine* — English Translation by Father Fitzpatrick

* *The beginning of the Canon is placed in brackets in SOPRANO and TENOR.*

Thou_ bidd - est_ us our - selves be - stir And quit with Thee the sep - ul - chre.
5. E - ter - nal Shep - herd, who dost purge The flock in Thy bap - tis - mal surge:
This_ is_ the_ bath from which a - rise Pure thoughts, and where sin bur - ied lies.
6. Re - deem - er, on the Cross up - raised, Long ow - ing to our - selves, be praised
That_ there Thy_ Blood sal - va - tion's price Paid lav - ish - ly in sac - ri - fice.
7. May end - less worlds the glo - ries tell Of Christ, who van - quished death and hell;
And_ one_ e - ter - nal praise_ re - peat The Fa - ther and the Par - a - clete.

430 MELCOMBE — *Rex Sempiterne Domine* — English Translation by Archbishop Bagshawe

1. E - ter - nal King of Heav-en's hosts, Who didst the U - ni - verse cre - ate,
Who ev - er e - qual art with Him, From whom Thou dost o - rig - i - nate:
2. Thou gav - est when the earth was new, To Ad - am's race Thine im - age bright;
His bas - er clay Thou didst en-due With spir - it breath-ing love and light.
3. And, when man's race had been de - filed, By Sa - tan's en - vious fraud and hate,
Thou didst as - sume man's flesh, and man In his lost beau - ty re - in - state.
4. Thou, who wast once of Vir - gin born, Now from the tomb art born a - gain,

And our poor dead and bur - ied race, To bid to rise with Thee dost deign.
5. E - ter - nal Shep-herd, thou thy sheep Dost in bap - tis - mal wa - ters dye;
Here let our hearts their na - ture steep, Here let our vic - es bur - ied lie.
6. Thou—though to us the Cross was due— Wast nailed up - on its sa - cred wood,
And for sal - va - tion's price didst give, Un - spar - ing - ly Thy Pre - cious Blood.
7. Be God the Fa - ther glo - ri - fied, And He who rose, from death, His Son,
And Thou, the Ho - ly Par - a - clete, While ev - er - last - ing ag - es run.

 DUGUET — *Rex Sempiterne Domine* — English Translation by Archbishop Bagshawe

And our poor dead and bur - ied_ race, To bid to rise with Thee dost deign.
5. E - ter - nal Shep-herd, thou thy sheep Dost in bap - tis - mal wa - ters dye;
Here let our hearts their na - ture_ steep, Here let our vic - es bur - ied lie.
6. Thou— though to us the Cross was due—Wast nailed up - on its sa - cred wood,
And for sal - va - tion's price didst_ give, Un - spar - ing - ly Thy Pre - cious Blood.
7. Be God the Fa - ther glo - ri - fied, And He who rose, from death, His Son,
And Thou, the Ho - ly Par - a - clete, While ev - er - last - ing ag - es run.

1. E - ter - nal King of Heav-en's hosts, Who didst the U - ni - verse cre - ate,
Who ev - er e - qual art with Him, From whom Thou dost o - rig - i - nate:
2. Thou_ gav - est when the earth was new, To Ad - am's race Thine im - age_ bright;
His_ bas - er clay Thou didst en - due With spir - it breath-ing love and light.
3. And,_ when man's race had been de - filed, By Sa - tan's en - vious fraud and_ hate,
Thou didst as - sume man's flesh, and man In his lost beau - ty re - in - state.
4. Thou,_ who wast once of Vir - gin born, Now from the tomb art born a - gain,

And our poor dead and bur-ied race, To bid to rise with Thee dost deign.
5. E - ter - nal Shep-herd, thou thy sheep Dost in bap - tis - mal wa - ters dye;
Here let our hearts their na - ture steep, Here let our vic - es bur - ied lie.
6. Thou— though to us the Cross was due— Wast nailed up - on its sa - cred wood,
And for sal - va - tion's price didst give, Un - spar - ing - ly Thy Pre - cious Blood.
7. Be God the Fa - ther glo - ri - fied, And He who rose, from death, His Son,
And Thou, the Ho - ly Par - a - clete, While ev - er - last - ing ag - es run.

 HILDERSTONE — *Rex Sempiterne Domine* — English Translation by Archbishop Bagshawe

#158 has (optional) organ accompaniment at a lower key.

And our poor dead and bur - ied race, To bid to__ rise with Thee dost deign.
5. E - ter - nal Shep - herd, thou thy sheep Dost in bap - tis - mal wa - ters dye;
Here let our hearts their na - ture steep, Here let our__ vic - es bur - ied lie.
6. Thou— though to us the Cross was due— Wast nailed up - on its sa - cred wood,
And for sal - va - tion's price didst give, Un - spar - ing - ly Thy Pre - cious Blood.
7. Be God the Fa - ther glo - ri - fied, And He who rose, from death, His Son,
And Thou, the Ho - ly Par - a - clete, While ev - er - last - ing ag - es run.

1. E - ter - nal King of Heav-en's hosts, Who didst the U - ni - verse cre - ate,
Who ev - er e - qual art with Him, From whom Thou dost o - rig - i - nate:
2. Thou gav - est when the earth was new, To Ad - am's race Thine im-age bright;
His bas - er clay Thou didst en - due With spir - it breath - ing love and light.
3. And, when man's race had been de - filed, By Sa - tan's en - vious fraud and hate,
Thou didst as - sume man's flesh, and man In his lost beau - ty re - in - state.
4. Thou, who wast once of Vir - gin born, Now from the tomb art born a - gain,

And our poor dead and bur-ied race, To bid_ to rise with Thee dost deign.
5. E - ter - nal Shep - herd, thou thy sheep Dost in bap - tis - mal wa-ters dye;
Here let our hearts their na-ture steep, Here let_ our vic - es bur-ied lie.
6. Thou— though to us the Cross was due— Wast nailed up - on_ its sa-cred wood,
And for sal - va - tion's price didst give, Un - spar - ing - ly Thy Pre-cious Blood.
7. Be God the Fa - ther glo-ri - fied, And He who rose,_ from death, His Son,
And Thou, the Ho - ly Par-a - clete, While ev - er - last - ing ag-es run.

435 EISENACH — *Rex Sempiterne Domine* — English Translation by Archbishop Bagshawe

And our poor dead and bur - ied race, To bid to rise_ with Thee dost deign.
5. E - ter - nal Shep - herd, thou thy sheep Dost in bap - tis - mal wa - ters dye;
Here let our hearts their na - ture steep, Here let our vic - es bur - ied lie.
6. Thou— though to us the Cross was due— Wast nailed up - on its sa - cred wood,
And for sal - va - tion's price didst give, Un - spar - ing - ly_ Thy Pre - cious Blood.
7. Be_ God the Fa - ther glo - ri - fied, And He who rose, from death, His Son,
And Thou, the Ho - ly Par - a - clete, While ev - er - last - ing ag - es run.

1. E - ter - nal King of Heav - en's hosts, Who didst the U - ni - verse cre - ate,
Who ev - er e - qual art with Him, From whom Thou dost o - rig - i - nate:
2. Thou gav - est when the earth was new, To Ad - am's race Thine im - age bright;
His bas - er clay Thou didst en - due With spir - it breath - ing love and light.
3. And, when man's race had been de - filed, By Sa - tan's en - vious fraud and hate,
Thou didst as - sume man's flesh, and man In his lost beau - ty re - in - state.
4. Thou, who wast once of Vir - gin born, Now from the tomb art born a - gain,

#105 has (optional) organ accompaniment at a lower key.

PASSION CHORALE — *Salve Caput Cruentatum* — English Translation by Monsignor Knox

1. O sa - cred head ill - us - èd, By reed and bram - ble scarred,
That i - dle blows have bruis - èd, And mock - ing lips have marred,
How dimmed that eye so ten - der, How wan those cheeks ap - pear,
How o - ver - cast the splen - dor That an - gel hosts re - vere!
2. What mar - vel if thou lan - guish, Vig - or and vir - tue fled,
Wast - ed and spent with an - guish, And pale as are the dead?
O by thy foes' de - ri - sion, That death en - dured for me,

Grant that_ thy o - pen vi - sion A sin - ner's eyes may see.
3. Good Shep - herd, spent with lov - ing, Look on me, who_ have strayed,
Oft by those lips un - mov - ing With milk and hon - ey stayed;
Spurn not_ a sin - ner's cry - ing Nor from thy love out cast,
But rest_ thy head in dy - ing On these frail arms at last.
4. In this thy sa - cred Pas - sion O that some share_ had I!
O may thy Cross - 's fash - ion O'er - look me when I die!

For these_ dear pains that rack thee A sin - ner's thanks re - ceive;
O, lest_ in death I lack thee, A sin - ner's care re - lieve.
5. Since death must be my end - ing, In that dread hour_ of need,
My friend - less cause be - friend - ing, Lord, to my res - cue speed;
Thy - self,_ dear Je - sus, trace me That pas - sage to the grave,
And from_ thy Cross em - brace me With arms out - stretched to save.

SALVE CAPUT CRUENTATUM is the concluding section of a much longer work (*Salve Mundi Salutare*) attributed to St. Bernard of Clairvaux (d. 1153). Catholics know it as "O Sacred Head Surrounded," an English translation by Sir Henry W. Baker (d. 1877). In addition to Baker's, we have included translations by Msgr. Ronald Knox and Fr. Dominic Popplewell. The latter is noteworthy in that it matches the original meter, while Knox and Baker do not.

Baker's famous rendering is rather free, but does correspond to the original:

> Verse 1 ("O Sacred Head") conveys vv. 1-2, whose final words rhyme (*íllita, cúria*).
> Verse 2 ("I see Thy strength") conveys vv. 3-4, whose final words rhyme (*mácie, fácie*).
> Verse 3 ("In this Thy bitter Passion") conveys vv. 5-6, whose final words rhyme (*delíciis, bráchiis*).

Protestant hymnals favor translations of "O Haupt voll Blut und Wunden," a German version of *Salve Caput Cruentatum* by Lutheran minister Paul Gerhardt (d. 1676). Catholic hymnals, on the other hand, favor Baker's version—which translates the original Latin—and this hymn is almost never omitted, as demonstrated by a few examples:

> *Hosanna Catholic Hymn Book* (Fr. Bonvin, 1914) p. 58
> *Parochial Hymnal* (Fr. Rossini 1936) p. 23
> *Mount Mary Hymnal* (Sister Gisela, 1937) p. 39
> *Daily Hymn Book* (Society of St. John the Evangelist, 1948) p. 72
> *Cantate Omnes* (Catholic Choirmasters' Guild, 1952) #33
> *Catholic Hymns* (Fr. Selner, 1954) p. 65
> *Mediator Dei Hymnal* (1955) p. 26
> *Christ the King Hymnal* (Fr. Knauff, 1955) p. 42
> *Parish Hymnal* (Sisters of St. Joseph, 1957) p. 9
> *New Saint Basil Hymnal* (1958) p. 41
> *Hymns, Psalms, and Spiritual Canticles* (Dr. Marier, 1983) p. 364
> *Catholic Hymn Book* (London Oratory, 1998) p. 106

1. O Sa - cred Head, sur - round - ed By crown of pierc - ing thorn,
O Bleed - ing Head, so wound - ed, Re - viled, and put__ to scorn,
Death's pal - lid hue comes o'er Thee, The glow of life de - cays,
Yet An - gel hosts a - dore Thee, And trem - ble as they gaze.

2. I see Thy strength and vig - or All fad - ing in the strife,
And Death, with cru - el ri - gor, Be - reav - ing Thee of life;
O ag - o - ny of dy - ing, O love to sin - ners free;
Je - sus, all grace sup - ply - ing, O turn Thy Face on me.
3. In this Thy bit - ter Pas - sion, Good Shep - herd, think of me
With Thy most sweet com - pas - sion, Un - wor - thy though I be:

Be - neath Thy Cross a - bid - ing For - ev - er would I rest,
In Thy dear love con - fid - ing, And with Thy Pres - ence blest.
4. O Je - sus, I a - dore Thee, My thorn - crowned Lord and King;
I bow my heart be - fore Thee, Thy gra - cious Name I sing:
Thy Name that brought sal - va - tion, Thy Name, in life my stay,
My hope and con - so - la - tion When life shall fade a - way.

446 FORTESCUE — *Sancti Venite, Christi Corpus Sumite* — English Translation by Father Fortescue

1. Come all ye ho - ly, take the bod - y of your Lord,
Drink of his chal - ice, take the blood for you out-poured.
Saved by his bod - y, by his sa - cred blood, we raise
Grate - ful our voic - es un - to God in hymns of praise.
2. Christ our sal - va - tion, he who is the Son of God, Pur - chased our ran - som
by his cross and pre-cious blood. Dy - ing for all men, he the Lord pre -
pared this feast, Of - fered as vic - tim, of - fer - ing him - self as priest.

3. God to our fa - thers or - dered sac - ri - fice of old;
So he in sym - bols Christ the vic - tim true fore - told.
Source of all bright - ness, sole Re - deem - er of our race,
He to his ho - ly ser - vants gives a - bun - dant grace.
4. Come, who with pure hearts in the Sav - ior's word be - lieve;
Come, and par - tak - ing sav - ing grace from him re - ceive.

God our de - fend - er, guard - ian sure in this our strife,
Gives to his faith - ful af - ter death e - ter - nal life.
5. Bread come from heav - en gives he to the hun - ger - ing,
As for the thirst - y o - pens he the liv - ing spring.
Christ, source of all things, who here feeds us sin - ful men,
When this great day dawns, judge of all, will come a - gain.

1. San - cti ve - ní - te, Chri - sti cor - pus sú - mi - te,
san - ctum bi - bén - tes, quo red - ém - pti sán - gui - nem.
Sal - vá - ti Chri - sti cór - po - re et sán - gui - ne,
a quo re - fé - cti lau - des di - cá - mus De - o.
2. Da - tor sa - lú - tis, Chri-stus Fí - li - us De - i, mun - dum sal - vá - vit
per cru - cem et sán - gui - nem. Pro u - ni - vér - sis im - mo - lá - tus
Dó - mi - nus i - pse sa - cér - dos ex - í - stit et hó - sti - a.

3. Le - ge prae - cé - ptum im - mo - lá - ri hó - sti - as,
qua ad - um - brán - tur di - ví - na my - sté - ri - a.
Lu - cis in - dúl - tor et sal - vá - tor ó - mni - um
prae - clá - ram san - ctis lar - gí - tus est grá - ti - am.
4. Ac - cé - dant o - mnes pu - ra men - te cré - du - li, su - mant ae - tér - nam
sa - lú - tis cu - stó - di - am. San - ctó - rum cu - stos, re - ctor quo - que
Dó - mi - nus vi - tam pe - rén - nem lar - gí - tur cre - dén - ti - bus.

5. Cae - lé - stem pa - nem dat e - su - ri - én - ti - bus;
de fon - te vi - vo prae - bet si - ti - én - ti - bus.
Al - pha et Ó - me - ga i - pse Chri - stus Dó - mi - nus
ve - nit ven - tú - rus ju - di - cá - re hó - mi - nes.

 MANKATO — *Sancti Venite, Christi Corpus Sumite* — English Translation by Father Fortescue

Of - fered as vic - tim, of - fer - ing him - self as priest.
5. God to our fa - thers or - dered sac - ri - fice of old;
So he in sym - bols Christ the vic - tim true fore - told.
6. Source of all bright - ness, sole Re - deem - er of our race,
He to his ho - ly ser - vants gives a - bun - dant grace.
7. Come, who with pure hearts in the Sav - ior's word be - lieve;
Come, and par - tak - ing sav - ing grace from him re - ceive.

8. God our de - fend - er, guard - ian sure in this our strife,
Gives to his faith - ful af - ter death e - ter - nal life.
9. Bread come from heav - en gives he to the hun - ger - ing,
As for the thirst - y o - pens he the liv - ing spring.
10. Christ, source of all things, who here feeds us sin - ful men,
When this great day dawns, judge of all, will come a - gain.

1. San - cti ve - ní - te, Chri - sti cor - pus sú - mi - te,
san - ctum bi - bén - tes, quo red - ém - pti sán - gui - nem.
2. Sal - vá - ti Chri - sti cór - po - re et sán - gui - ne,
a quo re - fé - cti lau - des di - cá - mus De - o.
3. Da - tor sa - lú - tis, Chri - stus Fí - li - us De - i,
mun - dum sal - vá - vit per cru - cem et sán - gui - nem.

4. Pro u - ni - vér - sis im - mo - lá - tus Dó - mi - nus
i - pse sa - cér - dos ex - í - stit et hó - sti - a.
5. Le - ge prae - cé - ptum im - mo - lá - ri hó - sti - as,
qua ad - um - brán - tur di - ví - na my - sté - ri - a.
6. Lu - cis in - dúl - tor et sal - vá - tor ó - mni - um
prae - clá - ram san - ctis lar - gí - tus est grá - ti - am.
7. Ac - cé - dant o - mnes pu - ra men - te cré - du - li,

su - mant ae - tér - nam sa - lú - tis cu - stó - di - am.
8. San - ctó - rum cu - stos, re - ctor quo - que Dó - mi - nus
vi - tam pe - rén - nem lar - gí - tur cre - dén - ti - bus.
9. Cae - lé - stem pa - nem dat e - su - ri - én - ti - bus;
de fon - te vi - vo prae - bet si - ti - én - ti - bus.
10. Al - pha et Ó - me - ga i - pse Chri - stus Dó - mi - nus
ve - nit ven - tú - rus ju - di - cá - re hó - mi - nes.

1. Come all ye ho - ly, take the bod - y of your Lord, Drink of his
chal - ice, take the blood for you out - poured. Al - le - lu - ia.
2. Saved by his bod - y, by his sa - cred blood, we raise Grate - ful our
voic - es un - to God in hymns of praise. Al - le - lu - ia.
3. Christ our sal - va - tion, he who is the Son of God, Pur - chased our
ran - som by his cross and pre - cious blood. Al - le - lu - ia.

4. Dy - ing for all___ men, he the Lord pre - pared this feast, Of - fered as
vic - tim, of - fer - ing him - self as priest. Al - le - lu - - ia.
5. God to our fa - thers or - dered sac - ri - fice of old; So___ he in
sym - bols Christ the vic - tim true fore - told. Al - le - lu - ia.
6. Source of all bright - ness, sole Re - deem - er of our race, He___ to his
ho - ly ser - vants gives a - bun - dant grace. Al - le - lu - ia.
7. Come, who with pure___ hearts in the Sav - ior's word be - lieve; Come,___ and par -

tak - ing sav-ing grace from him re-ceive. Al - le - lu - - ia.
8. God our de - fend - er, guard-ian sure in this our strife, Gives__ to his
faith - ful af - ter death e - ter - nal life. Al - le - lu - - ia.
9. Bread come from heav - en gives he to the hun - ger - ing, As__ for the
thirst - y o-pens he the liv-ing spring. Al - le - lu - - ia.
10. Christ, source of all__ things, who here feeds us sin - ful men, When__ this great
day dawns, judge of all, will come a - gain. Al - le - lu - ia.

1. San - cti ve - ní - te, Chri-sti cor - pus sú - mi - te, san - ctum bi -
bén - tes, quo red - ém - pti sán - gui - nem. Al - le - lu - - ia.
2. Sal - vá - ti Chri - sti cór - po - re et sán - gui - ne, a quo re -
fé - cti lau - des di - cá - mus De - o. Al - le - lu - - ia.
3. Da - tor sa - lú - tis, Chri - stus Fí - li - us De - i, mun - dum sal -
vá - vit per cru - cem et sán - gui - nem. Al - le - lu - - ia.

4. Pro u - ni - vér - sis im - mo - lá - tus Dó - mi - nus i - pse sa -
cér - dos ex - í - stit et hó - sti - a. Al - le - lu - ia.
5. Le - ge prae - cé - ptum im - mo - lá - ri hó - sti - as, qua___ ad - um -
brán - tur di - ví - na my - sté - ri - a. Al - le - lu - ia.
6. Lu - cis in - dúl - tor et sal - vá - tor ó - mni - um prae - clá - ram
san - ctis lar - gí - tus est grá - ti - am. Al - le - lu - ia.
7. Ac - cé - dant o - mnes pu - ra men - te cré - du - li, su - mant ae -

tér - nam sa - lú - tis cu - stó - di - am. Al - le - lu - - ia.
8. San - ctó - rum cu - stos, re - ctor quo - que Dó - mi - nus vi - tam pe -
rén - nem lar - gí - tur cre - dén - ti - bus. Al - le - lu - ia.
9. Cae - lé - stem pa - nem dat e - su - ri - én - ti - bus; de fon - te
vi - vo prae - bet si - ti - én - ti - bus. Al - le - lu - - ia.
10. Al - pha et Ó - me - ga i - pse Chri - stus Dó - mi - nus ve - nit ven -
tú - rus ju - di - cá - re hó - mi - nes. Al - le - lu - - ia.

1. Come_ all ye ho - ly, take the bod - y of your Lord, Drink_
of his chal - ice, take the blood for you out-poured. Al - le - lu - ia.
2. Saved_ by his bod - y, by his sa - cred blood, we raise Grate -
ful our voic - es un - to God in hymns of praise. Al - le - lu - ia.
3. Christ_ our sal - va - tion, he who is the Son of God, Pur -
chased our ran - som by his cross and pre-cious blood. Al - le - lu - ia.
4. Dy - ing for all_ men, he the Lord pre - pared this feast, Of -

fered as vic - tim, of - fer - ing him - self as priest. Al - le - lu - ia.
5. God to our fa - thers or - dered sac - ri - fice of old; So
he in sym - bols Christ the vic - tim true fore - told. Al - le - lu - ia.
6. Source of all bright - ness, sole Re - deem - er of our race, He
to his ho - ly ser - vants gives a - bun - dant grace. Al - le - lu - ia.
7. Come, who with pure hearts in the Sav - ior's word be - lieve; Come,
and par - tak - ing sav - ing grace from him re - ceive. Al - le - lu - ia.

8. God__ our de - fend - er, guard-ian sure in this our strife, Gives_
to his faith - ful af - ter death e - ter - nal life. Al - le - lu - ia.
9. Bread__ come from heav - en gives he to the hun - ger - ing, As__
for the thirst - y o - pens he the liv - ing spring. Al - le - lu - ia.
10. Christ,__ source of all__ things, who here feeds us sin - ful men, When_
this great day__ dawns, judge of all, will come a - gain. Al - le - lu - ia.

1. San - cti ve - ní - te, Chri - sti cor - pus sú - mi - te, san -
ctum bi - bén - tes, quo red - ém - pti sán - gui - nem. Al - le - lu - ia.
2. Sal - vá - ti Chri - sti cór - po - re et sán - gui - ne, a
quo re - fé - cti lau - des di - cá - mus De - o. Al - le - lu - ia.
3. Da - tor sa - lú - tis, Chri - stus Fí - li - us De - i, mun -
dum sal - vá - vit per cru - cem et sán - gui - nem. Al - le - lu - ia.

4. Pro — u - ni - vér - sis im - mo - lá - tus Dó - mi - nus i -
pse sa - cér - dos ex - í - stit et hó - sti - a. Al - le - lu - ia.
5. Le - ge prae - cé - ptum im - mo - lá - ri hó - sti - as, qua —
ad - um - brán - tur di - ví - na my - sté - ri - a. Al - le - lu - ia.
6. Lu - cis in - dúl - tor et sal - vá - tor ó - mni - um prae -
clá - ram san - ctis lar - gí - tus est grá - ti - am. Al - le - lu - ia.
7. Ac - cé - dant o - mnes pu - ra men - te cré - du - li, su -

mant ae - tér - nam sa - lú - tis cu - stó - di - am. Al - le - lu - ia.
8. San - ctó - rum cu - stos, re - ctor quo - que Dó - mi - nus vi -
tam pe - rén - nem lar - gí - tur cre - dén - ti - bus. Al - le - lu - ia.
9. Cae - lé - stem pa - nem dat e - su - ri - én - ti - bus; de
fon - te vi - vo prae - bet si - ti - én - ti - bus. Al - le - lu - ia.
10. Al - pha et Ó - me - ga i - pse Chri - stus Dó - mi - nus ve -
nit ven - tú - rus ju - di - cá - re hó - mi - nes. Al - le - lu - ia.

ZAHN 5B — *Sancti Venite, Christi Corpus Sumite* — English Translation by Father Fortescue

1. Come_ all ye_ ho - ly, take the bod - y of your_ Lord,
Drink_ of his_ chal - ice, take the blood for you out - poured.
R. Chri - sti ca - ro_ ci - bus est.
2. Saved_ by his_ bod - y,
by his sa - cred blood, we_ raise
Grate - ful our_ voic - es
un - to God in hymns of_ praise.
R. Chri - sti ca - ro_ ci - bus est.
3. Christ_ our sal - va - tion, he who is the Son of_ God,

Pur - chased our ran - som by his cross and pre - cious blood.
R. Chri - sti ca - ro ci - bus est.
4. Dy - ing for all men,
he the Lord pre - pared this feast,
Of - fered as vic - tim,
of - fer-ing him - self as priest.
R. Chri - sti ca - ro ci - bus est.
5. God to our fa - thers or - dered sac - ri - fice of old;
So he in sym - bols Christ the vic - tim true fore - told.

R. Chri - sti ca - ro__ ci - bus est.
6. Source__ of all__ bright - ness,
sole Re-deem - er of our__ race,
He__ to his__ ho - ly
ser - vants gives a - bun - dant__ grace.
R. Chri - sti ca - ro__ ci - bus est.
7. Come,__ who with__ pure__ hearts in the Sav-ior's word be - lieve;
Come,_ and par - tak - ing sav - ing grace from him re - ceive.
R. Chri - sti ca - ro__ ci - bus est.
8. God__ our de - fend - er,

guard - ian sure in this our strife, Gives to his faith - ful
af - ter death e - ter - nal life. R. Chri - sti ca - ro ci - bus est.
9. Bread come from heav - en gives he to the hun - ger - ing,
As for the thirst - y o - pens he the liv - ing spring.
R. Chri - sti ca - ro ci - bus est.
10. Christ, source of all things,
who here feeds us sin - ful men, When this great day dawns,
judge of all, will come a - gain. R. Chri - sti ca - ro ci - bus est.

1. San - cti ve - ní - te, Chri - sti cor - pus sú - mi - te,
san - ctum bi - bén - tes, quo red - ém - pti sán - gui - nem.
R. Chri - sti ca - ro ci - bus est.
2. Sal - vá - ti Chri - sti
cór - po - re et sán - gui - ne, a quo re - fé - cti
lau - des di - cá - mus De - o.
R. Chri - sti ca - ro ci - bus est.
3. Da - tor sa - lú - tis, Chri - stus Fí - li - us De - i,

mun - dum sal - vá - vit per cru-cem et sán - gui - nem.
R. Chri - sti ca - ro ci - bus est.
4. Pro u - ni - vér - sis
im - mo - lá - tus Dó - mi - nus i - pse sa - cér - dos
ex - í - stit et hó - sti - a.
R. Chri - sti ca - ro ci - bus est.
5. Le - ge prae - cé - ptum im - mo - lá - ri hó - sti - as,
qua ad - um - brán - tur di - ví - na my - sté - ri - a.

R. Chri - sti ca - ro ci - bus est.
6. Lu - cis in - dúl - tor
et sal - vá - tor ó - mni - um
prae - clá - ram san - ctis
lar - gí - tus est grá - ti - am.
R. Chri - sti ca - ro ci - bus est.
7. Ac - cé - dant o - mnes
pu - ra men - te cré - du - li,
su - mant ae - tér - nam
sa - lú - tis cu - stó - di - am.
R. Chri - sti ca - ro ci - bus est.
8. San - ctó - rum cu - stos,

re - ctor quo - que Dó - mi - nus vi - tam pe - rén - nem
lar - gí - tur cre - dén - ti - bus. R. Chri - sti ca - ro ci - bus est.
9. Cae - lé - stem pa - nem dat e - su - ri - én - ti - bus;
de fon - te vi - vo prae - bet si - ti - én - ti - bus.
R. Chri - sti ca - ro ci - bus est.
10. Al - pha et Ó - me - ga
i - pse Chri - stus Dó - mi - nus ve - nit ven - tú - rus
ju - di - cá - re hó - mi - nes. R. Chri - sti ca - ro ci - bus est.

1. Come_ all ye ho - ly, take the bod - y of your Lord,
Drink___ of his chal - ice, take the blood for you out - poured.
2. Saved_ by his bod - y, by his sa - cred blood, we raise
Grate - ful our voic - es un - to God in hymns of praise.
3. Christ_ our sal - va - tion, he who is the Son of God,
Pur - chased our ran - som by his cross and pre - cious blood.
4. Dy - ing for all____ men, he the Lord pre - pared this feast,

Of - fered as vic - tim, of - fer - ing him - self as priest.
5. God_ to our fa - thers or - dered sac - ri - fice of old;
So_____ he in sym - bols Christ the vic - tim true fore - told.
6. Source_ of all bright - ness, sole Re - deem - er of our race,
He_____ to his ho - ly ser - vants gives a - bun - dant grace.
7. Come,_ who with pure___ hearts in the Sav - ior's word be - lieve;
Come,__ and par - tak - ing sav - ing grace from him re - ceive.

8. God our de - fend - er, guard - ian sure in this our strife,
Gives to his faith - ful af - ter death e - ter - nal life.
9. Bread come from heav - en gives he to the hun - ger - ing,
As for the thirst - y o - pens he the liv - ing spring.
10. Christ, source of all things, who here feeds us sin - ful men,
When this great day dawns, judge of all, will come a - gain.

1. San - cti ve - ní - te, Chri - sti cor - pus sú - mi - te,
san - ctum bi - bén - tes, quo red - ém - pti sán - gui - nem.
2. Sal - vá - ti Chri - sti cór - po - re et sán - gui - ne,
a quo re - fé - cti lau - des di - cá - mus De - o.
3. Da - tor sa - lú - tis, Chri - stus Fí - li - us De - i,
mun - dum sal - vá - vit per cru - cem et sán - gui - nem.

4. Pro u - ni - vér - sis im - mo - lá - tus Dó - mi - nus
i - pse sa - cér - dos ex - í - stit et hó - sti - a.
5. Le - ge prae - cé - ptum im - mo - lá - ri hó - sti - as,
qua ad - um - brán - tur di - ví - na my - sté - ri - a.
6. Lu - cis in - dúl - tor et sal - vá - tor ó - mni - um
prae - clá - ram san - ctis lar - gí - tus est grá - ti - am.
7. Ac - cé - dant o - mnes pu - ra men - te cré - du - li,

su - mant ae - tér - nam sa - lú - tis cu - stó - di - am.
8. San - ctó - rum cu - stos, re - ctor quo - que Dó - mi - nus
vi - tam pe - rén - nem lar - gí - tur cre - dén - ti - bus.
9. Cae - lé - stem pa - nem dat e - su - ri - én - ti - bus;
de fon - te vi - vo prae - bet si - ti - én - ti - bus.
10. Al - pha et Ó - me - ga i - pse Chri - stus Dó - mi - nus
ve - nit ven - tú - rus ju - di - cá - re hó - mi - nes.

HARTFORD 5B — *Sancti Venite, Christi Corpus Sumite* — English Translation by Father Fortescue

1. Come all ye ho - ly, take the bod - y__ of__ your Lord,
Drink of his chal - ice, take the blood for you out - poured.
2. Saved by his bod - y, by his sa - cred_ blood,_ we raise
Grate - ful our voic - es un - to God in hymns of praise.
3. Christ our sal - va - tion, he who is the__ Son_ of God,
Pur - chased our ran - som by his cross and pre - cious blood.
4. Dy - ing for all men, he the Lord pre - pared this feast,

Of - fered as vic - tim, of - fer - ing him - self as priest.
5. God to our fa - thers or - dered sac - ri - fice_ of old;
So he in sym - bols Christ the vic - tim true fore - told.
6. Source of all bright - ness, sole Re - deem - er___ of___ our race,
He to his ho - ly ser - vants gives a - bun - dant grace.
7. Come, who with pure hearts in the Sav - ior's_ word be - lieve;
Come, and par - tak - ing sav - ing grace from him re - ceive.

8. God our de - fend - er, guard - ian sure in this our strife,
Gives to his faith - ful af - ter death e - ter - nal life.
9. Bread come from heav - en gives he to the hun - ger - ing,
As for the thirst - y o - pens he the liv - ing spring.
10. Christ, source of all things, who here feeds us sin - ful men,
When this great day dawns, judge of all, will come a - gain.

1. San - cti ve - ní - te, Chri - sti cor - pus__ sú - mi - te,
san - ctum bi - bén - tes, quo red - ém - pti sán - gui - nem.
2. Sal - vá - ti Chri - sti cór - po - re et__ sán - gui - ne,
a quo re - fé - cti lau - des di - cá - mus De - o.
3. Da - tor sa - lú - tis, Chri - stus Fí - li - us__ De - i,
mun - dum sal - vá - vit per cru - cem et sán - gui - nem.

4. Pro u - ni - vér - sis im - mo - lá - tus Dó - mi - nus
i - pse sa - cér - dos ex - í - stit et hó - sti - a.
5. Le - ge prae - cé - ptum im - mo - lá - ri hó - sti - as,
qua ad - um - brán - tur di - ví - na my - sté - ri - a.
6. Lu - cis in - dúl - tor et sal - vá - tor ó - mni - um
prae - clá - ram san - ctis lar - gí - tus est grá - ti - am.
7. Ac - cé - dant o - mnes pu - ra men - te cré - du - li,

su - mant ae - tér - nam sa - lú - tis cu - stó - di - am.
8. San - ctó - rum cu - stos, re - ctor quo - que Dó - mi - nus
vi - tam pe - rén - nem lar - gí - tur cre - dén - ti - bus.
9. Cae - lé - stem pa - nem dat e - su - ri - én - ti - bus;
de fon - te vi - vo prae - bet si - ti - én - ti - bus.
10. Al - pha et Ó - me - ga i - pse Chri - stus Dó - mi - nus
ve - nit ven - tú - rus ju - di - cá - re hó - mi - nes.

1. Come all ye ho - ly, take the bod - y of your Lord,
Drink of his chal - ice, take the blood for you out- poured.
2. Saved by his bod - y, by his sa - cred blood, we raise
Grate - ful our voic - es un - to God in hymns of praise.
3. Christ our sal - va - tion, he who is the Son of God,
Pur - chased our ran - som by his cross and pre - cious blood.
4. Dy - ing for all men, he the Lord pre - pared this feast,

Of - fered as vic - tim, of - fer - ing him - self as priest.
5. God to our fa - thers or - dered sac - ri - fice of old;
So he in sym - bols Christ the vic - tim true fore - told.
6. Source of all bright - ness, sole Re - deem - er of our race,
He to his ho - ly ser - vants gives a - bun - dant grace.
7. Come, who with pure hearts in the Sav - ior's word be - lieve;
Come, and par - tak - ing sav - ing grace from him re - ceive.

8. God__ our de - fend - er, guard - ian sure in this our strife,
Gives__ to his faith - ful af - ter death e - ter - nal life.
9. Bread__ come from heav - en gives he to the hun - ger - ing,
As____ for the thirst - y o - pens he the liv - ing spring.
10. Christ,__ source of all__ things, who here feeds us sin - ful men,
When__ this great day__ dawns, judge of all, will come a - gain.

1. San - cti ve - ní - te, Chri - sti cor - pus sú - mi - te,
san - ctum bi - bén - tes, quo red - ém - pti sán - gui - nem.
2. Sal - vá - ti Chri - sti cór - po - re et sán - gui - ne,
a quo re - fé - cti lau - des di - cá - mus De - o.
3. Da - tor sa - lú - tis, Chri - stus Fí - li - us De - i,
mun - dum sal - vá - vit per cru - cem et sán - gui - nem.

4. Pro u - ni - vér - sis im - mo - lá - tus Dó - mi - nus
i - pse sa - cér - dos ex - í - stit et hó - sti - a.
5. Le - ge prae - cé - ptum im - mo - lá - ri hó - sti - as,
qua ad - um - brán - tur di - ví - na my - sté - ri - a.
6. Lu - cis in - dúl - tor et sal - vá - tor ó - mni - um
prae - clá - ram san - ctis lar - gí - tus est grá - ti - am.
7. Ac - cé - dant o - mnes pu - ra men - te cré - du - li,

su - mant ae - tér - nam sa - lú - tis cu - stó - di - am.
8. San - ctó - rum cu - stos, re - ctor quo - que Dó - mi - nus
vi - tam pe - rén - nem lar - gí - tur cre - dén - ti - bus.
9. Cae - lé - stem pa - nem dat e - su - ri - én - ti - bus;
de fon - te vi - vo prae - bet si - ti - én - ti - bus.
10. Al - pha et Ó - me - ga i - pse Chri - stus Dó - mi - nus
ve - nit ven - tú - rus ju - di - cá - re hó - mi - nes.

1. Come all ye ho - ly, take the bod - y of your Lord, Drink of his
chal - ice, take the blood for you out-poured. Al - le - lu - ia.
2. Saved by his bod - y, by his sa-cred blood, we raise Grate - ful our
voic - es un - to God in hymns of praise. Al - le - lu - ia.
3. Christ our sal - va - tion, he who is the Son of God, Pur - chased our
ran - som by his cross and pre-cious blood. Al - le - lu - ia.
4. Dy - ing for all men, he the Lord pre-pared this feast, Of - fered as

vic - tim, of - fer - ing__ him - self as priest. Al - le - lu - ia.
5. God to our fa - thers or-dered sac - ri - fice of old; So__ he in
sym - bols Christ the vic - tim true fore-told. Al - le - lu - ia.
6. Source of all bright - ness, sole Re-deem-er of our race, He__ to his
ho - ly ser-vants gives_ a - bun-dant grace. Al - le - lu - ia.
7. Come, who with pure__ hearts in the Sav-ior's word be-lieve; Come,_ and par -
tak - ing sav-ing grace from him re-ceive. Al - le - lu - ia.

8. God our de - fend - er, guard - ian sure in this our strife, Gives_ to his
faith - ful af - ter death e - ter - nal life. Al - le - lu - ia.
9. Bread come from heav - en gives he to the hun - ger - ing, As___ for the
thirst - y o - pens he___ the liv - ing spring. Al - le - lu - ia.
10. Christ, source of all___ things, who here feeds us sin - ful men, When this great
day___ dawns, judge of all,___ will come a - gain. Al - le - lu - ia.

1. San - cti ve - ní - te, Chri - sti cor - pus sú - mi - te, san - ctum bi -
bén - tes, quo red - ém - pti sán - gui - nem. Al - le - lu - ia.
2. Sal - vá - ti Chri - sti cór - po - re et sán - gui - ne, a quo re -
fé - cti lau - des di - cá - mus De - o. Al - le - lu - ia.
3. Da - tor sa - lú - tis, Chri - stus Fí - li - us De - i, mun - dum sal -
vá - vit per cru - cem et sán - gui - nem. Al - le - lu - ia.

4. Pro u - ni - vér - sis im - mo - lá - tus Dó - mi - nus i - pse sa -
cér - dos ex - í - stit et hó - sti - a. Al - le - lu - ia.
5. Le - ge prae - cé - ptum im - mo - lá - ri hó - sti - as, qua ad - um -
brán - tur di - ví - na my - sté - ri - a. Al - le - lu - ia.
6. Lu - cis in - dúl - tor et sal - vá - tor ó - mni - um prae - clá - ram
san - ctis lar - gí - tus est grá - ti - am. Al - le - lu - ia.
7. Ac - cé - dant o - mnes pu - ra men - te cré - du - li, su - mant ae -

tér - nam sa - lú - tis cu - stó - di - am. Al - le - lu - ia.
8. San - ctó - rum cu - stos, re - ctor quo - que Dó - mi - nus vi - tam pe -
rén - nem lar - gí - tur cre - dén - ti - bus. Al - le - lu - ia.
9. Cae - lé - stem pa - nem dat e - su - ri - én - ti - bus; de fon - te
vi - vo prae - bet si - ti - én - ti - bus. Al - le - lu - ia.
10. Al - pha et Ó - me - ga i - pse Chri - stus Dó - mi - nus ve - nit ven -
tú - rus ju - di - cá - re hó - mi - nes. Al - le - lu - ia.

464 CHRIST IST ERSTANDEN — *Sancti Venite* — English Translation by Father Fortescue

1. Come all ye ho - ly, take the bod - y of your Lord, Drink of his
chal - ice, take the blood for you out - poured. Ky - rie - léy - son. Refrain!
R. Al - le - lu - ia, al - le - lu - ia, al - le - lu - ia.
2. Saved by his bod - y, by his sa - cred blood, we raise Grate - ful our
voic - es un - to God in hymns of praise. Ky - rie - léy - son. Refrain!
3. Christ our sal - va - tion, he who is the Son of God, Pur - chased our
ran - som by his cross and pre - cious blood. Ky - rie - léy - son. Refrain!

4. Dy - ing for all men, he the Lord pre - pared this feast, Of - fered as
vic - tim, of - fer - ing him - self as priest. *Ky - rie - léy - son. Refrain!*
5. God to our fa - thers or - dered sac - ri - fice of old; So he in
sym - bols Christ the vic - tim true fore - told. *Ky - rie - léy - son. Refrain!*
6. Source of all bright - ness, sole Re - deem - er of our race, He to his
ho - ly ser - vants gives a - bun - dant grace. *Ky - rie - léy - son. Refrain!*
7. Come, who with pure hearts in the Sav - ior's word be - lieve; Come, and par -
tak - ing sav - ing grace from him re - ceive. *Ky - rie - léy - son. Refrain!*

8. God our de - fend - er, guard-ian sure in this our strife, Gives to his
faith - ful af - ter death e - ter - nal life.___ Ky - rie - léy - son.
R. Al - le - lu - ia, al - le - lu - ia, al - le - lu - ia.
9. Bread come from heav - en gives he to the hun - ger - ing, As for the
thirst - y o - pens he the liv - ing spring.___ Ky - rie - léy - son. Refrain!
10. Christ, source of all___ things, who here feeds us sin - ful men, When this great
day___ dawns, judge of all, will come a - gain.___ Ky - rie - léy - son. Refrain!

1. San - cti ve - ní - te, Chri - sti cor - pus sú - mi - te, san - ctum bi -
bén - tes, quo red - ém - pti sán - gui - nem. Ky - rie - léy - son.
R. Al - le - lu - ia, al - le - lu - ia, al - le - lu - ia.
2. Sal - vá - ti Chri - sti cór - po - re et sán - gui - ne, a quo re -
fé - cti lau - des di - cá - mus De - o. Ky - rie - léy - son. Refrain!
3. Da - tor sa - lú - tis, Chri - stus Fí - li - us De - i, mun - dum sal -
vá - vit per cru - cem et sán - gui - nem. Ky - rie - léy - son. Refrain!

4. Pro u - ni - vér - sis im - mo - lá - tus Dó - mi - nus i - pse sa -
cér - dos ex - í - stit et hó - sti - a. Ky - rie - léy - son.
R. Al - le - lu - ia, al - le - lu - ia, al - le - lu - ia.
5. Le - ge prae - cé - ptum im - mo - lá - ri hó - sti - as, qua ad - um -
brán - tur di - ví - na my - sté - ri - a. Ky - rie - léy - son. Refrain!
6. Lu - cis in - dúl - tor et sal - vá - tor ó - mni - um prae - clá - ram
san - ctis lar - gí - tus est grá - ti - am. Ky - rie - léy - son. Refrain!

7. Ac - cé - dant o - mnes pu - ra men - te cré - du - li, su - mant ae -
tér - nam sa - lú - tis cu - stó - di - am. Ky - rie - léy - son. Refrain!
8. San - ctó - rum cu - stos, re - ctor quo - que Dó - mi - nus vi - tam pe -
rén - nem lar - gí - tur cre - dén - ti - bus. Ky - rie - léy - son. Refrain!
9. Cae - lé - stem pa - nem dat e - su - ri - én - ti - bus; de fon - te
vi - vo prae - bet si - ti - én - ti - bus. Ky - rie - léy - son. Refrain!
10. Al - pha et Ó - me - ga i - pse Chri - stus Dó - mi - nus ve - nit ven -
tú - rus ju - di - cá - re hó - mi - nes. Ky - rie - léy - son. Refrain!

1. Ap - proach, ye just, and take The_ Bod - y of the Lord;
Your thirst of spir - it slake With His dear Blood out - poured.
2. For you that Blood was shed, That_ Bod - y sac - ri - ficed;
Now in this Ban - quet fed, Sing prais - es un - to Christ.
Extra: For by this Sac - ra - ment The_ Sav - ior plan - neth well
To snatch the pen - i - tent From out the jaws of hell;
3. Who, dy - ing on the Cross, By_ His own Flesh and Blood

Re - deemed the world from loss And gave it back to God.
4. For all on Cal - v'ry slain, He__ Vic - tim was, and Priest,
And still He doth re - main Both, in this Sa - cred Feast.
5. When in the An - cient Law A__ priest the vic - tim slew,
In type the proph - ets saw The Mys - t'ries of the New.
6. The Sav - ior and the Light Of__ all the hu - man race
Gives, in this Ho - ly Rite, A fount of end - less grace.

7. Draw nigh, be - liev - ing hearts, All pure and whol - ly shriv'n:
To you the Lord im - parts Him - self as pledge of heav'n.
8. By whom all crea - tures live, The Lord of life and death,
E - ter - nal life shall give To men of hum - ble faith,
9. And shall their hun - ger quench With liv - ing, heav'n-ly Bread,
Their thirst - ing spir - it drench With liv - ing foun - tains fed.
10. Al - pha - O - me - ga, when The course of time is sped,
Shall sure - ly come a - gain To judge the quick and dead.

1. Ap - proach, ye just, and take The Bod - y of the Lord;
Your thirst of spir - it slake With His dear Blood out - poured.
2. For you that Blood was shed, That Bod - y sac - ri - ficed;
Now in this Ban - quet fed, Sing prais - es un - to Christ.
Extra: For by this Sac - ra - ment The Sav - ior plan - neth well
To snatch the pen - i - tent From out the jaws of hell;
3. Who, dy - ing on the Cross, By His own Flesh and Blood

Re - deemed the world from loss And gave it back to God.
4. For all on Cal - v'ry slain, He Vic - tim was, and Priest,
And still He doth re - main Both, in this Sa - cred Feast.
5. When in the An - cient Law A priest the vic - tim slew,
In type the proph - ets saw The Mys - t'ries of the New.
6. The Sav - ior and the Light Of all the hu - man race
Gives, in this Ho - ly Rite, A fount of end - less grace.

7. Draw nigh, be - liev - ing hearts, All pure and whol - ly shriv'n:
To you the Lord im - parts Him - self_ as_ pledge of heav'n.
8. By whom all crea - tures live, The Lord of life and death, E - ter - nal
life shall give To men_ of_ hum - ble faith,
9. And shall their
hun - ger quench With liv - ing, heav'n-ly Bread, Their thirst-ing spir - it drench
With liv - ing_ foun - tains fed.
10. Al - pha - O - me - ga, when The course of
time is sped, Shall sure - ly come a - gain To judge the_ quick and dead.

 CLERMONT — *Sancti Venite, Christi Corpus Sumite* — English Translation by Monsignor Henry

1. Ap - proach, ye just, and take The Bod - y of the Lord;
Your thirst of spir - it slake With His dear Blood out - poured.
2. For you that Blood was shed, That Bod - y sac - ri - ficed;
Now in this Ban - quet fed, Sing prais - es un - to Christ.

* *A transposed organ accompaniment has been provided for optional use.*

Extra: For by this Sac - ra - ment The Sav - ior plan - neth well
To snatch the pen - i - tent From out the jaws of hell;
3. Who, dy - ing on the Cross, By His own Flesh and Blood
Re - deemed the world from loss And gave it back to God.
4. For all on Cal - v'ry slain, He Vic - tim was, and Priest,
And still He doth re - main Both, in this Sa - cred Feast.

5. When in the An - cient Law A priest the vic - tim slew,
In type the proph - ets saw The Mys - t'ries of the New.
6. The Sav - ior and the Light Of all the hu - man race
Gives, in this Ho - ly Rite, A fount of end - less grace.
7. Draw nigh, be - liev - ing hearts, All pure and whol - ly shriv'n:
To you the Lord im - parts Him - self as pledge of heav'n.

8. By whom all crea - tures live, The Lord of life and death,
E - ter - nal life shall give To men of hum - ble faith,
9. And shall their hun - ger quench With liv - ing, heav'n - ly Bread,
Their thirst - ing spir - it drench With liv - ing foun - tains fed.
10. Al - pha - O - me - ga, when The course of time is sped,
Shall sure - ly come a - gain To judge the quick and dead.

1. Draw nigh and take the Bod - y of the Lord And drink the ho - ly
Blood for you out - pour'd. By that pure Bod - y and that ho - ly Blood
Saved and re - freshed we ren - der thanks to God.
2. Sal - va - tion's
Giv - er, Christ, God's on - ly Son By His dear Cross and Blood the world hath
won. Of - fered was He for great - est and for least: Him - self the Vic - tim,
and Him - self the Priest.
3. Vic - tims were of - fered by the law of
old, Which in a type this heav'n - ly mys - t'ry told. He, Lord of

light, and Sav - ior of our race Hath giv - en to His saints a won - drous
grace.
4. Ap - proach ye then with faith - ful hearts sin - cere, And
take the safe - guard of sal - va - tion here. He that His saints in
this world rules and shields To all be - liev-ers life e - ter - nal yields.
5. He feeds the hun - gry with the Bread of Heav'n, And liv - ing
streams to those who thirst are giv'n. Al - pha and O - me - ga— to
whom shall bow All na - tions at the Doom— is with us now.

1. Draw nigh and take the Bod-y of the Lord And drink the ho - ly
Blood for you out-pour'd. By that pure Bod - y and that ho - ly Blood
Saved and re-freshed we ren-der thanks to God.
2. Sal - va-tion's
Giv - er, Christ, God's on - ly Son By His dear Cross and Blood the world hath
won. Of - fered was He for great-est and for least: Him - self the
Vic - tim, and Him-self the Priest.
3. Vic - tims were of - fered by the law of
old, Which in a type this heav'n-ly mys-t'ry told. He, Lord of

light, and Sav-ior of our race Hath_ giv-en to His saints a won-drous
grace.
4. Ap - proach ye then with faith-ful hearts sin - cere, And
take the safe - guard of sal-va-tion here. He that His saints in
this world rules and shields To___ all be - liev - ers life e - ter - nal yields.
5. He feeds the hun - gry with the Bread of Heav'n, And liv - ing streams
to those who thirst are giv'n. Al - pha and O - me -
ga— to whom shall bow All___ na-tions at the Doom— is with us now.

1. Draw nigh and take the Bod - y of the Lord And drink the ho - ly
Blood for you out - pour'd. By that pure Bod - y and that ho - ly Blood
Saved and re - freshed we ren - der thanks to God.
2. Sal - va - tion's Giv - er, Christ, God's on - ly Son By His dear Cross and Blood the world hath
won. Of - fered was He for great - est and for least: Him - self the
Vic - tim, and Him - self the Priest.
3. Vic - tims were of - fered by the law of old, Which in a type this heav'n-ly mys-t'ry told. He, Lord of

light, and Sav-ior of our race Hath giv-en to His saints a won-drous
grace.
4. Ap-proach ye then with faith-ful hearts sin-cere,
And take the safe-guard of sal-va-tion here. He that His saints
in this world rules and shields To all be-liev-ers life e-ter-nal
yields.
5. He feeds the hun-gry with the Bread of Heav'n, And liv-ing
streams to those who thirst are giv'n. Al-pha and O-me-ga— to
whom shall bow All na-tions at the Doom— is with us now.

1. Draw nigh and take the Bod - y of the Lord And drink the ho - ly
Blood for you out - pour'd. By that pure Bod - y and that ho - ly Blood
Saved and re - freshed we ren - der thanks to God.
2. Sal - va - tion's
Giv - er, Christ, God's on - ly Son By His dear Cross and Blood the world hath won.
Of - fered was He for great - est and for least: Him - self the Vic - tim,
and Him - self the Priest.
3. Vic - tims were of - fered by the law of old,
Which in a type this heav'n - ly mys - t'ry told. He, Lord of

light, and Sav - ior of our race Hath giv - en to His saints a
won - drous grace.
4. Ap - proach ye then with faith - ful hearts sin - cere,
And take the safe - guard of sal - va - tion here.
He that His
saints in this world rules and shields To all be - liev - ers life e -
ter - nal yields.
5. He feeds the hun - gry with the Bread of Heav'n,
And liv - ing streams to those who thirst are giv'n.
Al - pha and
O - me - ga—to whom shall bow All na - tions at the Doom—is with us now.

1. Draw nigh and take the Bod - y of the Lord And drink the ho - ly
Blood for you out - pour'd. By that pure Bod - y and that ho - ly Blood
Saved and re - freshed we ren - der thanks to God.
2. Sal - va-tion's Giv - er, Christ, God's on - ly Son By His dear Cross and Blood the world hath
won. Of - fered was He for great-est and for least: Him - self the Vic-tim,
and Him - self the Priest.
3. Vic - tims were of - fered by the law of
old, Which in a type this heav'n-ly mys-t'ry told. He, Lord of

light, and Sav - ior of our race Hath giv - en to His saints a
won - drous grace.
4. Ap - proach ye then with faith-ful hearts sin - cere,
And take the safe - guard of sal - va - tion here. He that His saints in
this world rules and shields To all be - liev - ers life e - ter - nal
yields.
5. He feeds the hun - gry with the Bread of Heav'n,
And liv - ing streams to those who thirst are giv'n. Al - pha and O - me -
ga— to whom shall bow All na - tions at the Doom— is with us now.

 FARLEY CASTLE — *Sancti Venite, Christi Corpus Sumite* — English Translation by Father Thurston

1. Draw nigh and take the Bod - y of the Lord And drink the ho - ly Blood for
you out - pour'd. By that pure Bod - y and that ho - ly Blood
Saved and re - freshed we ren - der thanks to God.
2. Sal - va - tion's
Giv - er, Christ, God's on - ly Son By His dear Cross and Blood the
world hath won. Of - fered was He for great - est and for least: Him - self the
Vic - tim, and Him - self the Priest.
3. Vic - tims were of - fered by the
law of old, Which in a type this heav'n-ly mys - t'ry told. He, Lord of

light, and Sav - ior of our race Hath giv - en to His saints a
won - drous grace.
4. Ap - proach ye then with faith - ful hearts sin - cere,
And take the safe - guard of sal - va - tion here. He that His
saints in this world rules and shields To all be - liev - ers life e -
ter - nal yields.
5. He feeds the hun - gry with the Bread of Heav'n,
And liv - ing streams to those who thirst are giv'n. Al - pha and O - me -
ga— to whom shall bow All na - tions at the Doom— is with us now.

1. At the Cross her sta - tion keep - ing, Stood the mourn - ful Moth - er weep - ing,
Close to Je - sus to the last.
2. Through her heart, his sor - row shar - ing,
All his bit - ter an - guish bear - ing,
Now at length the sword had pass'd.
3. Oh, how sad, how heav - y lad - en, Was that meek and bless - èd Maid - en,
God's true Moth - er un - de - filed.
4. Deep the well of her af - flic - tion
When she saw the Cru - ci - fix - ion Of her well be - lov - èd Son.
5. What man is there so un - feel - ing, Who, his heart to pit - y steel - ing,

* *A lower accompaniment is provided in the Brébeuf Organ Edition—for optional use.*

Could be - hold that sight un- moved?
6. Lives there one whose heart with an - guish
Fills not, thus to see her lan - guish,
Ag - o - niz - ing with her Son?
7. For the guilt that doomed his na - tion
Saw she Je - sus in pros - tra - tion
'Neath the scourg - es meek - ly bent;
8. Saw the Lord's A - noint - ed tak - en;
Saw her Child in death for - sak - en;
Heard his last ex - pir - ing cry.
9. Moth - er, fount whence love flows tru - est,
Let me know the pain thou knew - est,
Let me weep as thou hast wept;
10. Make me, lov - ing Christ, so love Him

That now, set - ting naught a - bove Him, To His Will my will may cleave.
11. Moth - er, eve - ry wound and trem - or Of the cru - ci - fied Re - deem - er,
Firm - ly fas - ten in my soul;
12. Since He deigns that all the mer - it
Of His wounds I should in - her - it All His pain with me di - vide.
13. Make me thy co - mourn - er tru - ly, For His cru - ci - fix - ion du - ly
Sorr' wing till my life is o'er:
14. Mine with thee be that sad sta - tion,
There to watch the great sal - va - tion Wrought up - on th'A - ton - ing Tree.
15. Vir - gin of all vir - gins fair - est, Share with me the pains thou bear - est,

Be thy crush - ing sor - rows mine.
16. Let me, mind - ful of His Pas - sion
Die in Christ, and, in some fash - ion,
Bear the wounds He bore for me.
17. All His bit - ter tor - ments feel - ing,
In the cross my spir - it reel - ing,
In His blood my sens - es drown.
18. Lest I burn in fires un - end - ing,
Sin - less Maid, my cause be - friend - ing,
Shield me at the judge - ment day.
19. Je - sus, when earth's shad - ows leave me,
Through thy Moth - er's prayers re - ceive me
With the palm of vic - to - ry.
20. When my bod - y lies for - sak - en
Let my ran - somed soul a - wak - en
Safe, in Par - a - dise, with thee.

1. Sta - bat Ma - ter do - lo - ró - sa
Jux - ta Cru - cem la - cri - mó - sa,
Dum pen - dé - bat Fí - li - us.
2. Cu - jus á - ni - mam ge - mén - tem,
Con - tri - stá - tam et do - lén - tem
Per - tran - sí - vit glá - di - us.
3. O quam tri - stis et af - flí - cta
Fu - it il - la be - ne - dí - cta
Ma - ter u - ni - gé - ni - ti!
4. Quae mae - ré - bat et do - lé - bat,
Pi - a Ma - ter, dum vi - dé - bat
Na - ti poe - nas ín - cli - ti.
5. Quis est ho - mo qui non fle - ret,
Ma - trem Chri - sti si vi - dé - ret

In tan - to sup - plí - ci - o?
6. Quis non pos - set con - tri - stá - ri,
Chri - sti Ma - trem con - tem - plá - ri
Do - lén - tem cum Fí - li - o?
7. Pro pec - cá - tis su - ae gen - tis,
Vi - dit Je - sum in tor - mén - tis,
Et fla - gél - lis súb - di - tum.
8. Vi - dit su - um dul - cem na - tum
Mo - ri - én - do de - so - lá - tum,
Dum e - mí - sit spí - ri - tum.
9. E - ja Ma - ter, fons a - mó - ris
Me sen - tí - re vim do - ló - ris
Fac, ut te - cum lú - ge - am.
10. Fac ut ár - de - at cor me - um

In a - mán - do Chri - stum De - um, Ut si - bi com - plá - ce - am.
11. San - cta Ma - ter, i - stud a - gas, Cru - ci - fí - xi fi - ge pla - gas
Cor - di me - o vá - li - de.
12. Tu - i na - ti vul - ne - rá - ti,
Tam di - gná - ti pro me pa - ti, Poe - nas me - cum dí - vi - de.
13. Fac me te - cum pi - e fle - re, Cru - ci - fí - xo con - do - lé - re,
Do - nec e - go víx - e - ro.
14. Jux - ta Cru - cem te - cum sta - re,
Et me ti - bi so - ci - á - re In plan - ctu de - sí - de - ro.
15. Vir - go vír - gi - num prae - clá - ra, Mi - hi jam non sis a - má - ra:

Fac me te - cum plán - ge - re.
16. Fac ut por - tem Chri - sti mor - tem
Pas - si - ó - nis fac con - sór - tem,
Et pla - gas re - có - le - re.
17. Fac me pla - gis vul - ne - rá - ri,
Fac me cru - ce i - ne - bri - á - ri,
Et cru - ó - re Fí - li - i.
18. Flam - mis ne u - rar suc - cén - sus,
Per te, Vír - go, sim de - fén - sus
In di - e ju - dí - ci - i.
19. Chri - ste, cum sit hinc ex - í - re,
Da per Ma - trem me ve - ní - re
Ad pal - mam vi - ctó - ri - ae.
20. Quan - do cor - pus mo - ri - é - tur,
Fac ut á - ni - mae do - né - tur
Pa - ra - dí - si gló - ri - a.

 ST CATHERINE — *Urbs Jerusalem Beata* — English Translation by Father Wallace

1. Cit - y Ce - les - tial, Sa - lem blest, Thy peace-ful vi - sion greets_ our eyes,
Thy walls on Christ's foun - da - tion rest, Thy tow'rs sur - mount the star - ry skies;
All like a bride en - gir - dled round With An - gels, who thy courts sur - round.
2. How hap-p'ly thou_ art wed - ded now, The Fa-ther's glo - ry is___ thy dow'r,
The Bride-groom's grace_ is on__ thy brow; A queen in beau - ty, rank,_ and pow'r,
Bound fast to Christ by nup - tial ties, A shin-ing tem - ple of the skies.
3. Thy gates, a - dorned_ with jew - els fair, Stand o - pen—all may en - ter in;

'Tis vir-tue must the heart pre-pare Of him who seeks thy courts to win,
Who for the love of Christ sus-tains Tor-ments His Ho-ly Will or-dains.
4. Stones which will form thy fear-some walls Stroke up-on stroke the chis-el hews,
The work-man's fre-quent ham-mer falls To make them fit-ting for his use;
Then deft-ly joins them each to each, Un-til thy tow'rs their sum-mit reach.
5. To God the Fa-ther, God Most High, Let all the world give hon-or meet;
And praise the Son with cease-less cry, And Ho-ly Ghost, the Par-a-clete,
To whom be pow-er, glo-ry, praise, Through lapse of ev-er-last-ing days.

 ST PHILIP — *Urbs Jerusalem Beata* — English Translation by Father Wallace

'Tis vir - tue must the heart_ pre - pare Of him who seeks_ thy courts to win,
Who for the love of Christ sus - tains Tor - ments His Ho - ly Will or - dains.
4. Stones which will form thy fear - some walls_ Stroke up - on stroke the chis - el hews,
The work - man's fre - quent ham - mer falls To make them fit - ting for his use;
Then deft - ly joins them each to each, Un - til thy tow'rs their sum - mit reach.
5. To God the Fa - ther, God Most High, Let all the world give hon - or meet;
And praise the Son with cease - less cry, And Ho - ly Ghost, the Par - a - clete,
To whom be pow'r, glo - ry, and praise, Through lapse of ev - er - last - ing days.

 VATER UNSER — *Urbs Jerusalem Beata* — English Translation by Father Wallace

1. Ce - les - tial Cit - y, Sa - lem blest, Thy peace - ful vi - sion greets our eyes,
Thy walls on Christ's foun - da - tion rest, Thy tow'rs sur - mount the star - ry skies;
All like a bride en - gir - dled round With An - gels, who thy courts sur - round.
2. How hap - p'ly thou art wed - ded now, The Fa - ther's glo - ry is thy dow'r,
The Bride - groom's grace is on thy brow; A queen in beau - ty, rank, and pow'r,
Bound fast to Christ by nup - tial ties, A shin - ing tem - ple of the skies.
3. Thy gates, a - dorned with jew - els fair, Stand o - pen— all may en - ter in;

'Tis vir - tue must the heart pre - pare Of him who seeks thy courts to win,
Who for the love of Christ sus - tains Tor - ments His Ho - ly Will or - dains.
4. Stones which will form thy fear - some walls Stroke up - on stroke the chis - el hews,
The work-man's fre - quent ham - mer falls To make them fit - ting for his use;
Then deft - ly joins them each to each, Un - til thy tow'rs their sum - mit reach.
5. To God the Fa - ther, God Most High, Let all the world give hon - or meet;
And praise the Son with cease-less cry, And Ho - ly Ghost, the Par - a - clete,
To whom be pow - er, glo - ry, praise, Through lapse of ev - er - last - ing days.

493 ANGELS' SONG 8E — *Urbs Jerusalem Beata* — English Translation by Father Wallace

'Tis vir-tue must the heart pre-pare Of him who seeks thy courts to win,
Who for the love of Christ sus-tains Tor-ments His Ho-ly Will or-dains.
4. Stones which will form thy fear-some walls Stroke up-on stroke the chis-el hews,
The work-man's fre-quent ham-mer falls To make them fit-ting for his use;
Then deft-ly joins them each to each, Un-til thy tow'rs their sum-mit reach.
5. To God the Fa-ther, God Most High, Let all the world give hon-or meet;
And praise the Son with cease-less cry, And Ho-ly Ghost, the Par-a-clete,
To whom be pow-er, glo-ry, praise, Through lapse of ev-er-last-ing days.

494 STELLA — *Urbs Jerusalem Beata* — English Translation by Father Wallace

'Tis vir - tue must the heart_ pre - pare Of him_ who seeks thy courts to win,
Who for_ the love of Christ_ sus - tains Tor - ments His Ho - ly Will or - dains.
4. Stones which_ will form thy fear - some walls Stroke up - on stroke the chis - el hews,
The work - man's fre - quent ham - mer falls To make them fit - ting for his use;
Then deft - ly joins them each_ to each, Un - til_ thy tow'rs_their sum - mit reach.
5. To God_ the Fa - ther, God_ Most High, Let all_ the world_ give hon - or meet;
And praise_ the Son with cease - less cry, And Ho - ly Ghost, the Par - a - clete,
To whom_ be pow - er, glo - ry, praise, Through lapse of ev - er - last-ing days.

500 CUPERTINO — *Veni Creator Spiritus* — English Translation by Father Fitzpatrick

1. Come, O Cre - a - tor - Spir - it, deign Our minds to vis - it, which are Thine;
Fill with Thy heav'n - ly grace a - gain Our hearts, which are Thy work di - vine.
2. The gift of God who reigns a - bove, Thou, who art called the Par - a - clete;
His liv - ing fount, His fire, His love, His unc - tion to the spir - it sweet.
3. Fin - ger of God's right hand art Thou; Thou dost a sev'n - fold gift im - part;
The Fa - ther's prom - ise, du - ly now En - rich - ing fal - t'ring tongues, Thou art.
4. Il - lu - mine Thou these minds of ours; Up - on our hearts Thy love out - pour,

Strength-en with Thine im - mor - tal pow'rs Our mor - tal weak-ness ev - er - more.
5. Our en - e - my drive far a - way; On us forth-with Thy peace be-stow,
If Thou but lead us day by day, No e - vil paths our feet shall go.
6. The Fa-ther un - to us make known, Make known His on - ly Son, no less,
And let us ev - er Thee a - lone The spir - it of Them both con - fess.
7. To God the Fa - ther glo - ry be, And to the Son, who from the dead
A - rose; like - wise e - ter - nal - ly The Par - a - clete be hal - low - èd.

503 IOANNES — *Veni Creator Spiritus* — English Translation by Campbell of Skerrington

1. Cre - a - tor-Spir - it, Lord of grace, Make Thou our hearts_ Thy dwell - ing place,
And with Thy might ce - les - tial, aid_ The souls of those_ whom Thou hast made.
2. Come from the Throne of God_ a - bove, O Par - a - clete, O ho - ly Dove;
Come, oil of glad - ness, cleans-ing fire_ And liv - ing spring of pure_ de - sire.
3. O Fin - ger of the Hand di - vine, The sev'n - fold gifts_ of grace are Thine,
And touched by Thee_ the lips_ pro - claim All praise to God's_ most ho - ly name.
4. Then to our souls Thy light im - part, And give Thy love_ to ev - 'ry heart;

Turn all our weak - ness in - to might, O Thou the source_ of life_ and light.
5. Far from us keep our cru - el foe, And peace from Thine own hand be - stow;
Up - held by Thee, our strength and guide, No e - vil can_ our steps be - tide.
6. Spir - it of faith, on us_ be - stow The Fa - ther and_ the Son to know;
And of the Twain, the Spir - it, Thee— E - ter - nal One,_ e - ter - nal Three.
7. To God the Fa - ther let_ us sing; To God the Son,_ our Ris - en King;
And e - qual - ly_ with these a - dore_ The Spir - it, God_ for ev - er - more.

1. Cre - a - tor - Spir - it, Lord of grace, Make Thou our
hearts Thy dwell-ing - place, And with Thy might ce - les - tial, aid
The souls of those whom Thou hast made. Al - le - lu - ia.
2. Come from the Throne of God a - bove, O Par - a -
clete, O ho - ly Dove; Come, oil of glad - ness, cleans - ing fire
And liv - ing spring of pure de - sire. Al - le - lu - ia.

3. O Fin - ger of the Hand di - vine, The sev'n - fold
gifts of grace are Thine, And touched by Thee the lips pro - claim
All praise to God's most ho - ly name. Al - le - lu - ia.
4. Then to our souls Thy light im - part, And give Thy
love to ev - 'ry heart; Turn all our weak - ness in - to might,
O Thou the source of life and light. Al - le - lu - ia.

5. Far from us keep our cru - el foe, And peace from
Thine own hand be - stow; Up - held_ by Thee, our strength and guide,
No e - vil can our steps be - tide. Al - le - lu - ia.
6. Spir - it of faith, on us___ be - stow The Fa - ther
and the Son to know; And of___ the Twain, the Spir - it, Thee—
E - ter - nal One, e - ter - nal Three. Al - le - lu - ia.

7. To God the Fa - ther let__ us sing; To God the
Son, our Ris - en King; And e - qual - ly__ with these a - dore
The Spir - it, God for ev - er - more. Al - le - lu - ia.

505 EISENACH — *Veni Creator Spiritus* — English Translation by Campbell of Skerrington

Turn all our weak - ness in - to might, O Thou the source of life and light.
5. Far__ from us keep our cru - el foe, And peace from Thine own hand be-stow;
Up - held by Thee, our strength and guide, No e - vil can__ our steps be - tide.
6. Spir - it of faith, on us be - stow The Fa-ther and the Son to know;
And of the Twain, the Spir - it, Thee— E - ter - nal One,__ e - ter - nal Three.
7. To__ God the Fa-ther let us sing; To God the Son, our Ris - en King;
And e - qual - ly with these a - dore The Spir - it, God__ for ev - er - more.

1. Cre - a - tor - Spir - it, Lord of grace, Make Thou our hearts Thy dwell - ing - place,
And with Thy might ce - les - tial, aid The souls of those whom Thou hast made.
2. Come from the Throne of God a - bove, O Par - a - clete, O ho - ly Dove;
Come, oil of glad - ness, cleans - ing fire And liv - ing spring of pure de - sire.
3. O Fin - ger of the Hand di - vine, The sev'n - fold gifts of grace are Thine,
And touched by Thee the lips pro - claim All praise to God's most ho - ly name.
4. Then to our souls Thy light im - part, And give Thy love to ev - 'ry heart;

Turn all our weak - ness in - to might, O Thou the source of life and light.
5. Far from us keep our cru - el foe, And peace from Thine own hand be - stow;
Up - held by Thee, our strength and guide, No e - vil can our steps be - tide.
6. Spir - it of faith, on us be - stow The Fa - ther and the Son to know;
And of the Twain, the Spir - it, Thee— E - ter - nal One, e - ter - nal Three.
7. To God the Fa - ther let us sing; To God the Son, our Ris - en King;
And e - qual - ly with these a - dore The Spir - it, God for ev - er - more.

507 WHITEHALL — *Veni Creator Spiritus* — English Translation by Campbell of Skerrington

Turn all our weak - ness in - to might, O Thou the source of life and light.
5. Far from us keep our cru - el foe, And peace from Thine own hand be - stow;
Up - held by Thee, our strength and guide, No e - vil can our steps be - tide.
6. Spir - it of faith, on us be - stow The Fa - ther and the Son to know;
And of the Twain, the Spir - it, Thee— E - ter - nal One, e - ter - nal Three.
7. To God the Fa - ther let us sing; To God the Son, our Ris - en King;
And e - qual - ly with these a - dore The Spir - it, God for ev - er - more.

1. Cre - a - tor - Spir - it, Lord of grace, Make Thou our hearts Thy dwell - ing - place,
And with Thy might ce - les - tial, aid The souls of those whom Thou hast made.
2. Come from the Throne of God a - bove, O Par - a - clete, O ho - ly Dove;
Come, oil of glad - ness, cleans - ing fire And liv - ing spring of pure de - sire.
3. O Fin - ger of the Hand di - vine, The sev'n - fold gifts of grace are Thine,
And touched by Thee the lips pro - claim All praise to God's most ho - ly name.
4. Then to our souls Thy light im - part, And give Thy love to ev - 'ry heart;

(♮)
Turn all our weak-ness in - to might, O Thou the source of life and light.
5. Far from us keep our cru - el foe, And peace from Thine own hand be - stow;
(♮)
Up - held by Thee, our strength and guide, No e - vil can our steps be - tide.
6. Spir - it of faith, on us be - stow The Fa - ther and the Son to know;
(♮)
And of the Twain, the Spir - it, Thee— E - ter - nal One, e - ter - nal Three.
7. To God the Fa - ther let us sing; To God the Son, our Ris - en King;
(♮)
And e - qual - ly with these a - dore The Spir - it, God for ev - er - more.

 LAMBILLOTTE — *Veni Creator Spiritus* — Translation (abridged) by Father Caswall

1. Come, Ho - ly Ghost, Cre - a - tor blest, And in our hearts take
up Thy rest; Come with Thy grace and heav'n - ly aid, To fill the
hearts which Thou hast made, To fill the hearts which Thou hast made.
2. O Com - fort - er, to Thee we cry, Thou heav'n - ly gift of
God most high, Thou Font of life and Fire of love, And sweet a -
noint - ing from a - bove, And sweet a - noint - ing from a - bove.

3. O Ho - ly Ghost, through Thee a - lone, Know we the Fa - ther
and the Son; Be this our firm un - chang - ing creed, That Thou dost
from them both pro - ceed, That Thou dost from them both pro - ceed.
4. Praise we the Lord, Fa - ther and Son, And Ho - ly Spir - it,
with them one; And may the Son on us be - stow All gifts that
from the Spir - it flow, All gifts that from the Spir - it flow.

516 NUN KOMM DER HEIDEN HEILAND — *Veni Redemptor Gentium* — English Transl. by Reynolds

1. Sav - ior of the na - tions, come; Vir - gin's Son, here make Thy home!
Mar - vel now, O heav'n and_ earth, That the Lord chose such_ a birth.
2. Not by hu - man flesh_ and blood, By the Spir - it of our God
Was the Word of God made_ flesh— Wom - an's Off - spring, pure_ and fresh.
3. Won - drous birth! O won - drous Child Of the Vir - gin un - de - filed!
Though by all the world dis - owned, Still to be in heav'n en - throned.
4. From the Fa - ther forth_ He came And re - turn - eth to the same,

Cap - tive lead - ing death and hell— High the song of tri - umph swell!
5. Thou, the Fa - ther's on - ly Son, Hast o'er sin the vic - t'ry won.
Bound - less shall Thy king - dom be; When shall we its glo - ries see?
6. Bright - ly doth Thy man - ger shine, Glo - rious is its light di - vine.
Let not sin o'er cloud this light; Ev - er be our faith thus bright.
7. Praise to God the Fa - ther sing, Praise to God the Son, our King,
Praise to God the Spir - it be Ev - er and e - ter - nal - ly.

517 O HEILAND REISS — *Veni Redemptor Gentium* — English Translation by Neale

1. Come, Thou Re-deem - er of the earth, And man - i - fest Thy vir-gin - birth:
Let ev-'ry age a - dor - ing fall; Such birth be - fits the God of all.
2. Be - got - ten of no hu-man will, But of the Spir - it, Thou art still
The Word of God in flesh ar-rayed, The prom-ised fruit to men dis - played.
3. The vir - gin womb that bur-den gained With vir-gin hon - or all un - stained;
The ban-ners there of vir - tue glow; God in His tem - ple dwells be - low.
4. Forth from His cham - ber go-eth He, That roy - al home of pu-ri - ty,
A giant in two - fold sub - stance one, Re-joic-ing now His course to run.

5. From God the Fa - ther He pro - ceeds, To God the Fa - ther back He speeds;
His course He runs to death and hell, Re-turn-ing on God's throne to dwell.
6. To God the Fa - ther e-qual, Word, Thy mor-tal ves - ture on Thee gird;
The weak-ness of our flesh at length Sus-tain-ing by Thy change-less strength.
7. Thy cra - dle here shall glit-ter bright, And dark-ness breathe a new-er light,
Where end-less faith shall shine se-rene, And twi-light nev - er in-ter - vene.
8. All hon - or, laud and glo-ry be, O Je-sus, Vir - gin-born, to Thee:
All hon-or, as is ev - er meet, To Fa-ther and to Par-a - clete.

519 AMYOT — *Veni Sancte Spiritus* — English Translation by Father Caswall

1. Ho - ly Spir - it, Lord of light, From the clear ce - les - tial height
Thy pure beam - ing ra - diance give: Come, Thou Fa - ther_ of the poor;
Come, with treas - ures which en - dure; Come, Thou Light of all that live.
2. Thou, of all con - sol - ers best, Thou, the soul's de - light - some guest,
Dost re - fresh - ing peace be- stow; Thou in toil art_ com - fort sweet;
Pleas - ant cool - ness in the heat; Sol - ace in the midst of woe.
3. Light im - mor - tal, light di - vine, Vis - it Thou these hearts of thine,

And our in - most be - ing fill. If Thou take thy_ grace a - way, Noth - ing pure in
man will stay; All his good is turn'd to ill.
4. Heal our wounds; our
strength re - new; On our dry - ness pour thy dew; Wash the stains of guilt a -
way: Bend the stub - born_ heart and will; Melt the fro - zen, warm the chill;
Guide the steps that go a - stray.
5. Thou, on those who ev - er - more
Thee con - fess and Thee a - dore, In Thy sev'n - fold gifts de - scend: Give them com - fort_
when they die; Give them life with Thee on high; Give them joys that nev - er end.

1. The Word pro - ceed - ing from a - bove, Yet leav - ing not the Fa - ther's side,
Goes forth un - to his work of love And comes to life's great e - ven - tide.
2. A mem - ber of his cho - sen band Would hand him o - ver to his foes:
Be - fore his death, him - self he hands As food of life to whom he chose.
3. To them be - neath two forms he gave His flesh and blood, com - plete and whole,
That man, of two - fold sub - stance made, Be fed in bod - y and in soul.

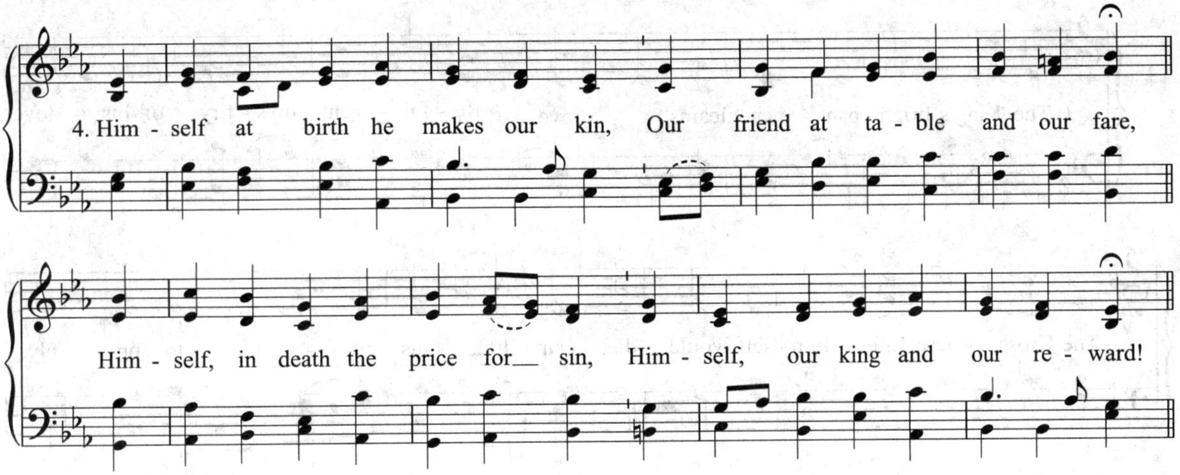
4. Him - self at birth he makes our kin, Our friend at ta - ble and our fare,
Him - self, in death the price for___ sin, Him - self, our king and our re - ward!

O Salutáris Hóstia

5. O sav - ing Vic - tim, op - 'ning wide The gate of Heav'n to man be - low,
Our foes press on from ev' - ry___ side, Thine aid sup - ply, Thy strength be - stow.
6. To Thy great Name be end - less praise, Im - mor - tal God - head, One in Three;
O grant us end - less length of___ days In our true na - tive land, with Thee.

529 NOTRE DAME — *Vexilla Regis Prodeunt* — English Translation by Father Husenbeth

1. The King's bright ban - ner gleams a - bove, Re - ful - gent mys - t'ry of his love,
The Cross, where Life him - self would die, Our life,_ thus dy - ing, to sup - ply.
2. The spear's sharp point laid o - pen wide That source of grace,_ his sa - cred side,
When forth with wa - ter streamed his blood To wash_ our souls, a sav - ing flood.
3. Ful - filled was that by Da - vid's tongue, Pro - phet - ic, once_ to na - tions sung:
That God in af - ter - ag - es should Reign Mon - arch from the Cross-'s wood.
4. O beau - teous tree, thy branch - es shine, Em - pur - pled by_ our king di - vine,

Pre-ferred his sa - cred limbs to bear, Such hon - or wor - thiest deemed to share.
5. Blest Cross, to grate - ful souls en - deared, Our ran - som on thine arms was reared,
And when thy bal - ance proved its worth, It snatched from hell the sons of earth.
In these most sol - emn Pas-sion days
6. O Cross, with hope the Chris-tian prays, Re - joic - ing in these pas-chal days,
Grace for the guilt - y and the just, Through Christ, our sole re - source and trust.
7. Blest Trin - i - ty, sal - va-tion's spring, Thy praise may eve - ry spir-it sing;
And where the Cross - 's tri-umphs glow, The Cross - 's glo - rious crown be - stow.

1. The King's bright ban - ner gleams a - bove, Re - ful - gent mys - t'ry of his love,
The Cross, where Life him - self would die, Our life, thus dy - ing, to sup - ply.
2. The spear's sharp point laid o - pen wide That source of grace, his sa - cred side,
When forth with wa - ter streamed his blood To wash our souls, a sav - ing flood.
3. Ful - filled was that by Da - vid's tongue, Pro - phet - ic, once to na - tions sung:
That God in af - ter - ag - es should Reign Mon - arch from the Cross - 's wood.
4. O beau - teous tree, thy branch - es shine, Em - pur - pled by our king di - vine,

Pre - ferred his sa - cred limbs to bear, Such hon - or wor - thiest deemed to share.
5. Blest Cross, to grate - ful souls en - deared, Our ran - som on thine arms was reared,
And when thy bal - ance proved its worth, It snatched from hell the sons of earth.
In these most sol - emn Pas - sion days
6. O Cross, with hope the Chris - tian prays, Re - joic - ing in these pas - chal days,
Grace for the guilt - y and the just, Through Christ, our sole re - source and trust.
7. Blest Trin - i - ty, sal - va - tion's spring, Thy praise may eve - ry spir - it sing;
And where the Cross - 's tri - umphs glow, The Cross - 's glo - rious crown be - stow.

 IOANNES — *Vexilla Regis Prodeunt* — English Translation by Father Husenbeth

Pre - ferred his sa - cred limbs to bear, Such hon - or wor - thiest deemed to share.
5. Blest Cross, to grate - ful souls en deared, Our ran - som on__ thine arms was reared,
And when thy bal - ance proved its worth, It snatched from hell__ the sons__ of earth.
In these most sol - emn Pas - sion days
6. O Cross, with hope the Chris-tian prays, Re - joic - ing in__ these pas - chal days,
Grace for the guilt - y and__ the just,__ Through Christ, our sole__ re - source and trust.
7. Blest Trin - i - ty, sal - va - tion's spring, Thy praise may eve - ry spir - it sing;
And where the Cross - 's tri - umphs glow, The Cross - 's glo - rious crown be - stow.

1. The King's bright ban - ner gleams a - bove, Re - ful - gent mys - t'ry of his love,
The Cross, where Life him - self would die, Our life, thus dy - ing, to sup - ply.
2. The spear's sharp point laid o - pen wide That source of grace, his sa - cred side,
When forth with wa - ter streamed his blood To wash our souls, a sav - ing flood.
3. Ful - filled was that by Da - vid's tongue, Pro - phet - ic, once to na - tions sung:
That God in af - ter - ag - es should Reign Mon - arch from the Cross - 's wood.
4. O beau - teous tree, thy branch - es shine, Em - pur - pled by our king di - vine,

Pre - ferred his sa - cred limbs to bear, Such hon - or wor - thiest deemed to share.
5. Blest Cross, to grate - ful souls en - deared, Our ran - som on thine arms was reared,
And when thy bal - ance proved its worth, It snatched from hell the sons of earth.
In these most sol - emn Pas - sion days
6. O Cross, with hope the Chris - tian prays, Re - joic - ing in these pas - chal days,
Grace for the guilt - y and the just, Through Christ, our sole re - source and trust.
7. Blest Trin - i - ty, sal - va - tion's spring, Thy praise may eve - ry spir - it sing;
And where the Cross - 's tri - umphs glow, The Cross - 's glo - rious crown be - stow.

 WAREHAM — *Vexilla Regis Prodeunt* — English Translation by Father Husenbeth

Pre - ferred his_ sa - cred limbs to bear, Such hon - or wor - thiest deemed to share.
5. Blest Cross, to grate - ful souls en deared, Our ran - som on_ thine arms was reared,
And when thy_ bal - ance proved its worth, It_ snatched from hell_ the sons_ of earth.
In these most sol - emn Pas - sion days
6. O Cross, with hope the Chris - tian prays, Re - joic - ing in_ these pas - chal days,
Grace for_ the_ guilt - y and the just, Through Christ, our sole_ re - source and trust.
7. Blest Trin - i - ty, sal - va - tion's spring, Thy praise may eve - ry spir - it sing;
And where the_ Cross - 's tri - umphs glow, The Cross - 's glo - rious crown be - stow.

1. The King's bright ban-ner gleams a-bove, Re-ful-gent mys-t'ry of his love,
The Cross, where Life him-self would die, Our life, thus dy-ing, to sup-ply.
2. The spear's sharp point laid o-pen wide That source of grace, his sa-cred side,
When forth with wa-ter streamed his blood To wash our souls, a sav-ing flood.
3. Ful-filled was that by Da-vid's tongue, Pro-phet-ic, once to na-tions sung:
That God in af-ter-ag-es should Reign Mon-arch from the Cross-'s wood.
4. O beau-teous tree, thy branch-es shine, Em-pur-pled by our king di-vine,

Pre - ferred his sa - cred limbs to bear, Such hon - or wor - thiest deemed to share.
5. Blest Cross, to grate-ful souls en-deared, Our ran-som on thine arms was reared,
And when thy bal-ance proved its worth, It snatched from hell the__ sons of earth.
In these most sol - emn Pas - sion days
6. O Cross, with hope the Chris-tian prays, Re - joic - ing in these pas - chal days,
Grace for the guilt - y and the just, Through Christ, our sole re - source and trust.
7. Blest Trin - i - ty, sal - va-tion's spring, Thy praise may eve - ry spir - it sing;
And where the Cross-'s tri - umphs glow, The Cross-'s glo - rious crown be - stow.

AGINCOURT — *Vexilla Regis Prodeunt* — English Translation by Campbell of Skerrington

1. The King of kings his ban - ner rears, The mys - ter - y of love ap - pears, The Lord of life re - signs his breath, And dy - ing ran - soms all from death.
2. Though bowed his head and closed his eyes, The love he bears us nev - er dies; And min - gled now, more liv - ing flows The stream that life on all be - stows.
3. What proph - ets sang in heav'n-ly strain, A king who should for ev - er reign, Be - hold up - on his pur - ple throne, Let all the earth his

scep - ter own.
4. O hon - ored cross, O beau-teous tree,
In E - den's bow'rs was_ none like thee;
What glo - ry may_ with thine com - pare
The Lord, the King of kings to bear?
5. Blest bal - ance, on whose arms is weighed
The price for our_ re - demp-tion paid—
The ran - som dear_ of sin-ful men,
To bring us back to God a - gain.
6. To thee, O Christ, for man be - trayed,
Be end - less praise and_ glo-ry paid;
The Fa - ther e - qual - ly a - dore,
And Ho - ly Spir - it ev - er - more.

538 ROGERS PARK — *Vexilla Regis Prodeunt* — English Translation by Dayman

1. The King's bright ban - ners for-ward go The mys - t'ry of the Cross to show,
Where God - In - car - nate death en-dured, And life by death for man pro - cured.
2. With out-stretch'd hands, trans fix'd and torn With bleed - ing brow and crown of thorn,
The One, the will - ing Vic-tim see, Self-sac - ri - ficed, man-kind to free.
3. Pierc'd by the spear His sa-cred side For us sent forth a min-gled tide,
A cleans - ing and a sav-ing flood, Thence flowed the Wa-ter and the Blood.
4. Ful-filled is all that saints of old In true pro-phet-ic song fore-told,
Th'ac-curs - èd Tree be-comes a Throne, Whence reigns our King, the Lord a - lone.

5. True Tree of Life! O Tree most fair, Or-dained those ho-ly limbs to bear,
In roy - al maj - es - ty it stood, Em-pur - pled with a Sav - ior's Blood.
6. Up - on its arms, ex-tend-ed wide, The sin - less One for sin-ners died,
The ran - som of the world to pay, He spoils the spoil-er of his prey.
7. Pris-'ners of hope, Thy Cross we hail, Christ, by this sign may we pre-vail,
Saints find Thy glo - ry here re-veal'd, And pen - i-tents their par - don seal'd.
8. To Thee, E - ter - nal Three in One, By all that breathe be hom-age done,
By that mys - te - rious Cross re-store, And guide us, safe for ev - er - more.

539 DUGUET — *Vexilla Regis Prodeunt* — English Translation by Dayman

5. True Tree of Life! O Tree most fair, Or - dained those ho - ly limbs to bear,
In roy - al maj - es - ty it__ stood, Em - pur - pled with a Sav - ior's Blood.
6. Up - on its arms, ex - tend - ed wide, The sin - less One for sin - ners died,
The ran - som of the world to__ pay, He spoils the spoil - er of his prey.
7. Pris - 'ners of hope, Thy Cross we hail, Christ, by this sign may we pre - vail,
Saints find Thy glo - ry here re - veal'd, And pen - i - tents their par - don seal'd.
8. To Thee, E - ter - nal Three in One, By all that breathe be hom - age done,
By that mys - te - rious Cross re - store, And guide us, safe for ev - er - more.

 WHITEHALL — *Vexilla Regis Prodeunt* — English Translation by Dayman

#102 has (optional) organ accompaniment at a higher key.

5. True Tree of Life! O Tree most fair, Or - dained those ho - ly limbs to bear,
In roy - al maj - es - ty it stood, Em - pur - pled with a Sav - ior's Blood.
6. Up - on its arms, ex - tend - ed wide, The sin - less One for sin - ners died,
The ran - som of the world to pay, He spoils the spoil - er of his prey.
7. Pris - 'ners of hope, Thy Cross we hail, Christ, by this sign may we pre - vail,
Saints find Thy glo - ry here re - veal'd, And pen - i - tents their par - don seal'd.
8. To Thee, E - ter - nal Three in One, By all that breathe be hom - age done,
By that mys - te - rious Cross re - store, And guide us, safe for ev - er - more.

541 EISENACH — *Vexilla Regis Prodeunt* — English Translation by Dayman

5. True__ Tree of Life! O Tree most fair, Or - dained those ho - ly limbs to bear,
In roy - al maj - es - ty it stood, Em - pur - pled with_ a Sav - ior's Blood.
6. Up - on its arms, ex - tend - ed wide, The sin - less One for sin - ners died,
The ran - som of the world to pay, He spoils the spoil - er of his prey.
7. Pris - 'ners of hope, Thy Cross we hail, Christ, by this sign may we pre - vail,
Saints find Thy glo - ry here re - veal'd, And pen - i - tents_ their par - don seal'd.
8. To__ Thee, E - ter - nal Three in One, By all that breathe be hom - age done,
By that mys - te - rious Cross re - store, And guide us, safe_ for ev - er - more.

542 MELCOMBE — *Vexilla Regis Prodeunt* — English Translation by Dayman

5. True Tree of Life! O Tree most fair, Or - dained those ho - ly limbs to bear,
In roy - al maj - es - ty it stood, Em - pur - pled with a Sav - ior's Blood.
6. Up - on its arms, ex - tend - ed wide, The sin - less One for sin - ners died,
The ran - som of the world to pay, He spoils the spoil - er of his prey.
7. Pris - 'ners of hope, Thy Cross we hail, Christ, by this sign may we pre - vail,
Saints find Thy glo - ry here re - veal'd, And pen - i - tents their par - don seal'd.
8. To Thee, E - ter - nal Three in One, By all that breathe be hom - age done,
By that mys - te - rious Cross re - store, And guide us, safe for ev - er - more.

543 KEMPEN — *Vexilla Regis Prodeunt* — English Translation by Dayman

5. True Tree of Life! O Tree most fair, Or - dained_ those ho - ly limbs to bear,
In roy - al maj - es - ty it stood, Em - pur - pled with_ a Sav - ior's Blood.
6. Up - on its arms, ex - tend - ed wide, The sin - less One for sin - ners died,
The ran - som of the world to pay, He spoils the spoil - er of_ his prey.
7. Pris - 'ners of hope, Thy Cross we hail, Christ, by_ this sign may we_ pre - vail,
Saints find Thy glo - ry here re - veal'd, And pen - i - tents_ their par - don seal'd.
8. To Thee, E - ter - nal Three in One, By all_ that breathe be hom - age done,
By that mys - te - rious Cross re - store, And guide us, safe_ for ev - er - more.

1. The King's bright ban - ners for - ward go The mys - t'ry of the Cross to show,
Where God - In - car - nate death en - dured, And life by death for man pro - cured.
2. With out - stretch'd hands, trans - fix'd and torn With bleed - ing brow and crown of thorn,
The One, the will - ing Vic - tim see, Self - sac - ri - ficed, man - kind to free.
3. Pierc'd by the spear His sa - cred side For us sent forth a min - gled tide,
A cleans - ing and a sav - ing flood, Thence flowed the Wa - ter and the Blood.
4. Ful - filled is all that saints of old In true pro - phet - ic song fore - told,
Th'ac - curs - èd Tree be - comes a Throne, Whence reigns our King, the Lord a - lone.

5. True Tree of Life! O Tree most fair, Or - dained those ho - ly limbs to bear,
In roy - al maj - es - ty it stood, Em - pur - pled with a Sav - ior's Blood.
6. Up - on its arms, ex - tend - ed wide, The sin - less One for sin - ners died,
The ran - som of the world to pay, He spoils the spoil - er of his prey.
7. Pris - 'ners of hope, Thy Cross we hail, Christ, by this sign may we pre - vail,
Saints find Thy glo - ry here re - veal'd, And pen - i - tents their par - don seal'd.
8. To Thee, E - ter - nal Three in One, By all that breathe be hom - age done,
By that mys - te - rious Cross re - store, And guide us, safe for ev - er - more.

 WINCHESTER NEW — *Vexilla Regis Prodeunt* — English Translation by Dayman

5. True Tree of Life! O Tree most fair, Or - dained those ho - ly limbs to bear,
In roy - al maj - es - ty it stood, Em - pur - pled with a Sav - ior's Blood.
6. Up - on its arms, ex - tend - ed wide, The sin - less One for sin - ners died,
The ran - som of the world to pay, He spoils the spoil - er of his prey.
7. Pris - 'ners of hope, Thy Cross we hail, Christ, by this sign may we pre - vail,
Saints find Thy glo - ry here re - veal'd, And pen - i - tents their par - don seal'd.
8. To Thee, E - ter - nal Three in One, By all that breathe be hom - age done,
By that mys - te - rious Cross re - store, And guide us, safe for ev - er - more.

1. The King's bright ban - ners for-ward go The mys - t'ry of the_ Cross to show,
Where God - In - car - nate death_ en - dured, And life by death for man_ pro - cured.
2. With out - stretch'd hands, trans - fix'd and torn With bleed - ing brow and_ crown of thorn,
The One, the will - ing Vic - tim see, Self - sac - ri - ficed, man - kind to free.
3. Pierc'd by the spear His sa - cred side For us sent forth a_ min - gled tide,
A cleans - ing and_ a sav - ing flood, Thence flowed the Wa - ter and_ the Blood.
4. Ful - filled is all that saints of old In true pro - phet - ic_ song fore - told,
Th'ac - curs - èd Tree_ be - comes a Throne, Whence reigns our King, the Lord_ a - lone.

5. True Tree of Life! O Tree most fair, Or - dained those ho - ly__ limbs to bear,
In roy - al maj - es - ty__ it stood, Em - pur-pled with a Sav - ior's Blood.
6. Up - on its arms, ex - tend - ed wide, The sin - less One for__ sin - ners died,
The ran - som of__ the world_ to pay, He spoils the spoil - er of__ his prey.
7. Pris - 'ners of hope, Thy Cross we hail, Christ, by this sign may_ we pre - vail,
Saints find Thy glo - ry here_ re - veal'd, And pen - i - tents their par - don seal'd.
8. To Thee, E - ter - nal Three in One, By all that breathe be__ hom - age done,
By that mys - te - rious Cross re - store, And guide us, safe for ev - er - more.

553 NOTRE DAME — *Victis Sibi Cognomina* — English Translation by Chambers

1. From con - quered realms let ty - rants claim The hon - ors of an
earth - ly name; A bet - ter ti - tle, Christ, to Thee, Is drawn from
those whom Thou dost free.
2. To none but Thine can man ap -
peal His fa - tal mal - a - dies to heal; Naught else can dy - ing
souls re - store, And life im - part for ev - er - more.
3. With blood that
Name at first was bought, With blood was our re - demp - tion wrought; Shall
e - vil to such mad - ness grow This price - less treas - ure to fore - go?

4. No high - er hon - or can we claim Than suf - f'ring for that
sa - cred Name; By it death shall not bit - ter be, But pre - cious,
when en - dured for Thee!
5. O Thou, whom we de - light to call
Our Sav - ior, Je - sus, Lord of all; O heark - en, as with
thank-ful voice We in Thy glo - rious Name re - joice.
6. Je - sus, to
Thee the Vir-gin's Son, Be ev - er - last - ing hom-age done; To
God the Fa - ther we re - peat The same, and to the Par - a - clete.

1. From con - quered realms let ty - rants claim The hon - ors of an earth - ly name;
A bet - ter ti - tle, Christ, to Thee, Is drawn from those whom Thou dost free.
2. To none but Thine can man ap - peal His fa - tal mal - a - dies to heal;
Naught else can dy - ing souls re - store, And life im - part for ev - er - more.
3. With blood that Name at first was bought, With blood was our re - demp - tion wrought;
Shall e - vil to such mad - ness grow This price - less treas - ure to fore - go?

#18 has (optional) organ accompaniment at a higher key.

4. No high - er hon - or can we claim Than suf - f'ring for that_ sa - cred Name;
By it death shall not bit - ter be, But pre - cious, when en - dured_ for Thee!
5. O Thou, whom we de - light to call Our Sav - ior, Je - sus,_ Lord of all;
O heark - en, as_ with thank - ful voice We in Thy glo - rious Name_ re - joice.
6. Je - sus, to Thee the Vir - gin's Son, Be ev - er - last - ing_ hom - age done;
To God the Fa - ther we_ re - peat The same, and to the Par - a - clete.

555 IOANNES — *Victis Sibi Cognomina* — English Translation by Chambers

4. No high - er hon - or can_ we claim Than suf - f'ring for_ that sa - cred Name; By it death shall_ not bit - ter be,_ But pre - cious, when en - dured for Thee!
5. O Thou, whom we de - light_ to call Our Sav - ior, Je - sus, Lord of all; O heark - en, as_ with thank - ful voice We in Thy glo - rious Name_ re - joice.
6. Je - sus, to Thee the Vir - gin's Son, Be ev - er - last - ing hom - age done; To God the Fa - ther we_ re - peat_ The same, and to_ the Par - a - clete.

1. From con-quered realms let ty - rants claim The hon - ors of an earth - ly name;
A bet - ter ti - tle, Christ, to Thee, Is drawn from those whom Thou dost free.
2. To none but Thine can man ap - peal His fa - tal mal - a - dies to heal;
Naught else can dy - ing souls re - store, And life im - part for ev - er - more.
3. With blood that Name at first was bought, With blood was our re - demp - tion wrought;
Shall e - vil to such mad - ness grow This price-less treas - ure to fore - go?

#286 has (optional) organ accompaniment at a lower key.

4. No high - er hon - or can we claim Than suf - f'ring for that sa - cred Name;
By it death shall not bit - ter be, But pre - cious, when en - dured for Thee!
5. O Thou, whom we de - light to call Our Sav - ior, Je - sus, Lord of all;
O heark - en, as with thank - ful voice We in Thy glo - rious Name re - joice.
6. Je - sus, to Thee the Vir - gin's Son, Be ev - er - last - ing hom - age done;
To God the Fa - ther we re - peat The same, and to the Par - a - clete.

558 PASCHAL LAMB — *Victis Sibi Cognomina* — English Translation by Chandler

1. Con - qu'ring kings their ti - tles take From the foes they cap - tive make;
Je - sus, by a nobl - er deed, From the thou - sands he hath freed.
For no oth - er Name is giv'n Un - to an - y un - der heav'n
Where - by souls in mor - tal strife Rise to gain e - ter - nal life.
2. That which Christ so hard - ly wrought, That which he so dear - ly bought,
That sal - va - tion, mor - tals, say, Will you mad - ly cast a - way?

Ra - ther glad - ly for that name Bear the cross, en - dure the shame;
Suf - fer with him joy - ful - ly, Death, through him, is vic - to - ry.
3. Dost thou, Je - sus, con - de - scend To be called the sin - ners' friend?
Ours then it shall al - ways be Thus to make our boast of thee.
Glo - ry to the Fa - ther be; Glo - ry, Vir - gin - born, to thee;
Glo - ry to the Ho - ly Ghost, Ev - er from the heav'n - ly host.

559 ST GEORGE — *Victis Sibi Cognomina* — English Translation by Chandler

Ra - ther glad - ly for that name Bear the cross, en - dure the shame;
Suf - fer with him joy - ful - ly, Death, through him, is vic - to - ry.
3. Dost thou, Je - sus, con - de - scend To be called the sin - ners' friend?
Ours then it shall al - ways be Thus to make our boast of thee.
Glo - ry to the Fa - ther be; Glo - ry, Vir - gin - born, to thee;
Glo - ry to the Ho - ly Ghost, Ev - er from the heav'n - ly host.

1. Con - qu'ring kings their ti - tles take From the foes they cap - tive make;
Je - sus, by a nobl - er deed, From the thou - sands he hath freed.
For no oth - er Name is giv'n Un - to an - y un - der heav'n
Where - by souls in mor - tal strife Rise to gain e - ter - nal life.
2. That which Christ so hard - ly wrought, That which he so dear - ly bought,
That sal - va - tion, mor - tals, say, Will you mad - ly cast a - way?

Ra - ther glad - ly for that name Bear the cross, en - dure the shame;
Suf - fer with him joy - ful - ly, Death, through him, is vic - to - ry.
3. Dost thou, Je - sus, con - de-scend To be called the sin - ners' friend?
Ours then it shall al - ways be Thus to make our boast of thee.
Glo - ry to the Fa - ther be; Glo - ry, Vir - gin - born, to thee;
Glo - ry to the Ho - ly Ghost, Ev - er from the heav'n - ly host.

561 ORIENTIS PARTIBUS — *Victis Sibi Cognomina* — English Translation by Chandler

1. Con - qu'ring kings their ti - tles take From the foes they cap - tive make; Je - sus,
by a nobl - er deed, From the thou - sands he hath freed. Al - le - lu - ia.
2. For no oth - er Name is giv'n Un - to an - y un - der heav'n Where - by
souls in mor - tal strife Rise to gain e - ter - nal life. Al - le - lu - ia.
3. That which Christ so hard - ly wrought, That which he so dear - ly bought, That sal -
va - tion, mor - tals, say, Will you mad - ly cast a - way? Al - le - lu - ia.

4. Ra - ther glad - ly for that name Bear the cross, en - dure the shame; Suf - fer
with him joy - ful - ly, Death, through him, is vic - to - ry. Al - le - lu - ia.
5. Dost thou, Je - sus, con - de - scend To be called the sin - ners' friend? Ours then it shall
al - ways be Thus to make our boast of thee. Al - le - lu - ia.
6. Glo - ry to the Fa - ther be; Glo - ry, Vir - gin - born, to thee; Glo - ry to the
Ho - ly Ghost, Ev - er from the heav'n - ly host. Al - le - lu - ia.

1. Con - qu'ring kings their ti - tles take From the foes they cap - tive make; Je - sus,
by a nobl - er deed, From the thou - sands he hath freed. Al - le - lu - ia.
2. For no oth - er Name is giv'n Un - to an - y un - der heav'n Where - by
souls in mor - tal strife Rise to gain e - ter - nal life. Al - le - lu - ia.
3. That which Christ so hard - ly wrought, That which he so dear - ly bought, That sal -
va - tion, mor - tals, say, Will you mad - ly cast a - way? Al - le - lu - ia.

4. Ra - ther glad - ly for that name Bear the cross, en - dure the shame; Suf - fer
with him joy - ful - ly, Death, through him, is vic - to - ry. Al - le - lu - ia.
5. Dost thou, Je - sus, con - de - scend To be called the sin - ners' friend? Ours then
it shall al - ways be Thus to make our boast of thee. Al - le - lu - ia.
6. Glo - ry to the Fa - ther be; Glo - ry, Vir - gin - born, to thee; Glo - ry
to the Ho - ly Ghost, Ev - er from the heav'n - ly host. Al - le - lu - ia.

1. Con - qu'ring kings their ti - tles take From the foes they cap - tive make;
Je - sus, by a nobl - er deed, From the thou - sands he hath freed.
For no oth - er Name is giv'n Un - to an - y un - der heav'n
Where - by souls in mor - tal strife Rise to gain e - ter - nal life.
2. That which Christ so hard - ly wrought, That which he so dear - ly bought,
That sal - va - tion, mor - tals, say, Will you mad - ly cast a - way?

Ra - ther glad - ly for that name Bear the cross, en - dure the shame;
Suf - fer with him joy - ful - ly, Death, through him, is vic - to - ry.
3. Dost thou, Je - sus, con - de - scend To be called the sin - ners' friend?
Ours then it shall al - ways be Thus to make our boast of thee.
Glo - ry to the Fa - ther be; Glo - ry, Vir - gin - born, to thee;
Glo - ry to the Ho - ly Ghost, Ev - er from the heav'n - ly host.

1. Con - qu'ring kings their ti - tles take From the foes they cap - tive make;
Je - sus, by a nobl - er deed, From the__ thou - sands he hath freed.
2. For no oth - er Name is giv'n Un - to an - y un - der heav'n
Where - by souls in mor - tal strife Rise to__ gain e - ter - nal life.
3. That which Christ so hard - ly wrought, That which he so dear - ly bought,
That sal - va - tion, mor - tals, say, Will you__ mad - ly cast a - way?

4. Ra - ther glad - ly for that name Bear the cross, en - dure the shame;
Suf - fer with him joy - ful - ly, Death, through him, is vic - to - ry.
5. Dost thou, Jesus, con - de - scend To be called the sin - ners' friend?
Ours then it shall al - ways be Thus to make our boast of thee.
6. Glo - ry to the Fa - ther be; Glo - ry, Vir - gin - born, to thee;
Glo - ry to the Ho - ly Ghost, Ev - er from the heav'n - ly host.

Ladies
1. O come, O come, Em - ma - nu - el, And ran - som cap - tive
Men
1. O come, O come, Em - ma - nu - el, And ran - som cap - tive
Organ
L
Is - ra - el, That mourns in lone - ly ex - ile
M
Is - ra - el, That mourns in lone - ly ex - ile
O

This accompaniment cannot be sung without organ accompaniment. • The men should be softer than the ladies.

L
here, Un - til the Son of God ap - pear.
M
here, Un - til the Son of God ap - pear.
O
R. Re - joice, re -
R. Re - joice, re -
L
joice! Em - ma - nu - el shall come to thee, O Is - ra - el.
M
joice! Em - ma - nu - el shall come to thee, O Is - ra - el.
O

L
2. O come, of Gen - tile hearts the King, A world that needs thee
M
2. O come, of Gen - tile hearts the King, A world that needs thee
O
L
ran - som - ing, And save thy ser - vants, who con - fess With
M
ran - som - ing, And save thy ser - vants, who con - fess With
O

This accompaniment cannot be sung without organ accompaniment. • The men should be softer than the ladies.

L
hum - bled hearts their faith - less - ness.
M
hum - bled hearts their faith - less - ness.
O
R. Re - joice, re -
R. Re - joice, re -
L
joice! Em - ma - nu - el shall come to thee, O Is - ra - el.
M
joice! Em - ma - nu - el shall come to thee, O Is - ra - el.
O

L
3. O come, thou Day - star seen on high, With heal - ing for our
M
3. O come, thou Day - star seen on high, With heal - ing for our
O
L
hearts draw nigh; Do thou the mists of night dis - pel, And
M
hearts draw nigh; Do thou the mists of night dis - pel, And
O

This accompaniment cannot be sung without organ accompaniment. • The men should be softer than the ladies.

L
death's fore - bod - ing dark - ness quell.
R. Re - joice, re -
M
death's fore - bod - ing dark - ness quell.
R. Re - joice, re -
O
L
joice! Em - ma - nu - el shall come to thee, O Is - ra - el.
M
joice! Em - ma - nu - el shall come to thee, O Is - ra - el.
O

L
4. O come, thou Key of Da - vid's store, Un - lock the heav'n - ly
M
4. O come, thou Key of Da - vid's store, Un - lock the heav'n - ly
O
L
gates once more; Safe jour - ney to thy courts be - stow, And
M
gates once more; Safe jour - ney to thy courts be - stow, And
O

This accompaniment cannot be sung without organ accompaniment. • The men should be softer than the ladies.

L
shut the way that leads be - low.
M
shut the way that leads be - low.
O
R. Re - joice, re -
R. Re - joice, re -
L
joice! Em - ma - nu - el shall come to thee, O Is - ra - el.
M
joice! Em - ma - nu - el shall come to thee, O Is - ra - el.
O

L
5. O come, Thou Rod of Jes - - se, free Thine own from Sa - tan's
M
5. O come, Thou Rod of Jes - se, free Thine own from Sa - tan's
O
L
tyr - an - ny; From depths of hell Thy peo - ple save, And
M
tyr - an - ny; From depths of hell Thy peo - ple save, And
O

This accompaniment cannot be sung without organ accompaniment. • The men should be softer than the ladies.

L
give them vic - t'ry o'er the grave.
M
give them vic - t'ry o'er the grave.
O
R. Re - joice, re -
R. Re - joice, re -
L
joice! Em - ma - nu - el shall come to thee, O Is - ra - el.
M
joice! Em - ma - nu - el shall come to thee, O Is - ra - el.
O

L
6. O come, thou ev - er - last - ing Lord, Who once by Is - rael's host a - dored
M
6. O come, thou ev - er - last - ing Lord, Who once by Is - rael's host a - dored
O
L
Thy ten com - mand - ments mad - est known, In maj - es - ty of glo - ry shown. R.
M
Thy ten com - mand - ments mad - est known, In maj - es - ty of glo - ry shown. R.
O

This accompaniment cannot be sung without organ accompaniment. • The men should be softer than the ladies.

L
7. O come, thou Wis-dom whose de - cree Doth gov - ern all things peace - ful - ly;
M
7. O come, thou Wis-dom whose de - cree Doth gov - ern all things peace - ful - ly;
O
L
The way of pru - dence here be - low And life here - af - ter deign to show. R.
M
The way of pru - dence here be - low And life here - af - ter deign to show. R.
O

1. On Jor-dan's bank the Bap-tist's cry An-nounc-es that the Lord is nigh;
A-wake and heark-en, for He brings Glad tid-ings of the King of kings!
2. Then cleansed be ev-'ry soul from sin; Make straight the way of God with-in;
Pre-pare we in our hearts a home Where such a might-y Guest may come.

* *A transposed organ accompaniment has been provided for optional use.*

3. For Thou art our sal - va - tion, Lord, Our ref - uge, and our great re - ward;
With - out Thy grace our souls must fade, And with - er like a flow'r de - cayed.
4. To heal the sick stretch out Thy hand, And bid the fall - en sin - ner stand;
Shine forth, and let Thy light re - store Earth's own true love - li - ness once more.
5. All praise, e - ter - nal Son, to Thee, Whose ad - vent sets Thy peo - ple free,
Whom with the Fa - ther we a - dore And Ho - ly Ghost for - ev - er - more.

655 MERTON — *En Clara Vox Redarguit* — English Translation by Father Fitzpatrick

1. Hark! a voice, in ur - gent warn - ing, Clear - ly rings the dark - ness through;
Cast a way your dreams, 'tis morn - ing; Christ is shin - ing down on you.
2. Star - tled at the sol - emn warn - ing Let the earth - bound soul a - rise;
Christ, her Sun, all sloth dis - pel - ling, Shines up - on the morn - ing skies.

* *A transposed organ accompaniment has been provided for optional use.*

3. T'ward us, lo! the Lamb ad - vanc - es, Free - ly all our debt to pay:
One in words that grief en - hanc - es, Let us all for par - don pray.
4. And when next He comes, re - ful - gent, Girdl - ing all the world with fear,
May He, as a Judge in - dul - gent, Shield us, though our guilt is clear.
5. Glo - ry, pow'r, and praise un - end - ing To the Fa - ther and the Son,
And the Par - a - clete, as - cend - ing While e - ter - nal ag - es run.

656 SEÁN 8M — *Instantis Adventum Dei* — Father Coffin

1. The com - ing of our God Our_ thoughts must now em - ploy;
Then let us meet him on the road With hymns of ho - ly joy.
2. The ev - er - last - ing Son In - car - nate soon shall be:
He will a ser - vant's form put on, To make his peo - ple free.
3. Daugh - ter of Zi - on, rise To_ greet thine in - fant King;
Nor let thy stub - born heart de - spise The par - don he doth bring.

4. In glo - ry from his throne A - gain will Christ de - scend,
And sum - mon all that are his own To joys that nev - er end.
5. Be - fore that dread - ful day May_ all our sin be gone;
May the old man be put a - way, And the new man put on.
6. Our joy - ful prais - es sing To_ Christ, who set us free;
Like trib - ute to the Fa - ther bring, And, Ho - ly Ghost, to thee.

1. O come, Di - vine Mes - si - ah, The world in si - lence waits the day
When hope shall sing its tri - umph, And sad - ness flee a - way.
R. Dear Sav - ior, haste! Come, come to earth. Dis - pel the
night and show Thy face, And bid us hail the dawn of grace.
O come, Di - vine Mes - si - ah, The world in si - lence waits the day
When hope shall sing its tri - umph, And sad - ness flee a - way.
2. O Thou whom na - tions sighed for, Whom priest and proph - et long fore - told,
Wilt break the cap - tive fet - ters, Re - deem the long - lost fold. *Refrain!*

HELMSLEY — "Lo! He Comes With Clouds Descending" 658

1. Lo! he comes with clouds de - scend - ing, Once for
fa - vored sin - ners slain; Thou - sand thou - sand saints at - tend - ing
Swell the tri - umph of his train: Al - le - lu - ia, al - le -
lu - ia, al - le - lu - ia! God ap - pears, on earth to reign.
2. Eve - ry eye shall now be - hold him Robed in
dread - ful maj - es - ty; Those who set at nought and sold him,
Pierced and nailed him to the tree, Deep - ly wail - ing, deep - ly
wail - ing, deep - ly wail - ing Shall the true Mes - si - ah see.

3. Those dear_ to - kens_ of_ his_ Pas - sion Still his
daz - zling bod - y_ bears, Cause of_ end - less_ ex - ul - ta - tion
To his ran - somed wor - ship - pers:_ With_ what rap - ture, with_ what
rap - ture, with_ what rap - ture, Gaze we_ on those glo - rious scars!
4. Yea, A - men!_ let_ all_ a - dore_ thee, High on
thine e - ter - nal_ throne; Sav - ior,_ take_ the_ pow'r_ and_ glo - ry:
Claim the king - dom for_ thine own:_ O_ come quick - ly, O_ come
quick - ly, O_ come quick - ly! Al - le - lu - ia! Come, Lord, come!

1. The heav - ens, Sav - ior, o - pen tear: down, down from heav - en fleet-ly fare!
Tear thou from heav - en gate and door: tear thou, nor lock nor bolt leave more.
2. A dew, O God, from heav - en send: down in the dew, O Sav - ior, wend.
Break - ing, ye clouds, un - bur - den - ing, show - er on Ja - cob's house the King.
3. A - non, O earth, thy shoots be seen, that hill and vale may grow all green.
Forth then, O earth, this blos - som bring: out of the earth, O Sav - ior, spring!

4. The on - ly store of hope world - wide,
and the one balm, where dost thou bide?
Yea, from the high - est hall re - move,
balm in this vale of tears to prove.
5. Thou sun and star, O fair and bright,
glad - ly would we en - joy thy sight!
Rise up, O sun: thy glow with - drawn,
all of us sit in gloom for - lorn.
6. Here we en - dure the grav - est want:
un - end - ing death doth us con - front.
Come, lead us with a might - y hand
from wretch - ed - ness to our home - land!

1. Come, thou long - ex - pect - ed Je - sus, Born to set thy peo - ple free,
From our fears and sins re - lease us, Let us find our rest in thee.
2. Is - rael's strength and con - so - la - tion, Hope of all the earth thou art,
Dear De - sire of eve - ry na - tion, Joy of ev - 'ry long - ing heart.
3. Born thy peo - ple to de - liv - er, Born a Child and yet a King,
Born to reign in us for ev - er, Now thy gra - cious king - dom bring.
4. Hon - or, glo - ry, vir - tue, mer - it, To the Fa - ther and the Son,
With the co - e - ter - nal Spir - it, While e - ter - nal ag - es run.

1. Hark! the her - ald an - gels sing___ Glo - ry to the new - born King;
Peace on earth and mer - cy mild,___ God and sin - ners rec - on - ciled:
Joy - ful all ye na - tions rise,___ Join the tri - umph of the skies,___
With the an - gel - ic host pro - claim, Christ is___ born in Beth - le - hem.
R. Hark! the her - ald an - gels sing Glo - ry___ to the new - born King.
2. Christ, by high - est heav'n a - dored,_ Christ, the ev - er - last - ing Lord,
Late in time be - hold him come__ Off - spring of a Vir - gin's womb!

Veiled in flesh the God-head see,
Hail the in-car-nate De-i-ty!
Pleased as man with man to dwell,
Je-sus, our Em-ma-nu-el.
R. Hark! the her-ald an-gels sing
Glo-ry to the new-born King.
3. Hail the heav'n-born Prince of Peace!
Hail the Sun of Right-eous-ness!
Light and life to all he brings,
Ris'n with heal-ing in his wings;
Mild he lays his glo-ry by,
Born that man no more may die,
Born to raise the sons of earth,
Born to give them sec-ond birth. Refrain!

1. Joy to the world! the Lord is come: Let earth re - ceive her
King; Let ev - 'ry heart pre - pare Him room,
And heav'n and na - ture sing, And heav'n and na - ture sing,
And heav'n and na - ture sing, And heav'n and na -
And heav'n, and heav'n and na - ture sing.
ture sing,
2. Joy to the earth! the Sav - ior reigns: Let men their songs em -
ploy, While fields and floods, rocks, hills, and plains

Re - peat the sound - ing joy, Re - peat the sound - ing joy,
Re - peat the sound - ing joy, Re - peat the sound -
Re - peat, re - peat, the sound - ing joy.
ing joy,
3. No more let sins and sor - rows grow, Nor thorns in - fest the
ground; He comes to make His bless - ings flow
Far as the curse is found, Far as the curse is found,
Far as the curse is found, Far as the curse
Far as, far as, the curse is found.
is found,

4. He rules the world with truth and grace, And makes the na - tions
prove The glo - ries of His right - eous - ness,
And won - ders of His love, And won - ders of His love,
And won - ders of His love, And won - ders of
And won - ders, won - ders of His love.
His love,
5. His name shall be the Prince of Peace, The ev - er - last - ing
Lord, The Won - der - ful, the Coun - sel - lor,

* *A transposed organ accompaniment has been provided for optional use.*

The God by all a - dored, The_ God by all a - dored,
The God by all a - dored, The God by all
The_ God,_ the God_ by all a - dored.
a - dored,

665 IN DULCI JUBILO — *In Dulci Jubilo (14th century)*

1. Good Chris - tian men, re - joice With heart and soul and voice;
Give ye heed to what we say: Je - sus Christ is born to - day!
Ox and ass be - fore him bow, And he is in the man - ger now.
Christ is born to - day! Christ is born to - day!
2. Good Chris - tian men, re - joice With heart and soul and voice;
Now ye hear of end - less bliss: Je - sus Christ was born for this!

He has o - pened heav - en's door, And man is blest for - ev - er - more.
Christ was born for this! Christ was born for this!
3. Good Chris - tian men, re - joice With heart and soul and voice;
Now ye need not fear the grave: Je - sus Christ was born to save!
Calls you one and calls you all, To gain his ev - er - last - ing hall.
Christ was born to save! Christ was born to save!

1. Once in roy - al Da - vid's cit - y Stood a low - ly cat - tle_ shed,
Where a Moth - er laid_ her_ Ba - by In a man - ger for_ His_ bed:
Mar - y was that Moth - er mild, Je - sus Christ her lit - tle_ Child.
2. He came down to earth_ from_ heav - en, Who is God and Lord_ of_ all,
And His shel - ter was_ a_ sta - ble, And His cra - dle was_ a_ stall;
With the poor, and mean, and low - ly, Lived on earth our Sav - ior_ ho - ly.

3. And, through all His won - drous child - hood He would hon - or and_ o - bey,
Love and watch the low - ly__ Maid - en, In whose gen - tle arms_ He__ lay;
Chris - tian chil - dren all must be Mild, o - be - dient, good_ as__ He.
4. For He is our child - hood's pat - tern, Day by day like us__ He__ grew,
He was lit - tle, weak, and__ help - less, Tears and smiles like us__ He__ knew;
And He feel - eth for our sad - ness, And He shar - eth in__ our_ glad - ness.

5. And our eyes at last shall see Him, Through His own re - deem - ing love,
For that Child so dear and gen - tle Is our Lord in heav'n a - bove;
And He leads His chil - dren on To the place where He is gone.
6. Not in that poor low - ly sta - ble, With the ox - en stand - ing by,
We shall see Him; but in heav - en, Set at God's right hand on high;
Where like stars His chil - dren crowned All in white shall wait a - round.

1. An - gels we have heard on high, Sweet - ly sing - ing o'er the plain;
And the moun - tains in re - ply Ech - o - ing their joy - ous strain:
R. Gló - - - - - - - - - ri - a, in ex - cél - sis De - - o!
Gló - - - - - - - - - ri - a, in ex - cél - sis De - o!
2. Shep - herds, why this ju - bi - lee? Why your glad - some strain pro - long?
Say what may the tid - ings be Which in - spire your heav'n - ly song. Refrain!
3. Come to Beth - le - hem and see Him, whose birth the an - gels sing;
Come, a - dore on bend - ed knee, Christ the Lord, the new - born King. Refrain!

1. God rest you mer - ry, Gen - tle - men, Let noth - ing you dis - may,
For Je - sus Christ our Sav - ior Was born up - on this day,
To save us all from Sa - tan's pow'r When we were gone a - stray.
Refrain: O tid - ings of com - fort and joy, com-fort and
joy; O tid - ings of com - fort and joy!
2. From God our heav'n-ly Fa - ther A bless-èd an-gel came, And un - to cer-tain shep - herds
Brought tid-ings of the same, How that in Beth - le - hem was born The Son of God by name. R.
3. "Fear not," then said the an - gel, "Let noth - ing you af - fright,

This day is born a Sav - ior, Of a pure Vir - gin bright,
To free all those who trust in him From Sa - tan's pow'r and might." *Refrain!*
4. And when to Beth - le - hem they came, Where - at this in - fant lay,
They found him in a man - ger, Where ox - en feed on hay;
His moth - er Mar - y kneel - ing, Un - to the Lord did pray. *Refrain!*
5. Now to the Lord sing prais - es, All you with - in this place,
And with true love and broth - er - hood Each oth - er now em - brace;
This ho - ly tide of Christ - mas Doth bring re - deem - ing grace. *Refrain!*

670 ADESTE FIDELES — *Adeste Fideles, Laeti Triumphantes* — English Translation by Father Oakeley

1. O come, all ye faith - ful, Joy - ful and tri - um - phant, O come ye, O come ye to
Beth - le - hem; Come and be - hold him, Born the King of an - gels;
R. O come, let us a - dore him, O come, let us a - dore him,
O come, let us a - dore him, Christ the Lord.
2. God - head of God - head, Light of Light e - ter - nal, Him doth a Maid - en
birth ac - cord: True God, and made not, But in - deed be - got - ten:
R. O come, let us a - dore him, O come, let us a - dore him,
O come, let us a - dore him, Christ the Lord.

3. Sing, choirs of an - gels, Sing in ex - ul - ta - tion, Sing, all ye cit - i - zens of
heav'n a - bove! Glo - ry to God, all glo - ry in the high - est;
R. O come, let us a - dore him, O come, let us a - dore him,
O come, let us a - dore him, Christ the Lord.
4. Yea, Lord, we greet thee, Born this hap - py morn - ing; Je - sus, to thee be
glo - ry giv'n; Word of the Fa - ther, Now in flesh ap - pear - ing;
R. O come, let us a - dore him, O come, let us a - dore him,
O come, let us a - dore him, Christ the Lord.

671 ADESTE FIDELES — *Adeste Fideles, Laeti Triumphantes* — **Textus originalis Latinus**

1. Ad - é - ste, fi - dé - les, Lae - ti tri - um - phán - tes; Ve - ní - te, ve - ní - te in
Béth - le - hem; Na - tum vi - dé - te Re - gem an - ge - ló - rum:
R. Ve - ní - te a - do - ré - mus, ve - ní - te a - do - ré - mus,
ve - ní - te a - do - ré - mus Dó - mi - num.
2. De - um de De - o, Lu - men de lú - mi - ne, Ge - stant pu - él - lae
ví - sce - ra; De - um ve - rum, Gé - ni - tum, non fa - ctum:
R. Ve - ní - te a - do - ré - mus, ve - ní - te a - do - ré - mus,
ve - ní - te a - do - ré - mus Dó - mi - num.

3. Can - tet nunc I - o! Cho - rus an - ge - ló - rum: Can - tet nunc au - la cae -
lé - sti - um: Gló - ri - a, gló - ri - a, In ex - cél - sis De - o!
R. Ve - ní - te a - do - ré - mus, ve - ní - te a - do - ré - mus,
ve - ní - te a - do - ré - mus Dó - mi - num.
4. Er - go qui na - tus Di - e ho - di - ér - na. Je - su ti - bi sit
gló - ri - a: Pa - tris ae - tér - ni Ver - bum ca - ro fa - ctum!
R. Ve - ní - te a - do - ré - mus, ve - ní - te a - do - ré - mus,
ve - ní - te a - do - ré - mus Dó - mi - num.

672 ALL SAINTS 8B — *Puer Natus Est Nobis* ("Bright and joyful is the morn…")

1. Bright and joy - ful is the morn, For to_ us a Child is born;
From the high - est_ realms of_ Heav'n, Un - to us_ a Son is giv'n.
2. On His shoul - der He shall bear Pow'r and_ maj - es - ty, and wear
On His ves - ture_ and His_ thigh, Names most aw - ful, names most high.
3. Won - der - ful in coun - sel He, The in - car - nate De - i - ty;
Sire of ag - es,_ ne'er to_ cease, King of kings, and Prince of Peace.
4. Come and wor - ship at His feet; Yield to_ Christ the hom - age meet;
From His man - ger_ to His_ throne, Hom - age due_ to God a - lone.

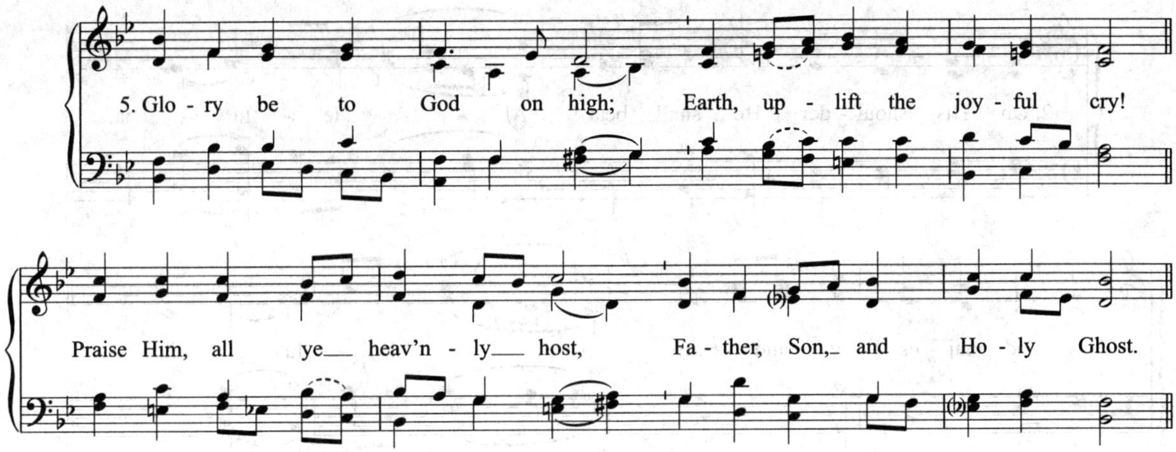
5. Glo - ry be to God on high; Earth, up - lift the joy - ful cry!
Praise Him, all ye heav'n - ly host, Fa - ther, Son, and Ho - ly Ghost.

LLANFAIR — *Puer Natus Est Nobis* ("Bright and joyful is the morn...")

1. Bright and joy - ful is the morn, Al - le - lu - ia.
For to us a Child is born; Al - le - lu - ia.
From the high - est realms of Heav'n, Al - le - lu - ia.
Un - to us a Son is giv'n. Al - le - lu - ia.

2. On His shoul - der He shall_ bear Al - - le - lu - ia.
Pow'r and maj - es - ty, and_ wear Al - - le - lu - ia.
On His ves - ture and_ His_ thigh, Al - le - lu - ia.
Names most aw - ful, names most_ high. Al - - le - lu - ia.
3. Won - der - ful in coun - sel_ He, Al - - le - lu - ia.
The in - car - nate De - i - ty; Al - le - lu - ia.
Sire of ag - es, ne'er_ to_ cease, Al - le - lu - ia.

King of kings, and Prince of__ Peace. Al - - le - lu - ia.
4. Come and wor-ship at His__ feet; Al - le - lu - ia.
Yield to Christ the hom-age__ meet; Al - - le - lu - ia.
From His man-ger to___ His__ throne, Al - le - lu - ia.
Hom-age due to God a - lone. Al - - le - lu - ia.
5. Glo-ry be to God on__ high; Al - - le - lu - ia.
Earth, up-lift the joy-ful__ cry! Al - -le - lu - ia.

Praise Him, all ye heav'n - ly___ host, Al - le - lu - ia.
Fa - ther, Son, and Ho - ly___ Ghost. Al - le - lu - ia.

CULBACH — *Puer Natus Est Nobis* ("Bright and joyful is the morn…")

1. Bright and joy - ful is the morn, For to us a Child is born;
From the high - est realms of Heav'n, Un - to us a Son is giv'n.
2. On His shoul - der He shall bear Pow'r and maj - es - ty, and wear
On His ves - ture and His thigh, Names most aw - ful, names most high.

3. Won - der - ful in coun - sel He, The in - car - nate De - i - ty;
Sire of ag - es, ne'er to cease, King of kings, and Prince of Peace.
4. Come and wor - ship at His feet; Yield to Christ the hom - age meet;
From His man - ger to His throne, Hom - age due to God a - lone.
5. Glo - ry be to God on high; Earth, up - lift the joy - ful cry!
Praise Him, all ye heav'n - ly host, Fa - ther, Son, and Ho - ly Ghost.

1. The first No-ël the Angel did say Was to certain poor Shep-herds in fields as they lay;
In fields where they lay keep-ing their sheep On a cold win-ter's night that was so deep.
R. No - ël, No - ël, No - ël, No - ël, Born is the King of Is - ra - el.
2. They look - èd up and saw a Star Shin-ing in the East be - yond them far,
And to the earth it gave great light, And so it con - tin-ued both day and night. R.
3. And by the light of that same Star, Three Wise Men came from coun - try far;
To seek for a King was their in - tent, And to fol-low the Star wher-ev - er it went. R.

4. This Star drew nigh to the North West, O - ver Beth - le - hem it took its rest;
And there it did both stop and stay, Right o - ver the place where Je - sus lay. R.
5. Then en - ter'd in those Wise Men three Most rev - 'rent - ly up - on their knee,
And of - fer'd there, in his pres - ence, Both gold, and myrrh, and frank - in - cense. R.
6. Then let us all with one ac - cord Sing prais - es to our heav - en - ly Lord;
That hath made heav'n and earth of nought, And with his blood man - kind hath bought.
R. No - ël, No - ël, No - ël, No - ël, Born is the King of Is - ra - el.

677 GREENSLEEVES — "What Child Is This?"

1. What child is this, who, laid to rest On Mar - y's lap is sleep - ing?
Whom an - gels greet with an - thems sweet, While shep - herds watch are keep - ing?
This, this is Christ the King, Whom shep - herds guard and an - gels sing;
Haste, haste, to bring Him laud, The Babe, the son of Mar - y.
2. Why lies He in such mean es - tate Where ox and ass are feed - ing?
Good Chris - tian, fear: for sin - ners here The si - lent Word is plead - ing.
Optional: Nails, spear shall pierce Him through, The cross be borne, for me, for you:

Hail, hail the Word made flesh, The Babe, the son of Mar - y.
3. So bring Him in - cense, gold and myrrh, Come, peas - ant, king to own Him;
The King of kings sal - va - tion brings, Let lov - ing hearts en - throne Him.
Optional: Raise, raise the song on high, The Vir - gin sings her lull - a - by:
Joy, joy, for Christ is born, The Babe, the son of Mar - y.

Some choirmasters use "This, this is Christ the King…" as the Refrain.

Others choose to use a different refrain each time, here called "optional."

1. Si - lent night, ho - ly night, All is calm, all is bright
Round yon Vir - gin Moth - er and Child. Ho - ly In - fant, so ten - der and mild,
Sleep in heav - en - ly peace,
Sleep in heav - en - ly peace.
2. Si - lent night, ho - ly night, Shep - herds quake at the sight;
Glo - ries stream from heav - en a - far. Heav’n - ly hosts sing Al - le - lu - ia;
Christ, the Sav - ior, is born,
Christ, the Sav - ior, is born!
3. Si - lent night, ho - ly night, Son of God, love’s pure light
Ra - diant beams from Thy ho - ly face, With the dawn of re - deem - ing grace,

Je - sus, Lord, at Thy birth,
Je - sus, Lord, at Thy birth!

The following verses may be used for the Epiphany:

e1. Si - lent night, ho - ly night, Guid - ing Star, lend thy light;
See the east - ern wise men bring Gifts and hom - age to our King!
Christ the Sav - ior is here,
Christ the Sav - ior is here!
e2. Si - lent night, ho - ly night, Won - drous Star, lend thy light;
With the an - gels let us sing Al - le - lu - ia to our King!
Christ the Sav - ior is here,
Christ the Sav - ior is here!

1. Bright - est and best of the sons of the morn - ing,
Dawn on our dark - ness and lend us thine aid;
Star of the East, the ho - ri - zon a - dorn - ing,
Guide where our in - fant Re - deem - er is laid.
2. Cold on his cra - dle the dew - drops are shin - ing,
Low lies his head with the beasts of the stall:
An - gels a - dore him in slum - ber re - clin - ing,
Mak - er and Mon - arch and Sav - ior of all.

3. Say, shall we yield him, in cost - ly de - vo - tion, O - dors of
E - dom and of - f'rings di - vine? Gems of the moun - tain and pearls
of the o - cean, Myrrh from the for - est or gold from the mine?
4. Vain - ly we of - fer each am - ple ob - la - tion, Vain - ly with
gifts would his fa - vor se - cure; Rich - er by far is the heart's
ad - o - ra - tion, Dear - er to God are the prayers of the poor.

After Verse 4, the first verse is repeated: "Brightest and best of the sons..."

 DIX — “As With Gladness, Men Of Old”

1. As with__ glad - ness, men of old Did the guid - ing star be - hold,
As with__ joy they hailed its light Lead - ing on - ward, beam - ing bright,
So, most glo - rious Lord, may we Ev - er - more be led to Thee.
2. As with__ joy - ful steps they sped To that low - ly man - ger - bed,
There to__ bend the knee be - fore Him whom heav’n and earth a - dore,
So may we with will - ing feet Ev - er seek Thy mer - cy - seat.
3. As they__ of - fered gifts most rare At that man - ger rude and bare;

So may we with ho - ly joy, Pure and free from sin's al - loy,
All our cost - liest treas - ures bring, Christ, to Thee, our heav'n - ly king.
4. Ho - ly Je - sus, eve - ry day Keep us in the nar - row way;
And, when earth - ly things are past, Bring our ran - somed souls at last
Where they need no star to guide, Where no clouds Thy glo - ry hide.
5. In the heav'n - ly coun - try bright, Need they no cre - at - ed light;
Thou its Light, its Joy, its Crown, Thou its Sun which goes not down:
There for - ev - er may we sing Al - le - lu - ias to our King!

681 ST GEORGE — "Songs Of Thankfulness And Praise"

1. Songs of thank - ful - ness and praise, Je - sus, Lord, to Thee we raise,
Man - i - fest - ed by the star To the sag - es from a - far;
Branch of roy - al Da - vid's stem In Thy birth at Beth - le - hem;
An - thems be to Thee ad - dressed, God in man made man - i - fest.
2. Man - i - fest at Jor - dan's stream, Proph - et, Priest, and King su - preme;
And at Ca - na, wed - ding guest, In Thy God - head man - i - fest;
Man - i - fest in pow'r di - vine, Chang - ing wa - ter in - to wine;
An - thems be to Thee ad - dressed, God in man made man - i - fest.

3. Man - i - fest in mak - ing whole Pal - sied limbs and faint - ing soul;
Man - i - fest in val - iant fight, Quell - ing all the dev - il's might;
Man - i - fest in gra - cious will, Ev - er bring - ing good from ill;
An - thems be to Thee ad-dressed, God in man made man - i - fest.
4. Grant us grace to see Thee, Lord, Mir - rored in Thy ho - ly Word;
May we im - i - tate Thee now, And be pure, as pure art Thou;
That we like to Thee may be At Thy great E - piph - a - ny;
And may praise Thee, ev - er blest, God in man made man - i - fest.

1. Sole hope of all the world and Lord,
Be - stow - er of the great re - ward,
Re - ceive the prayers thy ser - vants raise
Mixt with meet psalms and chants of praise.
2. And though our con - science doth pro - claim Our deep trans - gres - sions
and our shame, Cleanse us, O God, we hum - bly plead,
From sins of thought and word and deed.

3. Our sins re - mem - ber thou no more: For - give: thou art of might - y pow'r:
So take up - on thee, Lord, our care That pure in heart we make our prayer.
4. There - fore ac - cept, O Lord, this tide Of fast which thou hast sanc - ti - fied,
That we may reach by mys - tic ways The sac - ra - ments of Pas - chal days.
5. May he who is the three - fold Lord On us con - fer this high re - ward,
In whom so long as worlds a - bide One on - ly God is glo - ri - fied.

For this hymn, we strongly recommend placing all ladies on the Soprano Line, all men on the Tenor Line, and organ accompaniment.

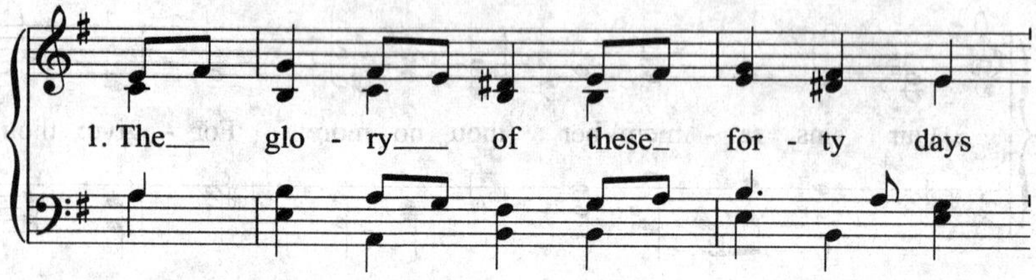
1. The glo - ry of these for - ty days

We cel - e - brate with songs of praise; For Christ, by Whom all
things were made, Him - self has fast - ed and has prayed.
2. A - lone and fast - ing Mo - ses saw
The lov - ing God who gave the law; And to E - li - jah,
fast - ing, came The steeds and char - i - ots of flame.
3. So Dan - iel trained his mys - tic sight,

De - liv - ered from the li - ons' might; And John, the Bride - groom's
friend, be - came The her - ald of Mes - si - ah's Name.
4. Then grant us, Lord, like them to be
Full oft in fast and prayer with Thee; Our spir - its strength - en
with Thy grace, And give us joy to see Thy face.
5. O Fa - ther, Son, and Spir - it blest, To Thee be eve - ry prayer ad - dressed,
Who art in three - fold Name a - dored, From age to age, the on - ly Lord.

1. For - ty days and for - ty nights
Thou wert fast - ing in the wild;
For - ty days and for - ty nights
Tempt - ed, and yet un - de - filed.
2. Should not we Thy sor - row share, And from
earth - ly joys ab - stain,
Fast - ing with un - ceas - ing
prayer,
Glad with Thee to suf - fer pain?

3. Then if Sa - tan on us press, Flesh or spir - it to as - sail,
Vic - tor in the wil - der - ness, Grant we may not faint nor fail.
4. So shall we have peace di - vine; Ho - lier glad - ness ours shall be;
Round us, too, shall an - gels shine, Such as min - is - tered to Thee.
5. Keep, O keep us, Sav - ior dear, Ev - er con - stant by Thy side;
That with Thee we may ap - pear At th'e - ter - nal East - er - tide.

1. Lord, who through - out these for - ty days
For us didst fast and pray,
Teach us with Thee to mourn our sins,
And close by Thee to stay.
2. As Thou with Sa - tan didst con - tend, And
didst the vic - t'ry win,
O give us strength in
Thee to fight, In Thee to con - quer sin.

3. As Thou didst hun - ger bear and thirst, So teach us, gra - cious Lord,
To die to self, and dai - ly live By Thy most ho - ly word.
4. And through these days of pen - i - tence, And
through Thy Pas - sion - tide, For - ev - er - more, in
life and death, O Lord, with us a - bide.
5. A - bide with us that when this life Of suf - fer - ing is past,
An East - er of un - end - ing joy We may at - tain at last.

1. O love, how deep, how broad, how high!
How pass - ing thought__ and__ fan - ta - sy
That God, the Son__ of God, should take
Our mor - tal form for mor - tals' sake!
2. He sent no an - gel to our race Of high - er
or__ of__ low - er place, But wore the robe__ of
hu - man frame, And he him - self to this world came.

3. For us bap - tized, for us he bore His ho - ly fast_ and_ hun - gered sore;
For us temp - ta - tion sharp he knew; For us the tempt - er o - ver - threw.
4. For us to wick - ed men be - trayed, Scourged, mocked,_ in
crown_ of__ thorn ar - rayed; For us he bore__ the
Cross -'s death; For us at length gave up his breath.
5. For us he rose from death a - gain, For us__ he went on_ high to reign,
For us he sent_ his Spir - it here To guide, to strength - en, and to cheer.

687 ROCKINGHAM — "When I Survey The Wondrous Cross"

1. When I sur - vey the won - drous Cross, On which the Prince of
glo - ry died, My rich - est gain I count but loss,
And pour con - tempt on all my pride.
2. For - bid it,
Lord, that I should boast Save in the death of Christ my God;
All the vain things that charm me most, I sac - ri -
fice them to his Blood.
3. See from his head, his
hands, his feet, Sor - row and love flow min - gled down;

Did e'er such love and sor - row meet Or thorns com - pose so rich a crown?
4. His dy - ing crim - son like a robe, Spreads o'er his bod - y on the Tree;
Then am I dead to all the globe, And all the globe is dead to me.
5. Were the whole realm of na - ture mine, That were a pre - sent far too small;
Love so a - maz - ing, so di - vine, De - mands my soul, my life, my all.

1. O come and mourn with me a - while;
See, Mar - y calls us to her side;
O come and let us mourn with her;
Je - sus, our love, is cru - ci - fied.
2. Have we no tears to shed for him,
While sol - diers scoff and crowds de - ride?
Ah! look how pa - tient - ly he hangs;
Je - sus, our love, is cru - ci - fied.
3. How fast his feet and hands are nailed,
His bless-èd tongue with thirst is tied;
His fail - ing eyes are blind with blood;
Je - sus, our love, is cru - ci - fied.

4. Sev'n times he spoke, sev'n words of love, And all three hours his si - lence cried
For mer - cy on the souls of men; Je - sus, our love, is cru - ci - fied.
5. O break, O break, hard heart of mine. Thy weak self-love and guilt - y pride
His Pi - late and his Ju - das were; Je - sus, our love, is cru - ci - fied.
6. A bro - ken heart, a fount of tears, Ask, and they will not be de - nied;
A bro - ken heart love's cra - dle is; Je - sus, our love, is cru - ci - fied.
7. O love of God! O sin of man! In this dread act your strength is tried;
And vic - to - ry re - mains with love; Je - sus, our love, is cru - ci - fied.

689 LOVE UNKNOWN — "My Song Is Love Unknown"

1. My song is love un - known, My Sav - ior's love to
me, Love to the love - less shown, That they might
love - ly be. O who am I, That
for my sake My Lord should take Frail flesh, and die?
2. Christ came from his blest throne, Sal - va - tion to be -
stow: But peo - ple scorned, and none The longed - for
Christ— would know: But O, my Friend, My
Friend in - deed, Who at my need His life did spend!

3. Some - times they strew his way, And his sweet prais - es
sing; Re - sound - ing all the day Ho - san - nas
to their King: Then "Cru - ci - fy!" Is
all their breath, And for his death They thirst and cry.
4. They rise, and needs will have My dear Lord made a -
way; A mur - der - er they save, The Prince of
Life they slay, Yet cheer - ful he To
suf - f'ring goes, That he his foes From thence might free.

5. In life, no house, no home, My Lord on earth might have; In death no friend - ly tomb But what a stran - ger gave. What may I say? Heav'n was his home; But mine the tomb Where - in he lay.
6. Here might I stay and sing, No sto - ry so di - vine; Nev - er was love, dear King, Nev - er was grief like thine. This is my Friend, In Whose sweet praise I all my days Could glad - ly spend.

1. Who - e'er to vir - tue think - eth hard the way,
Be - cause we must have war con - tin - u - al
A - gainst the world, the flesh, the dev'l, that aye
Would force our souls in - to their bond and thrall;
Let him re - mem - ber— choose what way he shall,
E'en from the world it - self he must sus - tain
La - bor and grief, ad - ver - si - ty and pain.

2. Con - sid - er well, how fool - ish 'tis and vain, To look for heav'n through pleas - ure and de -
light, Since Christ, our lead - er and our sov - er - eign, As - cend - ed thith - er but by man - ly
fight, And bit - ter pas - sion: say, would it be right, Your - selves his faith - ful
foll - 'wers to re - cord, Yet stand on terms far bet - ter than your Lord?
3. What - e'er good work thou dost, with la - bor do: The la - bor goes, the good - ness doth re -
main; If thou do ill, with pleas - ure join'd there - to, The pleas - ure which thine e - vil works con -
tain Gli - deth a - way—thou mayst it not re - tain: Deep in thy soul the
e - vil cleaves be - hind, With pain of heart, and heav - i - ness of mind.

4. Con - sid - er well, that, both by night and day, While we so bus - i - ly pro - vide and
care For our dis - port, our rev - el, and our play, For pleas - ant mel - o - dy and dain - ty
fare, Death steal - eth on full sli - ly; un - a - ware He lieth at hand, and
shall us all sur - prise, We know not when, nor where, nor in what wise.
5. When fierce temp - ta - tions threat thy soul with loss, Think on his Pas - sion and the bit - ter
pain, Think on the mor - tal an - guish of the Cross, Think on Christ's blood let out at eve - ry
vein, Think of his pre - cious heart all rent in twain: For thy re - demp - tion
think all this was wrought; Nor be that lost which He so dear - ly bought!

1. Ah, ho - ly Je - sus, how hast thou of - fend - ed, That man to
judge thee hath in hate pre - tend - ed? By foes de - rid - ed,
by thine own re - ject - ed, O most af - flict - ed.
2. Who was the guilt - y? Who brought this up - on thee? A - las! my
trea - son, Je - sus, hath un - done thee. 'Twas I, Lord Je - sus,
I it was de - nied thee: I cru - ci - fied thee.
3. Lo, the good Shep - herd for the sheep is of - fered; The slave hath

sin - nèd, and the Son hath suf - fered; For man's a - tone - ment,
while he noth - ing heed - eth, God in - ter - ced - eth.
4. For me, kind Je - sus, was thine in - car - na - tion, Thy mor - tal
sor - row, and thy life's ob - la - tion; Thy death of an - guish
and thy bit - ter Pas - sion, For my sal - va - tion.
5. There - fore, kind Je - sus, since I can - not pay thee, I do a -
dore thee, and will ev - er pray thee, Think on thy pit - y
and thy love un - swerv - ing, Not my de - serv - ing.

CRUCIFER — "Lift High The Cross"

R. Lift high the Cross, the love of Christ pro - claim,
Till all the world a - dore his sa - cred name.
1. Come, Chris - tians, fol - low where the Mas - ter trod,
Our King vic - to - rious, Christ, the Son of God. R.
2. Led on their way by this tri - um - phant sign,
The hosts of God in con - qu'ring ranks com - bine. R.
3. Each new - born sol - dier of the Cru - ci - fied

Bears on his___ brow the seal of him who died. R.
4. O Lord, once lift - ed on the glo - rious tree,
As thou hast___ prom - ised, draw men un - to thee. R.
5. Let eve - ry race and eve - ry lan - guage tell
Of him who___ saves our souls from death and hell. R.
6. Set up thy throne, that earth's de - spair may cease
Be - neath the___ shad - ow of its heal - ing peace. R.

R. All glo - ry, laud and hon - or, To Thee, Re - deem - er, King,
To Whom the lips of chil - dren Made sweet Ho - san - nas ring.
1. Thou art the King of Is - ra - el, Thou Da - vid's roy - al Son,
Who in the Lord's name com - est, The King and Bless - èd One. Refrain!
2. The com - pa - ny of An - gels Are prais - ing Thee on high,
And mor - tal men, and all things Cre - at - ed make re - ply. Refrain!

3. The peo - ple of the He - brews With palms be - fore Thee went;
Our praise and prayer and an - thems Be - fore Thee we pre - sent. Refrain!
4. To Thee be - fore Thy pas - sion, They sang their hymns of praise;
To Thee now high ex - alt - ed Our mel - o - dy we raise. Refrain!
5. Thou didst ac - cept their prais - es; Ac - cept the prayers we bring,
Who in all good de - light - est, Thou good and gra - cious King. Refrain!

695 ST MARTIN — “Jesus, Meek And Lowly” — Father Collins

1. Je - sus, meek and low - ly, Sav - ior, pure and ho - ly,
On thy love re - ly - ing, Come I to thee fly - ing.
2. Prince of life and pow - er, My sal - va - tion's tow - er,
On the cross I view thee Call - ing sin - ners to thee.
3. There be - hold me gaz - ing At the sight a - maz - ing;
Bend - ing low be - fore thee, Help - less I a - dore thee.

4. See the red wounds stream - ing, With Christ's life - blood gleam - ing,
Blood for sin - ners flow - ing, Par - don free be - stow - ing.
5. Foun - tain rich in bless - ing, Christ's fond love ex - press - ing,
Thou my ach - ing sad - ness Turn - est in - to glad - ness.
6. Lord, in mer - cy guide me, Be thou e'er be - side me;
In thy ways di - rect me, 'Neath thy wings pro - tect me.

 KENMORE —*Vita Sanctorum, Decus Angelorum* — English Translation by McDougall

1. Life of thy saints and glo - ry of thine an - gels, Christ, who art
life of all who strive to love thee, Who by thy dy - ing
on the cross didst van - quish Death's min - i - stra - tion,
2. Save in these ho - ly days of peace thy ser - vants, Guard and sus -
tain by pledg - es of thy tri - umph, For now thy Pas - chal
feast through - out the wide world Joy they in keep - ing.
3. Now thou art Lord re - splend-ent in the high - est, And o'er the

heav - ens, God, thou art ex - alt - ed; Thence thou shalt
come, O God and man, in glo - ry, Judge, at the world's end.
4. Raise thou our hearts to know thee in thy beau - ty
Where thou dost sit at the high Fa-ther's right hand, Lest though we
rise thy per - fect jus - tice cast us In - to the dark - ness.
5. This may the Fa - ther grant us, Ho - ly Sav - ior;
This may he grant who is of both the Spir - it, With whom thou
reign - est, one in per - fect God - head, Un - to all ag - es.

697 PASCHAL LAMB —*Victimae Paschali Laudes* — Wipo of Burgundy

1. Christ the Lord is ris'n to - day, Chris - tians, haste your vows to pay;
Of - fer ye your prais - es meet At the Pas - chal Vic - tim's feet.
For the sheep the Lamb hath bled, Sin - less in the sin - ner's stead;
Christ the Lord is ris'n on high, Now he lives no more to die.
2. Christ, the Vic - tim un - de - filed, Man to God hath rec - on - ciled;
When in strange and aw - ful strife Met to - geth - er Death and Life.
Chris - tians, on this hap - py day Haste with joy your vows to pay;
Christ the Lord is ris'n on high, Now he lives no more to die.

3. Say, O won - d'ring Mar - y, say, What thou saw - est on thy way?
"I be - held, where Christ had lain, Emp - ty tomb and__ An - gels twain;
I be - held the glo - ry bright Of the ris - ing Lord of light:
Christ my hope is ris'n a - gain, Now he lives, and__ lives to reign."
4. Christ, who once for sin - ners bled, Now the first - born from the dead,
Thron'd in end - less might and pow'r Lives and reigns for__ ev - er - more.
Hail, e - ter - nal Hope on high! Hail, thou King of vic - to - ry!
Hail, thou Prince of Life a - dored! Help and save us,__ gra - cious Lord!

 AVE VIRGO VIRGINUM — "Come, Ye Faithful, Raise The Strain" — Saint John Damascene

1. Come, ye faith - ful, raise the strain Of tri - um - phant glad - ness;
God hath brought his Is - ra - el In - to joy from sad - ness;
Loosed from Phar - aoh's bit - ter yoke Ja - cob's sons and daugh - ters;
Led them with un - mois - tened foot Through the Red Sea wa - ters.
2. 'Tis the spring of souls to - day; Christ hath burst his pris - on,
And from three days' sleep in death As a sun hath ris - en;
All the win - ter of our sins, Long and dark, is fly - ing
From his light, to whom we give Laud and praise un - dy - ing.

3. Now the queen of sea - sons, bright With the day of splen - dor,
With the roy - al feast of feasts, Comes its joy to ren - der;
Comes to glad Je - ru - sa - lem, Who with true af - fec - tion
Wel - comes in un - wea - ried strains Je - sus' res - ur - rec - tion.
4. Nei - ther might the gates of death, Nor the tomb's dark por - tal,
Nor the watch - ers, nor the seal Hold thee as a mor - tal;
But to - day a - midst the twelve Thou didst stand, be - stow - ing
That thy peace which ev - er - more Pass - eth hu - man know - ing.

1. Je - sus Christ is ris'n to - day, Al - - le - lu - ia!
Our tri - um - phant ho - ly day, Al - - le - lu - ia!
Who did once up - on the cross, Al - - le - lu - ia!
Suf - fer to re - deem our loss. Al - - le - lu - ia!
2. Hymns of praise then let us sing, Al - - le - lu - ia!
Un - to Christ, our heav'n - ly King, Al - - le - lu - ia!

Who en - dured the Cross and grave, Al - - le - lu - ia!
Sin - ners_ to re - deem and save._ Al - - le - lu - ia!
3. But the pains which He en - dured,_ Al - - le - lu - ia!
Our sal - va - tion have pro - cured,_ Al - - le - lu - ia!
Now a - bove the sky He's King, Al - - le - lu - ia!
Where_ the_ an - gels ev - er sing._ Al - - le - lu - ia!

4. Sing we to our God a - bove,_ Al - - le - lu - ia!
Praise, e - ter - nal as His love,_ Al - - le - lu - ia!
Praise Him, all ye heav'n - ly host, Al - - le - lu - ia!
Fa - ther,_ Son, and Ho - ly Ghost._ Al - - le - lu - ia!

1. Let us re - joice right heart - i - ly, Al - le - lu - ia!
Mar - y of sighs and tears is free, Al - le - lu - ia!
Now all the mists have fled a - way, Al - le - lu - ia!
Where glows the cher - ished beam of day, Al - le - lu - ia!
R. Al - le - lu - ia, al - le - lu - ia, al - le - lu - ia.
2. Where then, O joy - a - mass - ing heart, Al - le - lu - ia!
Where is thy woe, where is thy smart? Al - le - lu - ia!
Well, heart, how well it goes with thee, Al - le - lu - ia!

Joy - filled to thy ca - pac - i - ty, Al - le - lu - ia!
R. Al - le - lu - ia, al - le - lu - ia, al - le - lu - ia.
3. Tell us, O Mar - y, Maid - en clean, Al - le - lu - ia!
This from thy Son dost thou not glean? Al - le - lu - ia!
Thy Son in - deed a - rose a - gain, Al - le - lu - ia!
Thy glad - ness makes no mar - vel then, Al - le - lu - ia!
R. Al - le - lu - ia, al - le - lu - ia, al - le - lu - ia.

4. Out of his wounds are run - ning forth, Al - le - lu - ia! Five lakes of
joy, five seas of mirth, Al - le - lu - ia! Joy that has flood - ed o - ver
thee, Al - le - lu - ia! And through thy heart gone cours - ing free,
Al - le - lu - ia! R. Al - le - lu - ia, al - le - lu - ia, al - le - lu - ia.
5. Now deep in joys thy heart is found, Al - le - lu - ia! And joy doth
more and more a - bound, Al - le - lu - ia! Vouch - safe a thought for us to
spare, Al - le - lu - ia! A drop with - al with us to share, Al - le -
lu - ia! R. Al - le - lu - ia, al - le - lu - ia, al - le - lu - ia.

701 LA ROCHELLE — *Aurora Caelum Purpurat* — English Translation by Campbell of Skerrington

1. The morn had spread her crim - son rays, When
rang the skies with shouts of praise; Earth joined the joy - ful
hymn to swell, That brought de - spair to van - quished hell.
2. He comes vic - to - rious from the grave, Who
died our sin - ful souls to save; He brings with Him to
light of day The saints who long im - pris - oned lay.

3. Let hymns of joy to grief suc - ceed: We know that Christ is ris'n in - deed;
We hear his white - robed an - gel's voice, And in our ris - en Lord re - joice.
4. With Christ we died, with Christ we rose, When at the font His name we chose;
Oh, nev - er - more let sin de - face Our souls en - robed in pas - chal grace.
5. To God the Fa - ther let us sing, To God the Son, our ris - en king,
And e - qual - ly let us a - dore The Spir - it, God for ev - er - more.

 SAVANNAH — "Love's Redeeming Work Is Done"

1. Love's re - deem - ing work is done; Fought the__ fight, the bat - tle won:
Lo, our Sun's e - clipse is o'er! Lo, he sets in__ blood no more!
2. Vain the__ stone, the watch,_ the seal, Christ has__ burst the gates_ of hell;
Death in vain for - bids his rise; Christ has o - pened Par - a - dise.

* *A transposed organ accompaniment has been provided for optional use.*

3. Lives again our glorious King; Where, O death, is now thy sting?
Dying once, he all doth save; Where thy victory, O grave?
4. Soar we now where Christ has led, Foll'wing our exalted Head;
Made like him, like him we rise; Ours the Cross, the grave, the skies.
5. Hail the Lord of earth and heav'n! Praise to thee by both be giv'n:
Thee we greet triumphant now; Hail, the Resurrection thou!

1. Hail the day that sees him rise, Al - - le - lu ia.
To the throne be - yond the skies. Al - - le - lu - ia.
Pas - chal Lamb for sin - ners giv'n Al - - le - lu - ia.
En - ters now the high - est heav'n. Al - - le - lu - ia.
2. There the glo - rious tri - umph waits; Al - - le - lu - ia.
Lift your heads, e - ter - nal gates! Al - - le - lu - ia.
He has van - quished death and sin; Al - - le - lu - ia.

Take the King of - glo - ry___ in. Al - le - lu - ia.
3. See! the heav'n its Lord re - ceives, Al - le - lu - ia.
Yet he loves the earth he___ leaves; Al - le - lu - ia.
Though re - turn - ing to___ his___ throne, Al - le - lu - ia.
Still he calls man - kind his___ own. Al - le - lu - ia.
4. See! he lifts his hands a - bove; Al - le - lu - ia.
See! he shows the prints of___ love: Al - le - lu - ia.

Hark! his gra - cious lips be - stow Al - - le - lu - ia.
Bless - ings on his Church be - low. Al - - le - lu - ia.
5. Still for us he in - ter - cedes; Al - - le - lu - ia.
His pre - vail - ing death he pleads; Al - - le - lu - ia.
Near him - self pre - pares our place, Al - - le - lu - ia.
Har - bin - ger of hu - man race. Al - - le - lu - ia.
6. Lord, though part - ed from our sight, Al - - le - lu - ia.

Far a - bove yon az - ure height, Al - le - lu - ia.
Grant our hearts may thith - er rise, Al - le - lu - ia.
Seek - ing thee be - yond the skies. Al - le - lu - ia.
7. There we shall with thee re - main, Al - le - lu - ia.
Part - ners of thine end - less reign; Al - le - lu - ia.
There thy face un - cloud - ed see, Al - le - lu - ia.
Find our heav'n of heav'ns in thee. Al - le - lu - ia.

705 BRESSANI — *Aeterne Rex Altissime, Redemptor* — English Translation by Father Fitzpatrick

1. E - ter - nal Mon - arch, King most high, Who art the world's Re - deem - er__ too,
O'er - come, to Thee did death sup - ply The tri - umph to Thy glo - ry due.
2. Thou__ mount-est now the star - ry way, Drawn thith - er by all Heav'n's de - mand,
For__ Heav'n, not man, in - vokes to - day, To rule its worlds, Thy hu - man hand.
3. That__ so this tri - une sys - tem all, The feats of Heav - en, earth and__ hell,
In__ hom - age may be - fore Thee fall And own Thee Lord, wher - e'er they dwell.
4. The__ An - gels trem - ble as they see Our mor - tal lot re - versed a - gain:

Flesh_ sinned; now flesh from sin doth free; As God the flesh of God doth reign.
5. Be_ here our joy, un - til we find That Thou a - bove art our re - ward,
Be - yond earth's joys of an - y kind, Who art the earth's one on - ly Lord.
6. To_ Thee we there - fore hum - bly cry Our sins in mer - cy to for - give,
To_ raise our hearts to Thee on high, Which by Thy loft - y grac - es live.
7. That_ when as Judge, the clouds being rent, Thou com'st, a sud - den dawn, once_ more,
Thou_ may'st re - mit our pun - ish - ment, And e - ven our lost crowns re - store.

 LASST UNS ERFREUEN — *Hymnum Canamus Gloriae* — Saint Bede the Venerable

1. A hymn of glo - ry let us sing; New songs through - out the world shall ring;
Al - le - lu - ia, al - le - lu - ia. Christ, by a road be - fore un - trod,
As - cend - eth to the throne of God. Al - le - lu - ia, al - le -
lu - ia, al - le - lu - ia, al - le - lu - ia, al - le - lu - - ia.
2. The ho - ly ap - os - tol - ic band Up - on the Mount of Ol - ives stand,
Al - le - lu - ia, al - le - lu - ia. And, with the Vir - gin - moth - er, see
Their Lord's re - splend - ent maj - es - ty. Al - le - lu - ia, al - le -
lu - ia, al - le - lu - ia, al - le - lu - ia, al - le - lu - - ia.

3. To whom the an-gels, draw - ing nigh: "Why stand and gaze up-on the sky?"
Al - le - lu - ia, al - le - lu - ia. "This is the Sav - ior," thus they say.
"This is His no - ble tri - umph day!" Al - le - lu - ia, al - le -
lu - ia, al - le - lu - ia, al - le - lu - ia, al - le - lu - ia.
4. "A - gain ye shall be - hold Him so As ye to - day have seen Him go;
Al - le - lu - ia, al - le - lu - ia. In glo-rious pomp as - cend - ing high,
Up to the por - tals of the sky." Al - le - lu - ia, al - le -
lu - ia, al - le - lu - ia, al - le - lu - ia, al - le - lu - ia.

5. Be Thou our joy and strong de - fense, Who art our fu - ture rec - om - pense:
Al - le - lu - ia, al - le - lu - ia. So shall the light that springs from Thee
Be ours through all e - ter - ni - ty. Al - le - lu - ia, al - le -
lu - ia, al - le - lu - ia, al - le - lu - ia, al - le - lu - ia.
6. O ris - en Christ, as - cend - ed Lord, All praise to Thee let earth ac - cord,
Al - le - lu - ia, al - le - lu - ia. Who art, while end - less ag - es run,
With Fa - ther and with Spir - it One. Al - le - lu - ia, al - le -
lu - ia, al - le - lu - ia, al - le - lu - ia, al - le - lu - ia.

WHITEHALL — *Nunc Sancte Nobis Spiritus* — English Translation by Cardinal Newman

1. Come, Ho - ly Ghost, who ev - er One Art with the Fa - ther and the Son;
Come, Ho - ly Ghost, our souls pos - sess With Thy full flood of ho - li - ness.

#102 has (optional) organ accompaniment at a higher key.

2. Let flesh, and heart, and lips, and mind, Sound forth our wit - ness to man - kind;
And love light up our mor - tal frame, Till oth - ers catch the liv - ing flame.
3. Thou ev - er - bless - èd Three in One, O Fa - ther and Co - e - qual Son,
O Ho - ly Ghost the Com - fort - er, Thy grace on Thy re - deemed con - fer.

1. Come down, O love di - vine, Seek Thou this soul_ of mine, And vis - it
it with Thine own ar - dor_ glow - ing. O Com - fort - er, draw near,
With - in my heart ap - pear, And kin - dle it, Thy ho - ly flame be -
stow - ing.
2. O let it free - ly burn, Till earth - ly
pas - sions turn To dust and ash - es in its heat con - sum - ing;
And let Thy glo - rious light Shine ev - er on my
sight, And clothe me round, the while my path il - lum - ing.

3. Let ho - ly char - i - ty Mine out - ward ves - ture be, And low - li -
ness be - come mine in - ner cloth - ing; True low - li - ness of heart,
Which takes the hum - bler part, And o'er its own short - com - ings weeps with
loath - ing.
4. And so the yearn - ing strong, With which the
soul will long, Shall far out - pass the pow'r of hu - man tell - ing;
For none can guess its grace, Till he be - come the
place Where - in the Ho - ly Spir - it makes His dwell - ing.

710 ALLES IST AN GOTTES SEGEN — *Qui Procedis Ab Utroque* — English Transl. by Monsignor Knox

1. Ho - ly Par - a - clete, life - giv - er, Who in love pro - ceed - est ev - er
From the Fa - ther, from the Son, Loose our tongues, thy prais - es learn - ing,
Fire our hearts, with ar - dors burn - ing From thy liv - ing flame be - gun.
2. Of thy gift is all man know - eth; To his feet thy guid - ance show - eth
Ways of jus - tice, paths of peace, Sin - ners hard - ened still re - ject - ing,
Sin - ners par - doned still pro - tect - ing By thy wis - dom's sure in - crease.
3. Thou canst change the heart of be - ing; Sac - ra - ments by thy de - cree - ing

Win their pow'r to___ heal and bless; Thou canst con - quer sin's il - lu - sion,
Thou canst put to quick con - fu - sion All our foes'_ de - ceit - ful - ness.
4. Thou, who cam - est down in old - en Time to com - fort and em - bold - en
Christ's a - pos - tles__ faint with fear, Send on us, thy com - fort need - ing,
Grace, our lit - tle worth ex - ceed - ing, Eve - ry faith - ful__ soul to cheer.
5. As the Fa - ther is, so thou art; As be - fore all worlds, so now art;
Praise to him,_ while ag - es live, With the Son whose blood hath bought us,
With thy - self, whose light hath taught us, We thy earth - ly__ ser - vants give.

711 GOTT VATER SEI GEPRIESEN — *Gott Vater Sei Gepriesen* — English Transl. by Fr. Rothensteiner

1. God Fa - ther, praise and glo - ry Thy chil - dren bring to Thee.
Good will and peace to man - kind Shall now_ for - ev - er be.
R. O most Ho - ly Trin - i - ty, Un - di - vid - ed_ U - ni - ty;
Ho - ly God, Might - y God, God Im - mor - tal, be a - dored.
2. And Thou, Lord Co - e - ter - nal, God's sole_ be - got - ten Son;
O Je - sus, King a - noint - ed, Who hast_ re - demp - tion won.

R. O most Ho - ly Trin - i - ty, Un - di - vid - ed U - ni - ty;
Ho - ly God, Might - y God, God Im - mor - tal, be a - dored.
3. O Ho - ly Ghost, Cre - a - tor, Thou Gift of God most high;
Life, love and ho - ly wis - dom, Our weak - ness now sup - ply.
R. O most Ho - ly Trin - i - ty, Un - di - vid - ed U - ni - ty;
Ho - ly God, Might - y God, God Im - mor - tal, be a - dored.

712 THAXTED — "To Thee, O Gracious Father" — Father Phillips

1. To___ thee, O gra - cious Fa - ther, we lift our lov - ing hearts;
to___ us the Bread of Heav - en e - ter - nal life im - parts.
We___ thank thee for thy fa - vor that___ marks us as thine own;
marks us as thine
Lord,___ keep us ev - er faith - ful, who come be - fore thy throne.
What_ love thou hast be - stowed on us, a love which makes us free!
It___ cleans - es us from ev' - ry sin, and keeps us close to thee.

2. To__ thee, O Christ our Sav - ior, we come for sav - ing grace;
we__ see how ten - der love__ is, by look - ing on thy face.
Keep__ us from all things hurt - ful by the pow - er of thy Cross;
pow - er of thy Cross;__
and__ help us to re - mem - ber our gain comes from thy loss.
What__ heav'n - ly Food is ours,__ Lord, this Food which makes us free!
It__ fills our hearts and makes us whole, and keeps us close to thee.

3. To thee, O Ho - ly Spir - it, we whis - per our de - sire;
our lives are emp - ty ves - sels: Lord, fill them with thy fire.
Make us thy faith - ful peo - ple who seek to do thy will;
seek to do thy will;
give us thy gifts of pow - er, our emp - ty hearts to fill.
What peace that pass - es ev'- ry thought, that peace which makes us free!
It ban - ish - es each doubt and fear, and keeps us close to thee.

4. From_ thee, O Tri - une God - head, sal - va - tion is come down;
A - tone - ment now is giv - en, man - kind re - ceives his crown.
In___ Sac - ra - ment tre - men - dous we___ touch e - ter - ni - ty;
touch e - ter - ni - ty;___
we___ love thee, God our Sav - ior: thou art our des - ti - ny.
O__ Fa - ther, Son, and Ho - ly Ghost, our faith shall nev - er cease!
In___ thee we have e - ter - nal life, and nev - er - end - ing peace.

 CUPERTINO — *Adesto Pater Domine* — English Translation by McDougall

1. Be pre - sent, Fa - ther, Lord of all, Thou Light that
art most wor - ship - ful, Be near us as our prayers we raise
And heart u - nites with mouth in praise.
2. And may thy Son, the Sole - be - got, The Co - e -
ter - nal, fail us not, Who hath re - deemed us on the Rood
And paid the price of his own blood.
3. And may the Ho - ly Ghost be nigh, The Com - fort -

er from thee on high, Who doth a - dorn our hum - ble race
With sev'n - fold mys - tic gifts of grace.
4. O ev - er - last - ing Trin - i - ty, And ev - er per - fect U - ni - ty,
Hear thou from heav'n thy sup - pliants' vows, And cleanse from
stains of sin their brows.
5. Laud, hon - or, might and
praise be done To God the Fa - ther and the Son, And to
the Ho - ly Par - a - clete Through end - less ag - es, as is meet.

1. Be pre - sent, Fa - ther, Lord of all, Thou Light that
art most wor - ship - ful, Be near us as our
prayers we raise And heart u - nites with mouth in praise.
2. And may thy Son, the Sole - be - got, The Co - e -
ter - nal, fail us not, Who hath re - deemed us
on the Rood And paid the price of his own blood.
3. And may the Ho - ly Ghost be nigh, The Com - fort -

er from thee on high, Who doth a - dorn our
hum - ble race With sev'n - fold mys - tic gifts of grace.
4. O ev - er - last - ing Trin - i - ty, And ev - er
per - fect U - ni - ty, Hear thou from heav'n thy
sup - pliants' vows, And cleanse from stains of sin their brows.
5. Laud, hon - or, might and praise be done To God the Fa - ther and the Son,
And to the Ho - ly Par - a - clete Through end - less ag - es, as is meet.

 ORIEL — "God Our Father, Lord Of Glory" — Father Phillips

1. God our Fa - ther, Lord of glo - ry, Thanks and praise we give to Thee;
In Thy mer - cy to our fa - thers, Thou didst bring them through the sea.
So by wa - ter hast Thou saved us, Now from Ad - am's sin set free.
2. Je - sus Christ, our Ris - en Sav - ior, Of Thy sac - ri - fice we sing;
As the lamb in an - cient mys - t'ry To Thy peo - ple life didst bring,
So in Eu - cha - ris - tic glo - ry, Thou, God's Lamb, art made our King.

3. Ho - ly Spir - it, Breath from heav - en, We Thy pre - cious gifts em - brace;
At cre - a - tion all things liv - ing Thou didst sanc - ti - fy with grace.
So may we, cre - a - tion's glo - ry, Be for Thee a dwell - ing place.
4. Lov - ing mer - cy of the Fa - ther, Sac - ri - fice of Christ the Son,
Quick - 'ning pow - er of the Spir - it: In us let Thy work be done!
May we rise to life e - ter - nal, That our Pas - chal joy be won.

718 REGENT SQUARE — "God Our Father, Lord Of Glory" — Father Phillips

3. Ho - ly Spir - it, Breath from heav - en, We Thy pre - cious gifts em - brace;
At cre - a - tion all things liv - ing Thou didst sanc - ti - fy with grace.
So may we, cre - a - tion's glo - ry, Be for Thee a dwell - ing place.
4. Lov - ing mer - cy of the Fa - ther, Sac - ri - fice of Christ the Son,
Quick - 'ning pow - er of the Spir - it: In us let Thy_ work be done!
May we rise to life e - ter - nal, That our Pas - chal joy be won.

719 DULCE CARMEN — "God Our Father, Lord Of Glory" — Father Phillips

3. Ho - ly Spir - it, Breath from heav - en, We Thy pre - cious gifts em - brace;
At cre - a - tion all things liv - ing Thou didst sanc - ti - fy with grace.
So may we, cre - a - tion's glo - ry, Be__ for__ Thee a dwell - ing place.
4. Lov - ing mer - cy of the Fa - ther, Sac - ri - fice of Christ the Son,
Quick - 'ning pow - er of the Spir - it: In us let__ Thy__ work be done!
May we rise to life e - ter - nal, That__ our__ Pas - chal joy be won.

722 LASST UNS ERFREUEN — “Almighty God, Majestic King” — Father Phillips

1. Al - might - y God, ma - jes - tic King, with joy - ful hearts thy peo - ple sing:
Al - le - lu - ia, al - le - lu - ia. For all good gifts we of - fer praise,
and ask thy bless - ings all our days: Al - le - lu - ia, al - le -
lu - ia, al - le - lu - ia, al - le - lu - ia, al - le - lu - ia.
2. Lord Je - sus Christ, E - ter - nal Son, who on the cross sal - va - tion won:
Al - le - lu - ia, al - le - lu - ia. Through thy great sac - ri - fice of love

we join our song with saints a - bove: Al - le - lu - ia, al - le -
lu - ia, al - le - lu - ia, al - le - lu - ia, al - le - lu - - ia.
3. O Ho - ly Spir - it, Light di - vine, dwell in these hearts and souls of thine:
Al - le - lu - ia, al - le - lu - ia. Keep us in peace and u - ni - ty
that with one voice our chant may be: Al - le - lu - ia, al - le -
lu - ia, al - le - lu - ia, al - le - lu - ia, al - le - lu - - ia.

1. We pray Thee, heav'n-ly Fa-ther, to hear us in Thy love,
and pour up-on Thy chil-dren the unc-tion from a-bove;
that so in love a-bid-ing, from all de-file-ment free,
all de-file-ment
we may in pure-ness of-fer a sac-ri-fice to Thee.
R.
R. O with thy ben-e-dic-tion up-on our souls out-poured,
may we nev-er cease in glad-ness to glo-ri-fy the Lord.
2. Be Thou our guide and help-er, Lord Je-sus Christ, we pray;

so___ may we well ap - proach Thee, if Thou wilt be the Way:
Thou,- ver - y Truth, hast prom - ised to___ help us in our strife,
help us in our
food___ of the wea - ry pil - grim, e - ter - nal source of Life. *Refrain!*
3. And___ Thou, cre - a - tor Spir - it, look on us, we are
Thine; re - new in us Thy grac - es, up - on our dark - ness shine;
un - wor - thy in our weak - ness, on___ Thee our hope is stayed,
Thee our hope is
and___ bless'd by Thy for - give - ness we will not be a - fraid. *Refrain!*

1. Fa - ther most ho - ly, gra - cious and for - giv - ing, Christ, high ex -
alt - ed, prince of our sal - va - tion, Spir - it of coun - sel,
nour - ish - ing cre - a - tion, God ev - er - liv - ing;
2. Trin - i - ty bless - èd, U - ni - ty un - sha - ken, On - ly true
God - head, sea of boun - ty end - less, Light of the an - gels,
suc - cor thou the friend - less, Shield the for - sak - en.

3. All things thou mad - est— noth - ing doth but preach thee, Serv - ing thee
ev - er in its course or - dain - èd We too would hymn thee;
this our prayer un - feign - èd Hear, we be - seech thee.
4. Bound - less thy praise be, whom no lim - it bound - eth, God in three
Per - sons, high in heav - en liv - ing, Where ad - o - ra - tion,
hom - age and thanks - giv - ing Ev - er re - sound - eth.

725 NON DIGNUS — "O Lord, I Am Not Worthy"

1. O___ Lord, I am not wor - thy That__ thou should'st come to me:
But__ speak the word of com - fort, My spir - it healed shall be.
2. And__ hum - bly I'll re - ceive thee, The__ bride-groom of my soul,
No__ more by sin to grieve thee Or fly thy sweet con - trol.
3. E - ter - nal Ho - ly Spir - it, Un - wor - thy though I be,
Pre - pare me to re - ceive him And trust the Word to me.

4. In - crease my faith, dear Je - sus, In___ thy Real Pres - ence here,
And___ make me feel most deep - ly That thou to me art near.
5. My___ hope in thee now strength - en, O___ Sav - ior of my soul,
Lest___ by temp - ta - tion blind - ed, I turn from my true goal.
6. O___ Sac - ra - ment most ho - ly, O___ Sac - ra - ment di - vine!
All___ praise and all thanks - giv - ing Be ev - 'ry mo - ment Thine.

1. O Je - sus, we a - dore thee, Who in thy love di - vine,
Con - ceal thy might - y God - head In forms of bread and wine.
R. O Sac - ra - ment most ho - ly, O Sac - ra - ment di - vine,
All praise and all thanks - giv - ing be ev - 'ry mo - ment thine!
2. O Je - sus we a - dore thee, Our Vic - tim and our Priest,
Whose pre - cious blood and bod - y Be - come our sa - cred feast. Refrain!

3. O Je - sus we a - dore thee, Our Sav - ior and our King,
And with the saints and an - gels, A hum - ble hom - age bring. *Refrain!*
4. O Je - sus, we a - dore thee; Come, live in us, we pray,
That all our thoughts and ac - tions Be thine a - lone to - day. *Refrain!*
5. O come, all you who la - bor In sor - row and in pain;
Come, eat this bread from heav - en, Your peace and strength re - gain. *Refrain!*

1. Je - sus, my Lord, my God, my all, How can I love Thee as I ought?
And how re - vere this won - drous gift, So far sur - pas - sing hope or thought?
R. Sweet Sac - ra - ment, we Thee a - dore! Oh, make us
love Thee more and more; Oh, make us love Thee more and more.
2. Had I but Mar - y's sin - less heart To love Thee with my dear - est King,
Oh, with what bursts of fer - vent praise Thy good - ness, Je - sus, would I sing! R.

3. Thy bod - y, soul,_ and God - head all;_ O mys - ter - y of love di - vine!
I can-not com - pass all_ I have,_ For all Thou hast and art are mine. R.
4. Sound, sound His prais - es high - er still,_ And come, ye an - gels, to our aid;
'Tis God, 'tis God,_ the ver - y God, Whose pow'r both man and an - gels made. R.
5. Je - sus, dear Pas - tor of_ the flock, We crowd in love a - bout Thy feet;
Our voic - es yearn_ to praise_ Thee, Lord, And joy - ful - ly Thy pres - ence greet. R.

1. Let all mor-tal flesh keep_ si - lence, And with fear and trem - bling_ stand;
Pon-der noth-ing earth - ly - mind - ed, For with bless-ing in his__ hand,
Christ our God to earth de - scend - eth, Our full hom-age to de - mand.
2. King of kings, yet born of__ Mar - y, As of old on earth he__ stood,
Lord of lords, in hu - man_ ves - ture— In the Bod - y and the__ Blood—
He will give to all the faith - ful His own self for heav'n - ly__ food.

3. Rank on rank the host of heav - en Spreads its van - guard on the way,
As the Light of light de - scend - eth From the realms of end - less day,
That the pow'rs of hell may van - ish As the dark - ness clears a - way.
4. At His feet the six - winged ser - aph; Cher - u - bim with sleep - less eye,
Veil their fac - es to the Pres - ence, As with cease - less voice they cry:
"Al - le - lu - ia, al - le - lu - ia, Al - le - lu - ia, Lord most high."

729 AURELIA — "O Jesus Christ, Remember" — Father Caswall

1. O Je - sus Christ, re - mem - ber, When Thou shalt come a - gain,
Up - on the clouds of Heav - en, With all Thy shin - ing train;
When ev - 'ry eye shall see Thee In De - i - ty re - vealed,
Who now up - on this al - tar In si - lence art con - cealed;
2. Re - mem - ber then, O Sav - ior, I sup - pli - cate of Thee,
That here I bowed be - fore Thee Up - on my bend - ed knee;

That here I owned Thy Pres - ence, And did not Thee de - ny;
And glo - ri - fied Thy great - ness Tho' hid from hu - man eye.
3. Ac - cept, Di - vine Re - deem - er, The hom - age of my praise;
Be Thou the light, and hon - or, And glo - ry of my days;
Be Thou my con - so - la - tion When death is draw - ing nigh;
Be Thou my on - ly treas - ure Through all e - ter - ni - ty.

 WESTMINSTER ABBEY F — "In The Presence Of The Blessed Sacrament"

1. Lord, en - throned in heav'n - ly splen - dor, First - be - got - ten from the dead,
Thou a - lone, our strong de - fend - er, Lift - est up thy peo - ple's head.
Al - le - lu - ia! Al - le - lu - ia! Je - sus, true and liv - ing Bread.
2. Here our humbl - est hom - age pay we; Here in lov - ing rev - 'rence bow;
Here for faith's dis - cern - ment pray we, Lest we fail to know thee now.
Al - le - lu - ia! Al - le - lu - ia! Thou art here, we ask not how.
3. Tho' the low - liest form doth veil thee As of old in Beth - le - hem,

Here as there thine an - gels hail thee, Branch and flow'r of Jes - se's stem.
Al - le - lu - ia! Al - le - lu - ia! We in wor - ship join with them.
4. Pas - chal Lamb, thine of - f'ring, fin - ished Once for all__ when thou wert slain,
In its full - ness un - di - min - ished Shall for ev - er - more re - main,
Al - le - lu - ia! Al - le - lu - ia! Cleans - ing souls from eve - ry stain.
5. Life - im - part - ing heav'n - ly Man - na, Strick - en Rock__ with stream - ing side,
Heav'n and earth with loud ho - san - na Wor - ship thee,__ the Lamb who died.
Al - le - lu - ia! Al - le - lu - ia! Ris'n, as - cend - ed, glo - ri - fied!

731 LAUDA ANIMA — "In The Presence Of The Blessed Sacrament"

Here as there thine an - gels hail thee, Branch and flow'r of Jes - se's stem.
Al - le - lu - ia! Al - le - lu - ia! We in wor - ship join with them.
4. Pas - chal Lamb, thine of - f'ring, fin - ished Once for all when thou wert slain,
In its full - ness un - di - min - ished Shall for ev - er - more re - main,
Al - le - lu - ia! Al - le - lu - ia! Cleans - ing souls from eve - ry stain.
5. Life - im - part - ing heav'n - ly Man - na, Strick - en Rock with stream - ing side,
Heav'n and earth with loud ho - san - na Wor - ship thee, the Lamb who died.
Al - le - lu - ia! Al - le - lu - ia! Ris'n, as - cend - ed, glo - ri - fied!

1. Lord, en - throned in heav'n - ly splen - dor, First - be - got - ten from the dead,
Thou a - lone, our strong de - fend - er, Lift - est up thy peo - ple's head.
Al - le - lu - ia! Al - le - lu - ia! Je - sus, true and liv - ing Bread.
2. Here our humbl - est hom - age pay we; Here in lov - ing rev - 'rence bow;
Here for faith's dis - cern - ment pray we, Lest we fail to know thee now.
Al - le - lu - ia! Al - le - lu - ia! Thou art here, we ask not how.
3. Tho' the low - liest form doth veil thee As of old in Beth - le - hem,

Here as there thine an - gels hail thee, Branch and flow'r of Jes - se's stem.
Al - le - lu - ia! Al - le - lu - ia! We in wor - ship join with them.
4. Pas - chal Lamb, thine of - f'ring, fin - ished Once for all when thou wert slain,
In its full - ness un - di - min - ished Shall for ev - er - more re - main,
Al - le - lu - ia! Al - le - lu - ia! Cleans - ing souls from eve - ry stain.
5. Life - im - part - ing heav'n - ly Man - na, Strick - en Rock with stream - ing side,
Heav'n and earth with loud ho - san - na Wor - ship thee, the Lamb who died.
Al - le - lu - ia! Al - le - lu - ia! Ris'n, as - cend - ed, glo - ri - fied!

1. Pa - nis an - gé - li - cus fit pa - nis hó - mi - num: Dat pa - nis
caé - li - cus fi - gú - ris tér - mi - num: O res mi - rá - bi - lis!
man - dú - cat Dó - mi - num Pau - per, sér - vus, et hú - mi - lis.
2. Te tri - na Dé - i - tas u - ná - que pó - sci - mus, Sic nos tu
ví - si - ta, sic - ut te có - li - mus: Per tu - as sé - mi - tas duc nos quo
tén - di - mus, Ad lu - cem quam in - há - bi - tas. A - men.

1. O Food the pil - grim need - eth, O Bread which an - gels feed - eth,
O Man - na from a - bove! The souls that hun - ger feed Thou,
The hearts that seek Thee lead Thou With Thy most_ ten - der love.
2. O Foun - tain ru - by - glow - ing, O Stream of love_ out - flow - ing
From Je - sus' pier - cèd side! This thought a - lone shall bless us,
This one de - sire pos - sess us, To drink of__ Thy sweet tide.
3. O Je - sus, by Thee bid - den, We here a - dore_ Thee, hid - den 'Neath forms of bread and wine.
Grant when the veil is riv - en, We may be - hold, in heav - en, Thy coun - te - nance di - vine.

736 O ESCA VIATORUM — *O Esca Viatorum*

1. O___ Food the pil - grim need - eth, O Bread which an - gels feed - eth, O
Man - na from a - bove! The souls that hun - ger__ feed Thou, The hearts that seek Thee_
lead Thou With Thy most ten - der__ love. With Thy most ten - der love.
2. O___ Foun - tain ru - by - glow - ing, O Stream of love out - flow - ing From
Je - sus' pier - cèd side! This thought a - lone shall bless us, This one de - sire pos -
sess us, To drink of Thy__ sweet tide. To drink of Thy sweet tide.
3. O___ Je - sus, by Thee bid - den, We here a - dore Thee, hid - den 'Neath

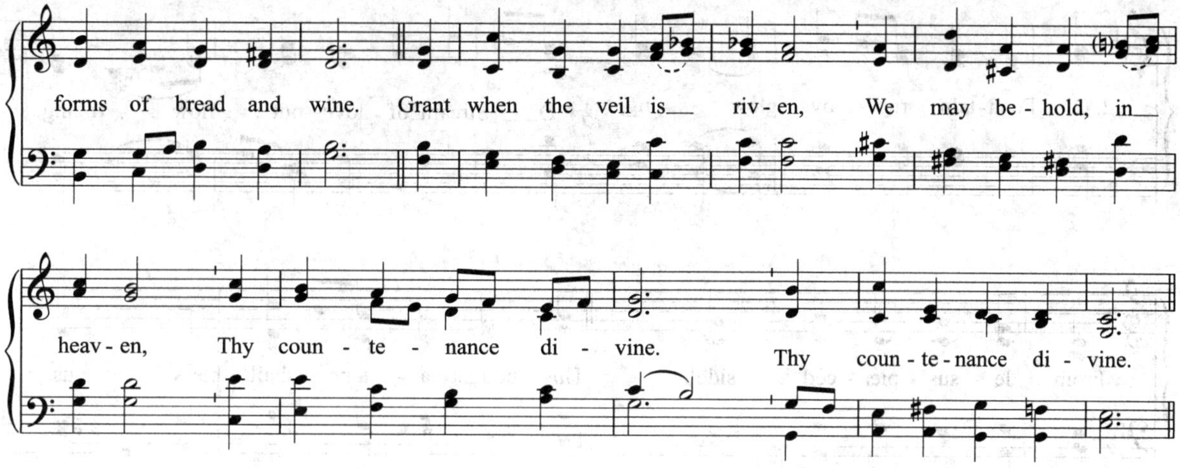
forms of bread and wine. Grant when the veil is__ riv-en, We may be-hold, in__
heav-en, Thy coun-te-nance di-vine. Thy coun-te-nance di-vine.

INNSBRUCK — *O Esca Viatorum*

1. O Food the pil-grim need-eth, O__ Bread which an-gels feed-eth,
O Man-na from a-bove! The souls that hun-ger feed Thou,
The__ hearts that seek Thee lead Thou With Thy__ most ten-der love.

2. O Foun-tain ru - by - glow - ing, O__ Stream of love out - flow - ing
From Je - sus' pier - cèd side! This thought a - lone__ shall bless us,
This__ one de - sire pos - sess us, To drink of Thy sweet tide.
3. O Je - sus, by__ Thee bid - den, We__ here a - dore Thee, hid - den
'Neath forms of bread and wine. Grant when the veil__ is riv - en,
We__ may be - hold, in heav - en, Thy coun - te - nance di - vine.

1. O pre - cious Lord, once born for us in sta - ble small and poor;
be born a - gain with - in our hearts, and there let us a - dore.
2. As once our Sav - ior thou didst come, both Man and God di - vine,
so now thou giv - est Flesh and Blood 'neath forms of bread and wine.
3. Sweet Fruit of Vir - gin Mar - y's womb, once hid from earth - ly sight,
may we thy chil - dren fruit - ful be, and show the world thy Light.
4. Now stay with us, Lord Je - sus Christ, in sol - emn Mys - ter - y,
that when our work on earth be done thy glo - ry we may see.

* Many other melodies and translations can be used for O Salutaris Hostia. For more options, search the index for "Verbum Supernum Prodiens" by St. Thomas Aquinas (d. 1274).

When singing SATB, many choirmasters will raise the pitch:

1. O sav - ing Vic - tim, op - 'ning wide The gate of Heav'n to man be - low,
1. O sa - lu - tá - ris hó - sti - a, Quae cae - li pan - dis ó - sti - um,
Our foes press on from ev' - ry__ side, Thine aid sup - ply, Thy strength be - stow.
Bel - la pre - munt ho - stí - li - a; Da ro - bur, fer au - xí - li - um.
2. To Thy great Name be end - less praise, Im - mor - tal God - head, One in Three;
2. U - ni tri - nó - que Dó - mi - no Sit sem - pi - tér - na gló - ri - a,
O grant us end - less length of__ days In our true na - tive land, with Thee.
Qui vi - tam si - ne tér - mi - no No - bis do - net in pá - tri - a.

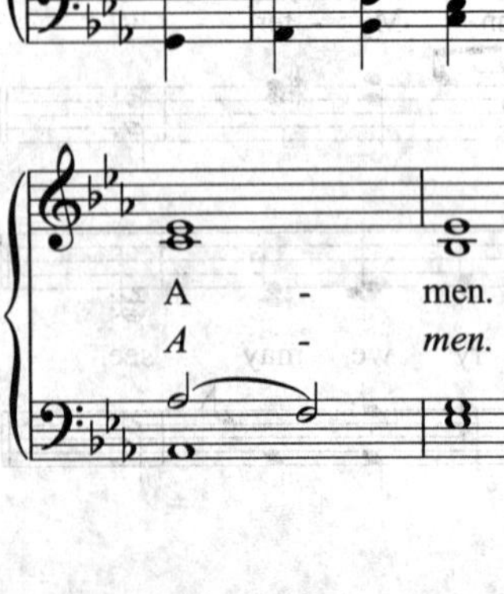
A - men.
A - men.

* Many other melodies and translations can be used for Tantum Ergo. Search the index for "Pange Lingua" by St. Thomas Aquinas (d. 1274).

Shortly before the blessing with the Sanctissimum, the "Tantum Ergo" is sung:

1. Down in ad - o - ra - tion fall - ing, This great Sac - ra - ment we hail;
1. Tan - tum er - go Sa - cra - mén - tum Ve - ne - ré - mur cér - nu - i:
O - ver an - cient forms of wor - ship New - er rites of grace pre - vail;
Et an - tí - quum do - cu - mén - tum No - vo ce - dat rí - tu - i:
Faith re - minds us Christ is pre - sent When our fee - ble sens - es fail.
Prae - stet fi - des sup - ple - mén - tum Sén - su - um de - fé - ctu - i.
2. To the Ev - er - last - ing Fa - ther, And the Son who reigns on high,
2. Ge - ni - tó - ri, Ge - ni - tó - que Laus et ju - bi - lá - ti - o,
With the Ho - ly Ghost pro - ceed - ing Forth from Each e - ter - nal - ly,
Sa - lus, ho - nor, vir - tus quo - que Sit et be - ne - dí - cti - o:
Be sal - va - tion, hon - or, bless - ing, Might, and end - less maj - es - ty. A - men.
Pro - ce - dén - ti ab u - tró - que Com - par sit lau - dá - ti - o. A - men.

740 AURELIA — "Behold Our Lord Transfigured" — Father Phillips

1. Be - hold our Lord trans - fig - ured, In Sac - ra - ment Di - vine;
His glo - ry deep - ly hid - den, 'Neath forms of Bread and Wine.
Our eyes of faith be - hold Him, Sal - va - tion is out - poured;
The Sav - ior dwells a - mong us, By ev - 'ry heart a - dored.
2. No long - er on the moun - tain With Pe - ter, James and John,
Our pre - cious Sav - ior bids us To walk where saints have gone.

He has no last - ing dwell - ing, Save in the hearts of men;
He feeds us with His Bod - y, To make us whole a - gain.
3. With Mo - ses and E - li - jah, We wor - ship Christ our King;
Lord, make our souls trans - fig - ured, Let us with an - gels sing.
Lead us in paths of glo - ry, Give tongues to sing thy praise;
Lord Je - sus, keep us faith - ful, Now and for all our days.

741 KING's LYNN — "Behold Our Lord Transfigured" — Father Phillips

He has no last - ing dwell - ing, Save in the hearts of men;
He feeds us with His Bod - y, To make us whole a - gain.
3. With Mo - ses and E - li - jah, We wor - ship Christ our King;
Lord, make our souls trans - fig - ured, Let us with an - gels sing.
Lead us in paths of glo - ry, Give tongues to sing thy praise;
Lord Je - sus, keep us faith - ful, Now and for all our days.

1. Be - hold our Lord trans - fig - ured, In Sac - ra - ment Di - vine;
His glo - ry deep - ly hid - den, 'Neath forms of Bread and Wine.
Our eyes of faith be - hold Him, Sal - va - tion is out - poured;
The Sav - ior dwells a - mong us, By ev - 'ry heart a - dored.
2. No long - er on the moun - tain With Pe - ter, James and John,
Our pre - cious Sav - ior bids us To walk where saints have gone.

He has no last - ing dwell - ing, Save in the hearts of men;
He feeds us with His Bod - y, To make us whole a - gain.
3. With Mo - ses and E - li - jah, We wor - ship Christ our King;
Lord, make our souls trans - fig - ured, Let us with an - gels sing.
Lead us in paths of glo - ry, Give tongues to sing thy praise;
Lord Je - sus, keep us faith - ful, Now and for all our days.

1. All ye who seek on Christ to gaze, Your eyes a - bove this world up - raise,
For there a to - ken you may_ see Of His e - ter - nal maj - es - ty.
2. A thing all glo - rious we be - hold, That knows no end and grows not old,
Ex - alt - ed, lim - it - less, sub - lime, And an - cient ere cre - a - tion's prime.

* *A transposed organ accompaniment has been provided for optional use.*

3. This is that King whose sov-'reign sway The Gen-tiles and the Jews o - bey,
To Abr-'ham prom - ised and de - creed To rule his num - 'rous faith - ful seed.
4. His wit - ness - es the Proph - ets are, And, there - with - al, from Heav'n a - jar,
His Fa - ther's wit - ness we re - ceive, Who bids us hear Him and be - lieve.
5. Be glo - ry, Je - sus, un - to Thee, Whom Thou dost let Thy chil - dren see,
Whom with the Fa - ther we a - dore And Ho - ly Ghost, for ev - er - more.

745 FESTAL SONG — *Quicumque Christum Quaeritis* — English Translation by Campbell of Skerrington

1. O ye, the tru - ly wise, Who in__ the Lord de - light,
Un - to the__ hills lift up your eyes, And see__ that glo - rious Sight.
2. O form sur - pas - sing far All love - li - ness of earth,
More an - cient_ than the morn - ing - star, In thy__ mys - te - rious birth.
3. Thou on - ly art our head, 'Tis thou__ whom we a - dore,
To faith - ful__ Abr - 'ham prom - is - èd A king__ for ev - er - more.

4. Proph - ets fore - told his birth, And wit - nessed when he came,
The Fa - ther speaks to all the earth To hear, and fear his name.
5. To low - ly hearts re - vealed, Our Sav - ior we a - dore,
Like trib - ute to the Fa - ther yield, And Spir - it ev - er - more.

746 POTSDAM — *Lux Alma, Jesu, Mentium* — English Translation by Cardinal Newman

1. Light of the anx - ious heart, Je - sus, Thou dost ap - pear,
To bid the gloom of guilt de - part, And shed Thy sweet - ness here.
2. Joy - ous is he, with whom, God's Word, Thou dost a - bide;
Sweet Light of our e - ter - nal home, To flesh - ly sense de - nied.
3. Bright - ness of God a - bove! Un - fath - om - a - ble grace!
Vouch - safe a pre - sent fount of love. To cleanse Thy cho - sen place.
4. To Thee, whom chil - dren see, The Fa - ther ev - er blest,
The Ho - ly Spir - it, One and Three, Be end - less praise ad - dressed.

1. Bless - èd Lamb, on Cal - v'ry's moun - tain Slain to take our sins a - way, Let the drops of
that rich foun - tain Our tre - men - dous ran - som pay: Sa - cred Sav - ior, Sa - cred
Sav - ior, Low - ly at thy feet we pray.
2. Bless - èd Lamb, vouch - safe us par -
don, In thy love our souls con - fide: By thy groans with - in the gar - den,
By the death which Thou hast died: Let thy Pas - sion, let thy Pas - sion Ev - er -
more with us a - bide!
3. So shall Peace, sweet Peace, be giv - en,
Pur - chase of thy pre - cious pain; So shall earth but lead to heav - en, Since for us the
Lamb was slain! Dear Re - deem - er, Dear Re - deem - er, Thou can'st not have died in vain.

1. Who is this from E - dom com - ing, he who out of Bos - ra fares,
in his bright a - dorn - ment shin - ing, cloth - ing crim - son - dyed who wears?
Who is he with val - or strid - ing, girt with might and maj - es - ty,
as a he - ro and de - fend - er, just re - quit - als to de - cree?
Word of God, the True, the Faith - ful, in his mouth a sharp - ened sword,
on his thigh and rai - ment writ - ten, King of kings, of lords the Lord.
2. Why is his ap - par - el rud - dy, like the vin - tage - tread - er's dress,
like the garb of those who tram - ple on the har - vest, wine to press?

Grape has nev - er stained his ves - ture: see, it is em - brued with blood,
that which has sub - dued the na - tions, sat - is - fied the wrath of God.
Man - y di - a - dems as - sum - ing, his a u - ni - ver - sal sway,
with a scep - ter forged of i - ron, whom all peo - ples will o - bey.
3. What are these, the wounds that pierce him, which we view up - on his hands:
what could be the mo - ti - va - tion that such cru - el - ty de - mands?
In the house of those who loved him have these hurts on him been dealt:
not by foes, nor yet by stran - gers, but by those with whom he dwelt!

This the Shep - herd has been strick - en for the scat - tered sheep for - lorn,
for our wrongs, and for our heal - ing, stripes and bruis - es he has borne.
4. He was once de - void of beau - ty, all his come - li - ness grown dim,
naught ap - pear - ing in his vis - age that would make us pleased with him.
He be - came a man of sor - rows, deep - ly down - cast and de - spised,
no re - spect to him ac - cord - ed, heav - en's arm un - rec - og - nized.
Like a lamb be - fore the shear - er, he con - tained his eve - ry cry,

all our ills and pangs he car - ried, led at his own_ will to die.
5. Now his face out - shines the day - star, o - ver - throws its blind - ing gaze;
now his wounds, five suns pre - sent - ing, all cre - at - ed_ sight a - maze;
now his blood, e - ter - nal ran - som, tes - ta - ment for ev - er - more,
peace be - stow - ing, par - don bring - ing, gold and sil - ver ren - ders_ poor.
Light un - broached his hab - i - ta - tion, like a robe that wraps him round,
Light is he, the world who made, in whom the world sal - va - tion found.

 ST BERNARD — *Quicumque Certum Quaeritis* — English Translation by Father Caswall

1. All ye who seek a comfort sure In trouble and distress,
Whatever sorrows vex the mind, Or guilt the soul oppress:
2. Jesus, who gave himself for you Upon the Cross to die,
Opens to you his Sacred Heart; Oh, to that Heart draw nigh.
3. Ye hear how kindly he invites; Ye hear his words so blest;
"All ye that labor, come to me, And I will give you rest."

4. What meek - er than the Sav - ior's Heart? As on the Cross he lay,
It did his mur - der - ers for - give And for their par - don pray.
5. O Heart, thou joy of saints on high, Thou hope of sin - ners here!
At - tract - ed by those lov - ing words, To thee I lift my prayer.
6. Wash thou my wounds in that dear Blood Which forth from thee doth
flow; New grace, new hope in - spire; a new And bet - ter heart be - stow.

751 FESTAL SONG — *Summi Parentis Filio* — English Translation by Father Caswall

1. To Christ, the Prince of Peace, And Son of God most high,
The Fa - ther of the world to come, Sing we with ho - ly joy.
2. Deep in his Heart for us The wound of love He bore;
That love, which still He kin - dles in The hearts that Him a - dore.
3. O Je - sus, Vic - tim blest, What else but love di - vine
Could Thee con - strain to o - pen thus That sa - cred Heart of thine?

4. O Fount of end - less life, O Spring of wa - ters clear,
O Flame ce - les - tial, cleans - ing all Who un - to Thee draw near!
5. Praise to the Fa - ther be; Praise to his on - ly Son;
Praise to the bless - èd Par - a - clete, While end - less ag - es run.

1. Crown him with man - y crowns, The Lamb up - on his throne;
Hark, how the heav'n - ly an - them_ drowns All mu - sic but its own:
A - wake, my soul, and sing Of him who died for thee,
And hail him as thy match - less King Through all e - ter - ni - ty.
2. Crown him the Vir - gin's Son, The God in - car - nate born,
Whose arm those crim - son tro - phies_ won Which now his brow a - dorn;

Fruit of the mys - tic Rose, As of that Rose the stem;
The Root, whence mer - cy ev - er flows, The Babe of Beth - le - hem.
3. Crown him the Lord of life, Who tri - umphed o'er the grave,
And rose vic - to - rious in the___ strife For those he came to save.
His glo - ries now we sing, Who died, and rose on high,
Who died e - ter - nal life to bring, And lives that death may die.
4. Crown him the Lord of love, Be - hold his hands and side,

Those wounds yet vis - i - ble a - bove In beau - ty glo - ri - fied:
No an - gel in the sky Can ful - ly bear that sight,
But down - ward bends his burn - ing eye At mys - ter - ies so bright.
5. Crown him the Lord of heav'n, En - throned in worlds a - bove;
Crown him the King, to whom is___ giv'n The won - drous name of Love;
Crown him with man - y crowns, As thrones be - fore him fall.
Crown him, ye kings, with man - y crowns, For he is King of all.

HILDERSTONE — *Te Saeculorum Principem* — English Translation by Father Fitzpatrick

1. The Prince of ag - es and of man, O Christ, we own that Thou art He:
Our minds, our hearts, nor will nor can Ac - knowl - edge_ an - y Lord but Thee.
2. The out - cry of the rab - ble rings: "We will not suf - fer Christ to reign";
But our voice, which tri - um - phant sings, Hails Thee as_ King Su - preme a - gain.
3. O Christ, who art the Prince of Peace, Re - bel - lious minds to Thee sub - ject,
And, in Thy love that doth not cease, Stray sheep in_ Thy one fold col - lect.
4. For this, up - on the gris - ly Tree Thou hang - est, with Thine arms out - spread,
The spear - thrust show - ing cru - el - ly Thy Heart where - in love's fires are red.

#158 has (optional) organ accompaniment at a lower key.

5. For this, like bread and wine in-deed, Up - on our al - tars Thou dost hide,
Out - pour - ing, for Thy chil-dren's need, Sal - va - tion__ from Thy wound-ed side.
6. With hon - ors, pub - lic as the skies, Let heads of na - tions Thee con - fess,
Let judge and states-man learn to prize, And laws and__ all the arts ex - press.
7. Let their in - sig - ni - a a - new Shine forth when kings to Thee sub - mit,
And may Thy scep - ter meek sub - due Our coun - try,__ and our homes, to it.
8. O'er eve - ry earth - ly mas - ter - y 'Tis Thine, O Je - sus, to pre - side:
With Fa - ther and with Spir - it be For end - less__ ag - es glo - ri - fied.

1. Hail Re - deem - er, King di - vine! Priest and Lamb, the throne is thine,
King, whose reign shall nev - er cease, Prince of ev - er - last - ing peace.
R. An - gels, Saints and na - tions sing "Praised be Je - sus Christ, our
King; Lord of life, earth, sky and sea, King of love on Cal - va - ry."
2. King most ho - ly, King of truth, Guide the low - ly, guide the youth;
Christ thou King of glo - ry bright, Be to us e - ter - nal light. R.
3. Shep - herd - King, o'er moun - tains steep, Home - ward bring the wand - 'ring sheep;

Shel - ter in one roy - al fold States and king - doms, new and old. R.
4. Crim - son streams, O King of grace, Drenched thy thorn - crowned head and face;
Floods of love's re - deem - ing tide Tore thy hands, thy feet, and side. R.
5. Eu - cha - ris - tic King, what love Draws thee dai - ly from a - bove,
Clad in signs of bread and wine: Feed us, lead us, keep us thine! R.
6. King, whose name cre - a - tion thrills, Rule our minds, our hearts, our wills,
Till in peace each na - tion rings With thy prais - es, King of kings. R.

1. Hail Re - deem - er, King di - vine! Priest and Lamb, the throne is thine,
King, whose reign shall nev - er cease, Prince of ev - er - last - ing peace.
R. An - gels, Saints and na - tions sing "Praised be Je - sus Christ, our King;
Lord of life, earth, sky and sea, King of love on___ Cal - va - ry."
2. King most ho - ly, King of truth, Guide the low - ly, guide the youth;
Christ thou King of glo - ry bright, Be to us e - ter - nal light. Refrain!
3. Shep - herd - King, o'er moun - tains steep, Home - ward bring the wand - 'ring sheep;

Shel - ter in one roy - al fold States and king - doms, new and old. Refrain!
4. Crim - son streams, O King of grace, Drenched thy thorn-crowned head and face;
Floods of love's re - deem - ing tide Tore thy hands, thy feet, and side. Refrain!
5. Eu - cha - ris - tic King, what love Draws thee dai - ly from a - bove,
Clad in signs of bread and wine: Feed us, lead us, keep us thine! Refrain!
6. King, whose name cre - a - tion thrills, Rule our minds, our hearts, our wills,
Till in peace each na - tion rings With thy prais - es, King of kings. Refrain!

1. Christ is King of earth and heav - en, Let his sub - jects all pro - claim
In the splen - dor of his tem - ple Hon - or to his ho - ly name.
Christ is King! No soul cre - at - ed Can re - fuse to bend the knee
To the God made Man who reign - eth, As 'twas prom - ised, from the tree.
2. Christ is King! Let hum - ble sor - row For our past ne - glect a - tone,
For the lack of faith - ful ser - vice To the Mas - ter whom we own.
Christ is King! Let joy and glad - ness Greet him; let his courts re - sound
With the praise of faith - ful sub - jects To his love in hon - or bound.

759 ICH GLAUB AN GOTT — “To Jesus Christ, Our Sovereign King”

1. To Je - sus Christ, our sov - ’reign King Who
is the world’s sal - va - tion, All praise and hom - age
do we bring And thanks and ad - o - ra - tion.
R. Christ Je - sus Vic - tor, Christ Je - sus Rul - er!
Christ Je - sus, Lord and Re - deem - er!
2. Thy reign ex - tend, O King be - nign, To

ev - 'ry land and na - tion; For in thy king - dom,
Lord di - vine, A - lone we find sal - va - tion. Refrain!
3. To thee and to thy Church, great King, We
pledge our hearts' ob - la - tion; Un - til be - fore thy
throne we sing, In end - less ju - bi - la - tion. Refrain!

1a. Hail, the world and heav - en's Queen, Rul - ing and re - fin - ing;
Hail, O crown of maid - en - hood, Star at mor - row shin - ing;
Hail, thou light di - vine - ly bright, Eve - ry grace com - bin - ing:
Has - ten, La - dy, bring - ing help To a world re - pin - ing.
2a. By the Lord be - yond all time Thou wert des - ig - nat - ed
Moth - er of his on - ly Word, By whom he cre - at - ed
Land, sea, sky; his beau - teous bride, Whom he dec - o - rat - ed,

So that Ad - am's crime to thee Nev - er was re - lat - ed.
1b. Sal - ve, mun - di Dó - mi - na, Cae - ló - rum Re - gí - na:
Sal - ve, Vir - go vír - gi - num, Stel - la ma - tu - tí - na. Sal - ve, ple - na grá - ti - a,
Cla - ra lux di - ví - na: Mun - di in au - xí - li - um, Dó - mi - na, fe - stí - na.
2b. Ab ae - tér - no Dó - mi - nus Te prae - or - di - ná - vit
Ma - trem u - ni - gé - ni - ti Ver - bi, quo cre - á - vit Ter - ram, pon - tum, aé - the - ra:
Te pul - chram or - ná - vit Si - bi spon - sam, A - dá - mus In qua non pec - cá - vit.

1a. Hail, the world and heav - en's Queen, Rul - ing and re - fin - ing;
Hail, O crown of maid - en - hood, Star at mor - row shin - ing;
Hail, thou light di - vine - ly bright, Eve - ry grace com - bin - ing:
Has - ten, La - dy, bring - ing help To a world re - pin - ing.
2a. By the Lord be - yond all time Thou wert des - ig - nat - ed Moth - er of his
on - ly Word, By whom he cre - at - ed Land, sea, sky; his beau - teous bride, Whom he dec - o -
rat - ed, So that Ad - am's crime to thee Nev - er was re - lat - ed.

1b. Sal - ve, mun - di Dó - mi - na, Cae - ló - rum Re - gí - na:
Sal - ve, Vir - go vír - gi - num, Stel - la ma - tu - tí - na.
Sal - ve, ple - na grá - ti - a, Cla - ra lux di - ví - na:
Mun - di in au - xí - li - um, Dó - mi - na, fe - stí - na.
2b. Ab ae - tér - no Dó - mi - nus Te prae - or - di - ná - vit Ma - trem u - ni -
gé - ni - ti Ver - bi, quo cre - á - vit Ter - ram, pon - tum, aé - the - ra: Te pul - chram or -
ná - vit Si - bi spon - sam, A - dá - mus In qua non pec - cá - vit.

1a. Hail, the world and heav-en's Queen, Rul-ing and re-fin-ing; Hail, O crown of
maid-en-hood, Star at mor-row shin-ing; Hail, thou light di-vine-ly bright,
Eve-ry grace com-bin-ing: Has-ten, La-dy, bring-ing help To a world re-pin-ing.
2a. By the Lord be-yond all time Thou wert des-ig-nat-ed Moth-er of his
on-ly Word, By whom he cre-at-ed Land, sea, sky; his beau-teous bride, Whom he
dec-o-rat-ed, So that Ad-am's crime to thee Nev-er was re-lat-ed.

1b. Sal - ve, mun - di Dó - mi - na, Cae - ló - rum Re - gí - na: Sal - ve, Vir - go
vír - gi - num, Stel - la ma - tu - tí - na. Sal - ve, ple - na grá - ti - a, Cla - ra
lux di - ví - na: Mun - di in au - xí - li - um, Dó - mi - na, fe - stí - na.
2b. Ab ae - tér - no Dó - mi - nus Te prae - or - di - ná - vit Ma - trem u - ni -
gé - ni - ti Ver - bi, quo cre - á - vit Ter - ram, pon - tum, aé - the - ra: Te pul -
chram or - ná - vit Si - bi spon - sam, A - dá - mus In qua non pec - cá - vit.

763 JESU LEIDEN PEIN UND TOD — *Salve Mundi Domina* — English Translation by Father Popplewell

1a. Hail, the world and heav - en's Queen, Rul - ing and re - fin - ing;
Hail, O crown of maid - en - hood, Star at mor - row shin - ing;
Hail, thou light di - vine - ly bright, Eve - ry grace_ com - bin - ing:
Has - ten, La - dy, bring - ing help To a world re - pin - ing.
2a. By the Lord be - yond all time Thou wert des - ig - nat - ed
Moth - er of his on - ly Word, By whom he cre - at - ed
Land, sea, sky; his beau - teous bride, Whom he dec - o - rat - ed,

So that Ad - am's crime to thee Nev - er was re - lat - ed.
1b. Sal - ve, mun - di Dó - mi - na, Cae - ló - rum Re - gí - na: Sal - ve, Vir - go
vír - gi - num, Stel - la ma - tu - tí - na. Sal - ve, ple - na grá - ti - a, Cla - ra
lux_ di - ví - na: Mun - di in au - xí - li - um, Dó - mi - na, fe - stí - na.
2b. Ab ae - tér - no Dó - mi - nus Te prae - or - di - ná - vit Ma - trem u - ni -
gé - ni - ti Ver - bi, quo cre - á - vit Ter - ram, pon - tum, aé - the - ra: Te pul -
chram_ or - ná - vit Si - bi spon - sam, A - dá - mus In qua non pec - cá - vit.

1a. Hail, the__ world and heav - en's Queen, Rul - ing and re - fin - ing;
Hail, O__ crown of maid - en - hood, Star at mor - row shin - ing;
Hail, thou light di - vine - ly bright, Eve - ry grace com - bin - ing:
Has - ten, La - dy, bring - ing help To a world re - pin - ing.
2a. By the__ Lord be - yond all time Thou wert des - ig - nat - ed
Moth - er__ of his on - ly Word, By whom he cre - at - ed
Land, sea, sky; his beau - teous bride, Whom he dec - o - rat - ed,

So that Ad - am's crime to thee Nev - er was re - lat - ed.
1b. Sal - ve, mun - di Dó - mi - na, Cae - ló - rum Re - gí - na: Sal - ve, Vir - go
vír - gi - num, Stel - la ma - tu - tí - na. Sal - ve, ple - na grá - ti - a, Cla - ra
lux di - ví - na: Mun - di in au - xí - li - um, Dó - mi - na, fe - stí - na.
2b. Ab ae - tér - no Dó - mi - nus Te prae - or - di - ná - vit Ma - trem u - ni -
gé - ni - ti Ver - bi, quo cre - á - vit Ter - ram, pon - tum, aé - the - ra: Te pul -
chram or - ná - vit Si - bi spon - sam, A - dá - mus In qua non pec - cá - vit.

765 EISENACH — "Pure Virgin, Hear Our Song Today" — Father Schrader

1. O gold - en Urn, O Fleece be - dewed,
Pure Vir - gin, hear our song to - day. O Bush a - blaze, yet
un - con - sumed, In - flame our hearts with love, we pray.
2. The knot that weep - ing Eve did tie,
You loosed, our joy - ful Moth - er true, That we, who once were
doomed to die Might live through Him Who lived through you.
3. A Tow - er ris - es from the ground;

Be - yond the drag - on's reach it soars: Where sin once reigned, let
grace a - bound! And light where dark - ness ruled be - fore.
4. Your mys - tic U - ni - corn now lays His Head up - on your lap and sighs,
Dear Maid - en, as with dole - ful gaze He spies the hunts - men draw - ing nigh.
5. Un - blem - ished Ewe, whose spot - less Lamb Was slain to spare a sin - ful race,
Guide freed - men to the prom - ised land, Where we shall see Him face to face.

1. Maid - en, yet a Moth - er, Daugh - ter of thy Son, High be - yond all
oth - er— Low - li - er is none; Thou the con - sum - ma - tion Planned by
God's de - cree, When our lost cre - a - tion Nobl - er rose in thee!
2. Thus his place pre - par - èd, He who all things made 'Mid his crea - tures
tar - ried, In thy bos - om laid; There his love he nour - ished,—
Warmth that gave in - crease To the Root whence flour - ished Our e - ter - nal peace.
3. Noon on Si - on's moun - tain Is thy char - i - ty; Hope its liv - ing foun - tain

Finds, on earth, in thee: La - dy, such thy pow - er, He, who grace would buy
Not as of thy dow - er, With-out wings would fly.
4. Nor a - lone thou
hear - est When thy name we hail; Of - ten thou art near - est When our voic - es
fail; Mir-rored in thy fash - ion All cre - a - tion's good, Mer-cy, might, com-pas - sion
Grace thy wom - an - hood.
5. La - dy, lest our vi - sion, Striv-ing heav'n-ward,
fail, Still let thy pe - ti - tion With thy Son pre - vail, Un - to whom all
mer - it, Pow'r and maj - es - ty With the Ho - ly Spir - it And the Fa - ther be.

 LAUDES MARIAE — *Omni Die, Dic Mariae* — English Translation by Father Bittleston

1. Dai - ly, dai - ly, sing to Mar - y, Sing, my soul, her prais - es due;
All her feasts, her ac - tions hon - or, With the heart's de - vo - tion true.
Lost in won-d'ring con - tem - pla - tion Be her maj - es - ty con - fessed:
Call her Moth - er, call her Vir - gin, Hap - py Moth - er, Vir - gin blest!
2. She is might - y in her plead - ing, Ten - der in her lov - ing care;
Ev - er watch - ful, un - der - stand - ing, All our sor - rows she will share.

Ad - vo - cate and lov - ing__ moth - er, Me - di - a - trix of all grace:
Heav - en's bless - ings she dis - pens - es On our sin - ful__ hu - man race.
3. Sing, my tongue, the Vir - gin's tro - phies, Who for us__ our Mak - er bore;
For the curse of old in - flict - ed, Peace and bless - ing to re - store.
Sing in songs of praise un - end - ing, Sing the world's ma - jes - tic Queen;
Wea - ry not nor faint in tell - ing All the gifts__ she__ gives to men.
4. All my sens - es, heart, af - fec - tions, Strive to sound__ her glo - ry forth:

Spread a - broad the sweet me - mo - rials Of the Vir - gin's price - less worth.
Where the voice of mu - sic thrill - ing, Where the tongue of el - o - quence,
That can ut - ter hymns be - seem - ing All her match - less ex - cel - lence?
5. All our grac - es flow from Mar - y; All then join her praise to sing:
Fair - est work of all cre - a - tion, Moth - er of cre - a - tion's King.
Sing in songs of peace un - end - ing, Call up - on her lov - ing - ly:
Seat of wis - dom, Gate of heav - en, Morn - ing star up - on the sea.

1. Thou, when deep - est night in - fer - nal Had for ag - es shroud - ed man,
Gav - est us that Light e - ter - nal Prom - ised since the world be - gan;
God in thee hath show - ered plen - ty On the hun - gry and the weak,
Send - ing back the might - y emp - ty, Set - ting up on high the meek.
2. Thine the prov - ince to de - liv - er Souls that deep in bond - age lie;
Thine to crush, and crush for ev - er, Life - de - stroy - ing her - e - sy;

Thine to show that earth - ly pleas - ures, All the world's en - chant - ing bloom,
Are out - ri - valled by the treas - ures Of the glo - rious life to come.
3. Thou to whom a Child was giv - en Great - er than the sons of men,
Com-ing down from high-est Heav - en To cre - ate this world a - gain:
By the hope thy name in - spi - res, By our doom, re - versed through thee,
Help us, Queen of An - gel cho - irs, Now and through e - ter - ni - ty.

1. Moth - er, yet a stain - less Vir - gin, He who deigned thy Son to be
Is the King of kings, and Mak - er Of the sky and earth and sea.
Bless we now that King Vic - to - rious Who doth thee for Moth - er own,
Born of thee for our Sal - va - tion, He our Health and Peace a - lone.
2. Now, through thee, on earth a - ris - ing Shines the new and heav'n - ly Light,
Driv - ing back the clouds and shad - ows Of the black and an - cient night.

Now the rich are weak and emp - ty, As thou said'st in song of old,
And the poor are filled with plen - ty, As thy proph - e - cy fore - told.
3. Sun and moon and stars a - dorn thee, Sin - less Eve, tri - um - phant sign;
Thou art she who crushed the ser - pent, Mar - y, pledge of life di - vine.
Cho - sen from e - ter - nal ag - es, Thou a - lone of all our race,
By thy Son's a - ton - ing mer - its Wast con - ceived in per - fect grace.

1. O glo-rious Maid, ex - alt - ed far Be - yond the light of burn - ing star, From him who
made thee thou hast won Grace to be Moth - er of his Son.
2. That which was lost in
hap-less Eve Thy ho - ly off - spring did re - trieve: The tear - worn sons of Ad - am's race
Through thee have seen the heav'n-ly place.
3. Thou wast the gate of heav'n's high Lord,
The door through which the light hath poured. Chris - tians re - joice, for through a Maid To
all man-kind is life con-veyed.
4. O Je - sus, Vir - gin - born, to thee E - ter - nal praise and
glo - ry be, Whom with the Fa - ther we a - dore And Ho - ly Spir - it, ev - er-more.

1. The glad - ness of thy Moth - er - hood, The an - guish of thy suf - fer - ing,
The glo - ry now that crowns thy __ brow, O Vir - gin - Moth - er, we would sing.
2. Hail, bless - èd Moth - er, full of joy In thy con - sent, thy vis - it too;
Joy in the birth of Christ on __ earth, Joy in Him lost and found a - new.
3. Hail thou, who in thine in - most heart, Didst bear, with spir - it full of grief,
Thy dear Son's ag - o - ny, and __ stripes, And thorns, and cross, of mar - tyrs chief.

4. Re - ful - gent in His tri - umph - ing, And in the Spir - it's tongues of flame:
Lit with the splen-dors of the_ King, All na - tions praise thy glo - rious name.
5. O come, ye na - tions, ros - es bring, Culled from these mys - ter - ies di - vine,
And for the Moth - er of your_ King With lov - ing hands your chap - lets twine.
6. We lay our hom - age at Thy feet, Lord Je - sus, Thou the Vir - gin's Son,
With Fa - ther and with Par - a - clete, Reign - ing while end - less ag - es run.

1. O thou who hang - est on the tree
With arms out - stretched in char - i - ty,
Grant us at thy blest moth - er's prayer
To meet thee on the heav'n - ly stair.
2. Love, and a sev'n - fold sor - row's dart
Be - side the cross trans - fixed thy heart;
La - dy of mer - cy, grant to us
To share that wound most dol - or - ous.

3. O Christ, thou sun that know'st no night,
That con - qu'rest death by death's own might,
Un - to thy ser - vants' hearts ap - pear
Now at thy bliss - ful moth - er's prayer.
4. Maid - en, who weep - est for thy son,
The bless - èd Sole - be - got - ten One,
Grant us the tears of love, we pray,
And wash our eve - ry stain a - way.
5. The God she bore with - in her womb
Is

laid with - in the rock - hewn tomb; Our souls en - chained by death of
yore, Lord, at thy Moth - er's prayer re - store.
6. Star of the sea most fair, we pray, That
guid'st us on life's nar - row way, No more by bonds of flesh op -
press'd, Grant us in Christ thy son to rest.
7. O Shep - herd of the sheep, thy praise A
thou - sand bands of an - gels raise; From all temp - ta - tion thine e -

lect At thy blest moth - er's prayer pro - tect.
8. Queen in the land of star - shin - ing Whose
prais - es ev - 'ry heart doth sing, When all our earth - ly praise is
done, Re - ward us with thy ben - i - son.
9. Glo - ry to Thee through all the earth, Lord
Je - sus, for thy vir - gin birth, With Fa - ther and with Spir - it
One While end - less ag - es on - ward run.

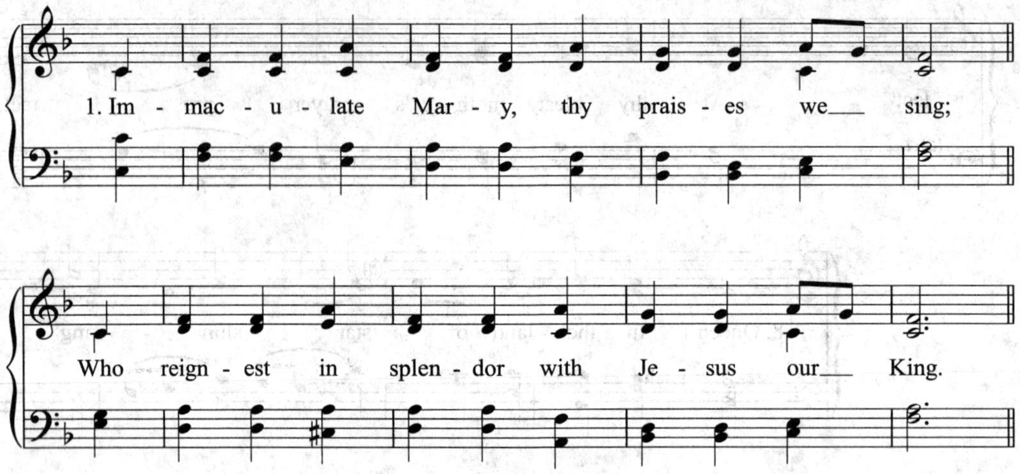
1. Im - mac - u - late Mar - y, thy prais - es we__ sing;
Who reign - est in splen - dor with Je - sus our__ King.

This Refrain is repeated after each verse:

R. A - ve, A - ve, A - ve Ma - rí - a!
A - ve, A - ve Ma - rí - - a!

2. In heav - en, the bless - èd thy glo - ry pro - claim;
On earth we, thy chil - dren, in - voke thy fair__ name.

3. Thy name is our pow - er, thy vir - tues our__ light,
Thy love is our com - fort, thy plead - ing our__ might.
4. We pray for our Moth - er, the Church up - on__ earth,
And bless, dear - est La - dy, the land of our__ birth.

The Refrain can also be sung in this way:

R. A - ve, A - ve, A - ve Ma - rí - a!
A - ve, A - ve, A - ve Ma - rí - a!

1. Our sec - ond Eve puts on her mor - tal shroud,
Earth breeds a heav'n for God's new dwell - ing - place;
Now ris - eth up E - li - as' lit - tle cloud,
That grow - ing shall dis - til the show'rs of grace;
Her be - ing now be - gins, who, ere she end,
Shall bring our good that shall our e - vil mend.
2. Both grace and na - ture did their force u - nite To make this Babe the sum of

all their best; Our most, her least; our mil - lion, but her mite—
She was at eas - iest rate worth all the rest: What grace to men, or
an - gels, God did part, Was all u - nit - ed in this In - fant's heart.
3. Four on - ly wights bred with - out fault are named, And all the rest con -
ceiv - èd were in sin; With - out both man and wife was Ad - am framed,
Of man, but not of wife, did Eve be - gin; Wife with - out touch of
man Christ's Moth - er was, Of man and wife this babe was bred in grace.

1. Spell E - va back and "A - ve" shall you find;
The first be - gan, the last re - versed our harms:
An an - gel's witch - ing words did E - va blind;
An an - gel's "A - ve" dis - en - chants the charms:
Death first by wom - an's weak - ness en - ter'd in,
In Wom - an's vir - tue life doth now be - gin.
2. O vir - gin blest, the heav'ns to thee in - cline, In thee their joy and

sov - 'reign they ag - nize; Too mean their glo - ry is to match with
thine, Whose chaste re - ceipt God more than heav'n did prize. Hail, fair - est
Heav'n, that heav'n and earth did bless, Where vir-tue's star, God's sun of jus - tice is!
3. With haugh - ty mind to God-head man as - pired, And was by pride from
place of pleas - ure chased; With lov - ing mind our man-hood God de - sired,
And as by love in great - er pleas - ure placed; Man la - b'ring
to as - cend pro-cured our fall; God yield-ing to de - scend cut off our thrall.

1. If sin be cap - tive, grace must find re - lease;
From curse of sin the in - no - cent is free;
Tomb, pris - on is for sin - ners that de - cease;
No tomb, but throne to guilt - less doth a - gree:
Though thralls of sin lie lin - g'ring in the grave.
Yet, fault - less corpse, with soul re - ward must have.
2. The daz - zled eye doth dim - mèd light re - quire, And dy - ing sights re -

pose in shroud - ing shades; But, ea - gles' eyes to bright - est light as -
pire, And liv - ing looks de - light in loft - y glades: Faint - wing - èd
fowl by ground do faint - ly fly, Our prince-ly Ea - gle mounts un - to the sky.
3. Gem to her worth, Spouse to her Love as - cends, Prince to her throne, Queen
to her heav'n - ly King, Whose court with sol - emn pomp on her at - tends,
And choirs of saints with greet - ing notes do sing; Earth ren - d'reth
up her un - de - serv - èd prey; Heav'n claims the right, and bears the prize a - way.

1. O san - ctís - si - ma, O pi - ís - si - ma, Dul - cis Vir - go Ma -
rí - - a!
Ma - ter a - má - ta, In - te - me - rá -
ta, O - ra, o - ra pro no - - bis!
2. Tu, so - lá - ti - um Et re - fú - gi - um, Vir - go Ma - ter Ma -
rí - - a!
Quid - quid o - ptá - mus, Per te spe - rá -
mus; O - ra, o - ra pro no - - bis!

3. Ec - ce dé - bi - les, Per - quam flé - bi-les, Sal - va nos, O Ma -
rí - a!
Tol - le lan - guó - res, Sa - na do - ló -
res; O - ra, o - ra pro no - bis!
4. Vir - go, ré - spi - ce, Ma - ter, á - spi - ce, Au - di nos, O Ma -
rí - a!
Tu, me - di - cí - nam, Por - tas di - ví -
nam; O - ra, o - ra pro no - bis.

 WHITEHALL — *Salve Regina, Mater Misericordiae* — Historic Catholic Translation (1687AD)

1. Hail to the Queen that reigns a - bove, Moth - er of Clem - en - cy and
Love: Hail, thou our Hope, Life, Sweet - ness: We, Eve's ban - ish'd
Chil - dren, cry to Thee.
2. We, from this wretch - ed Vale of
Tears Send Sighs and Groans un - to thine ears. O then, sweet
Ad - vo - cate, be - stow A pit - y ing look on us be - low.

#102 has (optional) organ accompaniment at a higher key.

3. Af - ter this Ex - ile, let us see Our Bless - èd Je - sus, born of Thee,
O mer - ci - ful, O pi - ous Maid! O gra - cious Mar - y! lend thine Aid.

1. Hail,_ Queen a - mong the heav'n - ly ones, O_____ Ma - rí - a!
a - lone the claim of earth - born sons, O_____ Ma - rí - a!
R. Cher - u - bim, tell out your glee, Ser - a - phim, now rev - el ye,
sing as one con - tin - ual - ly: Sal - ve, sal - ve, sal - ve_ Re - gí - na.
2. Moth - er of mer - cy, we en - treat, O_____ Ma - rí - a!
of___ par - don thou the Bear - er sweet, O_____ Ma - rí - a! Refrain!
3. Thou_ light of life and spring of grace, O_____ Ma - rí - a!

the cause of glad - ness to our race, O Ma - rí - a! Refrain!
4. Our La - dy, hail, our hope as well: O Ma - rí - a!
our wrong - ful un - der - tak - ings quell, O Ma - rí - a! Refrain!
5. Though ban - ished, lo to thee we cry, O Ma - rí - a!
with thee our hum - ble plead - ing ply, O Ma - rí - a! Refrain!
6. List thou to us, Eve's prog - e - ny, O Ma - rí - a!
who wretch - ed are but hope in thee, O Ma - rí - a! Refrain!

7. So___ then, thy mien upon us train, O___ Ma - rí - a!
nor___ us thy ser - vants yet dis - dain, O___ Ma - rí - a! Refrain!
8. Thine___ eyes do thou vouch - safe to turn— O___ Ma - rí - a!
t'ward___ us who for thy guid - ance yearn, O___ Ma - rí - a! Refrain!
9. Show___ him who is thy Son at last— O___ Ma - rí - a!
to___ us, this ban - ish - ment once past, O___ Ma - rí - a! Refrain!
R. Cher - u - bim, tell out your glee, Ser - a - phim, now rev - el ye,
sing as one con - tin - ual - ly: Sal - ve, sal - ve, sal - ve___ Re - gí - na.

 SALVE REGINA COELITUM — *Salve Regina, Mater Misericordiae*

1. Hail, Ho - ly Queen en - throned a - bove, O Ma - ri - a!
Hail, Moth-er of mer - cy and of love, O Ma - ri - a!
R. Tri - umph all ye cher - u - bim! Sing with us ye ser - a - phim!
Final Verse: R. An - gels, all your prais - es bring, Earth and heav - en, with us sing,
Heav'n and earth re - sound the hymn! Sal - ve, sal - ve, sal - ve, Re - gi - na!
All cre - a - tion ech - o - ing: Sal - ve, sal - ve, sal - ve, Re - gi - na!
2. Our life, our sweet - ness here be - low, O Ma - ri - a!
Our hope in sor - row and in woe, O Ma - ri - a! Refrain!
3. To thee we cry, poor sons of Eve, O Ma - ri - a!

To_ thee we sigh, we mourn, we grieve, O Ma - ri - a! *Refrain!*
4. This_ earth is but a vale of tears, O Ma - ri - a!
A_ place of ban - ish - ment and fears, O Ma - ri - a! *Refrain!*
5. Turn,_ then, most gra - cious Ad - vo - cate, O Ma - ri - a!
Toward us thine eyes com - pas - sion - ate, O Ma - ri - a! *Refrain!*
6. When_ this our ex - ile is com - plete, O Ma - ri - a!
Show_ us thy Son, our Je - sus sweet, O Ma - ri - a! *Refrain!*

1. No eye hath seen what joys the Saints ob - tain,
No ear hath heard what com - forts are pos - sessed;
No heart can think in what de - light they reign,
Nor pen ex - press their hap - py port of rest,
Where pleas - ure flows, and grief is nev - er seen.
Where good a - bounds, and ill is ban - ish'd clean.

2. Those sa - cred Saints re - main in per - fect peace.
Which Christ con - fessed, and walk - èd in His ways,
They shine in bliss, which now shall nev - er cease,
And to His Name do sing e - ter - nal praise:
Be - fore His throne in white they ev - er stand,
And car - ry palms of tri - umph in their hand.

3. A - bove them all the Vir - gin hath a place.
Which caused the world with com - fort to a - bound;
The beams do shine in her un - spot - ted face,
And with the stars her head is rich - ly crowned:
In glo - ry she all crea - tures pass - eth far,
The moon her shoes, the sun her gar - ments are.

4. Next a - bove her, and on a high - er throne,
Our Sav - ior in His Man - hood sit - teth here;
From Whom pro - ceeds all per - fect joy a - lone,
And in Whose Face all glo - ry doth ap - pear:
The Saints' de - light con - ceiv - èd can - not be
When they a Man the Lord of An - gels see.

FESTAL SONG — "For All Thy Saints, O Lord"

1. For all Thy saints, O Lord, Who strove_ in Thee to live,
Who fol - lowed Thee, o - beyed, a - dored, Our grate - ful hymn re - ceive.
2. For all Thy saints, O Lord, Who strove in Thee to die,
Who count - ed___ Thee their great Re - ward, Ac - cept_ our thank - ful cry.

3. They all in life and death, With Thee,_ their Lord, in view,
Learned from Thy_ Ho - ly Spir - it's breath To suf - fer and to do.
4. For this Thy name we bless And hum - bly pray that we
May fol - low_ them in ho - li - ness And live_ and die in Thee.
5. All might, all praise, be Thine, Fa - ther,_ co - e - qual Son,
And Spir - it,_ bond of love di - vine, While end - less ag - es run.

1. Bless - èd___ are the sons of God, They are bought with Christ's own Blood,
They are___ harm - less, meek, and mild. Ho - ly, hum - ble, un - de - filed.
R. With them num - ber'd may we be, Now and through e - ter - ni - ty!
2. They are___ lights up - on the earth, Chil - dren of a heav'n - ly birth;
Born of___ God, they hate all sin, God's pure seed re - mains with - in. Refrain!
3. Though they___ suf - fer much on earth, Stran - gers quite to this world's mirth,
They with___ love and peace are filled, They are by his Spir - it sealed. Refrain!

ALL SAINTS — *Wer Sind Die Von Gottes Throne* — English Translation by F. E. Cox

1. Who are these, like stars ap - pear - ing, These be - fore God's
throne who stand? Each a gold - en crown is wear - ing; Who
are all this glo - rious band? Al - le - lu - ia,
hark! they sing, Prais - ing loud their heav'n - ly king.
2. Who are these of daz - zling bright - ness, These in God's own
truth ar - rayed, Clad in robes of pur - est white - ness, Robes
whose lus - ter ne'er shall fade, Ne'er be touched by

time's rude hand— Whence comes all this glo - rious band?
3. These are they who have con-tend - ed For their Sav - ior's
hon - or long, Wres - tling on till life was end - ed, Fol -
l'wing not the sin - ful throng; These, who well the
fight sus - tained, Tri - umph through the Lamb have gained.
4. These are they whose hearts were riv - en, Sore with woe and

an - guish tried, Who in prayer full oft have striv - en With
the___ God they glo - ri - fied; Now, their pain - ful___
con - flict___ o'er, God has bid___ them weep no more.
5. These like priests have watched and wait - ed, Of - f'ring up to
Christ their will, Soul and bod - y con - se - crat - ed, Day
and___ night to serve Him still: Now in God's most___
ho - ly___ place Blest they stand___ be - fore His face.

1. O light that shone be - fore there rose cre - at - ed bright - ness, God the Son,
to - geth - er with the Fa - ther one, all things who gra - cious - ly dis - pose:
2. Our form with that of yours you wed, bred of a moth - er and a maid,
our cost - ly ran - som o - ver - paid when, lift - ed on the tree, you bled:
3. A right-eous man of Is - ra - el you led to make that maid his bride,
her child and her to guard and guide, to thwart the threats of earth or hell.
4. This car - pen - ter's re - put - ed heir were you, who built the cos - mic frame,
and, since the foe at - tacked the same, its dam - age ven - tured to re - pair.

5. His an - cient name - sake to pre - pare a - gainst the fam - ine wise - ly strove
and, pre - cious grain pre - served in trove, he thus pro - vid - ed sav - ing fare.
6. The lat - er Jo - seph kept the bread, the man - na true, di - vine - ly sent,
whose liv - ing flesh is nour - ish - ment to those he res - cues from the dead.
7. The Fa - ther's wis - dom, in his house his work you set a - bout to do,
which brought both grief and glad - ness to your fos - ter - fa - ther and his spouse.
8. To Naz - a - reth re - turn - ing thence, though na - ture hung up - on your will
the natu-'ral law you hon - ored still, your par - ents paid o - be - di - ence.

9. When came the hour to sat - is - fy the com - mon debt of Ad - am's race,
then with your bear - er, full of grace, you helped her hus - band well to die.
10. In bliss and glo - ry with-out end, O Jo - seph, pray for those who here
yet bide, and dan - gers have to fear, that heav - en shield them and be - friend.
11. Of fam - i - lies you are the stay, the Chur - ch's pa - tron, dev - ils' dread:
on these your in - flu - ence be shed, to strength - en good and ill al - lay.
12. To him who is both one and three, the spring of be - ing, high - est king,
let all he craft - ed prais - es ring in splen - dor for e - ter - ni - ty.

1. Ho - ly Jo - seph, In - ter - ces - sor, Un - to thee God's chil - dren sing;
Be our Pa - tron and Pro - tec - tor, To God's throne our prais - es bring.
2. Faith - ful Spouse of faith - ful Vir - gin, Lov - er of God's pu - ri - ty;
From thy wor - thy place in heav - en, Pray that we may faith - ful be.
3. Guard - ian of the Word In - car - nate, Si - lent guide of God's own Son;
Guard our hearts and lead us on - ward To the life that Christ has won.
4. Hum - ble man in loft - y sta - tion, God has shed His grace on thee;
Pray such grace to us be giv - en, That we live e - ter - nal - ly.

 MERTON — "Holy Joseph, Intercessor" — Father Phillips

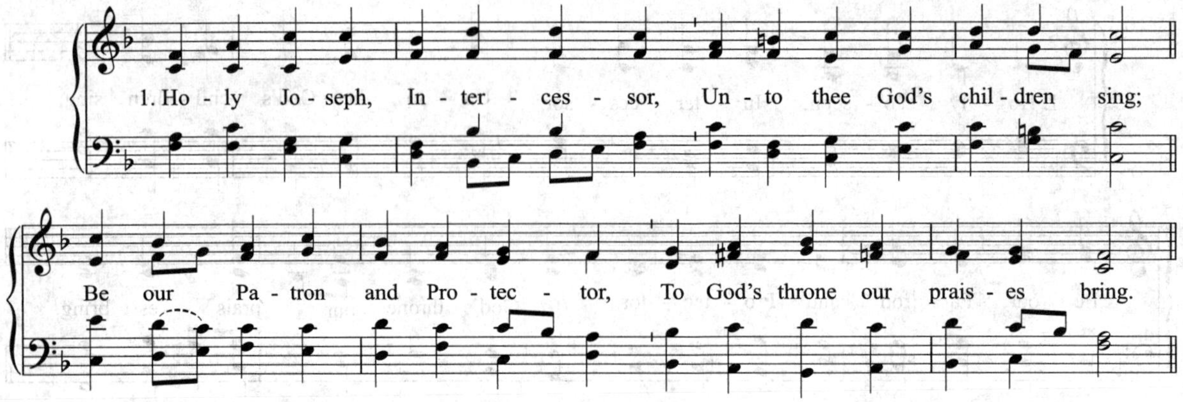
1. Ho - ly Jo - seph, In - ter - ces - sor, Un - to thee God's chil - dren sing;
Be our Pa - tron and Pro - tec - tor, To God's throne our prais - es bring.

#300 has (optional) organ accompaniment at a lower key.

2. Faith - ful Spouse of faith - ful Vir - gin, Lov - er of God's pu - ri - ty;
From thy wor - thy place in heav - en, Pray that we may faith - ful be.
3. Guard - ian of the Word In - car - nate, Si - lent guide of God's own Son;
Guard our hearts and lead us on - ward To the life that Christ has won.
4. Hum - ble man in lof - ty sta - tion, God has shed His grace on thee;
Pray such grace to us be giv - en, That we live e - ter - nal - ly.

1. Bless - èd Jo - seph, Guard - ian mild, Who didst love the Ho - ly Child,
Show thy love to us who pray, Shield us from all harm this day:
R. Fos - ter - fa - ther of the Word, Keep us close to Christ our Lord.
2. Great Saint Jo - seph, Pa - tron bold Of the Church from days of old,
Give us cour - age strong and new, To pro - claim God's Gos - pel true: Refrain!
3. He Whom thou didst guide in youth, We re - ceive in ver - y truth;
In this Sac - ra - ment of love, We are one with thee a - bove: Refrain!

1. Thou maid - en - moth - er's prog - e - ny, O Je - su, ho - ly Vir - gins' King,
we raise our low - ly hearts to thee, an - oth - er fruit - ful Vir - gin sing.
2. The glo - ry of her maid - en - head de - vot - ed to her Spouse di - vine,
in wed - lock mys - ti - cal, she bred the daugh - ters of a no - ble line.
3. The o - cean vast - ness brav - ing, fared her par - ents to a dis - tant shore,
by faith and love their child pre - pared to seek the pearl of hid - den store.
4. The lambs of Christ she saw be - reft of guid - ance and of nour - ish - ment:

his Cross to bear, all else she left, his Heart to please made all her bent.
5. His Prov - i - dence was all her fund, his Fos - ter - fa - ther all her ward;
all oth - er main - te - nance she shunned: her spir - it, all un - la - den, soared.
6. The stroke of glad - ness or of woe, when it be - fell, could nev - er change
her pur - pose, sway her to for - go her plight - ed faith, true love es - trange.
7. O bless - èd Mar - y, in the train of that fair Bride - groom, that great Lord,
the spot - less Lamb for sin-ners slain, pray him for us, grace to af - ford.

8. May he from eve - ry fell de - sign the pur - chase of his pain de - fend,
where his de - vice he bids to shine a - mid the stars, his mer - cy send.
9. The land that owns thy mor - tal birth be now the claim - ant of thy care,
and eve - ry clan of men on earth the heirs of thy de - serts and prayer.
10. Then to the boun - teous One - and - Three whence all things
are, where all things tend, true God - head, sov - 'reign
mas - ter - y, be praise and glo - ry with - out end.

1. Sim - ple saint and faith - ful priest, at this Eu - cha - ris - tic feast
we re - call thy ho - ly face, and with thee our__ Lord em - brace.
Give us true sim - plic - i - ty: pray for us, Saint An - tho - ny.
2. Word of God thou didst pro - claim; un - to thee God's Spir - it came,
bring - ing faith when thou didst preach, show - ing truth when_ thou didst teach.
May we speak words truth - ful - ly: pray for us Saint An - tho - ny.
3. Er - ror flees be - fore God's Light: through thy life Christ shin - eth bright,
show - ing men the way to peace, e - vil's hold from_ them re - lease.

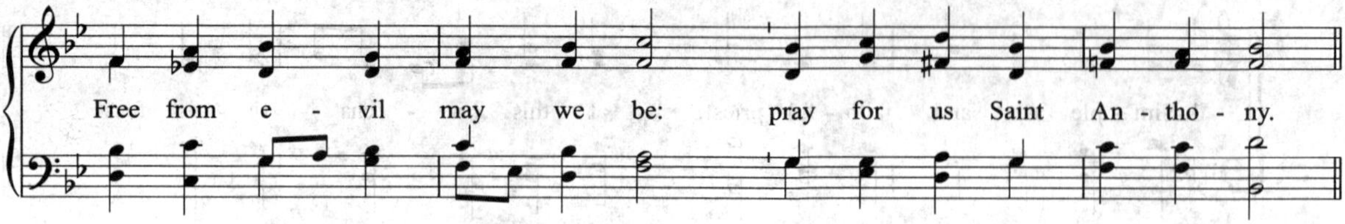
Free from e - vil may we be: pray for us Saint An - tho - ny.

ST FLAVIAN — "For The Dead" — Cardinal Newman

1. Help, Lord, the souls which Thou hast made, The souls to Thee so dear,
In pris - on for the debt un - paid Of sins com - mit - ted here.
2. Those ho - ly souls, they suf - fer on, Re - sign'd in heart and will,
Un - til Thy high be - hest is done, And jus - tice has its fill.
3. For dai - ly falls, for par - don'd crime, They joy to un - der - go

The shad - ow of Thy cross sub - lime, The rem - nant of Thy woe.
4. Oh, by their pa - tience of de - lay, Their hope a - mid their pain,
Their sa - cred zeal to burn a - way Dis - fig - ure - ment and stain;
5. Oh, by their fire of love, not less In keen - ness than the flame,
Oh, by their ver - y help - less - ness, Oh, by Thine own great Name,
6. Help, Lord, the souls which Thou hast made, The souls to Thee so dear,
In pris - on for the debt un - paid Of sins com - mit - ted here,

 ST COLUMBA 7M — “The King Of Love My Shepherd Is”

3
1. The_ King of love my_ shep - herd is, Whose good - ness fail - eth_ nev - er;
I noth - ing lack if I am his And he is mine for - ev - er.
3
2. Where_ streams of liv - ing_ wa - ter flow My ran - somed soul he_ lead - eth,
And where the ver - dant pas - tures grow With food ce - les - tial feed - eth.
3
3. Per - verse and fool - ish_ oft I strayed, But yet in love he_ sought me,
And on his shoul - der gen - tly laid, And home, re - joic - ing, brought me.

3
4. In__ death's dark vale I__ fear no ill With thee, dear Lord, be - side me;
Thy rod and staff my com - fort still, Thy cross be - fore to guide me.
3
5. Thou__ spread'st a ta - ble__ in my sight; Thine unc - tion, grace be - stow - eth;
And O what trans - port of de - light From thy pure chal - ice flow - eth!
3
6. And__ so through all the__ length of days Thy__ good - ness fail - eth__ nev - er;
Good Shep - herd, may I sing thy praise With - in thy house for - ev - er.

802 GROSSER GOTT — *Te Deum Laudamus* — English Translation by Father Walworth

1. Ho - ly God,_ we praise Thy name! Lord of all,__ we bow_ be - fore Thee;
All on earth_ Thy scep - ter claim, All in heav'n a - bove_ a - dore Thee;
In - fi - nite_ Thy vast do - main, Ev - er - last - ing is__ Thy reign.
In - fi - nite_ Thy vast do - main, Ev - er - last - ing is__ Thy reign.
2. Hark! the loud_ ce - les - tial hymn An - gel choirs a - bove_ are rais - ing;
Cher - u - bim_ and Ser - a - phim In un - ceas - ing cho - rus prais - ing,
Fill the_ heav'ns_ with sweet ac - cord: Ho - ly, ho - ly, ho - ly, Lord!
Fill the_ heav'ns_ with sweet ac - cord: Ho - ly, ho - ly, ho - ly, Lord!

3. Ho - ly Fa - ther, Ho - ly Son, Ho - ly Spir - it, Three_ we name Thee,
While in es - sence on - ly One, Un - di - vid - ed God_ we claim Thee,
And a - dor - ing bend the_ knee, While we own_ the mys - ter - y.
And a - dor - ing bend the_ knee, While we own_ the mys - ter - y.
4. Spare Thy peo - ple, Lord,_ we pray, By a thou - sand snares sur - round - ed:
Keep us free_ from sin_ to - day, Nev - er let_ us be_ con - found - ed;
Lo, I_ put_ my trust in_ Thee— Nev - er, Lord, a - ban - don me.
Lo, I_ put_ my trust in_ Thee— Nev - er, Lord, a - ban - don me.

803 LAUDATE DOMINUM — "Sing Praise To The Lord"

1. Sing praise to the Lord! praise God in the height; Re - joice in His
Word, you an - gels of light. O heav - ens, a - dore Him_ by___
whom you were made, And wor - ship be - fore_ Him in bright - ness ar - rayed.
2. Sing praise to the Lord! praise God on the earth, In tune - ful ac -
cord, all you of new birth; Praise Him who has brought you_ His_
grace from a - bove, Praise Him who has taught you to sing of His love.

3. Sing praise to the Lord! all things that give sound; Each ju - bi - lant
chord, re - ech - o a - round; Loud or - gans, His glo - ry tell
forth in deep tone, And trum - pets, the sto - ry of what He has done.
4. Sing praise to the Lord! thanks - giv - ing and song To Him be out -
poured all ag - es a - long; For love in cre - a - tion, for
heav - en re - stored, For grace of sal - va - tion, sing praise to the Lord!

804 RENDEZ À DIEU — *In Principio Creavit Deus* (Book of Genesis)

1. Foun - tain of full-ness, name of be - ing, one in thy God - head, per - sons three,
al - might - y arm, and eye all - see - ing, glad in thy bless - èd com - pa - ny:
from the be - gin - ning who hast bid - den the found - ing of do - min - ions twain,
o - pen to sense, or from it hid - den, bring - ing thee hon - or by their gain.
2. On the first day of thy cre - at - ing light sprang, o - bey - ing thy de - cree,
dark - ness from dark - ness sep - a - rat - ing, set - ting each night a bound - a - ry.

On the first day the Son, a - ris - ing, shed lus - ter on the som - ber tomb,
death, stale in tyr - an - ny, sur - pris - ing, fresh glo - ry sun - der - ing the gloom.
3. The vault su - per - nal took its sta - tion, keep - ing the wa - ters low and high;
now earth and sea, now veg - e - ta - tion, sun, moon and stars a - cross the sky.
Stead - fast in du - ty un - for - sak - en are, Lord, thy word and faith - ful love,
through pass - ing ag - es nev - er shak - en, fixed as the fir - ma - ment a - bove.

4. Eve - ning and morn-ing al - ter - nat - ing, o - cean and air were fraught with life,
down in the deep pro - lif - er - at - ing, a - mid the loft - y cur-rents rife.
Those sick of sin, phy - si-cian ho - ly, di - rect to pen - i - tence pro - found,
by vir - tue ris - ing, ev - er low - ly: so let thy heal-ing grace a - bound.
5. Cat - tle and sav-age beast were thriv - ing with those which crept a - long the land,
man, of thy mak-ing last ar - riv - ing, all else en - trust-ed to his hand:

formed of the clay, thine im-age bear - ing, a breath di - vine in vials of earth,
whose Prince, their vas - sal na - ture shar - ing, pau - pered him - self to mend their dearth.
6. Such was thy work, six days em - ploy - ment, heav - en and earth, with their ar - ray;
end - ing, their good-ness thine en - joy - ment, the sev-enth was thy rest-ing day.
Let us, all toil and care dis - card - ing, e - ter - nal sab-bath en - ter - ing,
thy face, whose sight is bliss, re - gard - ing, thy prais - es nev - er cease to sing.

1. Lead, kind - ly Light, a - mid th'en - cir - cling gloom, Lead
thou me on; The night is dark, and I am far from home,
Lead thou me on. Keep Thou my feet; I do not ask to
see The dis - tant scene; one step e - nough for me.
2. I was not ev - er thus, nor prayed that thou Shouldst
lead me on; I loved to choose and see my path; but now

Lead thou me on. I loved the gar - ish day, and, spite of
fears, Pride ruled my will; re - mem-ber not past years.
3. So long Thy pow'r hath blest me, sure it still Will
lead me on. O'er moor and fen, o'er crag and tor - rent, till
The night is gone. And with the morn those an - gel fac - es
smile Which I have loved long since, and lost a - while.

807 ST ANNE — "O God, Our Help In Ages Past" — (Psalm 89)

1. O God, our help in ag - es past, Our hope for years to come,
Our shel - ter from the storm - y blast, And our e - ter - nal home.
2. Be - neath the shad - ow of Thy throne Thy saints have dwelt se - cure;
Suf - fi - cient is Thine arm a - lone, And our de - fense is sure.
3. Be - fore the hills in or - der stood, Or earth re - ceived her frame,
From ev - er - last - ing Thou art God, To end - less years the same.

4. A thou - sand ag - es in Thy sight Are like an ev'n - ing gone;
Short as the watch that ends the night Be - fore the ris - ing sun.
5. Time, like an ev - er roll - ing stream, Bears all its sons a - way;
They fly, for - got - ten, as a dream Dies at the op'n - ing day.
6. O God, our help in ag - es past, Our hope for years to come,
Be Thou our guard while trou - bles last, And our e - ter - nal home.

808 REGENT SQUARE — *Angularis Fundamentum* — English Translation by Neale

1. Christ is made the sure foun-da - tion, Christ the head and cor - ner - stone;
Cho - sen of the Lord, and pre - cious, Bind - ing all the__ Church in one,
Ho - ly Zi - on's help for - ev - er, And her con - fi - dence a - lone.
2. All that ded - i - cat - ed cit - y, Dear - ly loved of God on high,
In ex - ult - ant ju - bi - la - tion, Pours per - pet - ual__ mel - o - dy,
God the One in Three a - dor - ing In glad hymns e - ter - nal - ly.
3. To this tem - ple, where we call Thee, Come, O Lord of Hosts, to - day;

With Thy wont - ed lov - ing - kind - ness Hear Thy ser - vants as they pray.
And Thy full - est ben - e - dic - tion Shed with - in its walls for aye.
4. Here vouch - safe to all Thy ser - vants What they ask of Thee to gain;
What they gain from Thee for - ev - er With the bless - èd to re - tain,
And here - af - ter in Thy glo - ry Ev - er - more with Thee to reign.
5. Laud and hon - or to the Fa - ther, Laud and hon - or to the Son,
Laud and hon - or to the Spir - it, Ev - er Three and ev - er One;
Con - sub - stan - tial, co - e - ter - nal, While un - end - ing ag - es run.

809 EWING — *Urbs Sion Aurea, Patria Lactea* — Bernard of Cluny

1. Je - ru - sa - lem the gold - en, With milk and hon - ey blest, Be - neath thy con - tem -
pla - tion Sink heart and voice op - prest. I know not, oh, I know not,
What joys a - wait us there, What ra - dian - cy of glo - ry, What bliss be - yond com - pare.
2. They stand, those halls of Zi - on, All ju - bi - lant with song,
And bright with man - y an an - gel, And all the mar - tyr throng;
The Prince is ev - er in them, The day - light is se - rene:
The pas - tures of the bless - èd Are decked in glo - rious sheen.

3. There is the throne of Da - vid; And there, from care re - leased,
The shout of them that tri - umph, The song of them that feast;
And they, who with their Lead - er, Have con - quer'd in the fight,
For ev - er and for ev - er Are clad in robes of white.
4. O sweet and bless - èd coun - try, The home of God's e - lect! O sweet and bless - èd
coun - try, That ea - ger hearts ex - pect! Je - sus, in mer - cy bring us
To that dear land of rest; Who art, with God the Fa - ther, and Spir - it, ev - er blest.

1. Lord Je - sus Christ, of joys and treas - ures rar - est, glow of the
Fa - ther's glo - ry, beam - ing bright, who have been made a child of men, the
fair - est, for to be in their midst was your de - light.
2. Al - ways to stay a - mong us is your pleas - ure, un - til the
world its fat - ed time should spend: ten - der - ness such as yours is, none could
mea - sure, lov - ing your own, and lov - ing to the end.
3. Though our first fa - ther fell, his kin - dred leav - ing un - der the

sway of death a fet-tered slave, your bonds of mer-cy brought forth from their
griev - ing those whom by Ad-am's cords you came to save.
4. Draw - ing all things, who are of all the mak - er, up - on the
cross up - lift - ed, all to heal, bear - ing a thirst that had one on - ly
slak - er: your precious blood out-poured to work our weal.
5. Good - ness di - vine and kind-ness man - i - fest - ed, you will not
quench the flax that smoul-ders frail, break not the reed that in - ju - ry has

wrest - ed, in whom the strong are shamed, the weak pre - vail.
6. There is no harm that lies be - yond your mend - ing, nor an - y
loss that you can - not re - store: hearts that are pure pre - serve in grace un -
end - ing, those sin has rav-aged mak - ing whole once more.
7. Once, hid - den God, a pil - grim peo - ple guid - ing, your tab - er -
nac - le told your pres-ence true: now too, Em - ma - nu - el, with us a -
bid - ing, you are the Word in flesh, nor yet in view.

8. Meal of the fa - vored, wine whence maid - ens flour - ish, vine that up -
holds its branch - es, lend - ing life, yield - ing it - self to rear them, and to
nour - ish, that they would thrive, in fruit - ful - ness be rife.
9. Hon - or and praise be of - fered with - out ceas - ing to the al -
might - y One, the ho - ly Three, Fa - ther, and Son, and Spir - it, still in -
creas - ing, be - fore the nev - er - fad - ing maj - es - ty.

HIGHWOOD — "Lord Jesus Christ, Of Joys And Treasures Rarest" — Father Popplewell

1. Lord Je - sus Christ, of joys and treas-ures rar - est, glow of the
Fa - ther's glo - ry, beam-ing bright, who have been made a child of
men, the fair - est, for to be in their midst was your de - light.
2. Al - ways to stay a - mong us is your pleas - ure, un - til the
world its fat - ed time should spend: ten - der-ness such as yours is,
none could mea - sure, lov - ing your own, and lov - ing to the end.
3. Though our first fa - ther fell, his kin-dred leav - ing un - der the

sway of death a fet-tered slave, your bonds of mer-cy brought forth
from their griev - ing those whom by Ad-am's cords you came to save.
4. Draw - ing all things, who are of all the mak - er, up - on the
cross up - lift - ed, all to heal, bear - ing a thirst that had one
on - ly slak - er: your pre - cious blood out - poured to work our weal.
5. Good - ness di - vine and kind-ness man - i - fest - ed, you will not
quench the flax that smoul - ders frail, break not the reed that in - ju -

ry has wrest - ed, in whom the strong are shamed, the weak pre - vail.
6. There is no harm that lies be - yond your mend - ing, nor an - y
loss that you can - not re - store: hearts that are pure pre - serve in
grace un - end - ing, those sin has rav - aged mak - ing whole once more.
7. Once, hid - den God, a pil - grim peo - ple guid - ing, your tab - er -
nac - le told your pres - ence true: now too, Em - ma - nu - el, with
us a - bid - ing, you are the Word in flesh, nor yet in view.

8. Meal of the fa - vored, wine whence maid - ens flour - ish, vine that up -
holds its branch - es, lend - ing life, yield - ing it - self to rear them,
and to nour - ish, that they would thrive, in fruit - ful - ness be rife.
9. Hon - or and praise be of - fered with - out ceas - ing to the al -
might - y One, the ho - ly Three, Fa - ther, and Son, and Spir - it,
still in - creas - ing, be - fore the nev - er - fad - ing maj - es - ty.

1. Lord Je - sus Christ, of joys and treas - ures rar - est, glow of the
Fa - ther's glo - ry, beam - ing bright, who have been made a child of
men, the fair - est, for to be in their midst was your de - light.
2. Al - ways to stay a - mong us is your pleas - ure, un - til the
world its fat - ed time should spend: ten - der - ness such as yours is,
none could mea - sure, lov - ing your own, and lov - ing to the end.
3. Though our first fa - ther fell, his kin - dred leav - ing un - der the

sway of death a fet - tered slave, your bonds of mer - cy brought forth
from their griev - ing those whom by Ad - am's cords you came to save.
4. Draw - ing all things, who are of all the mak - er, up - on the
cross up - lift - ed, all to heal, bear - ing a thirst that had one
on - ly slak - er: your pre - cious blood out - poured to work our weal.
5. Good - ness di - vine and kind - ness man - i - fest - ed, you will not
quench the flax that smoul - ders frail, break not the reed that in - ju -

ry has wrest - ed, in whom the strong are shamed, the weak pre - vail.
6. There is no harm that lies be - yond your mend - ing, nor an - y
loss that you can - not re - store: hearts that are pure pre - serve in
grace un - end - ing, those sin has rav - aged mak - ing whole once more.
7. Once, hid - den God, a pil - grim peo - ple guid - ing, your tab - er -
nac - le told your pres - ence true: now too, Em - ma - nu - el, with
us a - bid - ing, you are the Word in flesh, nor yet in view.

8. Meal of the fa - vored, wine whence maid - ens flour - ish, vine that up -
holds its branch - es, lend - ing life, yield - ing it - self to rear them,
and to nour - ish, that they would thrive, in fruit - ful - ness be rife.
9. Hon - or and praise be of - fered with - out ceas - ing to the al -
might - y One, the ho - ly Three, Fa - ther, and Son, and Spir - it,
still in - creas - ing, be - fore the nev - er - fad - ing maj - es - ty.

 FESTAL SONG — "The Earth Itself Declares" — Saint Philip Howard, Martyr of Jesus Christ

1. The earth it - self de - clares Thine hon - or and thy state;
It doth re - veal how thou for us, Didst all these things cre - ate.
2. The sky, the land, the sea, And all on earth be - low:
The glo - ry of thy wor - thy name Do with their prais - es show.
3. The ros - es that ap - pear So fair in out - ward sight,
The vi - o - lets which with their scent Do yield so great de - light.
4. The win - ter yields thee praise And sum - mer doth the same:

The sun, the__ moon, the stars, and all Do mag - ni - fy thy name.
5. The thun - der shows thy pow'r And light - ning which we see,
The snow and__ rain with won - der tell That none_ is like to thee.
6. The pearls, the pre - cious stones, The birds_ thy praise do sing;
The woods, the__ wells, and all de - lights, Which from_ this earth do spring.
7. Let us there - fore with praise Thy might - y works ex - press,
With heart and__ hand, with mind and all Which we__ from thee pos - sess.

1. Love di - vine, all - loves ex - cel - ling, Joy of heav'n to earth come down;
Fix in us thy hum - ble dwell - ing; All thy faith - ful mer - cies crown!
Je - sus, Thou art all com - pas - sion, Pure un - bound - ed love Thou art;
Vis - it us with Thy sal - va - tion; En - ter ev - 'ry trem - bling heart.
2. Come, Al - might - y to de - liv - er, Let us all Thy life re - ceive;
Sud - den - ly re - turn and nev - er, Nev - er more Thy tem - ples leave.

Thee we would be al - ways bless - ing, Serve Thee as Thy hosts a - bove,
Pray and praise Thee with - out ceas - ing, Glo - ry in Thy per - fect love.
3. Fin - ish, then, Thy new cre - a - tion; Pure and spot - less let us be.
Let us see Thy great sal - va - tion Per - fect - ly re - stored in Thee;
Changed from glo - ry in - to glo - ry, Till in heav'n we take our place,
Till we cast our crowns be - fore Thee, Lost in won - der, love, and praise.

820 ALL SAINTS — *O Splendor Aeterni Patris* — Father Coffin

1. Bright - ness of the Fa - ther's Glo - ry, God of God, and Light of Light,
Scat - ter with Thy per - fect knowl - edge All the shad - ows from our sight.
That they may be whol - ly Thine, Come with - in our souls to shine!
2. When our eyes grow dim and wea - ry May our souls on Thee de - pend,
Who with Thy right hand vouch - saf - est All Thy faith - ful to de - fend.
Lest they to the foe should yield, Stand our Cap - tain and our Shield.
3. When the bod - y's fee - ble na - ture Bows op - pressed with grief and pain,

Help our souls to rise un - in - jured, Soar - ing__ up to Thee a - gain,
Lift - ed on the__ wings of__ grace, Till at length they reach Thy Face.
4. On - ly Hope of man's sal - va - tion! Hear us—_ help us, when we pray;
Those, whom Thou by death hast pur-chased, Cast not__ in Thy wrath a - way.
Grant Thy venge - ance_ to sub - side, Lov - ing - kind - ness to pro - vide.
5. Praise and wor - ship to the Fa - ther, Praise and__ wor - ship to the Son,
Praise and wor - ship to the Spir - it, Now and__ ev - er - more be done:
Earth and Heav - en__ join, their_ song, Joy - ous, grate - ful, to pro - long.

1. Praise to the Ho - liest in the height, And in the depth be praise;
In all His words most won - der - ful, Most sure in all His ways.
2. O lov - ing wis - dom of our God! When all was sin and shame,
A sec - ond Ad - am to the fight And to the res - cue came.
3. O wis - est love! that flesh and blood, Which did in Ad - am fail,
Should strive a - fresh a - gainst the foe, Should strive and should pre - vail.

4. And that a high - er gift than grace Should flesh and blood re - fine,
God's Pres - ence and His ver - y Self, And Es - sence all di - vine.
5. O gen-'rous love! that He, who smote, In man for man the foe,
The dou - ble ag - o - ny in man For man should un - der - go;
6. And in the gar - den se - cret - ly, And on the Cross on
high, Should teach His breth - ren, and in - spire To
suf - fer and to die.
Verse 1 is repeated: "Praise to the Holiest…"

 SCHÖNSTER HERR JESU — *Schönster Herr Jesu (Jesuit Hymn)* — English Transl. by Fr. Popplewell

1. Lord Je - su fair - est, eve - ry lord who rul - est, God and Mar - y's_ Son who art,
thee would I cher - ish, hom - age would fur - nish, joy and rap - ture_ of my heart.
2. Thou who dost har - ness sole - ly all the fair - ness that doth earth_ and_ heav'n en - dow,
none else shall ev - er prove to me dear - er, Je - su dear - est_ mine, than thou.
3. Fair as the moon is, fair - er far the sun is, fair the stars are_ e - qual - ly;
nev - er was an - gel fin - er than Je - sus, nor more pure_ could be than he.

4. Fair find we sil-ver, pearls find e-ven fair-er, fair in-deed find gold a-gleam;
these now but glim-mer soon to grow dim-mer: ev-er-more will_ Je-sus beam.
5. Fair is each flow-er, fair-er still are child-er in men's fresh and_ ear-ly tide;
sure to for-do them, death doth pur-sue them: ev-er-more will_ Je-sus bide.
6. Lord Je-su dear-est, who yet here re-main-est in the ho-liest Sac-ra-ment,
Je-su, I pray thee, show us thy mer-cy now and when our_ lives are spent.

825 REGENT SQUARE — *Gloriosi Salvatoris Nominis Praeconia* — English Translation by Neale

1. To the name that brings sal - va - tion Hon - or, wor - ship, laud we pay;
That for man - y a gen - er - a - tion Hid in God's fore - knowl-edge lay,
But to ev - 'ry tongue and na - tion Ho - ly Church pro - claims to - day.
2. 'Tis the name of ad - o - ra - tion, 'Tis the name of vic - to - ry;
'Tis the name for med - i - ta - tion In the vale of mis - er - y;
'Tis the name for ven - er - a - tion By the cit - i - zens on high.

3. 'Tis the name by right ex - alt - ed O - ver ev - 'ry oth - er name:
That when we are sore as - sault - ed Puts our en - e - mies to shame:
Strength to them that else had halt - ed, Eyes to blind, and feet to lame.
4. Je - sus, we thy name a - dor - ing, Long to see thee as thou art:
Of thy clem - en - cy im - plor - ing So to write it in our heart,
That here - af - ter, up - ward soar - ing, We with an - gels may have part.

1. All crea - tures of our God and King, Lift up your voice and with us sing:
Al - le - lu - ia! Al - le - lu - ia! Thou burn - ing sun with gold - en beam,
Thou sil - ver moon with soft - er gleam: O___ praise Him! Al - le -
lu - ia! Al - le - lu - ia, al - le - lu - ia, al - le - lu - - ia!
2. Thou rush - ing wind that art so strong Ye clouds that sail in Heav'n a - long:
O___ praise Him! Al - le - lu - ia! Thou ris - ing moon, in praise re - joice,

Ye lights of ev'n - ing, find a voice: O___ praise Him! Al - le -
lu - ia! Al - le - lu - ia, al - le - lu - ia, al - le - lu - - ia!
3. Thou flow - ing wa - ter, pure and clear, Make mu - sic for thy Lord to hear:
O___ praise Him! Al - le - lu - ia! Thou fire so mas - ter - ful and bright,
That giv - est man both warmth and light: O___ praise Him! Al - le -
lu - ia! Al - le - lu - ia, al - le - lu - ia, al - le - lu - - ia!

4. And thou most kind and gen - tle death,
Wait - ing to hush our lat - est breath:
O praise Him! Al - le - lu - ia!
Thou lead - est home the child of God,
And Christ our Lord the way hath trod:
O praise Him! Al - le - lu - ia! Al - le -
lu - ia, al - le - lu - ia, al - le - lu - ia!

5. Let all things their cre - a - tor bless,
And wor - ship Him in hum - ble - ness:
O___ praise Him! Al - le - lu - ia!
Praise, praise the Fa - ther, praise the Son,
And praise the Spir - it, Three in One:
O___ praise Him! Al - le - lu - ia! Al - le -
lu - ia, al - le - lu - ia, al - le - lu - ia!

1. It is a splen - did thing To glo - ri - fy and praise
Our God, the Ev - er - last - ing Word, And Lord of end - less days.
2. The trem - bling cher - u - bim Be - fore Him fold their wings,
And all the heav'n - ly hosts a - dore The might - y King of kings.

* *A transposed organ accompaniment has been provided for optional use.*

3. We would our of - f'ring give, O Christ, to Thee we pray,
For Thou didst break the bands of death When dawned the glo - rious day.
4. To Thee, Thou Three in One, As - cend our songs di - vine;
One pow'r, one king - dom with - out end, And one do - min - ion Thine.
5. O Christ, the source of light, With light my soul in - spire;
Come, make my heart the bright a - bode Of Thy ce - les - tial fire.

1. O Star, for whose pure light the heav'n makes room, Hope of the
world thy death re - deemed and won, Though veiled thy ris - ing in a
Vir - gin's womb, Be - fore time was, the Fa - ther's Word and Son;
2. Strength - en the fee - ble; let thy Church be - low, Still lift - ing
un - re - prov - èd hands to heav'n, In worth - ier strains thy death - less
glo - ry show, And those free mer - cies count, thy grace hath giv'n.

3. Sus - tain our weak-ness, light our path ob - scure, Pierce the dull
shades of this dark night be - neath; Arm our frail thoughts a - gainst the
daz - zling lure Of those de - ceit - ful loves whose fruit is death.
4. Mys - te - rious Trin - i - ty, be end - less praise, Fa - ther, and
Son, and Ho - ly Spir - it, thine, Long as time's star this twi - light
world dis - plays, And when out - wea - ried suns no more shall shine.

1. Christ, the glo - ry of the sky, Christ, of earth the hope se - cure,
On - ly Son of God most high, Off-spring of a Maid - en pure.
2. Help us now Thy praise to sing; Grant our souls to know thy day:
Light and life them let it bring, Clouds and dark - ness burn a - way.
3. Day that dawns be - fore our eyes But that ver - y Light de - clares
Which the mind with strength sup - plies, World - ly night to brave pre - pares.

4. Pur - est Light, with - in us dwell, Nev - er from our souls de - part;
Come, the shades of earth dis - pel, Fill and pu - ri - fy the heart.
5. Faith in Him Whose name we bear In our heart of hearts a - bound;
Hope, thy bright - est torch pre - pare; All with ho - ly love be crowned.
6. Praise the Fa - ther, praise the Son, Spir - it blest, to Thee be praise;
To the God - head Three in One Glo - ry be through end - less days.

 WÜRTEMBURG — *Aeterna Caeli Gloria* — English Translation by Campbell of Skerrington

1. Christ, the glo - ry of the sky, Christ, of earth the hope se - cure,
On - ly Son of God most high, Off - spring of a Maid - en pure.
Al - le - lu - ia.
2. Help us now Thy praise to sing;
Grant our souls to know thy day: Light and life them let it bring,
Clouds and dark - ness burn a - way. Al - le - lu - ia.
3. Day that dawns be - fore our eyes But that ver - y Light de - clares Which the mind with
strength sup - plies, World - ly night to brave pre - pares. Al - le - lu - ia.

4. Pur - est Light, with - in us dwell, Nev - er from our souls de - part;
Come, the shades of earth dis - pel, Fill and pu - ri - fy the heart.
Al - le - lu - ia.
5. Faith in Him Whose name we bear
In our heart of hearts a - bound;
Hope, thy bright - est torch pre - pare;
All with ho - ly love be crowned.
Al - - le - lu - ia.
6. Praise the Fa - ther, praise the Son, Spir - it blest, to Thee be praise;
To the God - head Three in One Glo - ry be through end - less days.
Al - le - lu - ia.

1. Christ, the glo - ry of the sky, Christ, of earth the hope se - cure,
On - ly Son of God most high, Off-spring of a Maid - en pure.
2. Help us now Thy praise to sing; Grant our souls to know thy day:
Light and life them let it bring, Clouds and dark - ness burn a - way.
3. Day that dawns be - fore our eyes But that ver - y Light de - clares
Which the mind with strength sup - plies, World-ly night to brave pre - pares.

4. Pur - est Light, with - in us dwell, Nev - er from our souls de - part;
Come, the shades of earth dis - pel, Fill and pu - ri - fy the heart.
5. Faith in Him Whose name we bear In our heart of hearts a - bound;
Hope, thy bright - est torch pre - pare; All with ho - ly love be crowned.
6. Praise the Fa - ther, praise the Son, Spir - it blest, to Thee be praise;
To the God - head Three in One Glo - ry be through end - less days.

 KEINE SCHÖNHEIT HAT DIE WELT — *Aeterna Caeli Gloria* — English Translation by Campbell

1. Christ, the glo - ry of the sky, Christ, of earth_ the hope se-cure, On - ly Son of
God most high, Off - spring of_ a Maid - en pure. Al - le - lu - ia.
2. Help us now Thy praise to sing; Grant our souls_ to know thy day: Light and
life them let it bring, Clouds and dark - ness burn a - way. Al - le - lu - ia.
3. Day that dawns be - fore our eyes But that ver - y Light de-clares Which the mind with
strength sup-plies, World - ly night_ to brave pre-pares. Al - le - lu - ia.

4. Pur - est Light, with - in us dwell, Nev - er from_ our souls de - part; Come, the shades of
earth dis - pel, Fill and pu - ri - fy the heart. Al - le - lu - ia.
5. Faith in Him Whose name we bear In our heart of hearts a - bound; Hope, thy
bright - est torch pre - pare; All with ho - ly love be crowned. Al - le - lu - ia.
6. Praise the Fa - ther, praise the Son, Spir - it blest, to Thee be praise; To the
God - head Three in One Glo - ry be_ through end - less days. Al - le - lu - ia.

1. Christ, the glo - ry of the sky, Christ, of earth the hope se - cure,
On - ly Son of God most high, Off - spring of a Maid - en pure.
2. Help us now Thy praise to sing; Grant our souls to know thy day:
Light and life them let it bring, Clouds and dark - ness burn a - way.
3. Day that dawns be - fore our eyes But that ver - y Light de - clares
Which the mind with strength sup - plies, World - ly night to brave pre - pares.

4. Pur - est Light, with - in us dwell, Nev - er from our souls de - part;
Come, the shades of earth dis - pel, Fill and pu - ri - fy the heart.
5. Faith in Him Whose name we bear In our heart of hearts a - bound;
Hope, thy bright-est torch pre - pare; All with ho - ly love be crowned.
6. Praise the Fa - ther, praise the Son, Spir - it blest, to Thee be praise;
To the God-head Three in One Glo - ry be through end - less days.

1. Sanc - ti - fy me whol - ly, Soul of Christ a - dored;
Be my sure Sal - va - tion, Bod - y of the Lord;
Fill my yearn - ing spir - it, O Thou Blood un - priced:
Wash me, Sa - cred Wa - ter, From the side of Christ.
2. Pas - sion of my Sav - ior, Be my strength in need:
Good and gra - cious Je - sus, To my prayer give heed:

In Thy wounds most pre - cious, Let me ref - uge find:
All the en - vious pow - er Of the foe - man bind:
3. At death's fi - nal ho - ur, Call me to Thy face:
Bid me stand be - side Thee In the heav'n - ly place:
There with Saints and An - gels I shall sing to Thee
Through the count - less ag - es Of e - ter - ni - ty.

1. Soul of my Sav - ior, sanc - ti - fy my breast;
Bod - y of Christ, be Thou my sav - ing guest;
Blood of my Sav - ior, bathe me in Thy tide;
Wash me, ye wa - ters, flow - ing from His side.
2. Strength and pro - tec - tion may Thy Pas - sion be;
O bless - èd Je - sus, hear and an - swer me;

Deep in Thy wounds, Lord, hide and shel - ter me;
So___ shall I nev - er, nev - er part from Thee.
3. Save me from e - vil, make me Thine a - lone;
In my last mo - ments take me for Thine own;
Call me and bid me has - ten to Thy side,
That___ I may see Thee praised and glo - ri - fied.

839 NUN DANKET — Now Thank We All Our God

1. Now thank we all our God, With heart and hands and voic - es,
Who won-drous things hath done, In Whom His world re - joic - es;
Who from our moth - er's arms Hath bless'd us on our way
With count-less gifts of love, And still is ours to - day.
2. O may this boun-teous God Through all our life be near us,
With ev - er joy - ful hearts And bless-èd peace to cheer us;

And keep us in His grace, And guide us when per - plexed,
And free us from all ills
In this world in the next.
3. All praise and thanks to God The Fa - ther now be giv - en,
The Son, and Him Who reigns With Them in high - est heav - en,
E - ter - nal, Tri - une God, Whom earth and heav'n a - dore;
For thus it was, is now,
And shall be ev - er - more.

841 RUSTINGTON — "Alleluia, Sing To Jesus"

1. Al - le - lu - ia, sing to Je - sus, His the scep - ter, his the throne;
Al - le - lu - ia, his the tri - umph, His the vic - to - ry a - lone:
Hark! the songs of peace - ful Zi - on Thun - der like a might - y flood;
Je - sus, out of ev - 'ry na - tion, Hath re - deemed us by his Blood.
2. Al - le - lu - ia, not as or - phans Are we left in sor - row now;
Al - le - lu - ia, he is near us, Faith be - lieves, nor ques - tions how;
Though the cloud from sight re - ceived him When the for - ty days were o'er
Shall our hearts for - get His prom - ise, "I am with you ev - er - more"?

3. Al - le - lu - ia, Bread of an - gels, Thou on earth our Food, our stay;
Al - le - lu - ia, here the sin - ful Flee to thee from day to day;
In - ter - ces - sor, Friend of sin - ners, Earth's Re - deem - er, plead for me,
Where the songs of all the sin - less Sweep a - cross the crys - tal sea.
4. Al - le - lu - ia, King e - ter - nal, Thee the Lord of lords we own;
Al - le - lu - ia, born of Mar - y, Earth Thy foot - stool, heav'n thy throne:
Thou with - in the veil hast en - tered, Robed in flesh our great High Priest;
Thou on earth both Priest and Vic - tim In the Eu - cha - ris - tic Feast.

1. Sing praise to God Who reigns a - bove, The__ God of all cre - a - tion,
The God of pow'r, the God of love, The__ God of our sal - va - tion.
With heal-ing balm my soul is filled And eve - ry faith-less mur-mur stilled: R. To
God all praise and__ glo - ry.
2. What God's al-might-y pow'r hath made
His__ gra - cious mer - cy__ keep - eth, By morn-ing glow or eve - ning shade
His__ watch - ful eye ne'er sleep - eth; With - in the king-dom of His might,
Lo! all is just and all is right: R. To God all praise and__ glo - ry.

3. The Lord is nev - er far a - way, But__ through all grief dis - tress - ing,
An ev - er pre - sent help and stay, Our__ peace and joy and_ bless - ing.
As with a moth-er's ten-der hand, God gen - tly leads the cho-sen band: R. To
God all praise and_ glo - ry.
4. Let all who name Christ's ho - ly Name
Give__ God all praise and_ glo - ry; Let all who own His pow'r pro - claim
A - loud the won - drous sto - ry! Cast each false i - dol from its throne,
For Christ is Lord, and Christ a - lone: R. To God all praise and_ glo - ry.

 TRURO — "Lift Up Your Heads, Ye Mighty Gates" — (Psalm 23)

1. Lift up your heads, ye might - y gates; Be - hold, the
King of glo - ry waits; The King of kings is draw - ing
near; The Sav - ior of the world is here.
2. O blest the land, the cit - y blest, Where Christ the
Rul - er is con - fessed! O hap - py hearts and hap - py
homes To whom this King in tri - umph comes!

3. Fling wide the por - tals of your heart; Make it a
tem - ple, set a - part From earth - ly use for heav'n's em -
ploy, A - dorned with prayer and love and joy.
4. So come, my Sov - 'reign, en - ter in! Let new and
nobl - er life be - gin; Thy Ho - ly Spir - it guide us
on, Un - til the glo - rious crown be won.

1. God of mer - cy, God of grace, Show the bright - ness of Thy_ face;
Shine up - on us, Sav - ior, shine, Fill Thy Church with_ light di - vine;
And Thy sav - ing health ex - tend Un - to earth's re - mot - est end.

* *A transposed organ accompaniment has been provided for optional use.*

2. Let the peo - ple praise Thee, Lord! Be by all that live a - dored;
Let the na - tions shout and sing Glo - ry to their_ Sav - ior King,
At Thy feet their trib - ute pay, And Thy ho - ly will o - bey.
3. Let the peo - ple praise Thee, Lord! Earth shall then her fruits af - ford:
God to man His bless - ings give, Man to God de - vot - ed live;
All be - low, and all a - bove One in joy, and light, and love.

845 ELLACOMBE — "I Sing The Mighty Power Of God"

1. I sing the__ might - y pow'r of God, that made the moun-tains rise,
That spread the__ flow - ing seas a - broad, and built_ the loft - y skies.
I__ sing the wis - dom that or - dained the__ sun to rule the day;
The moon shines full at God's com - mand, and all__ the stars o - bey.
2. I sing the__ good - ness of the Lord, who filled the earth with food,
Who formed the__ crea - tures through the Word, and then_ pro - nounced them good.

Lord, how Thy won - ders are dis - played, wher - e'er I turn my eye,
If I sur - vey the ground I tread, or gaze_ up - on the sky.
3. There's not a___ plant or flow'r be - low, but makes Thy glo - ries known,
And clouds a - rise, and tem - pests blow, by or - der from Thy throne;
While all that bor - rows life from_ Thee is___ ev - er in Thy care;
And eve - ry - where that we can be, Thou, God_ art pre - sent there.

 LAUDA ANIMA — "Praise, My Soul, The King Of Heaven" — (Psalm 102)

1. Praise, my soul, the King of Heav - en; To His feet thy trib - ute bring.
Ran - somed, healed, re - stored, for - giv - en, Ev - er - more His prais - es sing:
Al - le - lu - ia, al - le - lu - ia; Praise the ev - er - last - ing King.
2. Praise Him for His grace and fa - vor To our fa - thers in dis - tress;
Praise Him still the same as ev - er, Slow to chide, and swift to bless.
Al - le - lu - ia, al - le - lu - ia; Glo - rious in His faith - ful - ness.

3. Fa - ther - like He tends and spares us; Well our fee - ble frame He knows;
In His hands He gen - tly bears us, Res - cues us from all our foes.
Al - le - lu - ia, al - le - lu - ia; Wide - ly yet His mer - cy flows.
4. An - gels, help us to a - dore Him; Ye be - hold Him face to face;
Sun and moon, bow down be - fore Him, Dwell - ers all in time and space.
Al - le - lu - ia, al - le - lu - ia; Praise with us the God of grace.

 ST ELIZABETH — *O Bello Dio, Signor Del Paradiso* — English Translation by Father Vaughan

1. O God of love - li - ness, O Lord of heav'n a - bove,
How wor - thy to pos - sess My heart's de - vot - ed love.
So sweet Thy coun - te - nance, So gra - cious to be - hold,
That on - ly glance were bliss un - told.
2. Thou art blest Three in One, Yet un - di - vid - ed still;
Thou art that One a - lone Whose love my heart can fill.

The heav'ns and earth be - low Were fash - ioned by Thy Word;
How great Thou art, O ho - ly Lord!
3. O Love - li - ness su - preme, And Beau - ty in - fi - nite!
O e - ver - flo - wing stream And o - cean of de - light!
O Life by which I live, My tru - est life a - bove,
I give Thee un - di - vid - ed love.

849 NICAEA — "Holy, Holy, Holy! Lord God Almighty"

1. Ho - ly, ho - ly, ho - ly! Lord God Al - might - y! Ear - ly in the
morn - ing our song shall rise to Thee;
Ho - ly, ho - ly, ho - ly,
mer - ci-ful and might - y! God in three Per - sons, bless-èd Trin - i - ty!
2. Ho - ly, ho - ly, ho - ly! All the saints a - dore Thee, Cast - ing down their
gold - en crowns a - round the glass - y sea;
Cher - u - bim and ser - a - phim
fall - ing down be - fore Thee, Who was, and is, and ev - er - more shall be.

3. Ho - ly, ho - ly, ho - ly! Though the dark - ness hide Thee, Though the eye of
sin - ful man Thy glo - ry may not see; On - ly Thou art ho - ly;
there is none be - side Thee, Per - fect in pow'r, in love, and pu - ri - ty.
4. Ho - ly, ho - ly, ho - ly! Lord God Al - might - y! All Thy works shall
praise Thy name, in earth, and sky, and sea; Ho - ly, ho - ly, ho - ly!
mer - ci - ful and might - y! God in three Per - sons, bless - èd Trin - i - ty!

1. Our hope a - lone, thy sov - 'reign Fa - ther's peer, Of earth and heav'n the
ev - er - last - ing day, Thou Word, our in - ward eyes to thee we
rear: O sav - ing God, look down on us, we pray.
2. Thy might - y grace as fire on us pour out; Thy voice re - sound - ing
rout the force of hell; Thou of the soul, whose frail - ty sees her
flout Thy laws, the le - thal sense - less - ness dis - pel.

3. Be gra - cious to a peo - ple who be - lieve, Now gath - ered, Christ, and
thee to bless who yearn: Their hymns, raised to thy death - less fame, re -
ceive, Then, with thy gifts re - plete, let them re - turn.
4. O Fa - ther, Son and Spir - it, God a - lone, The Ho - ly One, the
Word, their Bond di - vine, Our fer - vent prayer at - tend, whose em - pires
own Nor rise nor term, and self - il - lu - mined shine.

 FARLEY CASTLE — *Consors Paterni Luminis* — English Translation by Father Popplewell

1. Our hope a - lone, thy sov - 'reign Fa - ther's peer, Of earth and
heav'n the ev - er - last - ing day, Thou Word, our in - ward eyes to
thee we rear: O sav - ing God, look down on us, we pray.
2. Thy might - y grace as fire on us pour out; Thy voice re -
sound - ing rout the force of hell; Thou of the soul, whose frail - ty
sees her flout Thy laws, the le - thal sense - less - ness dis - pel.

3. Be gra - cious to a peo - ple who be - lieve, Now gath - ered,
Christ, and thee to bless who yearn: Their hymns, raised to thy death - less
fame, re - ceive, Then, with thy gifts re - plete, let them re - turn.
4. O Fa - ther, Son and Spir - it, God a - lone, The Ho - ly
One, the Word, their Bond di - vine, Our fer - vent prayer at - tend, whose
em - pires own Nor rise nor term, and self - il - lu - mined shine.

852 ST CATHERINE — "Faith Of Our Fathers, Holy Faith" — Father Faber

1. Faith of our fa - thers, liv - ing still, In spite of dun - geon, fire__ and sword;
O how our hearts_ beat high_ with joy Whe - ne'er we hear that glo - rious word:
Faith of our fa - thers, ho - ly faith! We will be true to thee till death.
2. Our fa - thers, chained_ in pris - ons dark, Were still in heart and con - science free;
And tru - ly blest__ would be___ our fate If we, like them, should die__ for thee.
Faith of our fa - thers, ho - ly faith! We will be true to thee till death.

3. Faith of our fa - thers! Mar - y's prayers Shall win all na - tions un - to thee;
And through the truth_ that comes_ from God Man-kind shall then in - deed_ be free.
Faith of our fa - thers, ho - ly faith! We will be true to thee till death.
4. Faith of our fa - thers! We_ will love Both friend and foe in all___ our strife;
And preach thee, too,_ as love_ knows how By kind-ly words and vir - tuous life.
Faith of our fa - thers, ho - ly faith! We will be true to thee till death.

853 LOBE DEN HERREN — "Praise To The Lord, The Almighty"

1. Praise to the Lord, the Al - might - y, the King of cre - a - tion! O my soul,
praise Him, for He is thy health and sal - va - tion! All ye who hear,
Now to His al - tar draw near, Join - ing in glad ad - o - ra - tion.
2. Praise to the Lord, who o'er all things so won-drous - ly reign - eth, Shel - ters thee
un - der His wings and so gen - tly sus - tain - eth! Hast thou not seen?
All that is need - ful hath been Grant - ed in what He or - dain - eth.

3. Praise to the Lord, who doth pros - per thy work and de - fend thee; Sure - ly His
good - ness and mer - cy here dai - ly at - tend thee: Pon - der a - new
What the Al - might - y can do, If with His love He be - friend thee.
4. Praise to the Lord! Oh, let all that is in me a - dore Him. All that hath
life and breath, come now with prais - es be - fore Him. Let the "A - men"
sound from His peo - ple a - gain, Now as we wor - ship be - fore Him.

1. Un - veil, O Lord, and on us shine In glo - ry and in grace;
This gaud - y world grows pale be - fore The beau - ty of Thy face.
2. Till Thou art seen, it seems to be A sort of fair - y ground,
Where suns un - set - ting light the sky, And flow'rs and fruits a - bound.
3. But when Thy keen - er, pur - er beam Is pour'd up - on our sight,
It los - es all its pow'r to charm, And what was day is night.

4. Its nobl - est toils are then the scourge Which made Thy blood to flow;
Its joys are but the treach - 'rous thorns Which cir - cled round Thy brow.
5. And thus, when we re - nounce for Thee Its rest - less aims and fears,
The ten - der mem-'ries of the past, The hopes of com - ing years,
6. Poor is our sac - ri - fice, whose eyes Are light - ed from a - bove;
We of - fer what we can - not keep, What we have ceased to love.

855 OLD HUNDREDTH — "All People That On Earth Do Dwell" — (Psalm 99)

1. All peo - ple that on earth do dwell, Sing to the Lord with cheer - ful voice.
Him serve with fear, His praise forth tell; Come ye be - fore Him and re - joice.
2. The Lord, ye know, is God in - deed; With - out our aid He did us make;
We are His folk, He doth us feed, And for His sheep He doth us take.
3. O en - ter then His gates with praise; Ap - proach with
joy His courts un - to; Praise, laud, and bless His Name

al - ways, For it is seem - ly so to do.
4. For why? the Lord our God is good; His mer - cy
is for ev - er sure; His truth at all times firm -
ly stood, And shall from age to age en - dure.
5. To Fa - ther, Son and Ho - ly Ghost, The God whom Heav'n and earth a - dore,
From men and from the an - gel host Be praise and glo - ry ev - er - more.

 RUSTINGTON — "Praise The Lord, Ye Heavens Adore Him"

1. Praise the Lord! ye heav'ns, a-dore Him; Praise Him, an - gels in the height;
Sun and moon, re - joice be-fore Him, Praise Him, all ye stars of light:
Praise the Lord! for He hath spo - ken, Worlds His might - y voice o - beyed;
Laws, which nev - er shall be bro - ken, For their guid - ance He hath made.
2. Praise the Lord! for He is glo - rious; Nev - er shall His prom - ise fail;
God hath made His saints vic - to - rious. Sin and death shall not pre - vail.

Praise the God of our sal - va - tion; Hosts on high, His pow'r pro - claim.
Heav'n and earth and all cre - a - tion, Laud and mag - ni - fy His name!
3. Wor - ship, hon - or, glo - ry, bless - ing, Lord, we of - fer un - to Thee;
Young and old, Thy praise ex - press - ing, In glad hom - age bend the knee.
All the saints in heav'n a - dore Thee; We would bow be - fore Thy throne.
As Thine an - gels serve be - fore Thee, So on earth Thy will be done.

1. Daugh - ter of Si - on, mark who rides a - mid ac - claim; whose chil - dren cry Ho -
san - na, hark, whose stones could tell his fame: Je - ru - sa - lem, whose doors would
grow more loft - y still, where might - y ju - bi - la - tion pours a - round the ho - ly hill!
2. Cel - e - brate Da - vid's heir, the Lord's a - noint - ed sing, with
gar - ments and with palms pre - pare the pro - gress of the king!
A lamb for slaugh - ter bound he choos - es to ap - pear, the
liv - ing God, with meek - ness crowned, whom hosts on high re - vere.

3. Glad - ly the Son di - vine in hu - man form de - scends to
car - ry out the rare de - sign that makes his foes his friends,
their mal - a - dy to heal, to purge its cause a - way and,
with the flesh he takes, to seal a cov - e - nant for aye.
4. Glo - ry to Christ a - bove and to the bless - èd tree on which he bled, com -
pelled by love, to set the fet - tered free! For him cre - a - tion waits: he
keeps his heav'n-ly seat, his awe - some ret - ri - bu - tion bates, ere all lie at his feet.

 CORONA — "The Living God, With Meekness Crowned" — Father Popplewell

1. Daugh - ter of Si - on, mark who rides a - mid ac - claim;
whose chil - dren cry Ho - san - na, hark, whose stones could tell his fame:
Je - ru - sa - lem, whose doors would grow more loft - y still,
where might - y ju - bi - la - tion pours a - round the ho - ly hill!
2. Cel - e - brate Da - vid's heir, the Lord's a - noint - ed sing,
with gar - ments and with palms pre - pare the pro - gress of the king!
A lamb for slaugh - ter bound he choos - es to ap - pear,
the liv - ing God, with meek - ness crowned, whom hosts on high re - vere.

3. Glad - ly the Son di - vine in hu - man form de - scends
to car - ry out the rare de - sign that makes his foes his friends,
their mal - a - dy to heal, to purge its cause a - way
and, with the flesh he takes, to seal a cov - e - nant for aye.
4. Glo - ry to Christ a - bove and to the bless - èd tree
on which he bled, com - pelled by love, to set the fet - tered free!
For him cre - a - tion waits: he keeps his heav'n - ly seat,
his awe - some ret - ri - bu - tion bates, ere all lie at his feet.

860 RUSTINGTON — "Glorious Things Of Thee Are Spoken" — (Isaias 33)

1. Glo - rious things of thee are spo - ken, Si - on, cit - y of our God;
He whose word can - not be bro - ken Formed thee for his own a - bode:
On the Rock of Ag - es found - ed, What can shake thy sure re - pose?
With sal - va - tion's walls sur - round - ed, Thou may'st smile at all thy foes.
2. See, the streams of liv - ing wa - ters, Spring - ing from e - ter - nal love,
Well sup - ply thy sons and daugh - ters, And all fear of want re - move:

Who can faint, while such a riv - er Ev - er will their thirst as - suage?
Grace, which like the Lord the Giv - er, Nev - er fails from age to age.
3. Sav - ior, if of Si - on's cit - y I through grace a mem - ber am,
Let the world de - ride or pit - y, I will glo - ry in thy name:
Fad - ing is the world - ling's pleas - ure, All his boast - ed pomp and show;
Sol - id joys and last - ing treas - ure None but Si - on's chil - dren know.

861 AUSTRIA — “Glorious Things Of Thee Are Spoken” — (Isaias 33)

Who can faint, while such a riv - er Ev - er will their thirst as- suage?
Grace, which like the Lord the Giv - er, Nev - er fails from age to age.
3. Sav - ior, if of Si - on's cit - y I through grace a mem - ber am,
Let the world de - ride or pit - y, I will glo - ry in thy name:
Fad - ing is the world - ling's pleas - ure, All his boast - ed pomp and show;
Sol - id joys and last - ing treas - ure None but Si - on's chil - dren know.

1. My God, ac - cept my heart this day, And make it al - ways Thine,
That I from Thee no more may stray, No more from Thee de - cline.
2. Be - fore the cross of Him Who died, Be - hold, I pros - trate fall:
Let ev - 'ry sin be cru - ci - fied, Let Christ be all in all.

* *A transposed organ accompaniment has been provided for optional use.*

3. A - noint me with Thy heav'n - ly grace, A - dopt me for Thine own,
That I may see Thy glo - rious face, And wor - ship at Thy throne.
4. May the dear blood once shed for me My blest a - tone - ment prove,
That I from first to last may be The pur - chase of Thy love.
5. Let ev - 'ry thought, and work, and word, To Thee be ev - er giv'n;
Then life shall be Thy ser - vice, Lord, And death the gate of heav'n.

ST RITA — "Jesus, Lord And Savior, Hear Me As I Pray" — Father Phillips

1. Je - sus, Lord and Sav - ior, hear me as I pray;
Je - sus, Son of Mar - y, stay with me to - day.
Je - sus, keep me faith - ful, lov - ing, good and true;
Je - sus, help me al - ways trust and fol - low you.
2. To all those a - round me, help me show my love; In my words and
ac - tions, like the saints a - bove; Guide me, dear Lord Je - sus, in my
work and play; Grant that I may please you, now and ev - 'ry day.

BRESSANI — *Rex Gloriose Martyrum* — English Translation by Fr. Caswall

1. O__ Thou, the Mar - tyrs' glo - rious King, Of Con - fes - sors the crown and__ prize;
Who__ dost to joys ce - les - tial bring Those who the joys of earth de - spise.
2. By__ all the praise thy Saints have won; By all their pains in days gone__ by;
By__ all the deeds which they have done; Hear Thou thy sup - pliant peo - ple's cry.
3. Thou__ dost a - mid thy Mar - tyrs fight; Thy Con - fes - sors Thou dost for - give;
May__ we find mer - cy in thy sight, And in thy sa - cred pres - ence live.
4. To__ God the Fa - ther glo - ry be, And to his sole - be - got - ten__ Son;
The__ same, O Ho - ly Ghost, to Thee, While ev - er - last - ing ag - es run.

865 THAXTED — *Deus Judicium Tuum Regi Da* — (Psalm 71)

1. Hail__ to the Lord's A - noint - ed, Great Da - vid's great - er Son!
Hail,__ in the time ap - point - ed, His reign on earth be - gun!
He__ comes to break op - pres - sion, To__ set the cap - tive free;
set the cap - tive free
To__ take a - way trans - gres - sion, And rule in eq - ui - ty.
R. To__ Him shall prayer un - ceas - ing And dai - ly vows as - cend;
His__ king - dom still in - creas - ing, A king - dom with - out end.
2. Kings__ shall bow down be - fore__ Him And gold and in - cense bring;

All__ na - tions shall a - dore__ Him, His praise all peo - ples sing; With__
off - 'rings of de - vo - tion Ships_ from the isles shall meet To__
from the isles shall meet
pour the wealth of o - cean In trib - ute at His feet. Refrain!
3. O'er__ eve - ry foe vic - to - rious, He on His throne shall rest,
From_ age to age more glo - rious, All bless-ing and all - blest. The__
tide of time shall nev - er His__ cov - e - nant re - move; His__
cov - e - nant re - move
Name shall stand for - ev - er, That name to us is Love. Refrain!

1. Firm - ly I be - lieve_ and tru - ly God is Three, and God is One;_
And_ I___ next ac - knowl - edge du - ly Man - hood tak - en by_ the Son.
2. And I trust and hope_ most ful - ly In that Man - hood cru - ci - fied;_
And_ each_ thought and deed_ un - ru - ly Do to death, as he_ has died.
3. Sim - ply to his grace_ and whol - ly Light and life and strength be - long,-
And_ I___ love su - preme - ly, sole - ly, Him the ho - ly, him_ the strong.

4. And I hold in ven - er - a - tion, For the love of him a - lone,
Ho - ly Church as his cre - a - tion, And her teach - ings are his own.
5. And I take with joy what - ev - er Now be - sets me, pain or fear,
And with a strong will I sev - er All the ties which bind me here.
6. Ad - o - ra - tion ay be giv - en, With and through th'an - gel - ic host,
To the God of earth and heav - en, Fa - ther, Son and Ho - ly Ghost.

 PASCHAL LAMB — "Solemn Hymn To The Son Of God" — Father Popplewell

1. Of the Fa - ther born a - lone, Heir co - re - gent of his throne,
Word he speaks e - ter - nal - ly, Mir - ror of his majes - ty:
Man to save, who man be - came, Pleased his ser - vile form to claim,
As a bless - èd Maid - en's child Earth to heav - en rec - on - ciled.
2. Ev - er God, in time a man, Lim - it - ed, whom none may span,
Know - ing all, whose wis - dom grew, Pas - chal Lamb and Shep - herd true:
Who by yield - ing won the strife, Who by dy - ing gar - nered life,
Who de - part - ed, but to bide With the Church, your cho - sen Bride.

3. Come for men to me - di - ate, Sov - 'reign Priest and Ad - vo - cate,
To your own who pledged to send, For their help, an - oth - er Friend:
With the Fa - ther in - ter - cede, Sin - less one, for sin - ners plead,
That the way of life they tread, By your grace to glo - ry led.
4. God al - might - y, three in one, Ho - ly Fa - ther, ho - ly Son,
With the ho - ly Par - a - clete, Let your works your praise re - peat:
To your most ex - alt - ed name Let un - fal - ter - ing ac - claim
From cre - at - ed things as - cend Now and ev - er, with - out end.

869 HEUSTIS — "Solemn Hymn To The Son Of God" — Father Popplewell

3. Come for men to me - di - ate, Sov - 'reign Priest and Ad - vo - cate,
To your own who pledged to send, For their help, an - oth - er Friend:
With the Fa - ther in - ter - cede, Sin - less one, for sin - ners plead,
That the way of life they tread, By your grace to glo - ry led.
4. God al - might - y, three in one, Ho - ly Fa - ther, ho - ly Son,
With the ho - ly Par - a - clete, Let your works your praise re - peat:
To your most ex - alt - ed name Let un - fal - ter - ing ac - claim
From cre - at - ed things as - cend Now and ev - er, with - out end.

 ST GEORGE — "Solemn Hymn To The Son Of God" — Father Popplewell

3. Come for men to me - di - ate, Sov - 'reign Priest and Ad - vo - cate,
To your own who pledged to send, For their help, an - oth - er Friend:
With the Fa - ther in - ter - cede, Sin - less one, for sin - ners plead,
That the way of life they tread, By your grace to glo - ry led.
4. God al - might - y, three in one, Ho - ly Fa - ther, ho - ly Son,
With the ho - ly Par - a - clete, Let your works your praise re - peat:
To your most ex - alt - ed name Let un - fal - ter - ing ac - claim
From cre - at - ed things as - cend Now and ev - er, with - out end.

871 SALZBURG — "Solemn Hymn To The Son Of God" — Father Popplewell

3. Come for men to me - di - ate, Sov - 'reign Priest and Ad - vo - cate,
To your own who pledged to send, For their help, an - oth - er Friend:
With the Fa - ther in - ter - cede, Sin - less one, for sin - ners plead,
That the way of life they tread, By your grace to glo - ry led.
4. God al - might - y, three in one, Ho - ly Fa - ther, ho - ly Son,
With the ho - ly Par - a - clete, Let your works your praise re - peat:
To your most ex - alt - ed name Let un - fal - ter - ing ac - claim
From cre - at - ed things as - cend Now and ev - er, with - out end.

872 CHRISTUS CHRISTUS CHRISTUS IST 7E — "Solemn Hymn To The Son Of God" — Fr. Popplewell

1. Of the Fa - ther born a - lone, Heir co - re - gent of his throne, Word he speaks e -
ter - nal - ly, Mir - ror of his maj - es - ty: Man to save, who man be - came, Pleased his
ser - vile form to claim, As a bless - èd Maid - en's child Earth to heav - en rec - on - ciled.
2. Ev - er God, in time a man, Lim - it - ed, whom none may span,
Know - ing all, whose wis - dom grew, Pas - chal Lamb and Shep - herd true:
Who by yield - ing won the strife, Who by dy - ing gar - nered life,
Who de - part - ed, but to bide With the Church, your cho - sen Bride.

3. Come for men to me - di - ate, Sov - 'reign Priest and Ad - vo - cate,
To your own who pledged to send, For their help, an - oth - er Friend:
With the Fa - ther in - ter - cede, Sin - less one, for sin - ners plead,
That the way of life they tread, By your grace to glo - ry led.
4. God al - might - y, three in one, Ho - ly Fa - ther, ho - ly Son, With the ho - ly Par - a-
clete, Let your works your praise re - peat: To your most ex - alt - ed name Let un-
fal - ter - ing ac - claim From cre - at - ed things as - cend Now and ev - er, with - out end.

873 WÜRTEMBURG — "Solemn Hymn To The Son Of God" — Father Popplewell

1. Of the Fa - ther born a - lone, Heir co - re - gent of his throne, Word he
speaks e - ter - nal - ly, Mir - ror of his maj - es - ty: Al - le - lu - ia.
2. Man to save, who man be - came, Pleased his ser - vile form to claim, As a
bless-èd Maid - en's child Earth to heav - en rec - on - ciled. Al - le - lu - ia.
3. Ev - er God, in time a man, Lim - it - ed, whom none may span, Know - ing
all, whose wis - dom grew, Pas - chal Lamb and Shep - herd true: Al - le - lu - ia.
4. Who by yield - ing won the strife, Who by dy - ing gar - nered life, Who de -
part - ed, but to bide With the Church, your cho - sen Bride. Al - le - lu - ia.

5. Come for men to me - di - ate, Sov-'reign Priest and Ad - vo - cate, To your own who
pledged to send, For their help, an - oth - er Friend: Al - le - lu - ia.
6. With the Fa - ther in - ter - cede, Sin - less one, for sin - ners plead, That the
way of life they tread, By your grace to glo - ry led. Al - le - lu - ia.
7. God al - might - y, three in one, Ho - ly Fa - ther, ho - ly Son, With the
ho - ly Par - a - clete, Let your works your praise re - peat: Al - le - lu - ia.
8. To your most ex - alt - ed name Let un - fal - ter - ing ac - claim From cre -
at - ed things as - cend Now and ev - er, with - out end. Al - le - lu - ia.

1. Of the Fa - ther born a - lone, Heir co - re - gent of his throne,
Word he speaks e - ter - nal - ly, Mir - ror of his maj - es - ty:
2. Man to save, who man__ be - came, Pleased his ser - vile form to claim,
As a bless - èd Maid - en’s__ child Earth to heav - en rec - on - ciled.
3. Ev - er God, in time__ a man, Lim - it - ed, whom none may span,
Know - ing all, whose wis - dom__ grew, Pas - chal Lamb and Shep - herd true:
4. Who by yield - ing won__ the strife, Who by dy - ing gar - nered life,
Who de - part - ed, but to__ bide With the Church, your cho - sen Bride.

5. Come for men to me - di - ate, Sov - 'reign Priest and Ad - vo - cate,
To your own who pledged to__ send, For their help, an - oth - er Friend:
6. With the Fa - ther in - ter - cede, Sin - less one, for sin - ners plead,
That the way of life they__ tread, By your grace to glo - ry led.
7. God al - might - y, three__ in one, Ho - ly Fa - ther, ho - ly Son,
With the ho - ly Par - a - clete, Let your works your praise__ re - peat:
8. To your most ex - alt - ed name Let un - fal - ter - ing ac - claim
From cre - at - ed things as - cend Now and ev - er, with - out end.

1. Of the Fa - ther born a - lone, Heir co - re - gent of his throne,
Word he speaks e - ter - nal - ly, Mir - ror of his maj - es - ty:
Al - le - lu - ia.
2. Man to save, who man be - came,
Pleased his ser - vile form to claim, As a bless - èd Maid - en's child
Earth to heav - en rec - on - ciled. Al - le - lu - ia.
3. Ev - er God, in time a man, Lim - it - ed, whom none may span,
Know - ing all, whose wis - dom grew, Pas - chal Lamb and Shep - herd true:

Al - - le - lu - ia.
4. Who by yield - ing
won the strife, Who by dy - ing gar - nered life, Who de - part - ed,
but to bide With the Church, your cho - sen Bride. Al - - le -
lu - ia.
5. Come for men to me - di - ate, Sov - 'reign
Priest and Ad - vo - cate, To your own who pledged to send,
For their help, an - oth - er Friend: Al - - le - lu - ia.
6. With the Fa - ther in - ter - cede, Sin - less one, for sin - ners plead,

That the way of life they tread, By your grace to glo - ry led.
Al - le - lu - ia.
7. God al - might - y,
three in one, Ho - ly Fa - ther, ho - ly Son, With the ho - ly
Par - a - clete, Let your works your praise re - peat: Al - le -
lu - ia.
8. To your most ex - alt - ed name
Let un - fal - ter - ing ac - claim From cre - at - ed things as - cend
Now and ev - er, with - out end. Al - le - lu - ia.

1. Of the Fa - ther born a - lone, Heir co - re - gent of his throne,
Word he speaks e - ter - nal - ly, Mir - ror of his maj - es - ty:
Man to save, who man be - came, Pleased his ser - vile form to claim,
As a bless - èd Maid - en's child Earth to heav - en rec - on - ciled.
2. Ev - er God, in time a man, Lim - it - ed, whom none may span,
Know - ing all, whose wis - dom grew, Pas - chal Lamb and Shep - herd true:

Who by yield - ing won the strife, Who by dy - ing gar - nered life,
Who de - part - ed, but to bide With the Church, your cho - sen Bride.
3. Come for men to me - di - ate, Sov-'reign Priest and Ad - vo - cate,
To your own who pledged to send, For their help, an - oth - er Friend:
With the Fa - ther in - ter - cede, Sin - less one, for sin - ners plead,
That the way of life they tread, By your grace to glo - ry led.

4. God al - might - y, three in one, Ho - ly Fa - ther, ho - ly Son,
With the ho - ly Par - a - clete, Let your works your praise re - peat:
To your most ex - alt - ed name Let un - fal - ter - ing ac - claim
From cre - at - ed things as - cend Now and ev - er, with - out end.

SAINT JEAN DE BRÉBEUF, PRAY FOR US AT GOD'S THRONE.

NOTICE: **"Text only hymns"** from the pew book do not appear in the Choral Supplement, since thousands of combinations are possible, depending on which melody is chosen. Various options are conveniently listed in the pew book, and "common melodies" are recommended. The following "text only" exceptions were made, and do appear in the Choral Supplement:

#653 • "O Come, O Come Emmanuel" (VENI EMMANUEL) 88 88 R

#683 • "The Glory Of These Forty Days" (SPIRES a.k.a. ERHALT UNS HERR) 88 88 (LM)

#838 • "Soul Of My Savior" (ANIMA CHRISTI 10A) 65 65 D

* * *

The following are given musical notation in the pew edition, but were **omitted** from the Choral Supplement since they are to be sung "German style" (unison + organ):

The page number given for a TITLE (English or foreign) refers to the first instance of that title in the Brébeuf pew edition. Page 190, for example, is given for *Maker Of The Starry Sphere*, because that is the first time it appears—yet optional melodies for that title continue to page 195.

Planning for the sacred liturgy should be done from the Brébeuf pew edition—not the Choral Supplement—for the following reasons: (1) The Choral Supplement contains an abridged version of the index, whereas the pew edition contains the full indices; (2) the pew edition contains extensive information about each hymn, including recommendations for each liturgical season; (3) hundreds of "unison hymns" appear in the pew edition **but not the SATB Choral Supplement.**

English Titles • Alphabetical

Planning for the sacred liturgy should be done from the Brébeuf pew edition—not the Choral Supplement—for the following reasons: (1) The Choral Supplement contains an abridged version of the index, whereas the pew edition contains the full indices; (2) the pew edition contains extensive information about each hymn, including recommendations for each liturgical season; (3) hundreds of "unison hymns" appear in the pew edition **but not the SATB Choral Supplement.**

Planning for the sacred liturgy should be done from the Brébeuf pew edition—not the Choral Supplement—for the following reasons: (1) The Choral Supplement contains an abridged version of the index, whereas the pew edition contains the full indices; (2) the pew edition contains extensive information about each hymn, including recommendations for each liturgical season; (3) hundreds of "unison hymns" appear in the pew edition **but not the SATB Choral Supplement.**

Planning for the sacred liturgy should be done from the Brébeuf pew edition—not the Choral Supplement—for the following reasons: (1) The Choral Supplement contains an abridged version of the index, whereas the pew edition contains the full indices; (2) the pew edition contains extensive information about each hymn, including recommendations for each liturgical season; (3) hundreds of "unison hymns" appear in the pew edition **but not the SATB Choral Supplement.**

Foreign Titles • Alphabetical

Italic titles are those modified by Pope Urban VIII in his 1631 reform

Planning for the sacred liturgy should be done from the Brébeuf pew edition—not the Choral Supplement—for the following reasons: (1) The Choral Supplement contains an abridged version of the index, whereas the pew edition contains the full indices; (2) the pew edition contains extensive information about each hymn, including recommendations for each liturgical season; (3) hundreds of "unison hymns" appear in the pew edition **but not the SATB Choral Supplement.**

Planning for the sacred liturgy should be done from the Brébeuf pew edition—not the Choral Supplement—for the following reasons: (1) The Choral Supplement contains an abridged version of the index, whereas the pew edition contains the full indices; (2) the pew edition contains extensive information about each hymn, including recommendations for each liturgical season; (3) hundreds of "unison hymns" appear in the pew edition **but not the SATB Choral Supplement.**

Hymn Tunes • Alphabetical

Planning for the sacred liturgy should be done from the Brébeuf pew edition—not the Choral Supplement—for the following reasons: (1) The Choral Supplement contains an abridged version of the index, whereas the pew edition contains the full indices; (2) the pew edition contains extensive information about each hymn, including recommendations for each liturgical season; (3) hundreds of "unison hymns" appear in the pew edition **but not the SATB Choral Supplement.**

Planning for the sacred liturgy should be done from the Brébeuf pew edition—not the Choral Supplement—for the following reasons: (1) The Choral Supplement contains an abridged version of the index, whereas the pew edition contains the full indices; (2) the pew edition contains extensive information about each hymn, including recommendations for each liturgical season; (3) hundreds of "unison hymns" appear in the pew edition **but not the SATB Choral Supplement.**

Hymn Tunes • Metrical

Planning for the sacred liturgy should be done from the Brébeuf pew edition—not the Choral Supplement—for the following reasons: (1) The Choral Supplement contains an abridged version of the index, whereas the pew edition contains the full indices; (2) the pew edition contains extensive information about each hymn, including recommendations for each liturgical season; (3) hundreds of "unison hymns" appear in the pew edition **but not the SATB Choral Supplement.**

Planning for the sacred liturgy should be done from the Brébeuf pew edition—not the Choral Supplement—for the following reasons: (1) The Choral Supplement contains an abridged version of the index, whereas the pew edition contains the full indices; (2) the pew edition contains extensive information about each hymn, including recommendations for each liturgical season; (3) hundreds of "unison hymns" appear in the pew edition **but not the SATB Choral Supplement.**